A Cross Section of Psychological Research

Journal Articles for Discussion and Evaluation

Andrea K. Milinki

Editor

 Pyrczak Publishing

P.O. Box 39731 • Los Angeles, CA 90039

Although the author and publisher have made every effort to ensure the accuracy and completeness of information contained in this book, we assume no responsibility for errors, inaccuracies, omissions, or any inconsistency herein. Any slights of people, places, or organizations are unintentional.

Editorial assistance provided by Elaine Fuess, Sharon Young, Brenda Koplin, Cheryl Alcorn, and Randall R. Bruce.

Cover:
Design by Robert Kibler and Larry Nichols.
Image by Wernher Krutein/Photovault.com.

Scanning services provided by Ken Ornburn.

Printed in the United States of America.
10 9 8 7 6 5 4 3 2 1   DOC   05 04 03 02 01 00 99

ISBN 1-884585-13-2

Table of Contents

Continued →

Introduction

This book is designed for students who are learning how to evaluate published psychological research. The 24 research articles in this collection provide the stimulus material for such a course.

Selection of the Articles

Several criteria were used in the selection of the articles. The first criterion was that the articles be comprehensible to students taking their first research methods course. Thus, to be selected, an article needed to illustrate straightforward designs and the use of basic statistics.

Second, the articles needed to deal with topics of interest to psychology majors. To apply this criterion, psychology students were given the titles and abstracts (i.e., summaries) of a number of articles to rate for interest. Only those that received moderate to high average ratings survived the screening of the initial pool of potential articles.

Third, the articles needed to illustrate a wide variety of approaches to research. You will notice in the table of contents that the articles represent 13 types of research such as Survey Research, Content Analysis, Correlational Research, True Experimental Research, and so on.

Finally, the articles needed to be drawn from a large number of different journals. Since each journal has its own genre as well as criteria for the selection of submissions for publication, students can get a taste of the wide variations in psychological research only by reading articles from a wide variety of journals. Application of this criterion resulted in 24 articles drawn from 18 different journals.

How to Use This Book

In the field tests, one or two articles were assigned for homework at each class meeting. Students were required to read the article(s) and answer the questions at the end of each one. At the next class meeting, the article(s) were discussed with the instructor leading the discussion. Other arrangements are, of course, possible. For example, each student might be responsible for leading the discussion of one of the articles after all members of the class have read it.

About the Questions at the End of Each Article

There are three types of questions at the end of each article. First, there are *Factual Questions*. The answers for these are explicitly stated in the articles. In addition to writing down the answers, students should record the line numbers where they found the answers. The line numbers will facilitate discussions if there are disagreements on what constitutes a correct answer to a question.

Second, there are *Questions for Discussion*. Because these are designed to stimulate classroom discussions, most of them ask for students' opinions on various decisions made by the researchers in conducting and writing up their research. In the field tests, these questions led to lively classroom discussions. Since professional researchers often debate such issues with each other, students should not be surprised by such debates taking place in their own classrooms.

Third, students are asked to make *Quality Ratings* for each article. This is done by applying eleven fundamental criteria for evaluating research. These criteria may be supplemented by the more extensive list presented in the Appendix or with lists of criteria that are found in some research methods textbooks.

Reading the Statistics in This Book

Students who have taken a statistics class as a prerequisite to their research methods class should feel quite comfortable with the overwhelming majority of statistics found in this collection because articles that contained large numbers of obscure or highly advanced statistics were excluded from this book.

Students who are learning about statistics for the first time in the course in which they are using this book may need some additional help from their instructors. Keep in mind that it is not realistic to expect instructors of a methods class to also teach a full-fledged course in statistical methods. Thus, there may be times when an instructor asks students to concentrate on the researcher's *interpretation* of statistics without getting bogged down in discussions of the theory underlying specific statistics. It is possible to focus on the interpretation instead of specific statistics because almost all researchers describe their results in words as well as numbers.

The Classification of the Articles

If you examine a number of psychological research methods textbooks, you will probably find that they all differ to some extent in their system for classifying various types of research. While some labels such as "true experiment," "qualitative research," and "survey" are common to almost all textbooks, others that you find in your textbook may be more idiosyncratic. In addition, some categories of research overlap each other. For example, when analyzing the results of a survey, a researcher may compute correlation coefficients, making it unclear whether it should be classified as a survey or as correlational research. An interesting classroom discussion topic is whether a given article can be classified as more than one type of research.

Acknowledgments

I am grateful to Mildred L. Patten, who is the author of a similar collection titled *Educational and Psychological Research: A Cross Section of Journal Articles for Analysis and Evaluation*. Her collection emphasizes broad issues of interest to both psychologists and educators, while this book places more emphasis on topics of interest to students preparing for careers as mental health professionals. Nevertheless, some structural elements of her book were employed in this one such as the inclusion of three types of questions at the end of each article. While I was preparing this book, she also provided me with advice on the criteria for selecting articles and on numerous technical matters.

I am indebted to the publishers who hold the copyrights to the articles in this book. Without their cooperation, it would not be possible to amass a collection such as you find here.

Andrea K. Milinki

Article 1

University Students' Reasons for *Not* Drinking: Relationship to Alcohol Consumption Level

ELLEN K. SLICKER
Middle Tennessee State University

ABSTRACT. The present study investigated the reasons university students have for *not* drinking on those occasions when they choose *not* to drink and whether those reasons differ with students' differing levels of alcohol consumption. Volunteer participants for the study were students (158 males, 245 females) from a mid-South state university. These students anonymously answered questions about the quantity and frequency of their alcohol consumption, and on this basis, four alcohol consumption level groups were formed (80.4% of the sample) in addition to abstainers (19.6% of the sample). Each student also responded to the question, "On those occasions when you *do not* drink (or drink very little), what is the *main* reason you make that decision?" A chi square test of independence indicated that reason for *not* drinking was significantly related to alcohol consumption level group, and separate chi square tests for goodness-of-fit revealed distinctly different reasons given for *not* drinking depending on the group's alcohol consumption level. Light drinkers endorsed religious-moral reasons significantly more often than the other groups, moderate drinkers chose safety reasons, while heavy drinkers indicated expense as their main reason for *not* drinking. The results of this unique study inform social and legislative policies for alcohol abuse prevention and intervention by indicating strategies that target the beliefs of the various alcohol consumption levels.

From *Journal of Alcohol and Drug Education*, 42, 83–102. Copyright © 1997 by the American Alcohol and Drug Information Foundation. Reprinted with permission.

Introduction

While data suggest that drinking on college campuses has declined somewhat over the past 15 years, alcohol abuse and the proportion of heavy drinkers (18–20%) in this population remain unchanged (Engs
5 & Hanson, 1988; Johnston, O'Malley, & Bachman, 1991; O'Hare, 1990). Alcohol appears to be the drug of choice on today's college campuses, predominantly due to the growing intolerance of and unavailability of "harder" drugs (Haberman, 1994; Johnson, Amatetti,
10 Funkhouser, & Johnson, 1988). From 80–90% of college students drink alcohol on a regular basis, many of whom meet criteria as alcohol abusers (Engs & Hanson, 1988; Haberman, 1994; Johnston et al., 1991). The number of alcohol users does not decline with age
15 during college, as studies have found that the percentage of users tends to grow over each of the college years for traditional students (O'Hare, 1990; Werch, Gorman, & Marty, 1987; Wiggins & Wiggins, 1987) with an increase in the percentage of heavy drinkers as
20 students progress through college (O'Hare, 1990). Of further concern is the finding that alcohol abuse in youth can be positively correlated with alcohol abuse in adulthood (Coate & Grossman, 1988). Although there may be more abstainers among the younger stu-
25 dents, among those who do drink, there is little, if any, difference in levels of alcohol consumption and in total reported alcohol-related problems between those who are under age 21 years and those who are 21 years or older (Engs & Hanson, 1988; O'Hare, 1990).
30 Currently in use are several presumed deterrents to alcohol abuse. Even though quite effective in teaching pertinent alcohol-related facts to youth, traditional alcohol abuse prevention programs of a didactic nature that attempt to increase knowledge or change attitudes
35 have not proven effective in changing drinking behavior (Moskowitz, 1989; Schall, Kemeny, & Maltzman, 1992; Smith & McCauley, 1991). Informing under-age students that drinking is illegal and that they will be arrested for drinking also has little impact on alcohol
40 practices (Engs & Hanson, 1988).
Religion is a social institution that has been found repeatedly to be a deterrent to alcohol use (Cochran, 1988; Hawks & Bahr, 1992; Schall et al., 1992), especially where secular controls are weak, such as at a
45 state university (Tittle & Welch, 1983). Further, it appears that religiosity has a stable inhibitory influence on a wide range of deviant behaviors (Cochran, 1991), particularly with regard to certain denominations (Hawks & Bahr, 1992).
50 Various legislative issues that attempt to control the availability of alcohol compose other potential deterrents to alcohol abuse. The Federal Uniform Drinking Age Act of July 1984 persuaded states that had previously lowered their drinking age to raise the legal age
55 to 21 years by October 1986 or lose thousands of dol-

lars in federal highway construction funds. However, even after this act officially took effect, no difference was found in alcohol consumption levels between those who were of legal age and those who were not 60 (O'Hare, 1990).

A second legislative measure that can impact availability of alcohol is higher cost of alcoholic beverages. Studies have found that even small increases in state taxes on alcohol decrease statewide alcohol consump- 65 tion level (Johnson et al., 1988; Lockhart, Beck, & Summons, 1993) as well as the number of alcohol-related traffic fatalities (Moskowitz, 1989; Nathan, 1988), and the number of youth who drive while intoxicated (Lockhart et al., 1993). However, many states 70 continue to ignore this potential deterrent.

Finally, it has been reported that the national campaign against drunk driving which peaked around 1985 had a significant impact on youth problem drinking, resulting in fewer alcohol-related traffic fatalities 75 (Coate & Grossman, 1988; Hingson, Howland, & Levenson, 1988; Tyron, 1992). While residual effects continue with those who passed through this age category in the early to mid 1980s, newer drivers have not been exposed to such strong informal social pressure to 80 not drive drunk (Hingson et al., 1988).

Many studies have considered the reasons why college students drink. These studies have investigated such variables as students' living situations and the contexts in which they drink (O'Hare, 1990), perceived 85 risk of alcohol-related misfortune (Smith & McCauley, 1991), internal attitudes that predict drinking (McCarty, Morrison, & Mills, 1983), students' attitudes toward alcohol (Tyron, 1992), situational determinants, such as social pressure or pleasant times, as 90 triggers for drinking (Carey, 1993), positive alcohol expectancies for drinking (Thombs, 1993), family background (Engs, 1990), family modeling (Bradley, Carman, & Petree, 1992), an avoidant, rather than problem-focused, style of coping (Fromme & Rivet, 95 1994), and time of day of drinking (Cutter & O'Farrell, 1984), to name a few. In spite of this plethora of research on reasons for drinking in the college population, few relevant studies have considered reasons for not drinking among college students.

100 In an early study, Demone (1973) found the major reasons for not drinking in his sample of adolescent high school males were health, safety, and expense. Later Barnes' (1981) study of high school adolescents revealed other reasons for not drinking such as prob- 105 lems with the law, loss of self-control, and problems with employment or school. Reeves and Draper (1984), again using a high school adolescent sample, found six reasons for not drinking, or reducing consumption, endorsed by the majority of their subjects who con- 110 sumed alcohol: maintain health, maintain self-respect, avoid parental disapproval, avoid disappointing family, maintain self-control, and maintain positive self-esteem. The abstainers in this study selected religion, bad taste, and dislike for the effects of drinking as their 115 major reasons for not drinking (Reeves & Draper, 1984).

Another offering found in the literature is one that considers reasons for not drinking in adult Hawaiians of various cultural backgrounds (Johnson, Schwitters, 120 Wilson, Nagoshi, & McClearn, 1985). In this study whites and Hawaiians living in Hawaii listed health and expense most often as reasons for not drinking, while Chinese Hawaiians and Japanese Hawaiians, for example, listed dislike of taste and lack of benefit from 125 drinking as their major reasons for not drinking.

Finally, Greenfield, Guydish, and Temple (1989) completed a study of West Coast universities through which they explored reasons for limiting drinking. They eliminated self-reported abstainers from their 130 analyses because those who abstain from drinking as a lifestyle tend to have markedly different reasons for doing so than do students who periodically limit their drinking. From their 17 survey questions, four factors emerged as reasons for not drinking: self-control (i.e., 135 "I like to feel in control of myself," "It's bad for my health," "I'm concerned about what people might think"), upbringing (i.e., "My religion discourages [or is against] drinking," "I'm part of a group that doesn't drink much," "I'm not old enough to drink legally"), 140 self-reform ("Someone suggested that I drink less," "I was embarrassed by something I said or did when drinking"), and performance ("Drinking interferes with my studies," "I wouldn't want to disappoint my parents"). Although not included in their survey, these 145 authors also found that intention to drive was the reason given as most important for not drinking by 77% of their sample. A second important reason, but one that they also omitted from their survey factor analysis, was taste of alcohol as a motive for not drinking.

150 Prevention techniques have proliferated as attempts have been made to find a means for reduction of the serious situation of problem drinking on university campuses. Given the potential usefulness, in terms of prevention, of discovering reasons for *not* drinking, it 155 was decided to investigate these reasons in a university population where drinking is the norm. This type of investigation is particularly important when attempting to build a prevention model (Reeves & Draper, 1984).

The *purposes of the present study* were to: (a) examine current patterns of alcohol use in a mid-South 160 university population, (b) discover which reasons university students endorse for *not* drinking on those occasions when they chose *not* to drink, (c) further discern whether students at varying levels of alcohol consumption have significantly different reasons for *not* drink- 165 ing, and (d) synthesize this information in light of current or potential alcohol abuse prevention measures that are viable for university students.

Method

Subjects

Participants in this study were 403 volunteer students from various psychology classes at a mid-South state university with enrollment of 17,000 students. These included psychology majors and minors as well as those students who were taking psychology classes to fulfill general studies requirements of the university or of their major. The group generally represented a cross section of all students at this university as most students are required to or voluntarily take classes in psychology. Because it is a state, not private, institution, most of the students who are enrolled at this university are from the middle socioeconomic class. The sample consisted of 39.2% males ($n = 158$) and 60.8% females ($n = 245$). Ethnic makeup was 84.7% white ($n = 341$), 12.9% African American ($n = 52$), and 2.4% from other ethnic backgrounds (mostly Asian, Hispanic American, Native American, and East Indian; $n = 10$). Ages of participants were as follows: 17–18 years: 19.1% ($n = 77$), 19–20 years: 17.9% ($n = 72$), 21–23 years: 40.2% ($n = 162$), 24–30 years: 12.9% ($n = 52$), and over 30 years: 9.9% ($n = 40$). The average age of all students at this university in the years studied was 24.1. There were 28.1% freshmen ($n = 112$), 14.5% sophomores ($n = 58$), 25.3% juniors ($n = 101$), 28.8% seniors ($n = 115$), and 3.3% graduate students ($n = 13$). Four students did not indicate their class status at the university. These percentages correspond to the university percentages as a whole.

Measures

Each participant completed an anonymous survey which included demographic information plus a question that asked, "On those occasions when you DO NOT drink (or drink very little) what is the MAIN reason you make this decision?" (See the Appendix at the end of this article.) The choices available were those that appeared most frequently in the literature as having been selected by a wide range of alcohol consumption level groups, thereby lending validity to their inclusion (Barnes, 1981; Greenfield et al., 1989; Johnson et al., 1985; Reeves & Draper, 1984). Additional items were generated by a similar sample in a prior pilot study by this investigator. This technique has previously been used successfully as a valid method of questionnaire construction (Reeves & Draper, 1984).

The students were also asked to report on their own alcohol consumption levels. This was completed by querying their frequency of drinking and the quantity of alcohol consumed at each occasion. On the basis of their responses, students were then classified into alcohol consumption level groups. While some investigators have used other more detailed and possibly more precise methods for this type of grouping (i.e., the time-line follow-back interview procedure), the quantity-frequency method from simple questionnaire self-report appears to result in similar grouping (Carey, 1993). Rules for division into groups were taken from Barnes (1978, 1981, 1984) with the exception of combining her two lightest drinking groups (infrequent and light) into one (light). Reliability and validity of this classification system have been demonstrated repeatedly by Barnes (1978, 1981, 1984). Internal consistency reliability (coefficient alpha) for the present classification system has been found at .83–.88 for older adolescents (including university students), with test-retest reliability at .85 for a two-week intervening time interval (university students; Slicker, 1996). Four consumption level groups resulted from the classification system in addition to the abstainers who were not used in the main chi square statistical analyses.

Procedure

Data collection extended over a three-week period early in the fall semester of 1993. Participants were asked to complete the questionnaire after they were informed that their participation was voluntary, that their responses were anonymous and confidential, and that results would be reported in group format only. All signed informed consent forms were separated from their response sheets. The questionnaire took approximately 10 minutes to complete, and participation rate was nearly 95%.

Results

The four consumption level groups were: light drinkers, moderate drinkers, moderately heavy drinkers, and heavy drinkers (Barnes, 1978, 1981, 1984). The *abstinent group* ($n = 79$; 19.6% of the total sample) consisted of those individuals who indicated that they never drink alcohol, leaving 80.4% who indicated that they do drink. For this study, *light drinkers* ($n = 159$; 39.4% of total) were designated as those who drink an average of 0–4 drinks once a month or less often or 0–2 drinks more often than once a month, but less often than once a week. *Moderate drinkers* ($n = 53$; 13.2% of total) were those who drink 1–2 drinks at a frequency of once a week or more often (i.e., daily), 3–4 drinks more often than once a month, but less than once a week, or 5 or more drinks once a month or less often. *Moderately heavy drinkers* ($n = 70$; 17.4% of total) were those who drink 3-4 drinks once a week or more, but not daily, or those who drink 5–10 drinks more often than once a month, but less than once a week. Finally, *heavy drinkers* ($n = 42$; 10.4% of total) were those whose consumption levels exceeded the criteria already mentioned both in frequency and amount consumed. This included drinking 3–4 drinks daily, 5–10 drinks once a week or more often, or drinking more than 10 drinks more often than once a month (i.e., weekly, daily). In this study, 18.9% ($n = 76$) of the total sample indicated that they have consumed (at any frequency) six or more drinks in one sitting (commonly referred to in the literature as "binge drinking").

Because of the sample size and the variety of comparisons made, a conservative alpha level of .005 was adopted to minimize Type I familywise errors. Initial analyses considered correlations among variables of interest such as alcohol consumption level and its components, quantity and frequency, and the demographic variables: age, gender, and ethnicity (see Table 1). Both alcohol consumption level and quantity of drinking at each occasion were significantly related to both age and gender, but neither was related to ethnicity. While frequency of drinking was related to quantity consumed at each sitting, frequency lacked a significant relationship to any of three demographic variables of interest: age, gender, or ethnicity.

Table 1

Correlation Matrix with Alcohol Consumption Variables and Demographic Variables

	1	2	3
1. Frequency of drinking			
2. Quantity at each occasion	.46**		
3. Alcohol consumption level	.81**	.80**	
4. Age	−.01	−.31**	−.21*
5. Gender[a]	−.21*	−.28**	−.31**
6. Ethnicity[b]	−.09	−.18	−.17

Note. $N = 324$; abstainers excluded. $*p < .001$ $**p < .0001$
[a]Male = 0, female = 1 [b]White = 0, African American = 1, "other" ethnic groups excluded

Of the total university sample ($N = 403$), 80.4% considered themselves to be drinkers (82.2% of the males and 79.2% of the females) while 19.6% considered themselves abstainers (17.8% of the males and 20.8% of the females). Although only 6.1% of all females in the study (7.7% of the drinking females) were found to be heavy drinkers, 17.1% of all the males (20.9% of the drinking males) fell in this category. The highly significant chi square for gender among the drinkers, $\chi^2(3, N = 323) = 33.85, p < .0001$, suggested that gender and alcohol consumption level were not independent variables, but were significantly related (see Table 2). Heavy drinking was nearly three times as prevalent in males as it was in females. In addition, there was no relationship found between abstainer versus drinker status and gender, $\chi^2(1, N= 402) = .54, p > .10$. This indicates that while females in this sample do not abstain in any greater proportions than do males, when they drink they do so more in moderation.

In order to consider the relationship between ethnicity and consumption level, it was necessary to exclude the "other" ethnic groups due to the small numbers in these groups. Only whites and African Americans were compared resulting in a chi square of $(3, N = 317) = 15.73, p < .001$ which suggested a significant relationship between alcohol consumption level and ethnicity (see Table 2). In fact, there were 5½ times as many white heavy drinkers as there were African Americans (14.4% vs. 2.6%). Proportionately, however, there were fewer than 1½ times as many African American abstainers as white (25.0% vs. 18.1%). The relationship between abstainers vs. drinker status and ethnicity was not significant, $\chi^2(1, N =393) = 1.36, p > .10$. In summary, while they do not necessarily abstain in greater proportions, African Americans in this sample drink more moderately than do whites. This difference in consumption levels appears to be related to the devout religious involvement of African Americans in the middle-South. Religion has been shown to serve as a protective factor against alcohol abuse in this population (Barnes, Farrell, & Banerjee, 1994).

In regard to age influences, there was no significant difference in consumption levels between those who were under age 21 years (the legal drinking age for this state) and those who were 21 years or older, $\chi^2(3, N = 324) = 6.25, p > .10$. This lack of relationship between age range and consumption level suggests that those students under age 21 years have drinking patterns that are similar to students 21 years of age and older. The relationship between abstainer vs. drinker status and age range resulted in $\chi^2(1, N = 403) = 5.22, p >.01$, suggesting no significant relationship between drinking status and age range. When broken down into the five smaller age groups, the chi square that emerged, $\chi^2(12, N = 324) = 26.50, p < .01$, suggested only a weak relationship between consumption level and age group (see Table 2), but no relationship emerged between drinking status (abstainer vs. drinker) and age group, $\chi^2(4, N = 403) = 7.96, p > .05$. These results show little difference overall in drinking patterns among the various age groups and no difference in proportion of abstainers among the five age groups. In viewing only those who drink, the age group with the greatest percentage of drinkers falling within the light consumption level was the over-30-years-of-age group, while the age group with the greatest percentage of heavy drinkers was the group of 19–20-year-olds. Observation suggests that as students in this sample age they are increasingly likely to be light to moderate drinkers. This result appears to be counter to the prior research indicating that young heavy drinkers often become older heavy drinkers (Coate & Grossman, 1988), but is consistent with Peele (1995) who noted that many people mature out of heavy drinking patterns.

A chi square procedure for independence was used to discover the relationship among the four consumption level groups and reasons for not drinking (see Table 3). Abstainers were excluded from these analyses due to a belief that there are theoretically divergent, more enduring, reasons for their abstention than are the more situational reasons mentioned by the drinkers. To combine the abstainers with the drinkers would unnecessarily confound the results. The overall chi square for independence, $\chi^2(27, N =324) = 71.64, p < .0001$, sug-

Table 2

Sample Characteristics in Percent (and Frequency) by Consumption Level for Drinkers with Chi Square Tests for Independence on Each Characteristic

| | Alcohol Consumption Level | | | | |
| | Light | Moderate | Mod/Heavy | Heavy | Total |
Characteristic	($n = 159$)	($n = 53$)	($n = 70$)	($n = 42$)	($N = 324$)
Male	34.1 (44)	12.4 (16)	32.6 (42)	20.9 (27)	39.9 (129)
Female	58.8 (114)	19.1 (37)	14.4 (28)	7.7 (15)	60.1 (194)
	$\chi^2(3, N = 323) = 33.85, p < .0001$				
White	44.8 (125)	18.6 (52)	22.2 (62)	14.4 (40)	88.0 (279)
African American	76.3 (29)	2.6 (1)	18.5 (7)	2.6 (1)	12.0 (38)
	$\chi^2(3, N = 317) = 15.73, p < .001^{a}$				
17–18 years	38.2 (21)	14.5 (8)	29.1 (16)	18.2 (10)	17.0 (55)
19–20 years	46.4 (26)	17.9 (10)	16.1 (9)	19.6 (11)	17.3 (56)
21–23 years	47.1 (66)	13.6 (19)	27.9 (39)	11.4 (16)	43.2 (140)
24–30 years	58.2 (25)	18.6 (8)	11.6 (5)	11.6 (5)	13.3 (43)
> 30 years	70.0 (21)	26.7 (8)	3.3 (1)	0.0 (0)	9.2 (30)
	$\chi^2(12, N = 324) = 26.50, p < .01$				
Age < 21 years	42.3 (47)	16.2 (18)	22.5 (25)	18.9 (21)	34.4 (111)
Age 21 or older	52.6 (112)	16.4 (35)	21.1 (45)	9.9 (21)	65.7 (213)
	$\chi^2(3, N = 324) = 6.25, p > .10$				
TOTAL	49.1 (159)	16.4 (53)	21.6 (70)	12.9 (42)	100.0 (324)

[a] "Other" ethnic groups excluded

375 gested that consumption level group and reason for not drinking were strongly related, and that there was a highly significant difference among consumption level groups in regard to main reason endorsed for not drinking when considering both genders together. This 380 model further suggested that 27% of the variance (Cramer's V) in reasons for not drinking, among the drinkers, was explained by level of alcohol consumption. Gender and reason for not drinking were themselves independent, $\chi^2(9, N = 323) = 10.20, p > .10$, 385 which suggests that no one reason was more attractive to one gender than it was to the other. In addition, ethnicity, age range, and university class status were also unrelated to reason for not drinking.

Further investigation via a series of individual chi 390 square tests for goodness-of-fit on each reason for not drinking indicated whether a particular reason was significantly more pertinent to one consumption level group than it was to the others (see Table 3). While overall, the *safety* reason was cited more than any other 395 reason (chosen by 24.7% of the total sample and 29.9% of the drinkers), it was most prevalent for the moderate drinkers (chosen by 35.9% of this group). All drinking groups chose this reason more often than did the abstainers (chosen by only 2.6%). The second most 400 popular reason given for choosing not to drink (chosen by 15.5% of the total sample and 17.9% of the drinkers) was need for *control* of one's self. A relatively equal distribution of respondents from each drinking group chose this reason, again, more often than did the 405 abstainers (chosen by 5.2% of the abstainers). The third most often chosen reason for not drinking among the

drinkers (chosen by 13.9%, but by only 11.2% of the total sample) involved need for *alertness*. This reason was chosen significantly less by the abstainers (0.0%) 410 than by the moderately heavy (21.7%) and heavy drinkers (21.4%), those who clearly are more likely to be affected by the potential for passing out. The fourth most popular reason for not drinking among drinkers (chosen by 11.1% of the drinkers and by 13.5% of the 415 total sample) was *health* concern. Health concern was the second most popular reason chosen by the abstainers (chosen by 23.4% of them), who chose this reason more often than did any of the drinking groups.

Although all other reasons were chosen by less than 420 10% of the drinkers, two additional reasons for not drinking produced significant results in the goodness-of-fit tests (see Table 3). First, *religious-moral* taboos, chosen by 15.2% of the total sample and by only 7.4% of the drinkers, was chosen by 46.8% of the abstainers 425 (their number one reason for not drinking). While 35.7% of abstaining men (6.4% of all males) chose religious beliefs, 53.1% of abstaining women (10.7% of all women) selected this as their main reason for not drinking. Among the drinkers, a significant chi square 430 goodness-of-fit test, $\chi^2(3, N = 324) = 15.36, p < .005$, indicated that alcohol consumption level was significantly related to this particular reason for not drinking, with the light drinkers choosing religious-moral taboos (chosen by 13.7% of them) significantly more often 435 than did the other drinking level groups.

The second reason for not drinking that produced a highly significant chi square goodness-of-fit test among the drinkers (chosen by 8.3% of the drinkers)

Table 3

Relationship of Reasons for Not Drinking to Alcohol Consumption Level in Percent (and Frequency) with Chi Square Tests for Goodness-of-fit

Reasons	Alcohol Consumption Level					χ^{2a}
	Light ($n = 159$)	Moderate ($n = 53$)	Mod/Heavy ($n = 70$)	Heavy ($n = 42$)	Total ($N = 324$)	
Religious-moral	13.7 (22)	3.8 (2)	1.5 (1)	0.0 (0)	7.4	15.36*
Taste	10.6 (17)	3.8 (2)	2.9 (2)	2.4 (1)	6.8	6.91
Health	13.7 (22)	13.2 (7)	5.8 (4)	7.1 (3)	11.4	3.58
Safety	31.3 (50)	35.9 (19)	29.0 (20)	19.1 (8)	29.9	2.44
Self-Control	15.0 (24)	20.7 (11)	20.3 (14)	21.4 (9)	17.9	1.51
Alertness	8.8 (14)	13.2 (7)	21.7 (15)	21.4 (9)	13.9	7.82
Expense	1.9 (3)	7.5 (4)	13.0 (9)	26.2 (11)	8.3	25.87**
Other[b]						1.61
Social Image	0.6 (1)	0.0 (0)	2.9 (2)	0.0 (0)	0.9	
Peers, family	2.5 (4)	1.9 (1)	0.0 (0)	0.0 (0)	1.5	
Availability	1.9 (3)	0.0 (0)	2.9 (2)	2.4 (1)	1.9	
Column Totals	100.0	100.0	100.0	100.0	100.0	

Chi Square test for independence, total model: $\chi^2(27, N = 324) = 71.64**$

[a]Chi square test for goodness-of-fit for each reason; $df = 3$
[b]Due to excessively small observed counts, the last three categories were collapsed into one for the goodness-of-fit test.
*$p < .05/10$ tests $= .005$ **$p < .0001$

was *expense*, $\chi^2(3, N = 324) = 25.87$, $p < .0001$. Although this reason was chosen by only 6.7% of the total sample, it was endorsed significantly more often by the heavy drinkers (26.2%) than by any of the other consumption level groups, a finding that strongly suggests that university students who are heavy drinkers are highly affected by the price of alcoholic beverages.

When considering reasons for not drinking by consumption level group, each group tended to have characteristic reasons for choosing not to drink. The most popular reasons (those endorsed by more than 15% of any group) were: for light drinkers—safety only; for moderate drinkers—safety and self-control; for moderately heavy drinkers—safety, alertness, and self-control; and for heavy drinkers—expense, alertness, self-control, and safety. Very few respondents from any of the drinking groups chose the following reasons for not drinking: dislike of *taste* (the third most often chosen reason by the abstainers, chosen by 20.8% of them), preservation of *social image, peer or family pressure* NOT to drink, and *lack of availability* because of being underage. Because the last three reasons were chosen so infrequently, these three were collapsed into one category for the goodness-of-fit test (see Table 3).

Discussion

Comparability of this Sample

The results of this study tend to concur with those of many prior studies, attesting to the reliability and validity of the alcohol consumption classification system used. The comparability of these results also suggests that the campus surveyed in the present study is similar to those campuses studied in the past, even though it is located in the Bible Belt South. For example, results of the present study find that 80.4% of the total sample drink alcohol as compared to 78.8% (Engs & Hanson, 1988), 90% (Haberman, 1994), 89% (Johnston et al., 1991), 81.5% (O'Hare, 1990), and 81.5% (Werch et al., 1987) in other studies. The percentages of men (82.2%) and women (79.2%) in this sample who drink are also similar to the findings of O'Hare (1990; 81.1% men, 81.6% women) and Werch et al. (1987; 80.3% men, 82.7% women). In addition, the absence of a significant difference in alcohol consumption levels between those age 21 years and older and those who are not yet 21 concurs with earlier results (O'Hare, 1990). The percentage of abstainers in the present study (19.6%) compares favorably to the results of Engs and Hanson (1988; 21.1%), O'Hare (1990; 18.5%), Werch et al. (1987; 18.5%), and Wiggins and Wiggins (1987; 20%). The present study finds that 17.8% of males and 20.8% of females abstain compared to O'Hare's (1990) 18.9% of males and 18.4% of females and Werch et al.'s (1987) 19.7% male and 17.3% female abstention. As in the Engs (1990) study, sophomores (typically 19 to 20 years of age) are the heaviest drinkers, and significant differences occur in alcohol consumption level due to gender and ethnicity. Whites are found to be heavier drinkers than African Americans both in the present study and in prior studies (O'Hare, 1990; Wechsler & McFadden, 1979). Werch et al. (1987) found three times as many heavy drinking males (21.3%) as females (7.1%) which compares proportionately to the present study (male heavy drinkers: 17.1%, female: 6.1%). Other studies designate binge drinking in similar terms (six or more drinks at one sitting, any frequency) which also lends itself to comparison. In the present study, 18.9% of the total sample are binge drinkers, compared to 20% in the Engs and Hanson (1988) study.

Implication of Reasons for Not Drinking

While numerous studies have considered university students' reasons *for* drinking, the present study sought to ascertain these students' reasons for *not* drinking on those occasions when they choose not to drink. By discerning their motivations for not drinking we are able to gain insight into possible preventative measures for reducing alcohol abuse among university students. Implication of these discovered relationships follow.

First, the need for *safety* (i.e., not driving after drinking) is clearly of major importance to all alcohol consumption level groups as it is the number one reason for not drinking listed overall as well as the number one reason listed by each of the drinking groups (with the exception of the heavy drinkers). This suggests a strong belief that injury of self or others is imminent when driving while intoxicated, in all groups except the heavy drinkers. The finding is also consistent with the Greenfield et al. (1989) study in that both samples revealed safety as their most important reason for not drinking. While there is not a significant difference among the various age groups nor among the consumption level groups regarding this reason, the moderate drinkers and those age 21–23 years tend to designate safety as most important more often than do all the other groups. This particular age cohort appears to have been affected most profoundly by the pronounced public media campaign of 10 years ago against drunk driving.

Since this safety reason for not drinking is the most powerful one, it seems logical to capitalize on this information in our efforts against alcohol abuse. First, some states have increased penalties for and enforcement of drunk driving laws. The sentences not only involve suspension or revocation of drivers' licenses, but also attendance at Victim Impact Panel meetings where the loved ones of those killed by drunk drivers confront the convicted offenders. Such programs, aimed at first-time offenders and those who have recently begun *experiencing* problems at home, at work, or at school, show promise (Nathan, 1988). Second, since the media campaign of 10 years ago had such apparent impact (Hingson et al., 1988), reawakening that channel to the intensity it once had would further inoculate the current cohort of young drivers, as well as future drivers, against driving drunk. Community organizations and consistent media presence with this message would keep public attention and social pressure focused on this issue in order to sustain behavioral change in the area of drunk driving as it has in other public areas (Hingson et al., 1988).

The second finding implicates underage drinking. Although the present study finds that 9.9% of the sample of students over age 21 years are heavy drinkers, a full 18.9% of the underage sample falls into this heavy drinking category as well. Only 1.5% (6 students) of the entire sample said that lack of *availability* of alcohol due to being underage was a problem. Clearly, the minimum drinking age legislation is not being adequately enforced. These laws are not significantly impacting this younger age range as demonstrated by the fact that almost twice as many of them are heavy drinkers as are those students who can buy alcohol legally. While lowering the drinking age apparently raises highway fatalities, raising the drinking age has had little positive impact on the university population in regard to alcohol consumption level. More effective enforcement of minimum drinking age laws both on and off campus could help curb this unrestricted accessibility as behavioral theories of choice suggest that alcohol consumption level varies inversely with direct constraints placed on access of alcohol (Vuchinich & Tucker, 1988).

Third, this axiom proffered by Vuchinich & Tucker (1988) can be applied not only to age eligibility for access, but also to the *affordability* of alcohol. It should not be surprising that raising the cost of alcoholic beverages has shown definitive promise as an alcohol abuse prevention measure (Coate & Grossman, 1988; Grossman, Coate, & Arluck, 1987). Results of the present study substantiate these findings as they indicate that there is a significant positive relationship between heavy drinking and endorsement of expense as a reason not to drink. Incidence of heavy and frequent drinking by youth is significantly and inversely related to the price of alcohol, affecting the frequent heavy drinkers even more than those who drink infrequently (Coate & Grossman, 1988; Cook & Tauchen, 1982; Grossman et al., 1987). Specifically, the heavy drinkers choose this as their reason for not drinking significantly more often than do any of the other groups. This means that if we were to substantially raise state and federal excise taxes on alcoholic beverages, the heavy drinkers (our main target group) would be most affected. Lockhart and colleagues (1993) have suggested that $7.50 per six-pack of beer is the point at which purchases drop off markedly. The raising of alcohol prices via heavier taxation could substantially impact the consumption level of this problem heavy drinking group, the group for which intervention is most needed.

The final implication that can be drawn from this study involves the impact of *religiosity* on alcohol consumption. Since nearly half of the abstinent group and 14% of the light drinkers cited a religious-moral reason for not drinking, it follows that self-reported religiosity apparently provides resiliency against alcohol use and abuse in a university population. This phenomenon is particularly evident in the Bible Belt South (Cochran, 1988; Sneed & Slicker, 1997). Although the mechanism of this connection between religion and abstinence is not evident from the present study, it has been suggested that the means through which religion works may be that of family values. For example, families who value components of a strong parent-adolescent relationship such as effective supervision of the adolescent, clear parent-adolescent communication, parental responsiveness to the adolescents (Barnes et al., 1994; Slicker, 1996), and appropriate parental modeling of drinking/nondrinking behaviors (Barnes, 1984) are significantly more likely to be high in religiosity than are families who are deficit in one or more of these values. Repeatedly studies have demonstrated that these components work to deter problem behaviors, such as alcohol abuse, in older adolescents (Barnes et al., 1994; Reeves & Draper, 1984; Slicker, 1996; Sneed & Slicker, 1997). Indirect intervention, intervention whose results will be evident only over time, involves bolstering parents and families with the skills for developing strong parent-adolescent relationships. Further study is warranted of the specific familial and parenting behaviors involved in providing this resiliency against alcohol abuse and of the mechanism of connection between religiosity and effective parenting.

Despite its demonstrated similarity to university populations from other parts of the country, caution should be exercised when generalizing the results of this study using psychology students from one mid-South university in the Bible Belt to other populations in other universities located in other regions of the country. That limitation aside, the results of this study can enlighten those who are in a position to create, to fund, and to enforce local programs.

Conclusions

The present study determined that significantly different reasons for not drinking are endorsed by various university alcohol consumption level groups. By capitalizing on these reasons, we can link students' belief systems to prevention/intervention programs. It has been found that interventions that increase perceived risk of negative effects in heavy drinkers may cause these drinkers to modify their beliefs about the consequences of their heavy drinking (McCarty et al., 1983). Currently, we are doing little to increase these perceived risks of negative effects as evidenced by a recent study indicating that although 36% of older adolescents admit to driving while intoxicated, only 3% have ever been arrested for this offense (Slicker, 1996). Rekindling persistent media presence and strengthening community action and legal action against driving drunk coupled with more effective and predicted enforcement of drunk driving laws could serve to increase heavy drinkers' beliefs in the inadvisability of driving drunk.

Legislation that increases excise taxes on alcohol, making its purchase economically prohibitive for heavy drinking university students, is another environmental technique that has been shown by economists to be effective in preventing alcohol abuse. Currently, a six-pack of beer (the favorite beverage of college students) can be purchased in grocery stores for little more than a six-pack of cola. The present study suggests that raising the price of alcohol would limit its availability to university students and would hit hardest in the heavy drinking group. Since it is clear that lack of availability of alcohol is an effective deterrent against alcohol abuse, limiting access to alcoholic beverages of underage drinkers is an option that is open for improved enforcement as well. Results of the present study suggest that few students under age 21 years currently feel the effect of restrictions on their ability to procure alcohol. Stiffer penalties for selling alcohol to, and buying alcohol for, minors is legislatively possible and could limit availability of alcohol to this underage population.

Finally, this study links periodic nondrinking in the light drinkers (and abstainers) predominantly to their religious/moral beliefs. Unlike the previously mentioned interventions, however, religion cannot be legislated. Change in the personal belief system of these students and their families will need to be made over the long term through consistent public school and community interventions with families of children and pre-adolescents, teaching parent-child relationship skills and effective parental monitoring skills.

Legislative and social strategies suggested by this research provide alternate prevention and intervention techniques that are our best defense against alcohol abuse. This study demonstrates for the first time that looking at students' reasons for *not* drinking is a viable direction from which to approach the widespread problem of alcohol abuse on university campuses.

References

Barnes, G. (1978). *Drinking patterns of youth in Genesee County*. Buffalo, NY: Research Institute on Alcoholism, New York State Division of Alcoholism and Alcohol Abuse.

Barnes, G. (1981). Drinking among adolescents: A subcultural phenomenon or a model of adult behaviors. *Adolescence, 16*, 211–229.

Barnes, G. (1984). Adolescent alcohol abuse and other problem behaviors: Their relationships and common parental influences. *Journal of Youth & Adolescence, 13*, 329–348.

Barnes, G., Farrell, M., & Banerjee, S. (1994). Family influences on alcohol abuse and other problem behaviors among black and white adolescents in a general population sample. *Journal of Research on Adolescents, 4*(2), 183–201.

Bradley, J., Carman, R., & Petree, A. (1992). Personal and social drinking motives, family drinking history, and problems associated with drinking in two university samples. *Journal of Drug Education, 22*(3), 195–202.

Carey, K. (1993). Situational determinants of heavy drinking among college students. *Journal of Counseling Psychology, 40*, 217–220.

Coate, D., & Grossman, M. (1988). Effects of alcohol beverage prices and legal drinking ages on youth alcohol use. *Journal of Law & Economics, 31*, 145–171.

Cochran, J. (1988). The effects of religiosity on secular and ascetic deviance. *Sociological Focus, 21*, 293–306.

Cochran, J. (1991). The effects of religiosity on adolescent self-reported frequency of drug and alcohol use. *Journal of Drug Issues, 22*, 91–104.

Cook, P., & Tauchen, G. (1982). The effect of liquor taxes on heavy drinking. *The Bell Journal of Economics, 13*, 379–390.

Cutter, H., & O'Farrell, T. (1984). Relationship between reasons for drinking and customary drinking behavior. *Journal of Studies on Alcohol, 45*, 321–325.

Demone, H. (1973). The nonuse and abuse of alcohol by the male adolescent. In *Proceedings of the 2nd Annual Alcoholism Conference* (pp. 24–32). Rockville, MD: NIAAA.

Engs, R. (1990). Family background of alcohol abuse and its relationship to alcohol consumption among college students: An unexpected finding. *Journal of Studies on Alcohol, 51*, 542–547.

Engs, R., & Hanson, D. (1988). University students' drinking patterns and problems: Examining the effects of raising the purchase age. *Public Health Reports, 103,* 667–673.

Fromme, K., & Rivet, K. (1994). Young adults' coping style as a predictor of their alcohol use and response to daily events. *Journal of Youth and Adolescence, 23,* 85–97.

Greenfield, T., Guydish, J., & Temple, M. (1989). Reasons students give for limiting drinking: A factor analysis with implications for research and practice. *Journal of Studies on Alcohol, 50,* 108–115.

Grossman, M., Coate, D., & Arluck, G. (1987). Price sensitivity of alcohol beverages in the United States: Youth and alcohol consumption. *Control issues in alcohol abuse prevention: Strategies for states and communities* (pp. 169–198). Greenwich, CT: JAI Press.

Haberman, S. (1994). A survey of alcohol and other drug use practices. *Journal of Alcohol & Drug Education, 39*(2), 85–100.

Hawks, R., & Bahr, S. (1992). Religion and drug use. *Journal of Drug Education, 22,* 1–8.

Hingson, R., Howland, J., & Levenson, S. (1988). Effects of legislative reform to reduce drunken driving and alcohol-related traffic fatalities. *Public Health Reports, 103,* 659–666.

Johnson, E., Amatetti, S., Funkhouser, J., & Johnson, S. (1988). Theories and models supporting prevention approaches to alcohol problems among youth. *Public Health Reports, 103,* 578–586.

Johnson, R., Schwitters, S., Wilson, J., Nagoshi, C., & McClearn, G. (1985). A cross-ethnic comparison of reasons given for using alcohol, not using alcohol, or ceasing to use alcohol. *Journal of Studies on Alcohol, 46,* 283–288.

Johnston, L., O'Malley, P., & Bachman, J. (1991). *Drug use among American high school seniors, college students, and young adults, 1975–1990,* Vol. II (pp. 139–149). Rockville, MD: U.S. Dept. of Health and Human Services.

Lockhart, S., Beck, K., & Summons, T. (1993). Impact of higher alcohol prices on alcohol-related attitudes and perceptions of suburban, middle-class youth. *Journal of Youth & Adolescence, 22,* 441–453.

McCarty, D., Morrison, S., & Mills, K. (1983). Attitudes, beliefs, and alcohol use: An analysis of relationships. *Journal of Studies on Alcohol, 44,* 328–341.

Moskowitz, J. (1989). The primary prevention of alcohol problems: A critical review of the research literature. *Journal of Studies on Alcohol, 50,* 54–88.

Nathan, P. (1988). Alcohol dependency prevention and early intervention. *Public Health Reports, 103,* 683–689.

O'Hare, T. (1990). Drinking in college: Consumption patterns, problems, sex differences, and legal drinking age. *Journal of Studies on Alcohol, 51,* 536–541.

Peele, S. (1995). *Discaring of America.* New York: Lexington.

Reeves, D., & Draper, T. (1984). Abstinence or decreasing consumption among adolescents: Importance of reasons. *International Journal of the Addictions, 19,* 819–825.

Schall, M., Kemeny, A., & Maltzman, I. (1992). Factors associated with alcohol use in university students. *Journal of Studies on Alcohol, 53,* 122–136.

Slicker, E. (1996). *Relationship of parenting style to behavioral adjustment in older adolescents.* Manuscript submitted for publication. Middle Tennessee State University, Murfreesboro.

Smith, R., & McCauley, C. (1991). Predictors of alcohol abuse behaviors of undergraduates. *Journal of Drug Education, 21,* 159–166.

Sneed, C., & Slicker, E. (1997). *Relationship of religiosity to substance use and risky sexual behavior in older adolescents.* Manuscript in preparation. Middle Tennessee State University, Murfreesboro.

Thombs, D. (1993). The differentially discriminating properties of alcohol expectancies for female and male drinkers. *Journal of Counseling & Development, 71,* 321–325.

Tittle, C., & Welch, M. (1983). Religiosity and deviance: Toward a contingency theory of constraining effects. *Social Forces, 61,* 653–682.

Tyron, G. (1992). Comparison of alcohol use by college students: 1983 and 1988. *Journal of Alcohol and Drug Education, 37*(2), 111–120.

Vuchinich, R., & Tucker, J. (1988). Contributions from behavior theories of choice to an analysis of alcohol abuse. *Journal of Abnormal Psychology, 97*(2), 181–195.

Wechsler, H., & McFadden, M. (1979). Drinking among college students in New England. *Journal of Studies on Alcohol, 40,* 969–996.

Werch, G., Gorman, D., & Marty, P. (1987). Relationship between alcohol consumption and alcohol problems in young adults. *Journal of Drug Education, 17,* 261–275.

Wiggins, J., & Wiggins, B. (1987). Drinking at a southern university: Its description and correlates. *Journal of Studies on Alcohol, 48,* 319–324.

Appendix

Directions: Please read *ALL CHOICES* before selecting *ONE* reason.

On those occasions when you *DO NOT DRINK* (or drink very little), what is the *MAIN* reason you make this decision?

1 = RELIGIOUS/MORAL CONCERNS	Example: A good Christian does not drink. My church forbids drinking. Drinking is a bad thing to do. Drinking is illegal for me.
2 = TASTE CONCERNS	Example: I don't like the taste of alcohol.
3 = HEALTH CONCERNS	Example: Drinking will make me sick. Drinking is not good for my body.
4 = SAFETY CONCERNS	Example: I don't drink when I have to drive a vehicle or operate machinery.
5 = CONTROL CONCERNS	Example: I don't drink when I have to be in control of my thinking, e.g., not make mistakes.
6 = ALERTNESS CONCERNS	Example: I don't drink when I need to be alert the next morning, or when I don't want to fall asleep or pass out drunk.
7 = SOCIAL IMAGE CONCERNS	Example: I don't drink when I don't want others to smell alcohol on my breath or see me intoxicated.
8 = PEER/FAMILY CONCERNS	Example: I feel peer pressure NOT to drink since my friends don't drink. No one in my family drinks, so I've never been exposed to drinking.
9 = ECONOMIC CONCERNS	Example: I don't drink when I can't afford to buy the alcohol.
10 = AVAILABILITY CONCERNS	Example: Since I'm underage, I can't usually get alcohol to drink.

Author Note: Grateful appreciation is extended to Jwa K. Kim for consulting with this author on statistical procedures and to James C. Tate for critiquing an earlier draft of this manuscript.

Address correspondence to: Ellen K. Slicker, Department of Psychology, Middle Tennessee State University, P.O. Box X081, Murfreesboro, TN 37132. eslicker@frank.mtsu.edu

Exercise for Article 1

Factual Questions

1. According to the researcher, there is a "plethora of research" on what topic?

2. In which lines does the researcher explicitly state the purposes of her research?

3. What reason does the researcher give for believing that her sample "generally represented a cross section of all students" at the university?

4. Was the survey anonymous?

5. Were the African Americans *or* the Whites more moderate in their drinking?

6. According to Table 3, *how many* of the "light" drinkers cited "safety" as a reason for not drinking?

7. What percentage of the sample said that lack of alcohol due to being underage was a problem?

Questions for Discussion

8. In your opinion, does the use of "volunteer" students affect the validity of this study? Explain. (See lines 169–170.)

9. If you had been in one of the psychology classes where this study was conducted, would you have agreed to participate? Why? Why not? (Note that in this study there was a 95% participation rate. See lines 244–246.)

10. According to Table 1, there is a correlation of –.31 between variable 2 (quantity at each occasion) and variable 4 (age). What is the meaning of this correlation coefficient?

11. Do the data in this study convince you that raising the cost of alcoholic beverages will cause a reduction in alcohol consumption by college students? Explain. (See lines 578–604.)

12. The researcher states that "caution should be exercised when generalizing the results of this study." Do you agree? Explain. (See lines 638–646.)

Quality Ratings

Directions: Indicate your level of agreement with each of the following statements by circling a number from 5 for strongly agree (SA) to 1 for strongly disagree (SD). If you believe an item is not applicable to this research article, leave it blank. Be prepared to explain your ratings.

A. The introduction establishes the importance of the study.

   SA   5   4   3   2   1   SD

B. The literature review establishes the context for the study.

   SA   5   4   3   2   1   SD

C. The research purpose, question, or hypothesis is clearly stated.

   SA   5   4   3   2   1   SD

D. The method of sampling is sound.

   SA   5   4   3   2   1   SD

E. Relevant demographics (for example, age, gender, and ethnicity) are described.

   SA   5   4   3   2   1   SD

F. Measurement procedures are adequate.

   SA   5   4   3   2   1   SD

G. All procedures have been described in sufficient detail to permit a replication of the study.

   SA   5   4   3   2   1   SD

H. The participants have been adequately protected from potential harm.

   SA   5   4   3   2   1   SD

I. The results are clearly described.

   SA   5   4   3   2   1   SD

J. The discussion/conclusion is appropriate.

   SA   5   4   3   2   1   SD

K. Despite any flaws, the report is worthy of publication.

   SA   5   4   3   2   1   SD

Article 2

Fatalism, Current Life Satisfaction, and Risk for HIV Infection Among Gay and Bisexual Men

SETH C. KALICHMAN
Georgia State University and
Center for AIDS Intervention Research,
Medical College of Wisconsin

JEFFREY A. KELLY
Center for AIDS Intervention Research,
Medical College of Wisconsin

MICHAEL MORGAN
Center for AIDS Intervention Research,
Medical College of Wisconsin

DAVID ROMPA
Center for AIDS Intervention Research,
Medical College of Wisconsin

ABSTRACT. This study surveyed 430 men at an urban gay pride celebration to assess fatalism, current life satisfaction, and perceived expected years of life among men who have sex with men. Analyses showed that men who engaged in unprotected anal intercourse outside of exclusive relationships reported a greater fatalistic outlook, were more dissatisfied with life, and perceived a shorter life for themselves than men who practiced only safer sex and men who were in exclusive relationships. Gay men in exclusive relationships scored higher than nonexclusively partnered gay men on the measure of current life satisfaction. These results suggest that efforts to prevent HIV infection among gay men should include building personal self-worth, support of long-term relationships, and future goal orientations.

From *Journal of Consulting and Clinical Psychology, 65,* 542–546. Copyright © 1997 by the American Psychological Association, Inc. Reprinted with permission.

Over 15 years after the first cases of AIDS were diagnosed, HIV has become well established in North America, with 40,000 to 80,000 new HIV infections contracted each year in the United States (Centers for
5 Disease Control and Prevention [CDC], 1995; Rosenberg, 1995). Although 71% of HIV infections worldwide have occurred among heterosexual men and women, and despite alarming increases in heterosexually transmitted U.S. HIV infections, the majority of
10 North Americans diagnosed with AIDS are men who have sex with men (CDC, 1995). Nearly 50% of gay and bisexual men in San Francisco became infected with HIV in the 1980s, with similar high rates of infections reported among gay and bisexual men in other
15 large cities (Torian et al., 1996). Given the high likelihood of HIV transmission during unprotected anal intercourse between male partners and a high prevalence of HIV infection, men who engage in unprotected anal intercourse outside of assuredly exclusive relationships
20 with partners of known HIV serostatus are extremely vulnerable to contracting HIV. Still, research shows that a significant number of gay and bisexual men continue to practice unprotected anal sex outside of monogamous relationships (Lemp et al., 1994; Osmond et
25 al., 1994).

Efforts to identify predictors of successful sexual risk reduction have drawn extensively on cognitive, motivational, and skills-based theoretical models (Bandura, 1994; Fishbein & Azjen, 1975), as well as con-
30 ceptual models specific to AIDS-preventive behavior (Catania, Kegeles, & Coates, 1990; Fisher & Fisher, 1992). Success in changing risk behaviors has been predicted by such psychological factors as perceived self-efficacy for making changes, strength of behavior
35 change intentions, favorable attitudes concerning condom use and other forms of safer sex, and sexual communication and assertiveness skills (Fisher, Fisher, & Rye, 1995). These factors are all associated with HIV risk reduction, but efforts to understand risk and assist
40 individuals to reduce risk requires attention to additional factors that influence risk behavior change and change maintenance.

A potentially important contributing factor to HIV risk that has received little attention is one's outlook
45 toward the future and experience of current life circumstances. Frutchey, Blankenship, Stall, and Henne (1995) reported that gay men in San Francisco who perceived themselves as lacking a future and held fatalistic views on AIDS were more likely to engage in
50 HIV risk-producing behaviors. These conclusions were based on in-depth interviews with men who reported high-risk sex. Rothspan and Read (1996) found that college students with positive views of the future practiced more methods of HIV risk reduction than fatalis-
55 tic students. Similarly, DiIorio, Parsons, Lehr, Adame, and Carlone (1993) reported that African American college students who had more constricted perceptions of their future were less likely to practice safer sex than more future-oriented students. Finally, Kalichman,

60 Rompa, and Muhammad (in press) found that scores on a fatalism scale significantly predicted engaging in sexual risk behaviors in a sample of low-income African American men. These findings converge to suggest that fatalistic thinking may characterize some persons 65 who engage in high-risk sexual practices.

There are several mechanisms through which life satisfaction and future outlook could influence HIV risk taking and risk reduction behavioral changes. Enacting behavior changes to reduce risk for HIV-AIDS 70 is difficult, it requires sustained vigilance against potential risk-producing situations, delaying or changing modes of sexual gratification, and it may result in partner resistance and relationship conflicts. Under such conditions, successful behavior change would only be 75 expected when individuals are satisfied with their lives and hold a strong positive outlook or expectancy for their future. In contrast, individuals who are dissatisfied with their lives and hold constricted outlooks for the future will likely have less motivation to adopt dif-80 ficult steps to reduce their risks. Other life-threatening risks, such as violence and drug use, have been associated with a negative world view and a constricted perspective of the future (Eron, Gentry, & Schlegel, 1994). It is likely that condom use and the adoption of 85 other steps toward HIV prevention will be greater among persons with a secure and positive outlook for the future given that they may have a greater sense of goals and aspirations.

The purpose of this research was to examine fatal-90 ism among men who have unprotected anal intercourse with men in nonexclusively partnered relationships. In addition, we sought to explore differences in perceived life expectancy and perceived current life satisfaction between gay men who reported abstinence or only 95 safer sex versus those who reported recent high-risk sexual behavior. Because whether an individual is in an exclusively partnered relationship may influence sexual behavior practices and the HIV risk associated with those practices, we also investigated the effects of rela-100 tionship status on life satisfaction and future outlook. We hypothesized that men who engaged in high-risk sex outside of exclusive relationships would be characterized by higher scores on a fatalism scale, lower present life satisfaction, and shortened expected length 105 of life.

Method

Participants

Four hundred thirty men were recruited at the June 1995 gay pride celebration in Milwaukee, Wisconsin, and were asked to complete anonymous surveys concerning HIV risk-associated sexual behaviors. This 110 festival was chosen as the site for data collection because of its size and the diversity of men who have sex with men who historically attend this event. Eighty-three percent of the sample was White, 9% African American, 4% Hispanic, and 4% of other ethnic back-115 grounds. The mean age of survey respondents was 33.2 years ($SD = 8.2$). The average number of years of completed education was 14.4 ($SD = 1.7$). Ninety-one percent of the sample identified themselves as exclusively gay, whereas the remaining 9% identified themselves 120 as bisexual.

Procedures and Measures

Potential participants were asked if they would complete a survey concerning HIV and AIDS requiring approximately 10 min. Over 90% of men approached agreed to complete the survey. Participant names were 125 not collected at any time during the survey. Participants were given gay pride novelty items, such as rainbow flags and key chains, in exchange for participating. The measures included demographic information, substance use, and HIV risk behavior and scales of fatalism and 130 life satisfaction. Each of these measures is described briefly below.

Demographics. Participants were asked their age, number of years of education, ethnicity, and whether they describe themselves as exclusively gay, bisexual, 135 or heterosexual. We also asked men if they were exclusively partnered, defined as being in a relationship with only one man for at least 6 months. Men also reported whether they had been tested for HIV antibodies and, if so, the results of their most recent test.

140 *Substance use and HIV risk behavior.* Substance use was assessed by asking participants the number of times that they had used alcohol and other drugs (marijuana, cocaine, and other substances) before engaging in sex in the previous 6 months. Responses 145 were recorded using open formats, requesting the number of occasions of substance use/sexual behavior in that time period, linking substance use to sexual behavior (Leigh & Stall, 1993). Open formats of this kind have been shown to increase response accuracy 150 (Catania, Gibson, Chitwood, & Coates, 1990).

We measured sexual behavior by asking participants to report the number of times they had engaged in anal intercourse, as the insertive partner and as the receptive partner, as well as the number of times they 155 used or did not use condoms during anal intercourse in the past 6 months. Insertive and receptive partner were combined to define a group of men who reported any unprotected anal intercourse in the previous 6 months. Participants also recorded the number of sexual part-160 ners with whom they had engaged in each behavior in the previous 6 months. Open-response formats were also used for the sexual behavior measure. Measures similar to those used in this study have been found reliable (Kauth, St. Lawrence, & Kelly, 1991).

165 *Fatalism.* Participants completed a measure of fatalistic thinking adapted from the Future Time Perspective Inventory (Heimberg, 1963), which has been found to predict safer sex practices in young heterosexual men (DiIorio et al., 1993). Responses to seven 170 items were reported on 7-point scales ranging from 1

(*completely disagree*) to 7 (*completely agree*). Items included "I look forward to the future with hope and enthusiasm" (reverse scored), "my future seems dark to me," "I expect that my plans for my future will change many times," "I don't know what kind of work I will do in the future," "The future seems very vague and uncertain to me," "I have great faith in the future" (reverse scored), and "sometimes I feel there is nothing new to look forward to in the future." The possible range of scores was 7 to 49, with higher scores representing greater fatalism. The seven-item Fatalism scale was reliable, with an internal consistency coefficient (alpha) of .70.

Life satisfaction. To assess self-perceived life satisfaction, we used eight items derived from the Quality of Life Inventory (Frisch, Cornell, Villanueva, & Retzlaff, 1992). Participants indicated how satisfied they were with their present income, love relationships, home, family relationships, friendships, sex life, job–career, and health. Responses to items were made on 6-point scales ranging from 1 (*not at all satisfied*) to 6 (*very satisfied*); the possible range of scores was 8 to 48, with high scores representing greater life satisfaction. The eight-item Life Satisfaction scale was reliable, $\alpha = .69$.

Perceived life expectancy. To assess perceptions of how much longer they believed they would live, we asked participants to estimate the age to which they expected to live. Current age was subtracted from this figure, and the difference was used to index perceived expected years of life.

Statistical Analyses

Participants were grouped according to whether they had engaged in unprotected anal intercourse in the past 6 months. We also partitioned the sample on the basis of current relationship status: exclusively partnered men and those not exclusively partnered. Being exclusively partnered was defined by self-identifying being in an exclusive relationship and reporting only one sex partner in the previous 6 months. Nonexclusively partnered men were defined by either reporting no sex partners or indicating that they had at least one male sex partner in the past 6 months but were not in an exclusive relationship. Seventy-five men indicated that they had multiple sex partners in the past 6 months but were now in exclusive relationships. These men were omitted from comparisons between relationship status groups to avoid confounding numbers of partners across relationship groups. This yielded 355 (83% of the sample) men included in the analyses. Groups were compared on dependent measures using 2 (engaged in unprotected anal intercourse vs. did not engage in unprotected anal intercourse) × 2 (exclusively partnered vs. not exclusively partnered) analyses of covariance (ANCOVA) controlling for participant age.

Because men who were HIV seropositive may differ in terms of their life satisfaction and future outlook in light of their illness and their expected years of life, we examined the distribution of HIV seropositive men across the four cells in the analysis. Results showed that HIV seropositive men were equally distributed across groups, $\chi^2(1, N = 355) = 0.30$, $p > .1$ (see Table 1). Thus, HIV serostatus did not introduce a confound in the study. Finally, for sexual and drug use variables where the distributions of behavior were highly skewed, data were transformed for parametric analyses using the formula $\log_{10}(x + 1)$ (Winer, 1971).

Results

Eighty-six percent of participants reported at least one male sex partner in the past 6 months. In the entire sample, 32% of men reported having unprotected insertive anal intercourse ($M = 3.5$, $SD = 12.01$), and 30% reported engaging in unprotected receptive anal intercourse ($M = 4.1$, $SD = 15.9$) in the past 6 months. Among men who engaged in any form of anal intercourse, a mean of 47% ($SD = 43.4$) of intercourse occasions were not protected by condoms. Ninety-two men (21%) reported use of condoms during all anal intercourse occasions. Among the 176 (41%) men who had engaged in any unprotected intercourse in the past 6 months, only 26% ($SD = 31.10$) of anal intercourse occasions were protected by condoms.

There was a significant association between engaging in unprotected anal intercourse and relationship status, $\chi^2(1, N = 355) = 30.01$, $p < .01$; 52% of men who engaged in unprotected anal intercourse were in exclusive relationships, whereas 25% of men who were not partnered reported this behavior. Forty-four (12%) men reported that they were HIV infected. Contingency table analyses failed to show associations between HIV serostatus and having engaged in recent risky sex or relationship status.

Substance Use in Relation to Sex

Controlling for participant age, ANCOVAs between risk and relationship status groups showed that men who had engaged in unprotected anal intercourse reported more use of both alcohol, $F(1, 336) = 28.49$, $p < .01$, and recreational drugs other than alcohol, $F(1, 336) = 12.15$, $p < .01$, in conjunction with sexual behavior. Relationship status groups did not differ with respect to substance use. However, there was a significant interaction with respect to recreational drug use, $F(1, 336) = 10.99$, $p < .01$; men who had engaged in unprotected intercourse with partners outside exclusive relationships reported greater drug use in association with sex (see Table 1).

Fatalism and Life Satisfaction

An ANCOVA conducted between risk groups and relationship status groups on the Fatalism scale, controlling for participant age, did not indicate main effects for having engaged in unprotected anal intercourse or relationship status. However, the interaction effect was significant, $F(1, 349) = 3.82$, $p < .05$; post

Table 1

Means (and Standard Deviations) for Alcohol and Drug Use During Sex, Fatalism, Life Satisfaction, Expected Years of Life, and Percentage of HIV-Seropositive Men Among HIV Risk and Relationship Status Groups

Measure	Did not engage in anal intercourse		Engaged in anal intercourse	
	Not partnered ($n = 178$)	Partnered ($n = 53$)	Not partnered ($n = 60$)	Partnered ($n = 64$)
Alcohol use before sex	4.3 (13.3)	7.8 (17.0)	11.6 (16.7)	12.1 (28.7)
Drug use before sex	1.5_a (6.9)	4.8_a (17.8)	12.6_b (40.9)	3.3_a (13.8)
Fatalism	22.1_a (7.1)	22.1_a (7.5)	24.2_b (8.1)	20.9_a (6.7)
Life satisfaction	32.1_a (7.6)	35.8_a (6.7)	30.6_b (7.6)	37.6_a (4.4)
Expected years of life*	41.6_b (19.0)	38.9 (18.5)	37.9_a (18.9)	46.5_b (16.4)
% HIV seropositive	9	11	15	8

Note. Means with different subscripts across rows are significantly different.
*Self-estimated age of death minus current age.

hoc tests showed that men who had engaged in unprotected anal intercourse outside of exclusive relationships scored higher on fatalism. With respect to life satisfaction, the main effect for having engaged in unprotected anal intercourse was not significant, but relationship status was significant, $F(1, 349) = 38.55, p < .01$; exclusively partnered men reported higher life satisfaction. The interaction effect was also significant, $F(1, 349) = 4.15, p < .05$; post hoc tests showed that men who had engaged in unprotected anal intercourse outside of exclusive relationships reported lower life satisfaction (see Table 1).

Perceived Life Expectancy

A 2 (Sexual Risk Behavior) × 2 (Relationship Status) ANCOVA for number of years of expected life, controlling for participant age, did not indicate main effects for either sexual risk or relationship status groups. Results did show a significant interaction between sexual risk behavior and relationship status groups, $F(1, 332) = 6.65, p < .01$; men who had engaged in unprotected anal intercourse and were not in an exclusive relationship expected to live a significantly shorter time than the other groups except men who were partnered and did not practice unprotected anal intercourse, where the difference was negligible (see Table 1).

Discussion

Most research conducted on factors related to high-risk sexual behavior and risk reduction behavior change has emphasized the role of psychological constructs closely and proximally related to the initiation of risk reduction such as AIDS risk knowledge, condom attitudes, behavior change intention and skills, and perceived risk reduction self-efficacy. Although these factors often predict risk reduction behavioral change, the present study's results indicate that broader contextual factors—including fatalistic outlook, uncertainty concerning the future, perceived short life expectancy, and current life dissatisfaction, also charac-

terize gay men who engage in HIV high-risk sexual behavior. To the extent that persons do not hold positive views for their future, and to the extent that life is currently lacking satisfaction, motivation to initiate and maintain risk reduction changes is likely to be weaker. It is not surprising that individuals would be most likely to take steps to preserve their well-being when they hold positive views of the future and when their present life circumstances are seen to merit wanting to live a long life. The present study's findings raise the disquieting but important possibility that some gay men may engage in high-risk sexual behavior because they do not perceive their future as promising or certain.

Of particular significance was the effect of relationship status in ameliorating these associations. Gay men in exclusively partnered relationships did not, for the most part, share the fatalistic and uncertain outlook of men not in exclusive relationships. Exclusively partnered men reported greater current life satisfaction than men who did not have primary relationships. Our findings indicating greater life satisfaction among partnered gay men relative to men not in exclusive relationships parallel similar findings of adjustment for persons in heterosexual relationships (Klerman, 1987). Whether having a stable partnered relationship produces greater present life satisfaction and a more positive future orientation, or whether gay men who already have these characteristics are more likely to enter and sustain exclusively partnered relationships, cannot be determined with this study's methodology.

Short-time horizon, fatalistic and uncertain future perspectives, and present life dissatisfaction appear related to risk in the present study. However, other interpretations concerning direction of effects are possible. For example, gay men who engage in unprotected anal intercourse outside exclusive relationships expected to live a shorter time than gay men who did not engage in risky sex. Although shorter perceived life expectancy might produce greater risk taking, it is also possible that those men who engage in high-risk be-

360 havior perceive that they may contract HIV and die at an earlier age than men who avoid risky behavior. It is also possible that factors not assessed in this study—including personality dispositions, sociocultural factors, internalized homophobia, or other dimensions—could account both for increased propensity to engage in high-risk sexual behavior and for life dissatisfaction and fatalistic or uncertain future

365 outlook. Also, our measure of fatalism may have tapped other constructs, such as pessimism or depression, neither of which were assessed in the present study. Further research will be needed to understand the mechanisms underlying these

370 relationships. The sample was one of convenience, predominantly White, and was recruited at a gay pride event. The sample may have underrepresented hidden and less self-accepting gay men since these persons would be less likely to attend a gay pride celebration. If

375 that is the case, the magnitude and prevalence of life dissatisfaction and negative life outlook indicators may actually be greater than those observed in this sample.

In spite of these limitations, the present findings carry several implications for HIV prevention efforts

380 with gay and bisexual men. One is the importance of more strongly embedding HIV risk reduction recommendations in the context of broader messages that affirm pride, self-esteem, and the belief that gay men deserve and can achieve long, productive, and gratify-

385 ing lives. HIV prevention efforts should emphasize contextual "reasons" for change, particularly as they relate to self-affirmation, pride, and positive expectations for the future, as well as technical aspects of risk reduction such as learning how to use condoms and

390 promoting positive attitudes about safer sex (Kalichman, Carey, & Johnson, 1996). HIV prevention interventions that strengthen these beliefs are more likely to provide frameworks and reasons for making and sustaining behavior change. These issues are likely

395 to be especially critical for young men who have sex with men because they are still experiencing a rapid increase in HIV infection incidence (Lemp et al., 1994; Osmond et al., 1994). As is true for other populations vulnerable to AIDS, continued HIV prevention efforts

400 among gay or bisexual men are likely to prove most successful and enduring when they occur in a broader social context that affirms self-worth, encourages personal pride, and supports personal decisions to establish stable relationships.

References

Bandura, A. (1994). Social cognitive theory and exercise of control over HIV infection. In R. DiClemente & J. Peterson (Eds.), *Preventing AIDS: Theories, methods, and behavioral interventions* (pp. 25–60). New York: Plenum.

Catania, J., Gibson, D., Chitwood, D., & Coates, T. (1990). Methodological problems in AIDS behavioral research: Influences on measurement error and participation bias in studies of sexual behavior. *Psychological Bulletin, 108,* 339–362.

Catania, J. A., Kegeles, S. M., & Coates, T. J. (1990). Toward an understanding of risk behavior: An AIDS risk reduction model (ARRM). *Health Education Quarterly, 17,* 53–72.

Centers for Disease Control and Prevention. (1995). *HIV/AIDS surveillance report: U.S. HIV and AIDS cases reported through December 1994.* Atlanta: Author.

DiIorio, C., Parsons, M., Lehr, S., Adame, D., & Carlone, J. (1993). Factors associated with use of safer sex practices among college freshmen. *Research in Nursing and Health, 16,* 343–350.

Eron, L. D., Gentry, J., & Schlegel, P. (1994). *Reason to hope: A psychological perspective on violence and youth.* Washington, DC: American Psychological Association.

Fishbein, M., & Azjen, I. (1975). *Belief, attitude, intention, and behavior: An introduction to theory and research.* Reading, MA: Addison-Wesley.

Fisher, J. D, & Fisher, W. A. (1992). Changing AIDS risk behavior. *Psychological Bulletin, 111,* 455–474.

Fisher, W. A., Fisher, J. D., & Rye, B. J. (1995). Understanding and promoting AIDS-preventive behavior: Insights from the theory of reasoned action. *Health Psychology, 14,* 255–264.

Frisch, M. B., Cornell, J., Villanueva, M., & Retzlaff, P. J. (1992). Clinical validation of the Quality of Life Inventory: A measure of life satisfaction for use in treatment planning and outcome assessment. *Psychological Assessment, 4,* 92–101.

Frutchey, C., Blankenship, W., Stall, R., & Henne, J. (1995). *Ability to envision a future predicts safe sex among gay men.* Unpublished manuscript.

Heimberg, L. K. (1963). *The measurement of future time perspective.* Unpublished doctoral dissertation. Nashville, TN: Vanderbilt University.

Kalichman, S. C., Carey, M. P., & Johnson, B. T. (1996). Prevention of sexually transmitted HIV infection: A meta-analytic review and critique of the theory-based intervention outcome literature. *Annals of Behavioral Medicine, 18,* 6–15.

Kalichman, S. C., Rompa, D., & Muhammad, A. (in press). Psychological predictors of risk for human immunodeficiency virus (HIV) infection among low-income inner-city men: A community-based survey. *Psychology and Health.*

Kauth, M., St. Lawrence, J., & Kelly, J. (1991). Reliability of retrospective assessments of sexual HIV risk behavior: A comparison of bi-weekly, three-month, and twelve-month self-reports. *AIDS Education and Prevention, 3,* 207–214.

Klerman, G. L. (1987). Clinical epidemiology of suicide. *Journal of Clinical Psychiatry, 48,* 33–38.

Leigh, B. C., & Stall, R. (1993). Substance use and risky sexual behavior for exposure to HIV: Issues in methodology, interpretation, and prevention. *American Psychologist, 48,* 1035–1045.

Lemp, G. F., Hirozawa, A. M., Givertz, D., Nicri, G. N., Anderson, L., Lindegren, M. L., Janssen, R. S., & Katz, M. (1994). Seroprevalence of HIV and risk behaviors among young homosexual and bisexual men: The San Francisco/Berkeley Young Men's Survey. *Journal of the American Medical Association, 272,* 449–454.

Osmond, D. H., Page, K., Wiley, J., Garrett, K., Sheppard, H. W., Moss, A. R., Schawrager, L., & Winkelstein, W. (1994). HIV infection in homosexual and bisexual men 18 to 29 years of age: The San Francisco young men's health study. *American Journal of Public Health, 84,* 1933–1937.

Rosenberg, P. S. (1995). Scope of the AIDS epidemic in the United States. *Science, 270,* 1372–1375.

Rothspan, S., & Read, S. J. (1996). Present versus future time perspective and HIV risk among heterosexual college students. *Health Psychology, 15,* 131–134.

Torian, L. V., Weisfuse, I. B., Makki, H. A., Benson, D., DiCamillo, L., Patel, P., & Toribio, F. (1996). Trends in HIV seroprevalence in men who have sex with men: New York City Department of Health sexually transmitted disease clinics, 1988–1993. *AIDS, 10,* 187–192.

Winer, B. J. (1971). *Statistical principles in experimental design.* New York: McGraw-Hill.

Note: This research was supported by a National Institute of Mental Health (NIMH) Center Grant P30 MH52776 and NIMH Grants R01 MH48286 and R01 MH53780.

About the authors: Seth C. Kalichman, Department of Psychology, Georgia State University, and Center for AIDS Intervention Research, Medical College of Wisconsin; Jeffrey A. Kelly, Michael Morgan, and David Rompa, Center for AIDS Intervention Research, Medical College of Wisconsin. Michael Morgan is now deceased.

Address correspondence to: Seth C. Kalichman, Department of Psychology, Georgia State University, University Plaza, Atlanta, GA 30303. Electronic mail may be sent via Internet to psysck@panther.gsu.edu

Exercise for Article 2

Factual Questions

1. What is the explicitly stated hypothesis for this study?

2. What was the average age of the respondents in this study?

3. What is the definition of "exclusively partnered?"

4. Do *higher scores* or *lower scores* indicate greater fatalism?

5. What percentage of the respondents reported using condoms during all anal intercourse occasions?

6. According to Table 1, which one of the four groups had the highest average incidence of engaging in drug use before sex?

7. According to Table 1, which one of the four groups had the lowest average life satisfaction score?

Questions for Discussion

8. Speculate on what the researchers mean by "reverse scored" as used in the paragraph in lines 165–183.

9. Are you surprised that over 90% of the men who were approached agreed to participate in the study given the potentially sensitive nature of the questions asked? Would you have expected such a high rate of participation? Explain.

10. The researchers note that their sample of "convenience" may have affected the results. Do you agree? (See lines 370–377.)

11. To what population(s), if any, would you be willing to generalize the results of this study?

12. If you were to conduct another study on the same topic, what changes in the research methodology would you make?

Quality Ratings

Directions: Indicate your level of agreement with each of the following statements by circling a number from 5 for strongly agree (SA) to 1 for strongly disagree (SD). If you believe an item is not applicable to this research article, leave it blank. Be prepared to explain your ratings.

A. The introduction establishes the importance of the study.

SA   5   4   3   2   1   SD

B. The literature review establishes the context for the study.

SA   5   4   3   2   1   SD

C. The research purpose, question, or hypothesis is clearly stated.

SA   5   4   3   2   1   SD

D. The method of sampling is sound.

SA   5   4   3   2   1   SD

E. Relevant demographics (for example, age, gender, and ethnicity) are described.

SA   5   4   3   2   1   SD

F. Measurement procedures are adequate.

SA   5   4   3   2   1   SD

G. All procedures have been described in sufficient detail to permit a replication of the study.

SA   5   4   3   2   1   SD

H. The participants have been adequately protected from potential harm.

SA   5   4   3   2   1   SD

I. The results are clearly described.

SA   5   4   3   2   1   SD

J. The discussion/conclusion is appropriate.

SA   5   4   3   2   1   SD

K. Despite any flaws, the report is worthy of publication.

SA   5   4   3   2   1   SD

Article 3

Implications of Racial Diversity in the Supervisor-Subordinate Relationship

SANDY JEANQUART-BARONE
Murray State University

ABSTRACT. This study addresses the impact of race on the supervisor-subordinate relationship. The purpose is to examine this relationship with minority subordinates reporting to both majority and minority group members. Using the subordinates needs framework identified by Baird and Kram (1983), 5 areas were addressed: supervisory support, developmental opportunities, procedural justice, acceptance or assimilation, and discrimination. The results indicated that African American subordinates with White supervisors experience less supervisory support, developmental opportunities, procedural justice, assimilation, and more discrimination than African American subordinates with African American supervisors.

From *Journal of Applied Social Psychology, 26,* 935–944.

The supervisor-subordinate relationship is the fundamental building block of the organization. A smooth working relationship without unnecessary tension between the supervisor and the subordinate is critical to
5 the organization since most of the initiatives and activities are taken at that level to achieve the organization's goals. The perceived attitudes and behaviors of the supervisor influence the attitudes and behaviors of the subordinates and vice versa. The effort expended
10 on the job and the subordinate's performance and satisfaction with work are also influenced by the attitudes and behaviors of the supervisor (Klimoski & Hayes, 1980). Despite the importance of the supervisor-subordinate relationship, little research focuses exclu-
15 sively on this relationship when the subordinate is an African American, with the exception of Tsui and O'Reilly (1989). This issue will become more and more important given the expected increase of minorities in the work force as predicted by Johnston and
20 Packer (1987).

The importance of addressing the impact of race on the supervisor-subordinate relationship is not only important because of the increasing numbers of minorities in organizations, but more so because supervisors dif-
25 fering in race have greater propensity for poor relations (Shuter, 1982; Tsui & O'Reilly, 1989). The purpose of this study is to examine the supervisor-subordinate relationship for African Americans reporting to Whites as compared to African Americans reporting to African
30 Americans. Examining these different effects will allow organizations to identify the specific areas of the supervisor-subordinate relationship that are prone to be problematic when subordinates differ in race from their supervisors. By identifying these areas, interventions
35 can be taken to allow virtually all employees a positive relationship with their supervisor.

Framework

The projected demographic changes can be expected to lead to an increase in the level of tension experienced by minority subordinates in organizations
40 since the dynamics of interactions between members differing in race are shown to be different from interactions among members of the same race (Shuter, 1982). People who differ in race have different socialization patterns, come from different backgrounds, pos-
45 sess different values (Foeman & Pressley, 1987), and quite possibly differ in their social interaction mode. These factors are likely to contribute to difficulties, especially between the supervisor and the subordinate (Dalton, 1959; Thompson, 1960) due to misperceptions
50 and personal prejudices.

In the supervisor-subordinate relationship, as in any relationship, both parties bring their own needs into the situation. Several needs of the subordinate were identified by Baird and Kram (1983). These needs include
55 the career support of the supervisor, developmental opportunities, accurate performance appraisals (procedural justice), and acceptance or assimilation into the majority work group of the organization. A final variable not included in the work of Baird and Kram, but
60 which has been found to be of concern to women and minorities, is shelter from discriminatory treatment from the subordinate's supervisor. Considerable research has shown that discrimination would be an issue for a minority subordinate. Using the variables that
65 Baird and Kram found to be pertinent in a healthy supervisor-subordinate relationship, this study examined these five variables (supervisory support, developmental opportunities, procedural justice, assimilation, and discrimination) when supervisors and subordinates
70 are both similar and dissimilar in terms of race.

Supervisory support refers to both the amount of

career guidance and information and the number of challenging work assignments that promote development. Using the work of Jones (1986) and Alderfer, Alderfer, Tucker, and Tucker (1980), it can be expected that African American subordinates will receive less support from their White supervisors. Jones found only 15% of the African Americans in his sample experienced a supportive climate, while Alderfer et al. found that African American employees do not receive as much important career information as do their White counterparts. While this research examined the experiences of African Americans reporting to Whites, research addressing African Americans reporting to African Americans is virtually nonexistent. However, when the supervisor is African American and has most likely had similar organizational experiences, the African American supervisor as opposed to the White supervisor may be more sensitized to the needs of the African American subordinate. Given this sensitivity, it could be expected that African Americans reporting to African Americans will experience higher levels of supervisory support than African Americans reporting to Whites.

Developmental opportunities are measured by the extent to which supervisors provide their subordinates with opportunities to improve skills and abilities through self-improvement seminars and challenging assignments. The work of Ilgen and Youtz (1986), Alderfer et al. (1980), and Nixon (1985) suggests that minorities in organizations receive fewer opportunities for training and development that prepare them for additional responsibilities. Again, this research is based on examining situations in which African Americans report to Whites. However, the African American supervisor may make extra efforts to ensure that African American subordinates are given opportunities for further development. Based on this, it can be expected that African Americans reporting to Whites will experience significantly fewer developmental opportunities than African Americans reporting to African Americans.

Procedural justice refers to the perceived fairness in the allocation of organizational rewards. While research examining procedural justice is limited, we can look at how supervisors evaluate the performance of subordinates. Kraiger and Ford (1985) in their meta-analysis, and more recently Greenhaus, Parasuraman, and Wormley (1990), found that the race of the rater and ratee did indeed influence performance evaluations. More specifically, it was found that African American employees were rated less favorably, especially when their rater was White. When this happens, it is quite likely that African American subordinates will perceive the appraisal process as unfair since the supervisor's evaluation is perceived as being inaccurate. Given these studies, it can be expected that African Americans reporting to Whites will perceive lower levels of procedural justice than African Americans reporting to African Americans.

Assimilation refers to the socialization or the acceptance of an individual into the informal networks of an organization (Teske & Nelson, 1974). Using the attraction-similarity paradigm, we can examine the dynamics of race in the assimilation process. The attraction-similarity paradigm suggests that people tend to be drawn to those who are similar to them in terms of demographic characteristics, activities, or attitudes (Byrne, Clore, & Worchel, 1966). Since the majority group in organizations is usually Whites, and since there are obvious differences between African Americans and Whites, it can be expected that African Americans as compared to Whites would experience more difficulties in being accepted by majority group members. Tsui and O'Reilly (1989) found that the more dissimilar the supervisor and subordinates are in terms of race and gender, the less effective the supervisor perceives the subordinate to be and the less the supervisor is attracted to the subordinate. These perceptions and attitudes are likely to contribute to distancing, aloofness, and related problems in the supervisor-subordinate relationship. Based on the above discussion, it is expected that African Americans reporting to Whites will experience significantly lower levels of assimilation than African Americans reporting to African Americans.

Discrimination is defined as making a distinction in favor of or against a person on the basis of the group, class, or category to which the individual belongs, rather than on actual merit (Webster, 1989). Biased perceptions and discriminatory treatment are most influenced by stereotypes held by individuals. Common stereotypes of African Americans include: "African Americans are trying to use Whites," "African Americans will always welcome and appreciate inclusion in White society," "All African Americans are alike in their attitudes and behaviors," and "African Americans are lazy and prefer not to work." These stereotypes portray African Americans in a negative light. While stereotypes abound for Whites as well, African Americans are more likely to be stifled by stereotypes than Whites, due in part to the greater number of Whites in the upper levels of organizations. Fernandez (1987) has shown that racist stereotypes are often carried into the organization, resulting in discriminatory treatment. Based on this discussion, it is suggested that African Americans reporting to Whites will experience significantly higher levels of discrimination than African Americans reporting to African Americans.

In sum, it is expected that African Americans reporting to African Americans will experience higher levels of supervisory support, developmental opportunities, procedural justice, assimilation, and lower levels of discrimination than African Americans reporting to Whites.

Table 1
Means, Standard Deviations, Reliabilities, and Source of Measures

Variable	Source of measure	Maximum possible	Number of items	M	SD	Cronbach's α	Split half reliability
Supervisory support	Greenhaus, Parasuraman, & Wormley (1990)	5	9	2.30	1.01	.95	.92
Developmental opportunities	Developed for study	5	3	2.69	1.05	.88	.80
Procedural justice	Folger & Konovsky (1989)	5	26	2.15	0.82	.94	.83
Assimilation	Hood (1989)	7	10	2.98	1.18	.84	.81
Discrimination	Adapted from ISR[a]	5	7	3.29	0.93	.89	.83

[a]ISR is the Institute for Social Research, the University of Michigan, Ann Arbor, 1973.

Method

Subjects

The population for this study was a national minority organization for federal government employees. This sample was selected due to its minority population. The cover letter of the questionnaire was written on the organization's letterhead and signed by the top executive. The survey ensured confidentiality to the respondents and was accompanied by a postage-paid envelope pre-addressed to the researcher. Of the 1,400 questionnaires that were sent, 163 were returned and 146 of those were from African American respondents. Due to the low response rate (12%), the demographic data of the respondents were compared to the demographic data of the population. Since no significant differences were apparent, subsequent analyses were run. According to King and Miles (1992), it is not uncommon for minorities to be less responsive to surveys than Whites. In fact, one respondent to the survey indicated that he/she filled out several surveys in the work place and nothing was done with the information. For many individuals when this happens, any surveys that are subsequently sent are perceived as a waste of time. Despite the response rate, this study is important since it is one of the first to examine the supervisory relationships of minorities using a national sample.

Table 2
Results of t Tests for Blacks Reporting to Blacks and Blacks Reporting to Whites

	M			
Variable	Blacks reporting to Blacks[a]	Blacks reporting to Whites[b]	t value	$p <$
Supervisory support	2.51	2.08	2.54	.005
Development opportunities	2.84	2.57	1.61	.05
Procedural justice	2.42	1.91	3.70	.0001
Assimilation	3.13	2.79	1.74	.04
Discrimination	3.13	3.50	−2.45	.005

[a]$n = 76$. [b]$n = 70$.

The sample was comprised only of African American employees, 26% of whom were clerks, 23% were postal carriers, 9% were general managers, and the remaining 42% held various other positions, including consultant, therapy technician, data technician, superintendent, nurse, and so on. Forty percent of the respondents were females. Thirty-nine percent of the respondents were between the ages of 41 and 50, with 29% being younger, and 32% being older. Forty-five percent of the respondents had attended some college, while 30% had at least a bachelor's degree. Thirty-one percent of the respondents had been employed by their organization between 19 and 25 years, and 46% were with the organization less than 19 years. Seventy-six (52%) of the respondents had an African American supervisor, and 70 (48%) respondents reported to a White supervisor.

Variables and Measures

Single-item questions tapped the demographic variables of gender, race, age, education, tenure in the job and organization, and race of supervisor. The measure and reliabilities for supervisory support, developmental opportunities, procedural justice, assimilation, and discrimination are provided in Table 1.

Data Analysis

The purpose of this study is to compare the relationship between African American subordinates reporting to African American supervisors and African American subordinates reporting to White supervisors. In order to achieve this objective, t tests were used to determine if there were significant differences in supervisory support, developmental opportunities, procedural justice, assimilation, and discrimination for African Americans reporting to African Americans and African Americans reporting to Whites.

Results

The means and standard deviations are also shown in Table 1. As can be seen, the supervisory support and the procedural justice experienced by the respondents are relatively low. Discrimination is moderately high at 3.29.

The results of the t tests are reported in Table 2. As can be seen, African Americans reporting to Whites experience significantly lower levels of supervisory support, fewer developmental opportunities, less pro-

19

cedural justice, and less assimilation and higher levels of discrimination than African Americans reporting to African Americans. The implications of this study will now be addressed.

Discussion

This study is one of the first to empirically contrast the relationship between African American subordinates reporting to African American supervisors and African American subordinates reporting to White supervisors. The results suggest that African American subordinates with White supervisors experience less supervisory support, fewer developmental opportunities, less procedural justice, less assimilation, and higher levels of discrimination. These results clearly indicate that supervisors are going to have to learn to better manage their subordinates who differ from them in terms of race.

The findings also have strong implications for organizations, especially in the context of the changing demographics of the work force. Organizations will have to have formal interventions to improve the relationships between supervisors and subordinates who differ in race if the organization wants to achieve high levels of productivity. Several suggestions are provided below.

One key intervention can occur in awareness training programs. These programs are similar to sensitivity training in that the program allows people to get in touch with their stereotypes and false assumptions about members of other races. Once they become aware of their stereotypes, the next step is the discovery of how these stereotypes influence their behaviors and decisions that result in subtle discrimination. The purpose is to encourage discussion and self-development to allow people to struggle with their prejudices in a safe environment. The goal of this technique is to change the attitudes of managers and to help them understand the dynamics of race.

While training is important, it is often not enough. Xerox found that training was a start, but unless something else was done to reinforce the newly acquired behavior, the old behavior continued to occur. It was only when Xerox tied their efforts at managing a diversified work force to the performance appraisal system that managers took the program seriously (Sessa, 1992). It was after this that Xerox noticed changes in the ways that minority employees were being managed.

A third intervention can occur with the organization's socialization process. A formal mentoring program for organizational members will help in the assimilation process as all members learn both the formal and the informal systems. This can also be expected to help the supervisor-subordinate relationship since supervisors perceive subordinates with mentors as more competent than subordinates without mentors (Kram, 1985).

While the above three interventions are generalized approaches, organization specific strategies are still required and should entail communicating with minorities in the organization. For instance, conduct an anonymous survey. Examine responses and identify areas that seem especially problematic for minority group members as well as majority group members. When these variables are identified and eliminated, all members benefit. Another aspect is to examine the turnover rate for specific groups of individuals. Exit interviews can then be conducted to identify processes or people that are racially biased.

The goal of this study was to compare the experiences of African American subordinates with White supervisors to African American subordinates with African American supervisors. Future research may also wish to examine the interaction of race and gender, as well as to look at how the cross-race supervisor-subordinate relationship can be altered by the presence of a mentor. While further research in this area is necessary, the results from this exploratory study suggest that the relationship between African American subordinates and their White supervisors requires improvements. These improvements can increase the competitive advantage of organizations, as well as productivity.

References

Alderfer, C. P., Alderfer, C. J., Tucker, L., & Tucker, R. (1980). Diagnosing race relations in management. *Journal of Applied Behavior Science, 27,* 135–166.

Baird, L. & Kram, K. E. (1983). Career dynamics: Managing the superior/subordinate relationship. *Organizational Dynamics, 11,* 46–64.

Byrne, D., Clore, G. L., Jr., & Worchel, P. (1966). The effect of economic similarity-dissimilarity as determinants of attraction. *Journal of Personality and Social Psychology, 51,* 1167–1170.

Dalton, M. (1959). *Men who manage.* New York, NY: John Wiley & Sons.

Fernandez, J. P. (1987). *Survival in the corporate fishbowl.* Lexington, MA: Lexington.

Foeman, A. K. & Pressley, G. (1987). Ethnic culture and corporate culture: Using Black style in organizations. *Communication Quarterly, 35,* 101–118.

Folger, R. & Konovsky, M. (1989). Effects of procedural justice and distributive justice on reactions to pay raise decisions. *Academy of Management Journal, 32,* 115–130.

Greenhaus, J. H., Parasuraman, S., & Wormley, W. M. (1990). Effects of race on organizational experiences, job performance evaluations, and career outcomes. *Academy of Management Journal, 33,* 64–86.

Hood, J. (1989). *Acculturation and assimilation as applied to the business organization.* Unpublished doctoral dissertation, University of Colorado at Boulder.

Ilgen, D. R. & Youtz, M. A. (1986). Factors affecting the evaluation and development of minorities in organizations. In K. Rowl & G. Ferris (Eds.), *Research in personnel and human resource management: A research annual* (pp. 307–337). Greenwich, CT: JAI.

Johnston, W. B. & Packer, A. E. (1987). *Workforce 2000.* Indianapolis, IN: Hudson Institute.

Jones, E. (1986). Black managers: The dream deferred. *Harvard Business Review, 64,* 84–93.

King, W. C. & Miles, E. W. (1992, August). *Questionnaire design, organizational diversity, and response rate: Does random distribution alone guarantee equal representation?* Presented at the 1992 National Academy of Management Meeting, Las Vegas, NV.

Klimoski, R. J. & Hayes, M. J. (1980). Leader behavior and subordinate motivation. *Personnel Psychology, 33,* 543–564.

Kraiger, K. & Ford, J. (1986). A meta-analysis of ratee race effects in performance ratings. *Journal of Applied Psychology, 70,* 56–65.

Kram, K. E. (1985). *Mentoring at work: Developmental relationships in organizational life.* Glenview, IL: Scott Foresman & Co.

Nixon, R. (1985). *Black managers in corporate America: Alienation or integration.* Washington, DC: National Urban League.

Sessa, V. I. (1992). Managing diversity at the Xerox Corporation: Balanced workforce goals and caucus groups. In Susan E. Jackson (Ed.), *Diversity in the workplace* (pp. 37–64). New York, NY: Guilford.

Shuter, R. (1982). Interaction of American Blacks and Whites in interracial and intraracial dyads. *Journal of Social Psychology, 117*, 45–52.

Teske, R. H. C. & Nelson, B. H. (1974). Acculturation and assimilation: A clarification. *American Ethnologist, 1*, 351–367.

Thompson, J. D. (1960). Organizational management of conflict. *Administrative Science Quarterly, 4*, 389–409.

Tsui, A. & O'Reilly, C. A. (1989). Beyond simple demographic effects: The importance of relational demography in superior-subordinate dyads. *Academy of Management Journal, 32*, 402–423.

Webster's encyclopedic unabridged dictionary of the English language. (1989). New York, NY: Portland House.

Address correspondence to: Sandy Jeanquart-Barone, Department of Management and Marketing, Murray State University, Murray, KY 42071.

Exercise for Article 3

Factual Questions

1. What is the dictionary (Webster) definition of *discrimination* cited in this article?

2. How many questionnaires were sent out? How many were returned?

3. Was the sample confined to one area of the nation?

4. There were how many items on the measure of discrimination?

5. What was the mean on supervisory support of Blacks reporting to Blacks? What was the mean on supervisory support of Blacks reporting to Whites?

6. Was the difference between the two means that you reported in response to question 5 statistically significant? If yes, at what probability level?

Questions for Discussion

7. Given that the cover letter was written on the organization's letterhead and signed by the top executive, would you have expected a higher rate of return? Explain.

8. Would it have been of interest to you to see the results analyzed separately for some of the demographic groups (e.g., separately for males and females)? Explain. (See lines 210–229 for the demographics collected in this study.)

9. Would you be willing to generalize the results of this study to employees who do *not* work for the federal government? Explain.

10. If you were to conduct another study on the same general topic, what changes in the research methodology, if any, would you make?

11. This research report is relatively short. If the journal had enough space to give the author a few additional pages in which to report on this research, which aspects of the research would you like to have more information on, if any?

Quality Ratings

Directions: Indicate your level of agreement with each of the following statements by circling a number from 5 for strongly agree (SA) to 1 for strongly disagree (SD). If you believe an item is not applicable to this research article, leave it blank. Be prepared to explain your ratings.

A. The introduction establishes the importance of the study.

   SA   5   4   3   2   1   SD

B. The literature review establishes the context for the study.

   SA   5   4   3   2   1   SD

C. The research purpose, question, or hypothesis is clearly stated.

   SA   5   4   3   2   1   SD

D. The method of sampling is sound.

   SA   5   4   3   2   1   SD

E. Relevant demographics (for example, age, gender, and ethnicity) are described.

   SA   5   4   3   2   1   SD

F. Measurement procedures are adequate.

   SA   5   4   3   2   1   SD

G. All procedures have been described in sufficient detail to permit a replication of the study.

   SA   5   4   3   2   1   SD

H. The participants have been adequately protected from potential harm.

   SA   5   4   3   2   1   SD

I. The results are clearly described.

   SA   5   4   3   2   1   SD

J. The discussion/conclusion is appropriate.

   SA   5   4   3   2   1   SD

K. Despite any flaws, the report is worthy of publication.

   SA   5   4   3   2   1   SD

Article 4

What Do Psychologists Know About Working with the Clergy? An Analysis of Eight APA Journals: 1991–1994

ANDREW J. WEAVER
Hawaii State Hospital

JUDITH A. SAMFORD
Hawaii State Hospital

AMY E. KLINE
Hawaii State Hospital

LEE ANN LUCAS
Hawaii State Hospital

DAVID B. LARSON
The National Institute
for Healthcare Research

HAROLD G. KOENIG
Duke University Medical Center

ABSTRACT. To better understand the role of clergy in relation to the practice of psychology, a systematic review of research on clergy in 8 major American Psychological Association journals was conducted. From 1991 to 1994, 4 of 2,468 (0.02%) quantitative studies considered clergy in their data. This examination of the literature suggests that psychology lacks an original empirical literature that can enable a scientific evaluation of the beneficial or harmful effects of clergy involvement in mental health care. Professional psychology should give greater consideration of and collaboration with clergy.

From *Professional Psychology: Research and Practice, 28,* 471–474. Copyright © 1997 by the American Psychological Association, Inc. Reprinted with permission.

One of the most creative and promising directions that professional psychology has taken is an increased interest in multidisciplinary collaboration (Hinshaw & DeLeon, 1995). Examples of professional collaboration
5 have been noted between psychology and a wide range of vocations, including family medicine (Bray & Rogers, 1995), geriatric medicine (McDowell, Burgio, Dombrowski, Locher, & Rodriguez, 1992), nursing (Abraham et al., 1991), and optometry (Biaggio &
10 Bittner, 1990).

However, there is one group of professionals that is rarely considered for collaboration with psychologists: the clergy. This deficit remains despite numerous studies over the past 35 years demonstrating that tens
15 of millions of Americans, or approximately 4 out of 10 who have mental health needs, seek assistance from members of the clergy in times of personal distress (Chalfant et al., 1990; Gurin, Veroff, & Feld, 1960; Veroff, Kulka, & Douvan, 1981; Weaver, 1995). The
20 National Institutes of Mental Health's Epidemiological Catchment Area Surveys found that clergy are more likely than psychologists or psychiatrists combined to have a person with a *Diagnostic and Statistical Manual*

of Mental Disorders (3rd ed., rev.) mental health diag-
25 nosis see them for assistance (Hohmann & Larson, 1993). This frequent use of the clergy by the public should not be a surprise, given the clergy's availability and accessibility and the high trust that Americans have in them (Gallup, 1990). Young adults rank clergy
30 higher in interpersonal skills, including warmth, caring, stability, and professionalism, than either psychologists or psychiatrists (Schindler, Berren, Hannah, Beigel, & Santiago, 1987).

According to the U.S. Department of Labor (1992),
35 there are approximately 312,000 Jewish and Christian clergy serving congregations in the United States (4,000 rabbis, 53,000 Catholic priests, and 255,000 Protestant pastors). In a recent review of 10 separate studies, clergy consistently reported that they devote an
40 average of 15% of their working time to pastoral counseling on the basis of a 40- to 60-hour work week (Weaver, 1995). This totals 148.2 million hours of counseling services a year, a volume of services that is roughly equivalent in time to each of the 77,000 mem-
45 bers of the American Psychological Association (APA) delivering services at 38.5 hours per week. This estimate does not take into account the nearly 100,000 nuns in full-time religious vocation in the Roman Catholic Church (Ebaugh, 1993), hospital chaplains, or
50 clergy and religious workers from other religious traditions (e.g., Christian Orthodox, Buddhism, Hinduism, and Islam) in the United States.

A Search for Relevant Research

We manually examined research on clergy (e.g., rabbis, ministers, priests, pastors, and chaplains) and
55 other religious workers (e.g., nuns, pastoral counselors, parish nurses, and parish social workers) published in eight APA-published journals. The study method was based on previous systematic reviews that have been conducted to document the use of religion as a variable
60 in psychiatry (Larson, Pattison, Blazer, Omran, & Kaplan, 1986), clinical geriatrics (Sherrill, Larson, &

Greenwold, 1993), and family medicine (Craigie, Liu, Larson, & Lyons, 1988). The eight journals examined were as follows: (a) *Developmental Psychology*, (b) the *Journal of Consulting and Clinical Psychology*, (c) the *Journal of Educational Psychology*, (d) the *Journal of Personality and Social Psychology*, (e) the *Journal of Counseling Psychology*, (f) *Psychology and Aging*, (g) *Professional Psychology: Research and Practice*, and (h) *American Psychologist*. Excluding *American Psychologist*, these journals published approximately half (48%) of the total published research output of APA journals during the time period 1991 to 1994 (Summary Report of Journal Operations: 1992, 1993). Each article was reviewed to determine if it contained either descriptive or inferential statistics that examined the role or use of religious professionals. We identified a total of 2,468 quantitative articles, of which a mere 4 empirical articles (or about 1 in 600) included and assessed the role of the clergy. Two of the four articles provided significant new data (Murstein & Fontaine, 1993; Pargament et al., 1991).

Implications for Professional Psychology

Our review of the published research literature revealed that, in terms of empirical research in psychology, examination of the clergy in relation to psychological and behavioral topics is extremely limited. For example, not 1 of the 265 empirical articles found in *Psychology and Aging* considered clergy in research relevant to elderly persons. Given that more than half (52%) of Americans who are 65 years of age or older attend worship on a weekly basis (Gallup, 1994) and that these older adults are more likely to seek help with mental health problems from clergy than from all mental health professionals combined (Koenig & Weaver, 1997), more psychological research investigating the role of clergy in the mental health care of older adults is needed.

In a parallel manner, no article in our sample considered the involvement of clergy in either the African American or Hispanic American communities despite the fact that Mollica, Streets, Boscarino, and Redlich (1986) found that African American pastors were much more likely to go into the community and seek out people in crisis than non-African American clergy, and Chalfant, Heller, Roberts, Briones, Aguirre-Hochbaum, and Farr (1990) found that Mexican Americans are more than twice as likely to seek clergy help with personal problems than psychologists and psychiatrists combined. Last, in three comprehensive reviews of rural psychology in our sample (Hargrove & Breazeale, 1993; Human & Wasem, 1991; Murray & Keller, 1991), none made reference to the central role clergy or religious communities have in rural mental health care (Rowles, 1986).

On a positive note, *Professional Psychology: Research and Practice* published one of the four identified articles: Pargament et al. (1991) described how academic psychology can enhance a working relationship between the religious and psychological communities. The article, which was well referenced to prior religious research, demonstrated how church and synagogue leaders might collaborate with consulting psychologists to improve their effectiveness. The authors lamented that "work with religious organizations may represent one of the last great taboos for professional psychology" (p. 403).

Professional psychologists should give serious consideration to expanding their contact with clergy in their community. Clergy are often in long-term relationships with individuals and their families, which enables the clergy to observe changes in behavior that may indicate early signs of distress. Furthermore, clergy are accessible helpers within communities who offer a sense of continuity with centuries of human history and an experience of being a part of something greater than oneself. Religious communities also have established patterns of responding to crises. Clergy can help psychologists gain access to family members in crisis who would otherwise not receive psychological care. Religious communities need to be linked with psychologists who are trained to provide preventive interventions for at-risk couples and families and who are skilled in working collaboratively with rabbis, priests, and ministers (Weaver, 1995). Rapid increases in the numbers of women clergy and psychologists offer new opportunities for these historically underrepresented groups to work together. Currently, one-third of the 60,000 seminary students in America are women, up from 10% in 1972 (Bedell, 1997).

Recommendations

It is clear that psychologists need more training in the clinical dynamics of religion. Studies indicate that few psychologists receive training in any aspect of religion or spirituality while in graduate school, and few seek postgraduate continuing education in those topics (Sheridan, Bullis, Adcock, Berlin, & Miller, 1992). A survey of 409 clinical psychologists who were members of the APA revealed that only 5% had religious or spiritual issues addressed in their professional training (Shafranske & Malony, 1990). In a national survey of counseling programs accredited by the APA, a somewhat higher one in four had a course component that at least minimally addressed religious or spiritual issues (Kelly, 1994). Last, a national survey of clinical training directors working in Association of Psychology Internship Centers indicated that none of their internship programs offered education or training in spiritual or religious issues, while at the same time almost three out of four of the training directors acknowledged that they addressed such issues in their own clinical practice (Lannert, 1991).

A lack of education in clinical training on religious issues or the role of clergy in mental health care may, in part, account for the limited collaboration between

the psychological and the religious communities. It is
175 also important to note that 5 out of 10 psychologists in
an academic setting reported having no religious preference, a figure more than seven times greater than that
found in the general population (50% vs. 7%, respectively) (Shafranske, 1996). For many academic psy-
180 chologists developing research and clinical training
programs, religion or the role of clergy in mental health
simply is outside their experience.

It is promising that recently a diverse group of
mental health educators, including psychologists (Sha-
185 franske, 1996; Sheridan, Wilmer, & Atcheson, 1994;
Stander, Piercy, Mackinnon, & Helmeke, 1994; Sansone, Khatain, & Rodenhauser, 1990), have argued that
their professions should address questions of cultural
and religious diversity and value-related religious con-
190 cerns within their curriculum requirements. In fact, as
of January 1996, all psychiatric residency programs in
the United States are required to address spiritual and
religious issues in their formal training (American
Medical Association, 1995).

195 Psychologists could be of significant service to the
community by training clergy, particularly ethnic-
minority pastors, in crisis intervention and preventive
mental health (Koenig & Weaver, 1997; Weaver &
Koenig, 1996; Weaver, Koenig, & Ochberg, 1996). Of
200 surveyed clergy, 70%–90% recognized a need and indicated a desire to have additional training in mental
health issues (Weaver, 1995). Given that one in three
psychologists reported a strong interest in religion,
many psychologists and clergy could benefit from bet-
205 ter education, communication, and collaboration (Bergin & Jensen, 1990). A recent national survey of marriage and family therapists indicated that they were
about as likely to have referrals from a member of the
clergy as from a physician, an employment assistance
210 program, or a managed care organization (Doherty &
Simmons, 1996).

It is important that the APA has taken a recent lead
in addressing the religious factor in professional psychology by producing a first-rate text titled *Religion*
215 *and the Clinical Practice of Psychology* (Shafranske,
1996). Although there is not a chapter on the role of
clergy working with psychologists, the volume is an
otherwise state-of-the-art assessment of religion in
psychological treatment by the foremost authorities in
220 the field. These scholars suggest that to ignore a social
phenomenon as widespread as religion and spirituality
is, in essence, to devalue a significant part of cultural
life and ethical experience.

References

Abraham, I. L., Thompson–Heisterman, A. A., Harrington, D. P., Smullen, D. E., Onega, L. L., Droney, E. G., Westerman, P. S., Manning, C. A., & Lictenberg, P. A. (1991). Outpatient psychogeriatric nursing services: An integrative model. *Archives of Psychiatric Nursing, 5*, 151–164.

American Medical Association (1995). *Graduate medical education directory 1995–1996: Program requirements for residency education in psychiatry.* Chicago: Author.

Bedell, K. B. (1997). *Yearbook of American and Canadian Churches, 1997.* Nashville, TN: Abingdon Press.

Bergin, A. E. & Jensen, J. P. (1990). Religiosity of psychotherapists: A national survey. *Psychotherapy, 27*, 3–6.

Biaggio, M. K. & Bittner, E. (1990). Psychology and optometry: Interaction and collaboration. *American Psychologist, 45*, 1313–1315.

Bray, J. H. & Rogers, J. C. (1995). Linking psychologists and family physicians for collaborative practice. *Professional Psychology: Research and Practice, 26*, 132–138.

Chalfant, H. P., Heller, P. L., Roberts, A., Briones, D., Aguirre–Hochbaum, S., & Farr, W. (1990). The clergy as a resource for those encountering psychological distress. *Review of Religious Research, 31*, 305–313.

Craigie, F. C., Liu, I. Y., Larson, D. B., & Lyons, J. S. (1988). A systematic analysis of religion variables in *The Journal of Family Practice*, 1976 to 1986. *The Journal of Family Practice, 27*, 509–513.

Doherty, W. J. & Simmons, D. S. (1996). Clinical practice patterns of marriage and family therapists: A national survey of therapists and their clients. *Journal of Marital and Family Therapy, 22*, 9–25.

Ebaugh, H. R. (1993). The growth and decline of Catholic religious orders of women worldwide. *Journal for the Scientific Study of Religion, 32*, 68–73.

Gallup, G. H. (1990). *Religion in America: 1990.* Princeton, NJ: The Gallup Organization.

Gallup, G. H. (1994). *Religion in America: 1994* (Suppl.). Princeton, NJ: The Gallup Organization.

Gurin, G., Veroff, J., & Feld, S. (1960). *Americans view their mental health: A nationwide interview survey.* New York: Wiley.

Hargrove, D. S., & Breazeale, R. L. (1993). Psychologists and rural services: Addressing a new agenda. *Professional Psychology: Research and Practice, 24*, 319–324.

Hinshaw, A. S. & DeLeon, P. H. (1995). Toward achieving multidisciplinary professional collaboration. *Professional Psychology: Research and Practice, 26*, 115–116.

Hohmann, A. A. & Larson, D. B. (1993). Psychiatric factors predicting use of clergy. In E. L. Worthington, Jr. (Ed.), *Psychotherapy and religious values* (pp. 71–84). Grand Rapids, MI: Baker Book House.

Human, J., & Wasem, C. (1991). Rural mental health in America. *American Psychologist, 46*, 232–239.

Kelly, E. W. (1994). The role of religion and spirituality in counselor education: A national survey. *Counselor Education and Supervision, 33*, 227–236.

Koenig, H. G. & Weaver, A. J. (1997). *Counseling troubled older adults–A handbook for clergy and religious caregivers.* Nashville, TN: Abingdon Press.

Lannert, J. L. (1991). Resistance and countertransference issues with spiritual and religious clients. *Journal of Humanistic Psychology, 31*(4), 68–76.

Larson, D. B., Pattison, E. M., Blazer, D. G., Omran, A. R., & Kaplan, B. H. (1986). Systematic analysis of research variables in four major psychiatric journals. *American Journal of Psychiatry, 143*, 329–334.

McDowell, J., Burgio, K. L., Dombrowski, M., Locher, J. L., & Rodriguez, E. (1992). An interdisciplinary approach to the assessment and behavioral treatment of urinary incontinence in geriatric outpatients. *Journal of the American Geriatric Society, 40*, 370–374.

Mollica, R. C., Streets, F. J., Boscarino, J., & Redlich, F. C. (1986). A community study of formal pastoral counseling activities of the clergy. *American Journal of Psychiatry, 143*, 323–328.

Murray, J. D., & Keller, P. A. (1991). Psychology and rural America: Current status and future directions. *American Psychologist, 46*, 220–231.

Murstein, B. I., & Fontaine, P. A. (1993). The public's knowledge about psychologists and other mental health professionals. *American Psychologist, 48*, 839–845.

Pargament, K. I., Falgout, K., Ensing, D. S., Reilly, B., Silverman, M., Van Haitsma, K., Olsen, H., & Warren, R. (1991). The congregation development program: Data-based consultation with churches and synagogues. *Professional Psychology: Research and Practice, 22*, 393–404.

Rowles, G. D. (1986). The rural elderly and the church. *Journal of Religion and Aging, 2*(1–2), 79–98.

Sansone, R. A., Khatain, K., & Rodenhauser, P. (1990). The role of religion in psychiatric education: A national survey. *Academic Psychiatry, 14*(1), 34–38.

Schindler, F., Berren, M. R., Hannah, M. T., Beigel, A., & Santiago, J. M. (1987). How the public perceives psychiatrists, psychologists, nonpsychiatric physicians, and members of the clergy. *Professional Psychology: Research and Practice, 18*, 371–376.

Shafranske, E. P. (1996). *Religion and the clinical practice of psychology.* Washington, DC: American Psychological Association.

Shafranske, E. P. & Malony, H. N. (1990). Clinical psychologists' religious and spiritual orientation and their practice of psychotherapy. *Psychotherapy, 27*(1), 72–78.

Sheridan, M. J., Bullis, R. K., Adcock, C. R., Berlin, S. D., & Miller, P. C. (1992). Practitioners' personal and professional attitudes and behaviors toward religion and spirituality. *Journal of Social Work Education, 28*(2), 190–203.

Sheridan, M. J., Wilmer, C. M., & Atcheson, L. (1994). Inclusion of content on religion and spirituality in the social work curriculum: A study of faculty views. *Journal of Social Work Education, 30*(3), 363–376.

Sherrill, K. A., Larson, D. B., & Greenwold, M. (1993). Is religion taboo in gerontology? Systematic review of research on religion in three major gerontology journals, 1985–1991. *The American Journal of Geriatric Psychiatry, 1*(2), 109–117.

Stander, V., Piercy, F. P., Mackinnon, D., & Helmeke, K. (1994). Spirituality, religion and family therapy: Competing or complementary worlds? *The American Journal of Family Therapy, 22*, 27–41.

Summary report of journal operations: 1992 (1993). *American Psychologist, 48*, 829–830.

United States Department of Labor (1992). *Occupational outlook handbook: United States Department of Labor*. Washington, DC: Bureau of Labor Statistics.

Veroff, J., Kulka, R. A., & Douvan, E. (1981). *Mental health in America: Patterns of help-seeking from 1957 to 1976*. New York: Basic Books.

Weaver, A. J. (1995). Has there been a failure to prepare and support parish-based clergy in their role as front-line community mental health workers? A review. *The Journal of Pastoral Care, 49*, 129–149.

Weaver, A. J., & Koenig, H. G. (1996). Elderly suicide, mental health professionals and the clergy. *Death Studies, 20*(5), 495–508.

Weaver, A. J., Koenig, H. G., & Ochberg, F. M. (1996). Posttraumatic stress, mental health professionals and the clergy. *Journal of Traumatic Stress, 9*(4), 861–870.

Acknowledgments: This article is dedicated to the Sacred Hearts priest Father Damien of Molokai, Hawaii, in thanksgiving for his 16 years of pastoral work among the lepers of Kalaupapa. He died a leper, Holy Week, 1889. We wish to express our gratitude to the Hawaii Psychological Research Consortium and to Lisa Iwamoto, head librarian at Hawaii State Hospital, for their generous help.

Address correspondence to: Andrew J. Weaver, Hawaii State Hospital, 45-710 Keaahala Road, Kaneohe, HI 96744. Electronic mail may be sent to aweaver@Hawaii.edu

Exercise for Article 4

Factual Questions

1. According to the literature review, how many Americans with mental health needs seek assistance from the clergy in times of personal distress?

2. Why should the frequent use of the clergy by the public not be a surprise?

3. Were parish social workers included in the definition of "clergy?"

4. The researchers examined how many journals for research on the clergy?

5. How many of the 2,468 quantitative articles were found to include and assess the role of the clergy?

6. Did any of the articles consider the involvement of the clergy in African American communities?

7. What is identified as a possible "last great taboo?"

Questions for Discussion

8. The researchers "manually" examined the journals. If you had conducted this study, would you have conducted a manual or electronic (i.e., computer-assisted) search? Explain.

9. Would you be interested in knowing the reason(s) why the particular journals listed in lines 63 through 70 were selected for this study? Explain.

10. The researchers considered only quantitative articles (with descriptive or inferential statistics). If you had conducted this study, would you have also limited it to quantitative articles? Explain.

11. Speculate on what the researchers mean by "significant new data." (See lines 80–82.)

12. In lines 150–151, the researchers state that "It is clear that psychologists need more training in the clinical dynamics of religion." Has this research report convinced you that this is true? Explain.

13. Is anything in this article especially interesting to you? Especially surprising? Explain.

Quality Ratings

Directions: Indicate your level of agreement with each of the following statements by circling a number from 5 for strongly agree (SA) to 1 for strongly disagree (SD). If you believe an item is not applicable to this research article, leave it blank. Be prepared to explain your ratings.

A. The introduction establishes the importance of the study.

SA 5 4 3 2 1 SD

B. The literature review establishes the context for the study.

SA 5 4 3 2 1 SD

C. The research purpose, question, or hypothesis is clearly stated.

SA 5 4 3 2 1 SD

D. The method of sampling is sound.

SA 5 4 3 2 1 SD

E. Relevant demographics (for example, age, gender, and ethnicity) are described.

SA 5 4 3 2 1 SD

F. Measurement procedures are adequate.

SA 5 4 3 2 1 SD

G. All procedures have been described in sufficient detail to permit a replication of the study.

SA 5 4 3 2 1 SD

H. The participants have been adequately protected from potential harm.

SA 5 4 3 2 1 SD

I. The results are clearly described.

SA   5   4   3   2   1   SD

J. The discussion/conclusion is appropriate.

SA   5   4   3   2   1   SD

K. Despite any flaws, the report is worthy of publication.

SA   5   4   3   2   1   SD

Article 5

Client Gender as a Process Variable in Marriage and Family Therapy: Are Women Clients Interrupted More Than Men Clients?

RONALD JAY WERNER-WILSON
Colorado State University

SHARON J. PRICE
University of Georgia

TONI S. ZIMMERMAN
Colorado State University

MEGAN J. MURPHY
Colorado State University

ABSTRACT. Influenced by language and therapeutic discourse as well as the feminist critique of marriage and family therapy, the authors conducted research to evaluate conversational power in marriage and family therapy. Research on interruptions has received the most empirical attention, so the authors examined videotaped therapy sessions to see if women clients were interrupted more than men clients. This strategy integrated scholarship on gender and conversation into research on marriage and family therapy process. Multivariate analysis of variance was used to examine the different treatment of women and men clients; gender of therapist was used as a control variable. Results indicated that marriage and family doctoral students interrupted women clients three times more than men clients.

From *Journal of Family Psychology, 11*, 373–377. Copyright © 1997 by the American Psychological Association, Inc. Reprinted with permission.

We conducted research to evaluate conversational power in marriage and family therapy. This research was influenced by two themes: language and therapeutic discourse as well as the feminist critique of marriage and family therapy. Empirical research has demonstrated that men and women use different conversational tactics in cross-gender interactions. Women, for example, frequently ask questions and follow-up on topics introduced by men; these tactics support conversation (Fishman, 1983). Men, on the other hand, are more likely to interrupt women and are more likely to successfully introduce a new topic of conversation; these are power tactics (Fishman, 1983). Research on interruptions has received the most empirical attention, so we examined videotaped therapy sessions to see if women clients were interrupted more than men clients. This strategy integrated scholarship on gender and conversation into research on marriage and family therapy process.

Relevant Literature
Conversation: The Currency of Therapy

From a social constructionist perspective, discourse defines social organization: The therapeutic system is a linguistic system that features the social construction of meaning between the client or clients and the therapist (Anderson & Goolishian, 1988). The therapist is principally responsible for the organization of therapeutic discourse, so she or he uses conversation to facilitate change (Anderson & Goolishian, 1988) or to maintain the status quo in a relationship (Avis, 1988; Davis, 1984; Goldner, 1988; Hare-Mustin, 1987, 1994).

Research on conversational strategies has supported the premise that therapists fundamentally shape therapeutic process. Viaro and Leonard (1983) examined videotaped therapy sessions in order to identify therapeutic rules. They suggested that the therapeutic setting provides therapists with conversational prerogatives (i.e., direct conversation, interrupt client) and identified four clinical implications: (a) therapists govern the process and organization of therapy, (b) therapists' prerogatives influence the rights of family members, (c) therapists maintain the central role in therapy, and (d) therapists are the source for all therapeutic rules (Viaro & Leonard, 1983). The present study examined the use of interruptions, a conversational prerogative.

Gender, Conversation, and Power

A linguistic approach to studying therapy is enhanced by an understanding of gender (Hare-Mustin, 1994; Hoffman, 1990). Therapeutic conversation features both competition for influence by each family member as well as negotiation for power between men and women (Avis, 1988; Davis, 1984; Goldner, 1988; Hare-Mustin, 1987). Men and women use different conversational strategies and receive different treatment in cross-gender dialogue. Because therapy is conversation, these differences may influence therapeutic process. Women are more likely to be interrupted in conversation than men (Smith-Lovin & Brody, 1989;

West & Zimmerman, 1983), so their efforts to participate in therapy may be disrupted.

An interruption is a power tactic, an overlap of speech that is disruptive or intrusive (West & Zimmerman, 1983; Zimmerman & West, 1975); it has been referred to as a small insult that establishes and maintains power differences (West & Zimmerman, 1983). Interruptions by men are rated as more appropriate than interruptions by women (Hawkins, 1988), and women are more likely to be interrupted in cross-gender conversations than in same-gender conversations (West & Zimmerman, 1983; Zimmerman & West, 1975). Responding to the explanation that men interrupt women because women talk more, West and Zimmerman found the same results when they controlled for amount of talk. Power, according to a review of research on interruptions, is the most important predictor of an interruption (Orcutt & Harvey, 1985; see also Kollock, Blumstein, & Schwartz, 1985). Gender is a diffuse status characteristic that influences power, which, in turn, influences interruptions (Orcutt & Harvey, 1985).

Purpose

If women and men therapy clients are treated differently—a possibility because gender influences conversation—clinicians could perpetuate inequality rather than serve as agents for change. We examined family therapy process to evaluate the use of interruptions by therapists, who have the prerogative to influence participants' rights (Viaro & Leonard, 1983), to see if women and men clients were treated differently. We used gender of therapist as an interaction effect because some research on individual counseling suggests that gender of therapist influences therapy. For example, research shows that a therapist's perception of therapy is influenced by gender of client: Men therapists report more problems than women therapists working with women clients, and men therapists are more likely than women therapists to describe clients negatively (see Nelson, 1993, for a thorough review of the literature).

Method

Participants

The sample for this study consisted of clients and therapists at a nonprofit marriage and family therapy clinic at a major Southern university. All therapists in this study were doctoral students in a marriage and family therapy program accredited by the American Association for Marriage and Family Therapy. Five women and seven men therapists contributed cases. This sample included 41 couples or families that included both an adult woman and man who attended a first session at the marriage and family therapy clinic. Participants were videotaped during their initial therapy session.

Procedures

Initial therapy sessions influence client expectations and lay the foundation for subsequent treatment. We examined the first therapy session to control for treatment duration. Therapy sessions have predictable stages (e.g., social, engagement, information collection, intervention, closure), so we examined multiple time points in the session. Three 5-min segments were coded for every client from early, middle, and later stages in the session: (a) 10 to 15-min segment, (b) 25 to 30-min segment, and (c) 40 to 45-min segment. Two senior-level undergraduate students, a man and a woman, who were naïve to the purpose of this research, coded videotapes from the first therapy session.

Coder training. Coders learned the coding scheme by practicing on tapes not featured in the sample until they achieved 80% agreement. The principal investigator in this study coded every fourth tape to determine criterion reliability. The coders maintained high interrater reliability (intraclass correlations were .96; based on Shrout & Fleiss, 1979).

Coding scheme. The transcripts were arranged with codes adjacent to each spoken turn to promote reliability by eliminating the need for coders to memorize codes: The coders viewed the video with the transcript and circled the appropriate code as they occurred during each speaking turn. A distinct set of codes was printed next to each speaker (e.g., therapist, woman client, man client), but each set of codes featured the same possible codes. For example, the therapist could interrupt either the woman or man client. Similarly, each client could interrupt either her or his partner or the therapist. In addition to enhancing reliability, this coding arrangement disguised the nature of the research project, because coders identified conversational strategies used by each speaker, not just the therapist.

Dependent Measure: Interruptions

Interruptions were distinguished from other forms of overlap such as supportive statements, which represent active listening skills. Statements that tailed off in tone or volume were not coded as interruptions because they represented invitations for reply.

It is possible that people who talk more are interrupted more, so we developed two measures to control for amount of client participation. First, we constructed a variable from the ratio of interruptions made by the therapist to the number of speaking turns taken by the client. Second, we constructed a variable from the ratio of interruptions made by the therapist to the number of words spoken by the client. These ratios provided standardized measures to examine therapist interruptions.

Results

We conducted multivariate analysis of variance (MANOVA) to examine the main effect and interaction effect of client gender and therapist gender on three measures of the dependent variable. We examined interaction effects because gender-linked conversational strategies might influence how therapists interact with clients. In addition, gender of therapist might influence the therapeutic process (Nelson, 1993). The mean values and standard deviations for therapist and client behaviors are presented in Table 1.

Table 1
Mean Values of Therapist and Client Behaviors by Gender of Client

Group	Man ($n = 41$) M	Man ($n = 41$) SD	Woman ($n = 41$) M	Woman ($n = 41$) SD
Therapist				
Interruptions	0.87	1.45	2.37	2.73
Interruptions (no. of client turns)	0.03	0.05	0.09	0.09
Interruptions (no. of client words)	0.0011	0.0017	0.0028	0.0026
Client				
No. of turns	22.80	15.68	25.90	13.01
No. of words	600.17	512.69	822.02	544.45

There was a significant difference for gender of client on all measures of interruption, including measures that controlled for number of turns and number of words (see Table 2). Neither gender of therapist nor the interaction of Gender of Client x Gender of Therapist was significant (see Table 2). Overall, marriage and family therapy doctoral students interrupted women clients three times more than men clients.

Table 2
Multivariate Analysis of Variance for Therapist Behaviors: Interruption (N = 82)

Dependent Variable	Source	$F(1, 78)$
Interruption	Client gender	9.10*
	Therapist gender	0.15
	Client Gender × Therapist Gender	0.39
Interruption (client turns)	Client gender	8.96*
	Therapist gender	0.03
	Client Gender × Therapist Gender	0.20
Interruption (client words)	Client gender	9.59*
	Therapist gender	0.01
	Client Gender × Therapist Gender	0.10

*$p < .01$.

Discussion

Previous research on gender as a process issue in marriage and family therapy has identified differences between men and women therapists as well as between men and women clients, but these differences do not seem to influence interruptions. Gender of therapist did not affect interruptions directed toward clients in this study. This finding is consistent with recent research

that suggests that modality (i.e., marital vs. family therapy) influences therapy process but gender of therapist does not (Werner-Wilson, 1995; Werner-Wilson, Price, & Zimmerman, 1996). Although gender of therapist does not influence therapy, results from this study provide additional information about the influence of client gender on the therapeutic process: Women clients are more likely to be interrupted than men clients. This finding suggests an ongoing need to consider the influence of gender as a process variable in marriage and family therapy.

Interruptions are power tactics that are influenced by gender in a variety of settings, including marriage and family therapy with student therapists. Although they are power tactics, interruptions may not reflect deliberate action by the therapist to exert power over the client. For example, therapists may block communication attempts by women clients in order to engage men clients who are often reluctant to engage in therapy. Although the effort to engage a reluctant client is meritorious, it should not occur at the expense of another participant. Interruptions may also reflect socialization: Therapists may interrupt women clients more because it is a common feature of conversation.

The findings from this study support what feminist scholars have recommended: (a) Research should incorporate gender themes and power analysis, (b) therapists should pay careful attention to their position in therapy, and (c) therapists should consider larger social forces (e.g., conversational conventions, power) and individual needs in therapy.

References

Anderson, H. & Goolishian, H. A. (1988). Human systems as linguistic systems: Preliminary and evolving ideas about the implications for clinical theory. *Family Process, 27,* 371–394.

Avis, J. M. (1988). Deepening awareness: A private study guide to feminism and family therapy. *Journal of Psychotherapy and the Family, 33,* 15–46.

Davis, K. (1984). The process of problem and (re)formulation in psychotherapy. *Sociology of Health and Illness, 8,* 44–74.

Fishman, P. M. (1983). Interaction: The work women do. In B. Thorne, C. Kramarae, & N. Henley (Eds.), *Language, gender and society* (pp. 89–101). Rowley, MA: Newbury House.

Goldner, V. (1988). Generation and gender: Normative and covert hierarchies. *Family Process, 27,* 17–31.

Hare-Mustin, R. T. (1987). The problem of gender in family therapy theory. *Family Process, 26,* 15–33.

Hare-Mustin, R. T. (1994). Discourses in the mirrored room: A postmodern analysis of therapy. *Family Process, 33,* 19–35.

Hawkins, K. (1988). Interruptions in task-oriented conversations: Effects of violations of expectations by males and females. *Women's Studies in Communication, 11,* 1–20.

Hoffman, L. (1990). Constructing realities: An art of lenses. *Family Process, 29,* 1–12.

Kollock, P., Blumstein, P., & Schwartz, P. (1985). Sex and power in interaction: Conversational privileges and duties. *American Sociological Review, 50,* 34–46.

Nelson, M. L. (1993). A current perspective on gender differences: Implications for research in counseling. *Journal of Counseling Psychology, 40,* 200–209.

Orcutt, J. D. & Harvey, L. K. (1985). Deviance, rule-breaking and male dominance in conversation. *Symbolic Interaction, 8,* 15–32.

Shrout, P. E. & Fleiss, J. L. (1979). Intraclass correlations: Uses in assessing rater reliability. *Psychological Bulletin, 2,* 420–428.

Smith-Lovin, L. & Brody, C. (1989). Interruptions in group discussions: The effects of gender and group composition. *American Sociological Review, 54,* 424–435.

Viaro, M. & Leonard, P. (1983). Getting and giving information: Analysis of a family-interview strategy. *Family Process, 22,* 27–42.

Werner-Wilson, R. J. (1995, November). *Client gender and the working alliance.* Paper presented at the American Association for Marriage and Family Therapy Annual Meeting, Baltimore, MD.

Werner-Wilson, R. J., Price, S. J., & Zimmerman, T S. (1996). *Is therapeutic topic influenced by gender in marriage and family therapy?* Manuscript submitted for publication.

West, C. & Zimmerman, D. H. (1983). Small insults: A study of interruptions in cross-sex conversations between unacquainted persons. In B. Thorne, C. Kramarae, & N. Henley (Eds.), *Language, gender and society* (pp. 103–117). Rowley, MA: Newbury House.

Zimmerman, D. H. & West, C. (1975). Sex-roles, interruptions and silences in conversation. In B. Thorne & N. Henley (Eds.), *Language and sex: Difference and dominance* (pp. 105–129). Rowley, MA: Newbury House.

Note: This research was funded, in part, by a grant from Platinum Mortgage Company, Jonesboro, Georgia.

About the authors: Ronald Jay Werner-Wilson, Toni S. Zimmerman, and Megan J. Murphy, Department of Human Development and Family Studies, Colorado State University; Sharon J. Price, Department of Child and Family Development, The University of Georgia. Megan J. Murphy is now at Department of Child and Family Development, The University of Georgia.

Address correspondence to: Ronald Jay Werner-Wilson, Department of Human Development and Family Studies, Colorado State University, Fort Collins, CO 80523. Electronic mail may be sent via the Internet to rjwilson@lamar.colostate.edu.

Exercise for Article 5

Factual Questions

1. What "has been referred to as a small insult that establishes and maintains power differences?"

2. How many of the therapists were women? How many were men?

3. The coders learned the coding scheme by practicing on tapes not used in the study until they reached what percentage of agreement?

4. Were statements that tailed off in tone or volume coded as interruptions? If yes, why? If no, why not?

5. What was the mean number of times that women were interrupted (without considering number of turns speaking or number of client words)?

6. When the researchers controlled for number of client words, was there still a significant difference in terms of number of therapist interruptions? If yes, at what probability level?

Questions for Discussion

7. Would you be interested in knowing more about the selection of the 41 cases and why they were attending therapy? Explain.

8. Do you think it was a good idea to control for treatment duration by examining only initial therapy sessions? Explain. (See lines 108–111.)

9. Do you think it was a good idea to keep the undergraduates who coded the videotapes naïve regarding the purpose of the study? Explain. (See lines 117–120.)

10. The researchers did not find a significant "Gender of Client by Gender of Therapist" interaction. That is, both male and female therapists were equally likely to interrupt female clients more often than male clients. (See lines 170–172 and Table 2). Does this result surprise you? Explain.

11. To what population(s), if any, would you be willing to generalize the results of this study?

12. If you were going to conduct another study on this topic, what changes in the research methodology would you make, if any?

Quality Ratings

Directions: Indicate your level of agreement with each of the following statements by circling a number from 5 for strongly agree (SA) to 1 for strongly disagree (SD). If you believe an item is not applicable to this research article, leave it blank. Be prepared to explain your ratings.

A. The introduction establishes the importance of the study.

SA   5   4   3   2   1   SD

B. The literature review establishes the context for the study.

SA   5   4   3   2   1   SD

C. The research purpose, question, or hypothesis is clearly stated.

SA   5   4   3   2   1   SD

D. The method of sampling is sound.

SA   5   4   3   2   1   SD

E. Relevant demographics (for example, age, gender, and ethnicity) are described.

SA   5   4   3   2   1   SD

F. Measurement procedures are adequate.

SA   5   4   3   2   1   SD

G. All procedures have been described in sufficient detail to permit a replication of the study.

SA   5   4   3   2   1   SD

Article 5   Client Gender as a Process Variable in Marriage and Family Therapy: Are Women Clients Interrupted More Than Men
Clients?

H. The participants have been adequately protected
from potential harm.

SA   5   4   3   2   1   SD

I. The results are clearly described.

SA   5   4   3   2   1   SD

J. The discussion/conclusion is appropriate.

SA   5   4   3   2   1   SD

K. Despite any flaws, the report is worthy of publication.

SA   5   4   3   2   1   SD

Article 6

An Unobtrusive Measure of Racial Behavior in a University Cafeteria

STEWART PAGE
University of Windsor
Windsor, Ontario, Canada

ABSTRACT. Observational data were gathered from a large university cafeteria for a period of 22 days, in l-hour periods per day, over one semester. Observations were made of the frequency with which Black and White cashiers were selected. Chi square analyses showed a significant association between a cashier's being Black and increased likelihood that she would not be selected. Some comments and comparisons are made with other research using similar measures.

From *Journal of Applied Social Psychology, 27,* 2172–2176.

The study of interracial behavior has long-standing familiarity to social and community psychologists, as well described in the classic writings of Kenneth Clark, Gordon Allport, Thomas Pettigrew, and others. Allport's (1958) *The Nature of Prejudice,* for example, remains one of the most frequently cited books on the issue, both within and without the discipline of psychology (Pettigrew, 1988). The dramatic effects of race as a variable in research have been demonstrated, for example, in a variety of situations assessing social influence and stigmatization. Many such studies have used some form of Bogardus' (1931, 1959) notion of *social distance* (social intimacy) measures of racial acceptance.

Observational and experimental studies of race have undoubtedly declined somewhat in recent times, while more pragmatic and biopolitical aspects such as equal opportunity, affirmative action, ethnic and cultural diversity, and so on have become more prominent. These issues are important, yet many aspects of interracial behavior remain incompletely understood.

One such aspect involves behavior in open situations; that is, those without racial demand characteristics or obligations (Orne, 1962). Moreover, the factor of race may also function differently at varying levels of awareness and in accordance with the extent of reactivity in measures used to observe it (e.g., Webb, Campbell, Schwartz, & Sechrest, 1966). For example, in a study which has now become a classic, Weitz (1972) administered a questionnaire assessing White-Black racial attitudes to a university population. For many of her subjects who had expressed egalitarian attitudes, Weitz nevertheless found that these same individuals showed subtly rejecting nonverbal behaviors when later placed in a laboratory situation requiring cooperative work alongside a Black individual. From a psychoanalytic perspective, Weitz referred to these results as supporting a *repressed-affect model* of racial behavior. In this view, racial behavior assessed reactively, such as with questionnaires or interviews, is typically egalitarian, yet may show "leakage," that is, negative aspects, when assessed nonreactively and unobtrusively. Similarly, in a series of studies (e.g., Page, 1995; Page & Day, 1990), we have found frequently that publicly advertised rental accommodation is likely to be described privately (thus unobservably) as "already rented" when landlords receive telephone inquiries from persons alleging to have some type of stigmatizing characteristic.

Although their study was not concerned directly with race, Hechtman and Rosenthal (1991) found, as another example of such leakage, that teachers showed more nonverbal warmth toward pupils for whom the teaching task was stereotypically gender appropriate (e.g., vocabulary items for girls; mechanical items for boys), as compared to when they taught a task which was gender inappropriate. Lott (1987), also in a nonracial context, similarly found that men did not show unfavorable attitudes toward women on paper-and-pencil measures. They did, however, in unobtrusively observed work situations, show subtle avoidance behaviors, more negative statements, and increased social distance specifically toward female coworkers. In a racial context, Taylor (1979) found that teachers' nonverbal behaviors varied subtly according to the race (White vs. Black) of their pupils in an unobtrusively observed teaching situation.

A long-standing difficulty in many studies remains that of generalization from laboratory-based research. The present study examined some aspects of racial behavior using a nonlaboratory (cafeteria) setting, whose essential functions are those of dining and socialization. Such settings generally carry no outward prescriptions or expectations regarding race, based on the tacit assumption that this factor indeed "does not

exist." The cafeteria setting is also one in which many behaviors, performed with little awareness or at low levels of intensity, may be unobtrusively observed. The speculative hypothesis was explored that a predomi-
80   nantly White population of customers, consisting mostly of undergraduate students, might select a White cashier more frequently than a Black cashier.

Method

Participants

During a recent semester, observations were made of a university population in a large public cafeteria at
85   the University of Windsor over a period of 22 (nonconsecutive) weekdays, excluding Fridays. A daily 1-hour observation period, from approximately noon until approximately 1 P.M. each day, was used.

Procedure

The spatial arrangement of the cafeteria was such
90   that once food items are collected and before entering the main eating area, customers must select a cashier from (usually) three choices during peak lunchtime hours throughout the academic year. Cashiers for the current period of observation were three females, lo-
95   cated at the end of three separate pathways, one of which must be selected by exiting customers. Distances to each cashier, from locations occupied by customers after selecting all food items, are approximately equal. In the eating area directly beyond the cashiers is a
100   counter area, containing a straight row of individual seats. A vertical partition attached to the front edge of the counter partially obscures the occupants of these seats from view. From one end of the counter, the activities of each cashier can be observed reliably and
105   unobtrusively.

Throughout the above time period, one of the three cashiers was Black; the remaining two were White. On the campus, as typical of Ontario universities generally, Black students form a distinct and visible minority
110   group.

A daily record was kept of the number of (non-Black) customers paying for food at each cashier. For consistency, observations were made only when three cashiers, at separate locations, were on duty. Individual
115   cashiers varied nonsystematically in their location from day to day. Cases in which a single person paid for one or more companions' food were counted as representing only a single customer. Cases where individuals only requested change or approached a cashier for rea-
120   sons other than paying for food were excluded. In general, therefore, a "unit" of observation was recorded and signaled, in most cases, when a cashier was observed extending her hand to return change. No subjective judgments or ratings were thus required; data
125   (Table 1) were gathered solely in the form of frequency counts.

Results and Discussion

Results, in terms of frequency of cashier selection,

are shown in Table 1. A goodness-of-fit (χ^2) analysis of the frequency data showed a significant tendency for
130   customers to select less frequently a cashier who was Black, $\chi^2(2, N = 9,713) = 6.57, p < .038$.

In order to evaluate further the possibility that a directional or spatial bias played some role in cashier selection, some additional data (covering 19 days; non-
135   Fridays) were gathered, during a different semester. For these data, all three cashiers were White. There was no significant location preference in selection, $\chi^2(2, N = 8,015) = 2.44, p < .296$.

In interpreting such results, one must exercise cau-
140   tion in view of certain limitations. One cannot know precisely what percentage of customers might have been included more than once over the total time period, nor does one have complete information about other factors in a university population which are ger-
145   mane to the issue of race. Moreover, populations such as the one observed in the present study consider themselves (and are considered) highly accepting, aware, and sensitive to matters concerning race, as congruent with commonly prevailing values and norms within a
150   North American university campus.

Table 1
Frequency of Cashier Selection by Race

Cashier	Frequency of selection
1 (White cashier)	3,320
2 (White cashier)	3,271
3 (Black cashier)	3,122
Cashier selection: Three White cashiers	
1	2,659
2	2,622
3	2,734

Yet there remain other, more abstract issues, still largely unresolved by social and community psychologists. One concerns Kelman's (1958) early distinctions between levels of attitude internalization, and between
155   the emotional, evaluative, and behavioral components of attitudes. Another concerns the unreliable, indeed sometimes disturbing, relationship between racial attitudes and racial behavior (Pettigrew, 1988). Another concerns the related issue of congruence between be-
160   haviors elicited under reactive conditions, in which they may be detected, and those which may be observed nonreactively and which may be performed at low levels of awareness. In this light, one is reminded of recent videotaped demonstrations on the ABC net-
165   work program *Prime Time Live,* in which Black "pseudoclients" were given false information about job availability, higher prices for used cars, and less accommodating service in stores. One is also reminded of LaPiere's (1934) classic study in which restaurateurs
170   indicated by telephone that Chinese couples would not be served, yet most such couples were served when

they actually entered the restaurants.

Again, while the factor of race may become a conspicuous factor in research situations where reactive measures or manipulations are used, its presence and effects in other situations may remain more insidious and ill-defined. Indeed, the present data reflect only frequency counts; that is, simple observations of human behavior. They seem sufficient, however, to illustrate the myth that race is irrelevant or does not exist in the context of everyday acts and social routines. Further research on the repressed affect model of racial behavior therefore seems clearly warranted.

References

Allport, G. (1958). *The nature of prejudice.* Garden City, NY: Doubleday Anchor Books.

Bogardus, E. (1931). *Fundamentals of social psychology.* New York, NY: Century Press.

Bogardus, E. (1959). *Social distance.* Yellow Springs, OH: Antioch.

Hechtman, S. & Rosenthal, R. (1991). Teacher gender and nonverbal behavior in the teaching of gender-stereotyped materials. *Journal of Applied Social Psychology, 21,* 446–459.

Kelman, H. (1958). Compliance, identification, and internalization: Three processes of attitude change. *Journal of Conflict Resolution, 2,* 51–60.

LaPiere, R. (1934). Attitudes versus actions. *Social Forces, 13,* 230–237.

Lott, B. (1987). Sexist discrimination as distancing behavior: A laboratory demonstration. *Psychology of Women Quarterly, 11,* 47–59.

Orne, M. (1962). On the social psychology of the psychological experiment: With particular reference to demand characteristics and their implications. *American Psychologist, 17,* 776–783.

Page, S. (1995). Effects of the mental illness label in 1993: Acceptance and rejection in the community. *Journal of Health and Social Behavior, 7,* 61–69.

Page, S. & Day, D. (1990). Acceptance of the "mentally ill" in Canadian society: Reality and illusion. *Canadian Journal of Community Mental Health, 9,* 51–61.

Pettigrew, T. (1988). The ultimate attribution error. In E. Aronson (Ed.), *The social animal* (pp. 325–344). New York, NY: W. H. Freeman.

Taylor, M. (1979). Race, sex, and the expression of self-fulfilling prophecies in a laboratory teaching situation. *Journal of Personality and Social Psychology, 37,* 897–912.

Webb, E., Campbell, D., Schwartz, R., & Sechrest, L. (1966). *Unobtrusive measures.* New York, NY: Rand-McNally.

Weitz, S. (1972). Attitude, voice, and behavior: A repressed affect model of interracial interaction. *Journal of Personality and Social Psychology, 24,* 14–21.

Address correspondence to: Stewart Page, Department of Psychology, University of Windsor, 401 Sunset, Windsor, Ontario N9B 3P4, Canada.

Exercise for Article 6

Factual Questions

1. According to the researcher, what is a "long-standing difficulty" in many studies?

2. What was the researcher's "speculative hypothesis?"

3. How many of the cashiers were Black?

4. How many times was the Black cashier selected?

5. What is the first "limitation" named by the researcher?

6. Were the differences among the three White (only) cashiers gathered during a different semester statistically significant?

Questions for Discussion

7. Beginning in line 50, the researcher cites two studies of gender discrimination. In your opinion, do they help establish the context for the present study on race? Explain.

8. The observations were made over a period of 22 days. Do you believe that is a sufficient number? Explain.

9. The researcher states that cashiers "varied in their location from day to day." Is this important information? Explain.

10. Is the comparison of the three White cashiers during a different semester an important part of this study? Explain. (See lines 132–138.)

11. Do you think that a replication of this study with a larger number of White and Black cashiers would be desirable? Explain.

12. Would you be willing to generalize the results of this study to your college or university cafeteria? Why? Why not?

Quality Ratings

Directions: Indicate your level of agreement with each of the following statements by circling a number from 5 for strongly agree (SA) to 1 for strongly disagree (SD). If you believe an item is not applicable to this research article, leave it blank. Be prepared to explain your ratings.

A. The introduction establishes the importance of the study.

   SA   5   4   3   2   1   SD

B. The literature review establishes the context for the study.

   SA   5   4   3   2   1   SD

C. The research purpose, question, or hypothesis is clearly stated.

   SA   5   4   3   2   1   SD

D. The method of sampling is sound.

   SA   5   4   3   2   1   SD

E. Relevant demographics (for example, age, gender, and ethnicity) are described.

> SA   5   4   3   2   1   SD

F. Measurement procedures are adequate.

> SA   5   4   3   2   1   SD

G. All procedures have been described in sufficient detail to permit a replication of the study.

> SA   5   4   3   2   1   SD

H. The participants have been adequately protected from potential harm.

> SA   5   4   3   2   1   SD

I. The results are clearly described.

> SA   5   4   3   2   1   SD

J. The discussion/conclusion is appropriate.

> SA   5   4   3   2   1   SD

K. Despite any flaws, the report is worthy of publication.

> SA   5   4   3   2   1   SD

Article 7

Chickasaw Native American Adolescent Mothers: Implications for Early Intervention Practices

ANNE McDONALD CULP
Oklahoma State University

VIRGINIA McCARTHICK
Oklahoma State University

ABSTRACT. Twenty-four adolescent mothers completed a cultural identity questionnaire and met with an observer in their homes to complete the HOME Scale. Analyses utilizing Pearson product-moment correlation coefficients found a significant relationship between high identity with the Native American culture and lower scores on verbal responsivity and on provision of material goods. These findings were expected given the Chickasaw values of quietness, reservation, and few worldly possessions. This study illustrates why cultural sensitivity is important for training and in practice when providing community services, such as early intervention.

From *Journal of Community Psychology, 25,* 513–518. Copyright © 1997 by John Wiley & Sons, Inc. Reprinted with permission.

Adolescent parenting practices have been found to differ when compared to older mothers, especially in the area of responsiveness and verbal interactions (Chase-Lansdale, Brooks-Gunn, & Palkoff, 1991; 5 Culp, Osofsky, & O'Brien, 1996), and stimulation in the home environment (see Luster & Mittelstaedt, 1993, for a review). In this regard, early interventions in home visitation have targeted first-time adolescent parents and have found effective results in better ma-10 ternal perception of empathic understanding toward children and increased understanding of adult roles in parenting (Culp, Culp, Blankemeyer, & Passmark, in press). Additionally, children of adolescent mothers benefit from early intervention by nurses in the areas of 15 reduced rate of child maltreatment, fewer accidents requiring emergency care, and better health throughout childhood (Olds & Kitzman, 1993). These findings have led many communities to implement early intervention programs for adolescent mothers. However, 20 there is little research on cultural differences that may affect the appropriateness and effectiveness of the intervention programs. Early intervention practices could continue to be refined by assessing the cultural identity of participants and consequently engage in intervention 25 practices within cultural contexts.

Many Native American values and beliefs define appropriate behavior by quietness, reserve, noninterference, and cooperation; and silence is a customary prac-tice of the American Indian (Ho, 1984). The Native 30 American relies upon indirect communication: eye contact is avoided as a means of showing respect (Burgess, 1978; Chisholm, 1983) and jumping into a conversation is considered offensive (Ho, 1984; Ryan, 1992). The Native American culture values controlling 35 emotions. The traditional demeanor is one of poise and self-containment.

Although children are taught to observe rather than to react, they are ever present at most social gatherings, and time spent with children is more important than 40 buying material goods for them (Burgess, 1978). Native American parents teach their children by participation and observation rather than by actual instruction and by buying materialistic goods. Verbalization of needs, wants, feelings, and intentions is not encouraged 45 because the needs of the group are more important than one's own needs (Ho, 1984).

Very little research specific to the Chickasaw tribe is available. However, the cultural characteristics of the Chickasaw individual has been documented: (a) the 50 individual uses nonverbal communication through body language, sign language, facial expression, silence, and respects personal space; (b) time is now and ever flowing, there is no need to hurry; (c) respect for elders and other adults (teachers) is shown not by 55 looking into their eyes, but rather, by glancing away; and (d) lack of belief in ownership—resources are to be shared among each other, not kept from those in need; a low emphasis on personal material wealth (Chickasaw Tribal Cultural Center, 1994; Milligan, 1976).

60 A study of Navajo mother-infant interaction measured consistent differences in comparisons with Anglo American mothers. It was found that during the first year of life, Navajo infants vocalized less than Anglo American infants, interaction with the mother was 65 shorter and mothers talked to and touched their infants less than Anglo mothers (Chisholm, 1983). The diverse language background and de-emphasis of verbal interaction practiced by Native Americans may hamper the development of language skills needed to succeed in 70 the majority culture's public educational system (Ho, 1984). Early studies on achievement (reviewed in Burgess, 1978) show that the educational potential of Native American children and non-Native American chil-

dren is equal at the school entrance level. Around the
75 eighth grade, Native American children fall behind non-Native American children on achievement scores. Education researchers often attribute this phenomenon to teaching style which encourages verbal assertiveness (Burgess, 1978). This lag in achievement may be par-
80 tially due to speech production. Knowing a tribal language and learning English as a second language may cause Native American children to use shorter sentences, omit adjectives, and use the English verb incorrectly (Burgess, 1978).

85 Ivey (1969) sampled 185 Cherokee, Choctaw, Creek, and Seminole children in an Indian residential elementary school to determine the influence of language upon reading and speech development. This study found a relationship between speech competency
90 and reading ability. The results showed that the students were deficient in reading, and the major contributing factor was defective speech. Guilmet (1977) found that Navajo children speak half as often as white children in the classroom. This lack of speech in the
95 classroom may be related to poor academic achievement. Teachers reveal a bias toward children with limited communication abilities (Rice, Hadley, & Alexander, 1993). When asked to assess a child's attributes (intelligence, social maturity) by listening to an audio
100 tape, they judge the children with limited communication abilities to be less capable than children without communication abilities, when, in fact, they are not.

In summary, adolescent mothers are at risk for poor parenting practices, and many communities are pro-
105 viding early home visitation intervention services to them. The expectation is that children of parents enrolled in intervention programs will experience healthy development: physically, cognitively, socially, and linguistically. However, adolescent mothers who iden-
110 tify with the Native American culture are likely to be a challenge for intervention professionals because they may be quiet, avoid eye contact, and communicate in an indirect way. This kind of communication may affect how the home visitor approaches the young
115 mother. In addition, the mother's quietness may influence her child's language acquisition and production, which, in turn, may influence school achievement.

This study investigated the relationship between the degree of cultural identity and the conditions of the
120 home environment of adolescent mothers. The variables of the home environment were verbal responsiveness and provision of materials to children. We hypothesized that high identity with the Native American culture will relate to less maternal verbal respon-
125 sivity and to low provision of manufactured learning materials in the home.

Method

Participants

The sample consisted of 24 adolescent mothers of which 16 were Native American, seven White, and one

African American and White. Of the Native American
130 mothers, 13 of the mothers were Chickasaw and 3 had close tribal affiliations.

All the mothers were less than 19 years of age at the time of their first child's birth. Eighty percent of the sample had annual incomes of less that $18,000; 53%
135 did not have high school degrees; 55% were not married. The children were less than 3 years of age with 80% less than 1 year old; 58% of the children had an older sibling.

Procedures

Mothers were recruited through parenting programs
140 in rural southwestern United States. A staff member who worked with the families described the study to the mothers and received consent for the researcher to meet them for a 90-minute visit at a time convenient to the mother and when the child was awake.

Measures

145 In addition to a basic demographic information form, two assessment instruments were used: The Home Observation for Measurement of the Environment (HOME; Caldwell & Bradley, 1984) and the Orthogonal Model of Cultural Assessment (Oetting &
150 Beauvias, 1991) were used.

The HOME Scale is an observation/interview measure of the quality of the social, emotional, and cognitive support available to the child in the home. The 45-item measure was developed for infants aged
155 0–3 years with each item scored in binary (yes–no) fashion. The 45 items are divided into six subscales: two of which were used in the study: (1) Emotional and Verbal Responsivity of the Mother, and (4) Provision of Play Materials. Reliability and validity of the
160 HOME Scale have been well documented. The scale is respected as a standard measure in the field of early environmental research with high predictive validity with studies predicting school-age social and cognitive development (Bradley & Caldwell, 1976a, 1976b;
165 1984; Bradley, Caldwell, & Rock, 1988). While administering the scale, the researcher attempted to put the parent at ease and care was taken not to ask questions in a threatening or judgmental manner.

The Orthogonal Model of Cultural Assessment
170 measures the degree to which an individual perceives his or her link with a particular culture. The measure allows for high or low identification with a particular culture, or any combination of bicultural identification. Six questions each require an answer for each culture
175 that is numeric and ranges from 1 (a lot) to 4 (none at all). The questions cover information on special activities that take place every year at particular times (such as holiday parties, special meals, religious activities, trips, or visits); cultural rules followed in everyday
180 family life and with the self; and if family success as well as their own future success exists in the culture. For the purpose of this study, only those scores relating to the Native American culture were used to calculate

the single Native American culture score. A score close to 1 is very high identity; a score close to 4 is very low identity. Reliability and validity studies have been carried out by Oetting and Beauvias (1991), and they report high concurrent validity among a sample of Native American youth and another cultural identity measure.

Results

Pearson product-moment correlation coefficients were used to analyze for relationships between cultural identity and the scores on verbal responsivity and provision of play materials. The Emotional and Verbal Responsivity Score covered 11 items, 7 of which were specific to conversation and verbalizations, 5 of which reflected the child receiving positive attention while the visitor was there. The possible range of scores was 0 to 11. The data in the study ranged from 2 to 10. Recall that a low score on the culture measure signifies high identity and a low HOME scale signifies low responsivity and provision. The results show a significant positive correlation (both scores are low). High Native American cultural identity relates to low verbal responsivity $r = .60, p = .001$.

The Provision of Play Materials score had 9 items which related to available toys: toys for muscle activity, for music, for simple eye-hand coordination, complex eye hand coordination, cuddly or role-playing toys. This scale had a potential range of 0 to 9 points. The data in this study ranged from 1 to 9. The results show a significant positive correlation between Native American cultural identity and learning materials, $r = .47; p = .01$.

Discussion

The purpose of this study was to investigate the relationship between Native American cultural identity and the home environment of Native American adolescent parents. The results of this study show significant support for the hypothesis which related high Native American cultural identity with low verbal responsivity and the provision of learning materials. Adolescent mothers who identified with the Native American culture had homes in which verbal initiations, responsivity, and spontaneous conversation with their children were low and the provision of manufactured learning materials was low. Since the research literature had documented that Native American children do not perform as well in school, it could be suggested that the study variables may have an important influence. Because the Chickasaw Native American mothers respect the values of their culture, it is of no surprise that scores on verbal responsivity and material possessions were low. This is a reflection of their cultural identity.

These data should be given serious consideration by community providers of intervention programs for Native American adolescent mothers. As indicated by Ho (1984), Guilmet (1977), Burgess (1978), and Ivey (1969), there is a concern for Native American children's language skills and academic success in school

and how teachers perceive low-level language users. This concern puts great emphasis on the need to intervene into the children's lives early. However, the intervention should be placed in a cultural context in which cultural identity is respected. Native American parents are concerned about school achievement. The parents worry about how much to compromise their cultural values and teachings (Burgess, 1978; Ryan, 1992). To facilitate the children's success in the majority culture public education system, community agency providers, educators, and parents need to share and discuss the information gleaned from Native American research studies and early intervention studies in which the specific parent-child activities are described that positively influence school achievement. Once this information is laid out in a clear way, the community service providers should listen and reflect what the Native American parents understand the studies to say. Parents should be given the time to explain how the information fits into their belief systems and if they might have methods that could be considered for implementation. The ideas generated by the parents could be used as a guide in developing creative ways to implement an early intervention program for the community Native American families. Service providers that are culturally sensitive will help ensure the program's success.

References

Bradley, R., & Caldwell, B. M. (1976a). The relation of infant's home environments to mental test performance at fifty-four months: A follow-up study. *Child Development, 47*, 1172–1174.

Bradley, R., & Caldwell, B. M. (1976b). Early home environments and changes in mental test performance in children 6–36 months. *Developmental Psychology, 12*(3), 93–97.

Bradley, R., Caldwell, B., & Rock, S. (1988). Home environment and school performance: A ten-year follow-up and examination of three models of environmental action. *Child Development, 59*, 852–867.

Burgess, B. (1978). Native American learning styles. In L. Morris (Ed.), *Extracting learning styles from social/cultural diversity. A study of five American minorities* (pp. 41–54). Norman, OK: Southwest Teacher Corps Network.

Caldwell, B., & Bradley, R. (1984). *Home observation for measurement of the environment: Administration manual.* Little Rock: University of Arkansas.

Chase-Lansdale, P. L., Brooks-Gunn, J., & Palkoff, R. L. (1991). Research and programs for adolescent mothers: Mission links and future promises. *Family Relations, 40*, 396–403.

Chickasaw Tribal Cultural Center (1994). *Cultural characteristics.* Unpublished brochure.

Chisholm, J. (1983). *Navajo infancy.* New York: Aldine Publishing Co.

Culp, A. M., Culp, R. E., Blankemeyer, M., Passmark, L. (in press). The effects of an early intervention parent education program on first-time parenting skills: Adolescent versus older mothers. *Infant Mental Health Journal.*

Culp, A. M., Osofsky, J. D., & O'Brien, M. (1996). Language patterns of adolescent and older mothers and their one-year old children: A comparative study. *First Language, 16*, 61–75.

Guilmet, G. (1977). The nonverbal American Indian child in the urban classroom (Doctoral dissertation, University of California, 1977). *Dissertation Abstracts International, 37* (10a), 6587A. (From Psychosocial Research in American Indian and Alaska Native Youth, 1984, Abstract No. 708515).

Ho, K. M. (1984). Family therapy with ethnic minorities. In A. Lauffer & C. Garvin (Eds.), *Sage Source Books for the Human Services Series* (pp. 69–122). Newbury Park, CA: Sage.

Ivey, L. P. (1969). Influence of Indian language on reading and speech development (Doctoral dissertation, University of Oklahoma, 1969). *Dissertation Abstracts International, 29* (08A), 2438A. (From Psychosocial Research in American Indian and Alaska Native Youth, 1984, Abstract No. 6901985).

Luster, T., & Mittelstaedt, M. (1993). Adolescent mothers. In T. Luster & L. Okagaki (Eds.), *Parenting: An Ecological Perspective* (pp. 69–99). Hillsdale, NJ: Erlbaum.

Milligan, D. (1976). *The Indian way.* Quannah, TX: Nortex Press.

Oetting, E., & Beauvias, F. (1991). Orthogonal cultural identification theory:

The cultural identification of minority adolescents. *The International Journal of Addictions, 25*, (5A & 6A), 655–685.

Olds, D., & Kitzman, H. (1993). Review of research on home visiting for pregnant women and parents of young children. *The Future of Children, 3*(3), 53–92.

Rice, M., Hadley, P., & Alexander, A. (1993). Social biases toward children with speech and language impairments: A correlative casual model of language limitations. *Applied Psycholinguistics, 14*, 445–471.

Ryan, J. (1992). Formal schooling and deculturalization: Nursing practice and the erosion of native communication styles. *The Alberta Journal of Educational Research, 38*, 91–103.

Acknowledgments: The authors would like to thank the families involved in the study and Pamela Carr for her thoughtful review of the manuscript.

Address correspondence to: Anne McDonald Culp, Department of Family Relations and Child Development, 243 Human Environmental Sciences, Oklahoma State University, Stillwater, OK 74078-6122.

Exercise for Article 7

Factual Questions

1. What is the explicitly stated hypothesis for this study?

2. How old were the mothers at the time of their first child's birth?

3. For what words does "HOME" stand?

4. How many of the Emotional and Verbal Responsivity of the Mother subscale items were specific to conversation and verbalizations?

5. Does a low HOME score indicate low responsivity and provision *or* does it indicate high responsivity and provision?

6. What is the value of the correlation coefficient for the relationship between Native American cultural identity and verbal responsivity? Is it statistically significant? If yes, at what probability level?

Questions for Discussion

7. If you had planned this study, would you have included White and African American adolescents? Why? Why not?

8. The participants in this study were recruited through parenting programs. Does this limit the generalizability of the findings? Explain.

9. The researchers do not present averages and measures of variability (such as means and standard deviations). In your opinion, is this an important omission? Explain.

10. In line 213, the researchers report a correlation coefficient of .47. Would you characterize this as representing a very strong relationship? If no, how would you characterize it?

11. If you were to conduct a similar study, what changes would you make in the research methodology, if any?

Quality Ratings

Directions: Indicate your level of agreement with each of the following statements by circling a number from 5 for strongly agree (SA) to 1 for strongly disagree (SD). If you believe an item is not applicable to this research article, leave it blank. Be prepared to explain your ratings.

A. The introduction establishes the importance of the study.

SA 5 4 3 2 1 SD

B. The literature review establishes the context for the study.

SA 5 4 3 2 1 SD

C. The research purpose, question, or hypothesis is clearly stated.

SA 5 4 3 2 1 SD

D. The method of sampling is sound.

SA 5 4 3 2 1 SD

E. Relevant demographics (for example, age, gender, and ethnicity) are described.

SA 5 4 3 2 1 SD

F. Measurement procedures are adequate.

SA 5 4 3 2 1 SD

G. All procedures have been described in sufficient detail to permit a replication of the study.

SA 5 4 3 2 1 SD

H. The participants have been adequately protected from potential harm.

SA 5 4 3 2 1 SD

I. The results are clearly described.

SA 5 4 3 2 1 SD

J. The discussion/conclusion is appropriate.

SA 5 4 3 2 1 SD

K. Despite any flaws, the report is worthy of publication.

SA 5 4 3 2 1 SD

Article 8

Understanding Shame in Adults: Retrospective Perceptions of Parental Bonding During Childhood

NITA LUTWAK
CUNY/Baruch College

JOSEPH R. FERRARI
DePaul University

ABSTRACT. The association between perceptions of parental-bonding style during childhood and moral affect of shame at young adulthood were examined with 264 women and 140 men (mean age [± *SD*] = 20.4 ± 1.6 years old). Shame affect was significantly positively related to fear of negative evaluation by others and social avoidance, and negatively related to recalled parental care in one's childhood. Multiple regression analyses indicated that maternal protectiveness, paternal care, fear of negative social evaluation, and social avoidance were significant predictors of shame, explaining 41% of the variance. Results support object relations theory, which states that shame is a moral affect associated with social evaluation apprehension and may have developmental implications for one's parental relations.

From *The Journal of Nervous and Mental Disease, 185*, 595–598. Copyright © 1997 by Williams & Wilkins. Reprinted with permission.

In the past decade, the role of shame has been given increased attention in the empirical-clinical literature as a potentially important emotion in a range of psychological disorders (Kohut, 1971; Lewis, 1971, 1987; Nathanson, 1987). Shame is a self-conscious emotion involving negative evaluations not of one's behavior but of one's entire self. When faced with negative events, it is the entire self that is painfully scrutinized and negatively evaluated. Clinical theory suggests that shame-prone individuals typically focus on how they believe others evaluate them negatively, and these apprehensions may promote social avoidance and anxiety (Harder and Zalma, 1990; Lewis, 1987; Lutwak and Ferrari, in press; Tangney et al., 1992). Studies have explored the determinants of shame, including a number of negative behavioral and cognitive tendencies such as anger arousal, depression, self-derogation, shyness, interpersonal anxiety, perfectionism, self-critical cognitions, and a diffuse-oriented self-identity (Harder and Zalma, 1990; Lutwak and Ferrari, 1996, in press; Lutwak et al., 1996; Tangney and Fischer, 1995).

The moral affect of shame has become a major focus of psychodynamically oriented conceptualizations (Tangney and Fischer, 1995). Object relation theory, which stresses the role of internalization of interpersonal experiences in psychopathologies (Greenberg and Mitchell, 1983; Tangney and Fischer, 1995), claims that shame arises from the unique role that parents play in a developing child. Within this framework, mother is considered the primary object of attachment and separation from her is one of the hallmarks of early development. The father is perceived as the first significant other outside the mother-child dyad that represents external reality (Kaywin, 1993). Essentially, this theoretical model states that early parental experiences become internalized in the process of personality formation and that later affective modes (such as shame) may be linked to the quality of these earlier object relations.

Studies demonstrated that individuals who recall early (perceived) negative parental experiences report maladjustments in their later personality styles, coping skills, and interpersonal relationships. As opposed to data recorded on direct, actual parent-child interactions, retrospective accounts of early childhood may involve selective memories, as well as selective reporting of those events. Nevertheless, retrospective studies indicate that adult chronic procrastinators, perfectionists, frequent indecisives, depressives, and substance abusers self-reported perceived poor parental care (Ferrari and Olivette, 1994; Flett et al., 1996; McCown et al., 1991). Negative perceptions of parental care recalled about childhood, in fact, have been associated with adult risk for psychopathology (Bornstein and O'Neill, 1992; Goldney, 1985), therapeutic processes and dynamics (Diamond et al., 1990), and predictive of recovery from maladjustments (Keitner et al., 1987; Vaughn and Leff, 1976).

This study examined the perceptions of parental bonding styles during childhood by individuals who reported the moral emotion of shame at young adulthood. The moral affect of shame was expected to be related to (and predictive of) negative evaluations by others and avoidance of social interactions, as clinical psychodynamic (object relations) theory would predict (Greenberg and Mitchell, 1983; Tangney and Fischer, 1995). To the extent that parental relations affect a person's development (Kaywin, 1993) and that shame is a negative affect concerning one's global perspective of himself or herself (Lewis, 1971), it also was expected that perceived negative parenting styles (e.g., low levels of affection) would predict shame among young adults. Furthermore, because the mother is believed to be the principal agent of affection and nurturance during childhood (Kaywin, 1993; Nathonson, 1987), it was predicted that increases in shame would be related to perceptions of low levels of maternal affection and care.

Methods

Participants

Young adults (264 women, 140 men) enrolled in a lower division psychology course at an urban, public, northeastern university were asked to participate in this study for extra course credit. Participants ranged in age from 18 to 28 (mean age = 20.4 ± 1.6 years old) and represented diverse ethnic identities (43% Asian-American, 18% Hispanic-American, 18% African-American, 15% Caucasian, 5% unidentified) and religious affiliations (29% Roman Catholic, 11% Buddhist, 10% Protestant, 6% Jewish, 3% Hindu, 2% Islamic, 38% unidentified).

Psychometric Measures

Hoblitzelle's (1982) 11 descriptive adjective Adapted Shame Scale (AS) was used to assess the moral affect of shame. Respondents described themselves along 7-point scales (1 = never true; 7 = always true) to each adjective. The shame scale has acceptable internal consistency (alpha $r = .83$) and temporal stability (retest $r = .93$) for a research tool and appropriate construct validity (Harder and Zalma, 1990; Hoblitzelle, 1982). Participants also completed Parker, Tupling, and Brown's (1979) 25-item Parental Bonding Instrument to measure perceptions of care and protection by one's parents received during childhood. Respondents report their perceptions separately for their mother and father during the first 16 years of life. Using 4-point rating scales (1 = very unlike, 4 = very like) to each item, respondents evaluate a "care" dimension (from affectionate, emotionally warm, and empathetic to neglecting, cold, and indifferent) and a "protective" dimension (from controlling, intrusive, and infantile to passive, independence, and autonomy) to yield maternal care (mC) and protectiveness (mP) and paternal care (pC) and protectiveness (pP) dimensions. The scale's authors report good internal consistency (.77) and temporal stability (.80) for the total scale score, and the instrument has been evaluated as a psychometrically valid measure of parental bonding (Gerlsman et al., 1990). Watson and Friend's (1969) 28-item, 5-point Social Avoidance Scale (SA) was used to examine whether individuals reported avoidance of social situations they perceived as potentially or actually distressful. The inventory has acceptable internal consistency (.87) and retest reliability (.82), as well as acceptable

validity (Watson and Friend, 1969). Participants also completed Leary's (1983) revised 23-item, 5-point Fear of Negative Evaluation Scale (FNE) to assess apprehension that others would evaluate oneself negatively. The scale's author reported an internal consistency of .79 and retest reliability of .75, as well as good construct and predictive validities.

Procedure

After signing and returning a consent form, participants completed demographic information (age, gender, ethnic identity, and religious preference) and the psychometric measures (in random order). Testing occurred at the beginning of the semester in groups of about 35 persons and took about 75 minutes to complete.

Results

There was no significant gender difference on the self-reported shame scores; therefore, no further gender comparisons were assessed. Scores on the seven self-reported measures were intercorrelated (Table 1). As expected, shame was significantly related to social avoidance and fear of negative social evaluation. Furthermore, although the magnitude of the coefficients was small, shame was significantly negatively related to both maternal and paternal care and affection and positively related to maternal protectiveness and control.

In addition, multiple regression analyses were performed to ascertain predictors of shame from the six other self-reported variables (entered: negative social evaluation, social avoidance, and parental care and protection separately for mother and father). Analyses indicated that the best predictors of shame were fear of negative social evaluation, social avoidance, low paternal care, and maternal protectiveness, $F(7,382) = 36.67$, $p < .001$. These variables explained 41% of the variance in shame ($R^2 = .41$).

Discussion

As expected, the results of this study were consistent with clinical models of moral affect (Lewis, 1971, 1987). Lindsay-Hartz (1984) and others (Harder and Zalma, 1990), for instance, claimed that feelings of shame about one's self may be related to self-consciousness over others' evaluations of one's self and experiences of anxiety in social or interpersonal contexts that may, in turn, elicit a social avoidance response. Participants in this study reported an association between shame affect and fear of negative social evaluation as well as social anxiety and interpersonal avoidance. In fact, both social interaction variables were significant predictors of shame. These results, then, support other studies that demonstrate a social interaction component to shame as a moral affect (Lutwak and Ferrari, 1996, in press; Tangney and Fischer, 1995).

Moreover, this study confirmed empirically a link

Table 1
Zero-order Correlation Coefficients between Self-reported Measures

Measure	AS	SA	FNE	mC	mP	pC	pP
Adaptive shame (AS)	[.83]						
Social avoidance (SA)	.457**	[.88]					
Negative social evaluation (FNE)	.453**	.440**	[.86]				
Maternal care (mC)	−.249*	−.189*	−.067	[.87]			
Maternal protectiveness (mP)	.196*	.084	.102	−.373**	[.83]		
Paternal care (pC)	−.225*	−.042	−.122	.412**	−.146	[.90]	
Paternal protectiveness (pP)	.137	.039	.111	−.163*	.371**	−.210	[.87]

(N = 404) *p ≤ > 01 **p ≤ .001
Values in brackets are coefficient alpha with this sample.

between perceptions of inadequate parental responsiveness during childhood and self-reported shame affect by adults (Kohut, 1978). The moral affect of shame was associated with memories of one's parents as demanding, overcontrolling, and nonnurturing. Specifically, individuals associated increases in shame with perceptions of their mother as neglectful, controlling, and affectionless and their father also as someone who did not express affection and warmth. These results were consistent with theoretical formulations suggesting that parental perceptions may be central to the formulation of the self and that early parenting experiences dispose one to anomalies in self-perception and psychopathology (Grinker, 1955; Lewinsohn and Rosenbaum, 1987).

Of course, this study does contain several methodological limitations. All participants were college students, raising the possibility that results may not be generalizable to other populations. Also, no questions were asked about blended families, number of siblings, or birth order, and all items were self-reported. Participants were required to recall past experiences with their parents, raising the possibility of selective memories in their retrospective reports. These results may simply reflect the fact that some people were more willing than others to acknowledge negative events and experiences. Future studies should conduct more in-depth, longitudinal assessments into different family structures and with participants from different age levels. Parental influences should be recorded from *actual* parent-child interactions, and measures of social desirability should be obtained.

Nevertheless, this study raised some interesting issues concerning social anxiety/avoidance, recollections of perceived parental bonding, and shame affect in adulthood. Clinicians should be attentive to information regarding client's avoidance of social interactions because social evaluation apprehension and avoidance were predictive of shame. Although nonclinical participants were used in this study, the fact that parental perceptions predicted shame (a negative moral affect) suggested that this information may help ascertain a potential source for the client's internal feelings of shame about themselves. Further research is needed to clarify further the antecedents and consequences of shame as a negative moral affect with clinical participants.

References

Bornstein RF, O'Neil RM (1992) Parental perceptions and psychopathology. *J Nerv Ment Dis* 180:475–483.

Diamond D, Kaslow N, Coonerty S, Blatt SJ (1990) Changes in separation-individuation and inter-subjectivity in long-term treatment. *Psychoanal Psychol* 7:363–397.

Ferrari JR, Olivette MJ (1994) Parental authority and the development of female dysfunctional procrastination. *J Res Pers* 28:87–100.

Flett G, Hewitt P, Singer A (1996) Perfectionism and parental authority styles. *Individ Psychol* 124:87–111.

Gerlsman C, Emmelkamp PM, Arrindell WA (1990) Anxiety depression and perception of early parenting: A meta-analysis. *Clin Psychol Rev* 10:251–277.

Goldney RD (1985) Parental representations in young women who attempt suicide. *Acta Psychiatr Scand* 72:230–232.

Greenberg JR, Mitchell SA (1983) *Object relations in psychoanalytic theory.* Cambridge, MA: Harvard University Press.

Grinker E (1955) Growth inertia and shame: Their therapeutic implications and dangers. *Int J Psychoanal* 36:242–253.

Harder DW, Zalma AZ (1990) Two promising shame and guilt scales: A construct validity comparison. *J Pers Assess* 55:729–745.

Hoblitzelle W (1982) *Developing a measure of shame and guilt and the role of shame in depression.* Unpublished dissertation, Yale University, New Haven, CT.

Kaywin R (1993) The theoretical contributions of Hans W. Loewald. *Psychoanal Study Child* 48:99–114.

Keitner GI, Miller IW, Epstein NB (1987) Family functioning and the course of major depression. *Compr Psychiatry* 28:54–64.

Kohut H (1971) *The analysis of the self.* New York: International Universities Press.

Kohut H (1978) *The search for the self.* New York: International Universities Press.

Leary MR (1983). A brief version of the Fear of Negative Evaluation Scale. *Pers Soc Psychol Bull* 9:371–376.

Lewinsohn PM, Rosenbaum M (1987) Recall of parental behavior by acute depressives, remitted depressives, and non-depressives. *J Pers Soc Psychol* 52:611–619.

Lewis HB (1971) *Shame and guilt in neurosis.* New York: International Universities Press.

Lewis HB (1987) Shame the "sleeper" in psychopathology. In HB Lewis (Ed), *The role of shame in symptom formation* (pp 1–28). Hillsdale, NJ: Erlbaum.

Lindsay-Hartz J (1984) Contrasting experiences of shame and guilt. *Am Behav Sci* 27:389–404.

Lutwak N, Ferrari JR (1996) Moral affect and cognitive processes. *Pers Individ Differ* 21:891–896.

Lutwak N, Ferrari JR (in press). Shame-related social anxiety: Replicating a link with various social interaction measures. *Anxiety, Stress, and Coping: An International Journal.*

Lutwak N, Ferrari JR, Cheek, JM (1996). *Shame-proneness, guilt-proneness, and self-identity: The role of orientation and processing style in moral affect.* Unpublished manuscript.

McCown W, Carise D, Johnson J (1991) Trait procrastination in adult children of alcohol abusers. *J Soc Behav Pers* 5:121–134.

Nathanson DL (1987) *The many faces of shame.* New York: Guilford.

Parker G, Tupling H, Brown LB (1979) A parental bonding instrument. *Br J Med Psychol* 42:1–10.

Tangney JP, Fischer KW (1995) *Self-conscious emotions: Shame, guilt, embarrassment, and pride.* New York: Guilford.

Tangney JP, Wagner PE, Gramzow R (1992) Proneness to shame, proneness to guilt, and psychopathology. *J Abnorm Psychol* 103:469–478.

Vaughn CE, Leff JP (1976) The influence of family and social factors on the course of psychiatric illness. *Br J Psychiatry* 29:125–137.

Watson D, Friend R (1969) Measurement of social evaluation anxiety. *J Consult Clin Psychol* 33:448–457.

About the authors: Nita Lutwak, Department of Psychology, CUNY/Baruch College, 17 Lexington Avenue, New York, NY 10010. Joseph R. Ferrari, Department of Psychology, DePaul University, 2219 North Kenmore Avenue, Chicago, IL, 60614-3504. Send reprint requests to Dr. Ferrari.

Exercise for Article 8

Factual Questions

1. Is "shame" defined as a self-conscious emotion involving one's behavior?

2. What is the reported value of the test-retest reliability coefficient (for temporal stability) for the Adapted Shame Scale?

3. Did the participants sign a consent form?

4. What is the value of the correlation coefficient for the relationship between AS and pC?

5. What is the value of the correlation coefficient for the relationship between maternal care and paternal care?

6. What percentage of the variance in shame was predicted in the multiple regression analysis by fear of negative social evaluation, social avoidance, low paternal care, and maternal protectiveness?

7. In Table 1, six different variables are correlated with AS. (See the column labeled AS.) Which one of these correlation coefficients represents the weakest relationship?

Questions for Discussion

8. The researchers mention the limitations of retrospective reports. (See lines 42–46 and lines 194–200.) Do you agree with the researchers? Explain.

9. The AS is described in lines 89–96. In your opinion, is the description adequate? Explain.

10. Speculate on why the researchers administered the psychometric measures "in random order."

11. The researchers do not present averages and measures of variability (such as means and standard de-

viations). In your opinion, is this an important omission? Explain.

12. Beginning in line 189, the researchers discuss methodological limitations. In your opinion, how serious is the first limitation they discuss? Explain.

Quality Ratings

Directions: Indicate your level of agreement with each of the following statements by circling a number from 5 for strongly agree (SA) to 1 for strongly disagree (SD). If you believe an item is not applicable to this research article, leave it blank. Be prepared to explain your ratings.

A. The introduction establishes the importance of the study.

SA   5   4   3   2   1   SD

B. The literature review establishes the context for the study.

SA   5   4   3   2   1   SD

C. The research purpose, question, or hypothesis is clearly stated.

SA   5   4   3   2   1   SD

D. The method of sampling is sound.

SA   5   4   3   2   1   SD

E. Relevant demographics (for example, age, gender, and ethnicity) are described.

SA   5   4   3   2   1   SD

F. Measurement procedures are adequate.

SA   5   4   3   2   1   SD

G. All procedures have been described in sufficient detail to permit a replication of the study.

SA   5   4   3   2   1   SD

H. The participants have been adequately protected from potential harm.

SA   5   4   3   2   1   SD

I. The results are clearly described.

SA   5   4   3   2   1   SD

J. The discussion/conclusion is appropriate.

SA   5   4   3   2   1   SD

K. Despite any flaws, the report is worthy of publication.

SA   5   4   3   2   1   SD

Article 9

Comparison of Education Versus Behavioral Skills Training Interventions in Lowering Sexual HIV-Risk Behavior of Substance-Dependent Adolescents

JANET S. ST. LAWRENCE
Jackson State University

KENNIS W. JEFFERSON
Jackson State University

EDNA ALLEYNE
Jackson State University

TED L. BRASFIELD
Jackson State University

ABSTRACT. Substance-dependent adolescents ($N = 34$) in a residential drug treatment facility received either a 6-session behavior skills training HIV-risk reduction intervention or standard HIV education. After the intervention, adolescents who received behavior skills training exhibited increased knowledge about HIV-AIDS, more favorable attitudes toward prevention and condom use, more internal locus of control, increased self-efficacy, increased recognition of HIV risk and decreases in high-risk sexual activity. Self-report data were corroborated by records for the treatment of sexually transmitted diseases. The results from this pilot demonstration effort suggest that skills training based on cognitive-behavioral principles may be effective in lowering high-risk adolescents' vulnerability to HIV infection and warrant evaluation in a controlled comparison with a larger sample.

From *Journal of Consulting and Clinical Psychology*, 63, 154–157.

The co-occurrence of juvenile delinquency, sexual behavior, and drug use among adolescents is well documented (Miller, Turner, & Moses, 1990). For decades, this triad has generated serious social and quality
5 of life concerns and now puts youths at jeopardy for adolescent-acquired HIV infection. Several studies reveal that adolescents are not changing their behavior in response to the threat of AIDS (DiClemente et al., 1992; Kegeles, Adler, & Irwin, 1988) because they
10 underestimate their risk, miscalculate their vulnerability, or feel impervious to negative outcomes (Quadrel, Fischhoff, & Davis, 1993). Despite the importance of HIV-prevention interventions for adolescents, little evaluation research is available to guide program de-
15 velopers regarding the content, timing, or format for risk reduction interventions targeting teenagers (St. Lawrence, 1993). One heuristic study evaluated a cog-

nitive intervention with minority youths (Schinke, Gordon, & Weston, 1990). Although the youths
20 learned problem-solving skills, their cognitive acquisition did not transfer into any measurable behavior changes lowering their HIV-infection risk. A more promising approach reported by Jemmott, Jemmott, and Fong (1992) found behavior skills training was
25 effective in lowering Black male adolescents' sexual risk behavior.

Given the limited number of empirically evaluated HIV risk-reduction programs for youth in general, it is not surprising that no published research to date has
30 evaluated prevention efforts for substance-dependent, sexually active, and conduct-disordered adolescents, although these youths may represent the apex of adolescents at risk for HIV. The purpose of the present demonstration study was to develop and evaluate, in
35 preliminary fashion, a cognitive-behavioral intervention's effectiveness in equipping substance-dependent adolescents with the interpersonal and technical skills necessary to lower risk and compare its outcome against a standard educational presentation.

Method

40 Participants in the present study were 34 adolescents in a residential treatment facility for substance-dependent youths. Ninety percent (90%) of the youths were court referred into treatment. The sample was 73% male, 26% female, 84% White, and 16% African
45 American. The mean age was 15.6 years (range, 13 to 17), and the mean grade level was 8.2. Eighty percent of the sample was sexually active, reporting a lifetime mean of 11.2 different sexual partners, and 15% were treated for a sexually transmitted disease in the previ-
50 ous 2 months. The study was conducted in Jackson, Mississippi, a city experiencing substantial increases in HIV seropositivity and AIDS. Informed consent was obtained separately from parents (or guardians) and

55 participants, and no one declined. All participants completed the intervention and the pre- and postintervention measures.

Pre- and postintervention, each participant completed measures using a code name devised by the adolescent. No personal identifying information was
60 collected to protect the participants' confidentiality. All measures were revised to a sixth-grade reading level, and the revisions were validated in earlier research (St. Lawrence, 1993; St. Lawrence et al., in press). The measures and Cronbach's alpha for this sample were as
65 follows: the AIDS Knowledge Test (Kelly, St. Lawrence, Hood, & Brasfield, 1989b; Cronbach's alpha for this sample = .76); Attitudes Toward HIV Prevention measure (Torabi & Yarber, 1992; Cronbach's alpha = .82 for this sample), Health Locus of Control Scale
70 (HLOC: Wallston, Wallston, & Devillis, 1978; Cronbach's alpha = .71); and Condom Attitude Scale—Revised (Sacco, Levine, Reed, & Thompson, 1991; St. Lawrence, 1993; Cronbach's alpha = .89). In addition to these paper-and-pencil inventories, each youth (a)
75 estimated his or her perceived risk for HIV infection on the basis of behavior in the previous 2 months and (b) rated his or her self-efficacy, using a 10-point Likert-type scale for both items. A risk behavior survey collected information about sexual behavior over 2
80 months pre- and postintervention. Residential status in the treatment program was consistent for both assessments.

Pre- and postintervention, each adolescent role played three simulated situations involving coercion to
85 engage in unprotected sexual intercourse, an invitation to engage in casual sex, and a partner who resisted condom use. Role play enactments were recorded and later rated by trained research assistants, who were not informed of the experimental condition or whether the
90 assessment was from pre- or postintervention. Four component skills and a global effectiveness rating were evaluated for each scene. Because of a mechanical malfunction, recordings from the education condition at postintervention were inaudible and could not be rated.
95 Mean interrater reliability was .96. A sample role play scene follows (role played with female participants):

Narration: You're just chillin' when this fine dude walks up and says he's had his eye on you and wants to get to know you better. He suggests the
100 two of you split and go over to his place. He says:

Prompt 1: Baby, come on. I can make you feel the earth move.
Prompt 2: You're not scared of a real man, are you?
105 *Prompt 3:* Baby, you can handle it. Let's go.

Group sessions were conducted weekly for 90 min over 6 weeks. Separate groups were conducted for male (2 groups per condition) and female (one group in each experimental condition) participants. All groups were
110 led by the same three group leaders, representative of the racial and gender demographics of the youths. All leaders followed a detailed procedural outline for each condition. Sessions were audiotape recorded and later rated for adherence to the protocol by a staff member
115 who was uninvolved in the program. No substantial departures from the prepared outlines were noted.

Standard Education Intervention

Three groups (*N* = 17) were randomly assigned to an education-only experimental condition ([EC] i.e., standard education intervention). This intervention
120 component provided participants with basic information didactically and through interactive game formats. Because of the youths' short attention span, didactic information was presented in short (less than 15 min) segments, followed by a "game" that required the
125 youths to use the information. Each game was followed by another didactic presentation that built on the previous module with games interspersed between modules. The games were adapted from television programs familiar to the youths (i.e., "HIV Feud" modeled on
130 "Family Feud") and names that were developmentally appealing (i.e., ''AIDS Busters''). Risk education was the sole focus of all six sessions, and no skills training was included or modeled in this experimental condition.

135 Abstinence was described as the only absolute protection from HIV infection. However, because more than 80% of the youths were sexually active, safer sex information was also provided. Sexual practices were presented along a risk continuum ranging from high
140 risk (e.g., unprotected intercourse) to moderate risk (intercourse when a latex condom and spermicide containing nonoxynol-9 are used) to no risk (activities that allow no bodily fluid exchange). Risk education was the sole content of all six sessions, and no behavior
145 skills training was included or modeled in this experimental condition.

Behavior Skills Training Intervention

Three groups (*N* = 17) participated in six sessions of behavior skills training (BST) that were developmentally
150 adapted from an intervention model that promoted lowered risk behavior in gay men and minority adolescents (Kelly, St. Lawrence, Hood, & Brasfield, 1989a, 1989b; St. Lawrence, Brasfield, Jefferson, & Alleyne, 1994) and included HIV education followed
155 by training and skill rehearsal in correct condom use, interpersonal communication skills, problem solving and self-management strategies. Risk education was provided in the first session using the same format that was described earlier. The second session focused on
160 condom use. Correct use was explained verbally and was then demonstrated with a cucumber, followed by a second demonstration using a penile model. This graduated sequence dissipated some of the initial nervousness and silliness that arose on participants' exposure to condoms at the beginning of the session. Each

45

participant also practiced and demonstrated condom use and was praised for correct use. Although the issue of training youths in condom use is socially sensitive, 80% of these youths were sexually active and 15% were treated for a sexually transmitted disease in each of the previous 2 months. Knowledge about self-protection was considered essential for those youths who would remain sexually active.

Three sessions provided training in assertion, partner negotiation, and communication skills. Youths observed the film *Are You with Me?* (Hoffman & Neema Barrett, 1991) to focus attention on issues relevant to partner negotiation and communication. Group leaders discussed and then modeled the specific skills and their use in situations that might arise and confer risk. Participants then practiced initiating discussion about HIV precautions, establishing partner agreement before considering sex, refusing coercions to engage in unsafe or unwanted sexual activities and outright refusal.

The final session emphasized problem solving and self-management strategies. Each youth identified past risky situations, noted the proximal factors that contributed to their risk behavior, and then developed and practiced an alternative way to deal with the high-risk antecedents in the future. For example, one group member decided to always have a "condom and a quarter." The condom was in the event of an unplanned sexual encounter, and the quarter was to call someone to come and get him if he wanted to escape from a situation. Cognitive self-management strategies such as self-affirmative statements were also taught and practiced. The intervention ended with participants' verbally identifying what they learned in the program, a change that he or she intended to make as a result, and specifically identifying how this change would be implemented. This enlisted participants into a public commitment as they behaviorally "contracted" to make changes and also provided peer models from within the group.

Participants in both conditions attended a mean of 5.8 sessions. Participants who missed a session because of illness received an individual make-up session before the next week's meeting.

Results and Discussion

Preliminary univariate and chi square tests found some significant differences between groups at pre-intervention. At pre-intervention, the BST participants obtained significantly lower scores on the Internal sub-scale of the HLOC, the Attitudes Toward HIV Prevention measure, the Condom Attitude Scale, a self-efficacy rating and perceptions of vulnerability to HIV infection. These preexisting differences are reflected in Table 1. There were no significant differences between male and female adolescents in knowledge, attitudes, or risk behavior with one exception. Male adolescents reported a higher mean number of sexual partners (the means for male and female adolescents were 1.9 and 1.4, respectively; $F[3, 60] = 5.61$, $p = .02$). Data from this demonstration project were subjected to statistical analysis, although the results should be interpreted with caution given the small sample size and the number of analyses reported. Univariate 2 (Condition) × 2 (Time) analyses of variance are reported in Table 1 and the pattern of change from pre- to postintervention was exceedingly consistent, providing promising support for the BST's impact.

Postintervention, youths in the BST intervention showed evidence of increased knowledge and internal locus of control scores, more favorable attitudes toward HIV prevention and condom use, increased self-efficacy, and greater recognition of personal vulnerability (all $p < .05$). Pre-intervention, these youths were significantly lower than the education condition on three of these measures, but were significantly higher than the education condition at postintervention. Analysis of the individual subscales of the Condom Attitude Scale revealed that, at postintervention, the youths in the BST intervention were more positive about the condom's impact on interpersonal relationships, exhibited more positive attitudes toward condom use, attached higher value to sexual safety in relationships, were less inhibited about using condoms, and perceived higher risk from unprotected sexual activity. Comparable changes were not evident in youths who participated in the information provision condition. Postintervention, these youths were significantly higher in self-efficacy than at pre-intervention and significantly lower in risk recognition than at pre-intervention or the BST participants at postintervention.

There were also significant differences between the experimental conditions in sexual risk behavior over 2-month periods at pre- and postintervention in the percentage of youths reporting: (a) coercions into unwanted sexual activity (EC: 7.7% to 15.4%; BST: 15.8% to 5.3%), (b) exchanging sex for money (EC: 7.7% to 15.4%; BST: 15.4% to none), (c) exchanging sex for drugs (EC: 15.4% to 23.1%; BST: 10.5% and 10.5%), (d) engaging in casual sex (EC: 15.4% to 23.1%; BST: 15.8% to 10.5%), or (e) engaging in sex with a partner they knew to be nonmonogamous (EC: 42.1% to 36.8%; BST: 46.2% to 7.7%) (all chi square tests attained $p < .05$).[1] The self-reported changes were substantiated by the residential treatment program's records for the number of sexually transmitted diseases that were treated each month. Six of the youths in each group required treatment for a sexually transmitted disease in the 2-months before entering the program. Postintervention, those who participated in the educational condition were unchanged ($n = 6$), whereas only one of the BST participants required treatment for a sexually transmitted disease in the 2 months after the intervention ended.

---

[1] Residential status was consistent for both time frames.

46

Table 1

Means, Standard Deviations, Significant Univariate Interactions and Post Hoc Tukey's Comparisons on Mean Paper-and-Pencil Measure Scores Between the Education and Behavior Skills Training Conditions at Pre- and Postintervention

| | M (SD) for: | | | | Interaction | |
| | Education | | Behavior skills training | | | |
Variable	Pre	Post	Pre	Post	F	p
AIDS Knowledge Test	19.8 (4.1)$_a$	19.5 (4.2)$_a$	18.8 (4.0)$_a$	21.6 (2.8)$_b$	2.58	.01
Health Locus of Control						
Internal subscale	22.4 (4.0)$_a$	23.2 (6.1)$_a$	20.1 (4.6)$_b$	25.3 (6.0)$_c$	4.03	.05
External subscale	23.4 (9.2)	23.3 (7.6)	23.3 (5.8)	20.9 (5.3)	1.10	ns
Attitudes toward HIV						
prevention	60.3 (6.4)$_a$	61.9 (7.5)$_a$	55.4 (8.6)$_b$	63.0 (5.5)$_c$	3.95	.05
Condom Attitude Scale	141.8 (25.2)$_a$	141.4 (39.9)$_a$	129.0 (35.6)$_b$	150.7 (33.4)$_c$	4.17	.05
Self-efficacy	8.1 (3.4)$_a$	8.9 (2.0)$_b$	7.7 (2.0)$_a$	9.8 (.6)$_c$	15.03	.0001
Perceptions of vulnerability	7.0 (2.1)$_a$	5.3 (3.7)$_b$	4.8 (3.1)$_b$	6.3 (2.9)$_a$	4.55	.04

Note. Different subscripts denote significant differences between means on Tukey post hoc tests. Pre = pre-intervention; Post = postintervention.

Table 2 summarizes the role play ratings for participants in the BST condition. Postintervention increases in all role play components and the overall effectiveness ratings were significant for participants in the BST condition (all $p < .05$). Unfortunately, because of a mechanical malfunction, there were no postintervention assessments from the education condition.

Table 2

Changes from Pre- to Postintervention in Masked Ratings of Interpersonal Skills in High-Risk Situations for Participants in the Behavior Skills Training Condition

Variable	Pre-intervention M (SD)	Postintervention M (SD)
Specific refusal of unsafe invitation or action	.4 (.8)	1.3 (2.0)
Provided a reason or rationale for refusal	.8 (.3)	1.8 (1.3)
Need for safety stated	.9 (1.5)	5.1 (2.4)
Proposed a lower risk alternative	.5 (1.2)	2.6 (2.3)
Global effectiveness rating	2.6 (2.5)	8.6 (2.4)

Note. Univariate results on all variables were significant on univariate analyses of variance (all $ps < .05$).

On their postintervention evaluations of the program, participants assigned mean ratings of 6.6 for the program's value and 6.4 to their comfort with the program staff on a 7-point scale ranging from 1 (*extremely poor–extremely little*) to 7 (*extremely good–a great deal*). All participants indicated that they would recommend the program to friends, and there were no significant differences between evaluations from youths in the two experimental conditions (both $p > .05$).

This uncontrolled demonstration project supports the potential usefulness of the BST intervention model.

All youths were simultaneously receiving treatment for substance abuse in a residential treatment program, based on an Alcoholics Anonymous treatment model that did not include skills training similar to the HIV risk reduction intervention, but contamination caused by informal exchanges between participants is a possibility. Although this study was successful in promoting risk behavior changes in substance-dependent adolescents who received BST, the durability of these changes is unknown. The intervention model appears promising, but more rigorous evaluation with a larger sample and longitudinal outcome evaluation is needed.

References

DiClemente, R. J., Durbin, M., Siegel, D., Krasnovsky, F., Lazarus, N., & Comacho, T. (1992). Determinants of condom use among junior high school students in a minority inner-city school district. *Pediatrics, 89,* 197–202.

Hoffman, J. (Producer), & Neema Barrett, N. (Director). (1991). *Are you with me?* [Film]. (Available from AIDSFILMS [Select Media], New York).

Jemmott, J. B., Jemmott, L. S., & Fong, G. T. (1992). Reductions in HIV risk-associated sexual behaviors among Black male adolescents: Effects of an AIDS prevention intervention. *American Journal of Public Health, 82,* 372–377.

Kegeles, S. M., Adler, N. E., & Irwin, C. E. (1988). Sexually active adolescents and condoms: Changes over the year in knowledge, attitudes, and use. *American Journal of Public Health, 78,* 460–461.

Kelly, J. A., St. Lawrence, J. S., Hood, H. V., & Brasfield, T. L. (1989a). Behavioral intervention to reduce AIDS-risk activities. *Journal of Consulting and Clinical Psychology, 57,* 60–67.

Kelly, J. A., St. Lawrence, J. S., Hood, H. V., & Brasfield, T. L. (1989b). An objective test of AIDS risk behavior knowledge: Scale development, validation, and norms. *Journal of Behavior Therapy and Experimental Psychiatry, 20,* 227–234.

Miller, C. F., Turner, C. F., & Moses, L. E. (Eds.) (1990). *AIDS: The second decade.* Washington, DC: National Academy Press.

Quadrel, M. J., Fischhoff, B., & Davis, W. (1993). Adolescent (in)vulnerability. *American Psychologist, 48,* 102–118.

Sacco, W. P., Levine, B., Reed, D. L., & Thompson, K. (1991). Attitudes about condom use as an AIDS-relevant behavior: Their factor structure and relation to condom use. *Psychological Assessment: A Journal of Consulting and Clinical Psychology, 3,* 272–276.

Schinke, S. P., Gordon, A. N., & Weston, R. E. (1990). Self-instruction to prevent HIV infection among African-American and Hispanic-American adolescents. *Journal of Consulting and Clinical Psychology, 58,* 432–436.

St. Lawrence, J. S. (1993). African-American adolescents' knowledge, health-related attitudes, sexual behavior, and contraceptive decisions: Implications for the prevention of adolescent HIV infection. *Journal of Consulting and Clinical Psychology, 61,* 104–112.

St. Lawrence, J. S., Brasfield, T. L., Jefferson, K. W., & Alleyne, E. (1944).

Social support as a factor in African-American adolescents' risk for teen pregnancy, sexually transmitted disease, and HIV infection. *Journal of Adolescent Research, 9*, 292–310.

St. Lawrence, J. S., Brasfield, T. L., Jefferson, K. W., Alleyne, E., O'Bannon, R. E., & Shirley, A. (in press). Cognitive-behavioral intervention to reduce African American adolescents' risk for HIV infection. *Journal of Consulting and Clinical Psychology.*

Torabi, M. R., & Yarber, W. (1992). Alternate forms of HIV prevention attitude scales for teenagers. *AIDS Education and Prevention, 4*, 172–182.

Wallston, K. A., Wallston, B. S., & Devillis R. (1978). Development of the multidimensional health locus of control (MHLOC) scales. *Health Education Monographs, 7*, 160–170.

Note: This research was supported by Grant MH48842 from the National Institute of Mental Health and by Grant DA08474 from the National Institute of Drug Abuse.

About the authors: Janet S. St. Lawrence, Kennis W. Jefferson, Edna Alleyne, and Ted L. Brasfield, Department of Psychology, Jackson State University.

Acknowledgments: We thank Clotie Graves, Monica Nelson, Rylander Lee, Brian Wilson, Angela Robertson, and the staff at The ARK for their assistance.

Address correspondence to: Janet S. St. Lawrence, Community Health Program, Department of Psychology, P.O. Box 17005, Jackson State University, Jackson, MS 39217-0105.

Exercise for Article 9

Factual Questions

1. According to the researchers, are there many empirically evaluated HIV risk-reduction programs?

2. What was the average age of the participants in this study?

3. The measures in this study were revised to be at what reading level?

4. On what variable were the male and female participants significantly different?

5. Which group (EC *or* BST) reported a reduction in exchanging sex for money?

6. What was the mean of the preintervention scores on the AIDS Knowledge Test for the BST group?

7. What was the standard deviation of the preintervention scores on the AIDS Knowledge Test for the BST group?

8. The differences between the pre-intervention and postintervention means in Table 2 are statistically significant at what probability level?

Questions for Discussion

9. The researchers use the term "Likert-type scale" in lines 77-78. What do you think this term means?

10. When the research assistants rated the role play enactments, they were not informed of the experimental condition or whether the assessment was pre- or postintervention. Is this an important feature of the study? Explain. (See lines 87-90.)

11. The researchers state that the leaders of the interventions "followed a detailed procedural outline for each condition." Was this a good idea? Would it have been better to allow each leader to modify the interventions as needed to meet the individual needs of the adolescents? Explain. (See lines 112-116.)

12. In addition to self-reports, the researchers examined records on the number of sexually transmitted diseases that were treated for participants in each intervention group. In your opinion, how important is this data? (See lines 266-275.)

13. The researchers state that the BST intervention model "appears promising." Do you agree? Explain. (See lines 302-307.)

Quality Ratings

Directions: Indicate your level of agreement with each of the following statements by circling a number from 5 for strongly agree (SA) to 1 for strongly disagree (SD). If you believe an item is not applicable to this research article, leave it blank. Be prepared to explain your ratings.

A. The introduction establishes the importance of the study.

   SA   5   4   3   2   1   SD

B. The literature review establishes the context for the study.

   SA   5   4   3   2   1   SD

C. The research purpose, question, or hypothesis is clearly stated.

   SA   5   4   3   2   1   SD

D. The method of sampling is sound.

   SA   5   4   3   2   1   SD

E. Relevant demographics (for example, age, gender, and ethnicity) are described.

   SA   5   4   3   2   1   SD

F. Measurement procedures are adequate.

   SA   5   4   3   2   1   SD

G. All procedures have been described in sufficient detail to permit a replication of the study.

   SA   5   4   3   2   1   SD

H. The participants have been adequately protected from potential harm.

SA   5   4   3   2   1   SD

I. The results are clearly described.

SA   5   4   3   2   1   SD

J. The discussion/conclusion is appropriate.

SA   5   4   3   2   1   SD

K. Despite any flaws, the report is worthy of publication.

SA   5   4   3   2   1   SD

Article 10

The Effects of Group Cohesiveness on Social Loafing and Social Compensation

STEVEN J. KARAU
Virginia Commonwealth University

KIPLING D. WILLIAMS
University of New South Wales

ABSTRACT. Individuals often engage in social loafing, exerting less effort on collective rather than individual tasks. Two experiments tested the hypothesis that social loafing can be reduced or eliminated when individuals work in cohesive rather than noncohesive groups. In Experiment 1, secretarial students typed both individually and collectively in simulated word-processing pools composed of either friends or strangers. In Experiment 2, dyads composed of either friends or strangers worked either coactively or collectively on an idea-generation task. Both studies supported the group cohesiveness hypothesis. Experiment 2 also suggested that individuals tend to engage in social compensation when working with coworkers who are low in ability. These findings are discussed in relation to S. J. Karau and K. D. Williams's (1993) Collective Effort Model.

From *Group Dynamics: Theory, Research, and Practice, 1,* 156–168. Copyright © 1997 by the American Psychological Association, Inc. Reprinted with permission.

Much of the world's work is accomplished by groups of individuals who work together on collective tasks in which member inputs are combined into a final product. For example, business committees combine
5 the contributions of individual members into a final report, symphony orchestras combine the sounds of individual musicians into a collective performance, and relay racing teams add the times of individual runners to get a team score. Intuition might suggest that indi-
10 viduals would be energized to work especially hard in groups. However, research has shown that individuals frequently reduce their efforts when working collectively—a phenomenon known as social loafing.

Formally, *social loafing* refers to the tendency for
15 individuals to exert less effort when working collectively (such that individual inputs are combined into a single group product) rather than individually or coactively (such that individuals work in the actual or implied presence of others, but inputs are not combined).
20 The results of more than 80 studies indicate that social loafing is a robust phenomenon that generalizes across a wide variety of tasks as well as most populations (for a review, see Karau & Williams, 1993). Although social loafing has been repeatedly demonstrated, several
25 factors have been found to moderate the effect. For

example, social loafing can be reduced or eliminated by increasing the degree to which individual or group inputs can be evaluated (Harkins & Szymanski, 1989; Szymanski & Harkins, 1987; Williams, Harkins, &
30 Latané, 1981), elevating the uniqueness of individual contributions (Harkins & Petty, 1982), or enhancing personal involvement with the task (Brickner, Harkins, & Ostrom, 1986).

However, one key factor that may have an espe-
35 cially profound impact—namely, group cohesiveness—has been disregarded. Almost all of the research on social loafing has examined noncohesive aggregates of strangers. This tendency to focus on such a narrow sample limits the ability to generalize results to natu-
40 rally occurring groups. Our research was designed to fill this gap by examining individual motivation within both cohesive and noncohesive groups. Although cohesiveness is a complex, possibly multidimensional construct (e.g., Tziner, 1982; Zaccaro & McCoy, 1988)
45 that has been defined and operationalized in a variety of ways (Evans & Jarvis, 1980), the majority of treatments of group cohesiveness have emphasized members' attraction to the group (Hogg, 1992; Lott & Lott, 1965). Thus, we defined *cohesiveness* as the degree to
50 which membership in the group was valuable or important to its members and *operationalized cohesiveness* in terms of membership in a group composed of either close friends or strangers. We hypothesized that social loafing would be reduced or eliminated in highly
55 cohesive groups.

Background
Collective Effort Model
We framed our hypotheses in terms of the Collective Effort Model (CEM; Karau & Williams, 1993). The CEM expands the basic assumptions of expectancy-value models of work motivation (e.g., Vroom,
60 1964) to the more complex realm of collective tasks and uses elements of social identity and self-evaluation theories to identify outcomes that people are likely to value in collective settings. The CEM suggests that individuals are only willing to work hard on a collec-
65 tive task to the degree that they expect their individual efforts to be instrumental in obtaining outcomes that they will personally value. When the outcomes tied to

the collective situation or the group's performance are not perceived as important, relevant, or meaningful,
70 individuals are unlikely to work hard. Moreover, even when the relevant outcomes are highly valued, individuals are not likely to work hard unless they expect their efforts to lead to performance that will be useful in obtaining those outcomes. Thus, working collec-
75 tively introduces a number of unique barriers to individual motivation because individual outcomes are affected by factors—such as the performance of other group members and the possible diffusion of group outcomes and consequences across members—in addi-
80 tion to one's own performance.

The CEM suggests that valued outcomes can consist of either objective outcomes, such as pay, or subjective outcomes, such as enjoyment, satisfaction, and feelings of belonging or of self-worth. Outcomes rele-
85 vant to self-evaluation may be particularly important for individual motivation on collective tasks because group performance settings produce the potential for self-evaluation from a variety of relevant sources (Breckler & Greenwald, 1986; Crocker & Luhtanen,
90 1990). Collective settings that provide information relevant to self-evaluation, whether from oneself, one's coworkers, one's boss, important reference groups, or other people, are likely to have strong implications for motivation. Cohesive groups or groups that individuals
95 strongly identify with and highly value are likely to enhance concern with self-evaluation, especially when related to group activities and outcomes. Consistent with this notion, theory and research on social identity and on social comparison and self-evaluation processes
100 in groups has repeatedly demonstrated that individuals maintain and enhance their self-evaluation by identifying with the positive attributes and accomplishments of groups and social categories to which they belong (Abrams & Hogg, 1990; Banaji & Prentice, 1994;
105 Goethals & Darley, 1987). Several recent analyses also suggest that some motivations—such as needs for social interaction, belonging, or connectedness—can only be fulfilled within the context of groups with at least a moderate level of cohesiveness (e.g., Caporael, Dawes,
110 Orbell, & van de Kragt, 1989). Indeed, Baumeister and Leary (1995) provided intriguing evidence that the need to belong and to establish and maintain strong interpersonal ties to groups may be one of the most fundamental, pervasive, and motivational aspects of the
115 human social condition. Taken as a whole, these perspectives provide converging support for the notion that individuals are more likely to value collective outcomes when working in cohesive groups or in groups with which they personally identify rather than in non-
120 cohesive groups. Thus, we predicted that, following the CEM, social loafing would be reduced or eliminated when individuals worked in cohesive groups under conditions in which their efforts would contribute to a favorable outcome for the group and its members.
125 The CEM also suggests that group cohesiveness

might have the potential to produce motivation gains under certain conditions. Specifically, if individuals value the collective outcomes associated with group performance and interaction more than the isolated
130 outcomes of their individual efforts, they may actually work harder collectively than coactively. Similarly, if a valued outcome is actually more reliant on individual efforts collectively than coactively, motivation gains might emerge. An example of the latter possibility is
135 the phenomenon of *social compensation*, in which individuals increase their efforts on collective tasks to compensate for the anticipated poor performance of other group members. Social compensation was documented in three experiments by Williams and Karau
140 (1991), who found that individuals actually worked harder collectively than coactively when they expected their coworker to perform poorly, based on either low interpersonal trust levels or confederate statements regarding effort or ability at the task. In contrast, par-
145 ticipants did not socially compensate for poorly performing coworkers when the task was low in meaningfulness, which is consistent with the CEM. Williams and Karau speculated that members of cohesive groups, who may attach special value to group out-
150 comes, may be especially willing to compensate for coworkers who perform poorly, although such increased effort might not persist over time if it is not reciprocated in some form. In Experiment 2, we included a manipulation of coworker ability to test this
155 hypothesis.

Relevant Empirical Evidence

Almost no research has directly examined group cohesiveness and social loafing. In fact, only three studies have either manipulated level of acquaintance with one's coworkers or examined individuals who
160 were clearly closely acquainted with one another. First, Shirakashi (1985) had Japanese students shout and clap in groups composed of either strangers or members of the students' sports club. Participants in both the high- and low-cohesiveness conditions worked equally hard
165 collectively and coactively (consistent, perhaps, with a cultural emphasis on collectivism), thereby leaving the cohesiveness question unanswered. Second, Hardy and Latané (1988) had high school cheerleaders perform a shouting task with another cheerleader from the same
170 or a different squad. Although all participants tended to reduce their collective efforts and there was no significant interaction between group cohesiveness and individual versus group work condition, the social loafing effect only reached significance in the low-
175 cohesiveness condition—providing initial, tentative support for the notion that group cohesiveness might at least reduce the absolute magnitude of social loafing. In a third study (Williams, Nida, Baca, & Latané, 1989), cohesiveness was not manipulated, but individ-
180 ual and group productivity was tested with existing teammates. Varsity intercollegiate swimmers competed

in individual and relay races in which individual times were either shouted out or not identified. Although all teams were relatively cohesive and composed of fairly close friends, individuals still tended to reduce their effort collectively when their times could not be identified. In contrast, when their times were identifiable, swimmers tended to increase their effort and work harder collectively than individually. However, neither of these simple trial-type effects (i.e., individual vs. collective) was significant, despite a significant interaction between identifiability and trial type. In summary, these studies have produced mixed results. The effects of cohesiveness, when present, have been fairly weak. Nevertheless, the lack of a significant loafing effect in several of the cohesive conditions within these studies may suggest that the tendency to loaf is at least partially reduced within cohesive groups.

Although direct evidence regarding group cohesiveness and social loafing is lacking, there is support for the related notion that concern for the group's evaluation can motivate individual members. Harkins and Szymanski (1989) found that participants were less likely to loaf when they believed the performance of their group was being compared with that of other groups and a clear standard was provided with which to make this comparison. Social loafing was eliminated, even in groups of strangers, when individuals were provided with an opportunity for self-validation through a group comparison. Working in cohesive groups may contribute even further to an individual's motive to obtain self-validation from one's important reference groups. Moreover, it is possible that such an increase in collective motivation would occur even in the presence of only a minimal or implied comparison or even when feedback about the group's performance is provided in the absence of an explicit comparison standard. Indeed, James and Greenberg (1989) found that students worked harder on an anagrams task when in-group salience (in terms of the students' university affiliation) was high and there was an implied comparison (with students at a rival university), even though an explicit comparison standard was not provided. James and Greenberg examined only coactive performance, however, preventing an analysis of the implications of in-group salience for collective motivation.

Indirect evidence that the value one attaches to a group may moderate social loafing is found in the results of several cross-cultural studies (e.g., Early, 1989; Gabrenya, Latané, & Wang, 1983; Gabrenya, Wang, & Latané, 1985; Shirakashi, 1985). Eastern or Asian culture is frequently characterized as group or socially oriented, whereas Western or North American culture is frequently characterized as individualistically oriented (e.g., Triandis, 1989). Thus, individuals in Eastern cultures may be more likely to attach importance to collective outcomes and, therefore, less likely to engage in social loafing. Although the results of individual studies are somewhat inconsistent, most studies have found that participants in countries such as Japan, Taiwan, and China either tend to loaf less than participants in the United States and Canada or do not loaf at all. Indeed, a recent meta-analysis of social loafing (Karau & Williams, 1993) confirmed that there is a significant tendency across studies for individuals from Eastern cultures to loaf less than those from Western cultures. Group cohesiveness could operate in a fashion similar to culture, contributing to member motivation by enhancing concern with group outcomes.

Of course, there is a large literature on group cohesiveness and group productivity that has implications for social loafing. This work has used a variety of conceptualizations of cohesiveness, examined a number of moderating conditions, and produced results that have varied across studies. A recent meta-analysis (Mullen & Copper, 1994) found support for a cohesiveness-productivity relationship, with a larger overall effect size for cohesion based on task commitment than on interpersonal attraction. These findings add support to the notion that individuals may work harder within cohesive groups, especially when they are committed to the group task. However, none of the studies in the larger cohesiveness literature has provided the necessary comparisons and controls for separating individual motivation from other input and process factors that may contribute to group performance.

Overview of the Present Research

Our theoretical analysis led to the hypothesis that group cohesiveness should serve to reduce or eliminate social loafing when individual inputs contribute to favorable group outcomes and when a comparison with other groups is available. We designed two studies to test this hypothesis. In Experiment 1, participants worked with either friends or strangers on a typing task, both individually and collectively. In Experiment 2, participants worked with either friends or strangers on an idea-generation task, either coactively or collectively. Coworker ability was also manipulated to provide an initial examination of the effect of expectations of coworker performance on individual effort in cohesive groups.

Experiment 1

Secretarial students at a vocational business college worked individually on a simulated typing pool task. On some trials, they were told that their inputs would be evaluated individually (individual condition); whereas on other trials, they were told that their inputs would be combined with those of three other typists (collective condition). Furthermore, on the group trials, half of the participants were told that their outputs were being combined with those of three friends (cohesive condition) and half were told that their outputs were being combined with those of three unnamed typists (noncohesive condition). We hypothesized that the tendency to engage in social loafing would be significantly reduced in cohesive groups.

Method

295   *Participants and design.* Participants were 30 students at the American Institute of Business (Des Moines, Iowa) in their last quarter of typing instruction, who volunteered at the request of their typing instructor. They were given no extra credit, although

300   their instructor expressed interest in the results. All participants were women between the ages of 19 and 24, with an average typing speed of 66.5 words per minute (range 42 to 90). Because the students all anticipated secretarial careers upon graduation, typing

305   was a meaningful task with important job-related consequences for this sample. A 2 (cohesiveness: cohesive or noncohesive) × 2 (work condition: individual or collective) mixed design was used, with cohesiveness as a between-subjects factor and work condition as a

310   within-subjects factor. Students were randomly assigned to one of two cohesiveness conditions (cohesive or noncohesive) and one of four orders of trial presentation (counterbalanced across cohesiveness conditions).

315   *Procedure.* After the students volunteered to participate, they were asked to write their name on an index card, along with the names of three classmates with whom they would most like to work. Each participant was assigned a time to report individually for

320   the experiment, which was conducted in a large conference room. On arrival, students were told that the researchers were interested in testing the capabilities of an inexpensive microcomputer to be used for word processing in small businesses. At the time, none of the

325   students had microcomputer or word-processing experience.[1]

The experimenter explained that he had hoped everyone would be able to work with the group of his or her choice and that he had tried to arrange it so that this

330   was possible. Half of the participants were told that they had, in fact, been assigned to the groups of their choice (cohesive condition), and the other half were told that, because of various problems due to different requests, they would not be working with the group of

335   their choice and would instead be randomly assigned to a group of people that was yet to be determined (noncohesive condition). Thus, group cohesiveness in this study was based on attraction to the group and probable importance of the group to the member. By manipu-

340   lating cohesiveness on the basis of membership in a group composed of friends versus strangers, we accomplished two important goals. First, the manipulation was powerful. Despite disagreements among researchers as to how cohesiveness should be conceptu-

345   alized (Hogg, 1992), all of the views suggest that groups of close friends are likely to have higher levels of cohesiveness than are groups of strangers. This manipulation is also likely to have more impact than a brief laboratory manipulation conducted on groups of

350   strangers. Second, the manipulation reflected multiple aspects of the construct of cohesiveness, thus increasing the chances that our results would be attributable to the general construct rather than an idiosyncratic component.

355   Each student was seated in front of a Radio Shack Model I TRS-80 microcomputer. Instructions, presented on the screen, informed the student that they would be testing a new, inexpensive microcomputer and would be asked to type as quickly as they could for

360   several time trials. On some trials the computer would record individual output, and on other trials it would combine individual outputs into a single group product to create a simulated word-processing pool. Participants were told that speed, not accuracy, was most im-

365   portant. Finally, they were told that, after they completed the trials, we would ask them for comments and suggestions regarding the keyboard and other aspects of the word processor.

Participants then typed one paragraph repeatedly in

370   four separate 10-min trials. At the beginning of each individual condition trial, the screen read, "You are working alone. Now that you know that your scores are not being combined but are being individually evaluated, type 'alone' and ENTER to continue." At the

375   beginning of each group condition trial, the screen read, "You are working with 3 others. Now that you know your work is being combined with 3 others, type 'group' and ENTER to continue." After completing the fourth trial, participants filled out a questionnaire that

380   contained manipulation checks and items to assess their impressions of the computer and task. They were then asked not to discuss the experiment with others and were excused. A debriefing session was held in the classroom after all sessions had been completed.

Results and Discussion

385   The students seemed extremely interested in the project and performed very conscientiously. After completing the task, participants uniformly commented on the ease or difficulty of the keyboard (most liked it), providing evidence that they believed the cover story.

390   The students typed an average of 57 words per minute (range = 37 to 83).

Manipulation checks. All questionnaire items were assessed using 100-point scales. Members of cohesive groups reported that they enjoyed pooling their efforts

395   more ($M = 66.87$) than did members of noncohesive groups ($M = 50.94$), $F(1, 22) = 4.53$, $p < .05$. In addition, participants reported that their outputs were more easily monitored when typing individually ($M = 71.17$) than collectively ($M = 57.87$), $F(1, 22) = 5.48$, $p < .05$,

[1] Experiment 1 is a previously unpublished study that was conducted in 1980 (Williams, 1981). It is included both to make the findings more accessible and because it was the direct conceptual and empirical precursor to our later work. Because Experiment 1 was conducted when microcomputers were first introduced, the students were very interested in testing and working with a microcomputer.

400 and that they had more control over the outcome when working individually ($M = 66.53$) than collectively ($M = 57.86$), $F(1, 22) = 4.88$, $p < .001$.

Performance data. Means and standard deviations for the performance data are presented in Table 1. As 405 predicted, there was a significant Cohesiveness × Work Condition interaction, $F(1, 22) = 5.36$, $p < .04$. Participants in the noncohesive condition tended to type more words per minute individually than collectively, whereas participants in the cohesive condition tended 410 to type more words per minute collectively than individually. However, neither work condition's simple effect was significant. Thus, our main hypothesis received modest support. There were no significant main effects of cohesiveness or of work condition on number 415 of words typed per minute.

Table 1
Mean Number of Words Typed per Minute as a Function of Group Cohesiveness and Work Condition

	Work condition	
Group cohesiveness	Individual	Collective
Noncohesive		
M	55.23	54.24
SD	12.67	13.88
Cohesive		
M	56.93	58.57
SD	8.47	9.91

Note. n per cell = 15.

These results provide initial support for the hypothesis that group cohesiveness moderates social loafing. When students thought their outputs were being combined with those of three unknown others, they 420 tended to work harder individually than collectively, which is consistent with research on social loafing. However, when students thought their outputs were being combined with those of three friends, they tended to work harder collectively than individually, produc-425 ing results similar to those found in research on social compensation. The resulting significant interaction supports the reasoning that people may work just as hard or even harder collectively as individually when they work with other members of a cohesive group. Of 430 course, Experiment 1 does not demonstrate that cohesiveness eliminates social loafing because members of noncohesive groups did not significantly reduce their collective effort. It is possible that a significant loafing effect did not emerge because the task was high in per-435 sonal involvement for this sample. Indeed, Brickner et al. (1986) found that individuals did not loaf on a task that was high in personal involvement. In Experiment 2, we used a task that was only moderate, rather than high, in personal involvement to counter this possibil-440 ity.

Our choice of a word-processing task might have also limited the interpretability of the findings somewhat. Although the word-processing task reflects an everyday application of collective effort on a task that 445 participants considered meaningful, typing speed and effort may not correspond directly. Increased effort by poor typists may produce errors that distract them from typing quickly. Fortunately, the typists in our sample were fairly skilled, suggesting that effort and produc-450 tivity should be closely related. Finally, unexpectedly assigning half of the participants to nonpreferred groups created the potential for a reactance that could conceivably have influenced performance. We controlled for these limitations in Experiment 2. Yet, de-455 spite these limitations, Experiment 1 represents an important, initial exploration of the effects of cohesiveness on individual effort in groups in a setting where performing well is important to the participants, and it also provides initial support for the notion that group 460 cohesiveness may moderate social loafing.

Experiment 2

We conducted a second experiment to provide a replication of our first experiment, to create a stronger test of the group cohesiveness hypothesis, and to allow for an initial examination of the effects of expectations 465 of coworker performance on motivation within cohesive groups. Members of mixed-sex dyads composed of either friends or strangers worked on an idea generation task either coactively or collectively. We also manipulated two levels of coworker ability (high or 470 low) using a note-passing technique. Note that the high-ability condition provided a conceptual replication of Experiment 1, whereas the low-ability condition allowed for an examination of social compensation and its relationship to group cohesiveness. We expected 475 that, consistent with our theoretical analysis and the results of Experiment 1, group cohesiveness would eliminate social loafing in the high-ability condition. In addition, we expected that, consistent with research on social compensation, members of noncohesive groups 480 would engage in social compensation and actually work harder collectively than coactively when working with coworkers who were low in ability. Finally, following Williams and Karau's (1991) suggestion that members of cohesive groups may be especially willing 485 to compensate for coworkers who perform poorly, we predicted that members of cohesive groups would also engage in social compensation when working with coworkers who were low in ability.

Method

Participants and design. Participants were 174 in-490 troductory psychology students at Purdue University who fulfilled partial course credit by their participation. Data from 10 participants were eliminated from the final analyses (4 expressed suspicion about the note-passing technique during debriefing, 3 expressed prior 495 familiarity with research on collective performance, and 3 did not properly follow the instructions for the task), resulting in a final sample of 164 participants (84 women and 80 men).

The experiment used a 2 (cohesiveness: cohesive-500 ness or noncohesive) × 2 (coworker ability: high or low) × 2 (work condition: coactive or collective) between-subjects factorial design. Individuals were randomly assigned to a work condition and to a coworker-ability condition. Gender did not significantly alter the pattern of results and was excluded as a factor in the final analyses.

Procedure. Participants were recruited by means of two sets of sign-up sheets with different experiment titles. One set requested only opposite gender friends or couples, whereas the other (which contained separate sheets for male and female students) listed only times for individuals. By using this method, we were able to obtain mixed gender dyads of either friends (cohesive) or strangers (noncohesive), without confounding cohesiveness with potential reactance created by assignment to an unfavorable group.

After their arrival at the laboratory, participants were greeted by the experimenter and seated at either of two adjacent desks. Between the desks were large cloth partitions that prevented participants from seeing one another. On each desk was a pair of headphones, a pen, and a box of blank slips of paper. The experimenter told participants that the purpose of the study was to examine "the effects of standardized communication on task perception." Participants were told that advances in technology had led to the creation of large electronic mail networks, many of which now offered banks of prewritten messages that users could select from to include in messages to save time and energy. They were told that, although use of such standardized messages was increasing, few researchers have examined the impact of such messages on how people perceive and approach various tasks. To simulate a standardized communication network, we allowed participants to choose 2 prewritten messages from a set of 10 to send to their coworker. No other communication was allowed. Furthermore, after exchanging messages with their coworker, the participants were asked to work on an idea-generation task to allow us to study the effects of standardized communication on task perception and performance.

The experimenter then explained the idea-generation task. This additive task was chosen for two reasons. First, effort would be directly related to performance. Second, the task could be presented in a meaningful way (i.e., it was plausible that the task could be associated with intelligence). The idea-generation task (e.g., Harkins & Petty, 1982) requires participants to come up with as many uses as possible for a given object in the time provided. In our study, participants were asked to generate as many uses as possible for a knife in a 12-min period. They were instructed to write each use on a separate slip of paper and to separately insert each slip into a box. In the coactive condition, a separate box with a small opening was placed in front of each participant. In the collective condition, a common box was placed between the desks so that each participant was able to place slips of

paper into the box through a small opening but was unable to monitor how many slips their coworker was placing inside. In the coactive condition, the experimenter told participants that we were interested in their individual scores and that these scores would be added up at the end of the session and each individual would be told how many uses they came up with. In the collective condition, the experimenter told participants that we were interested in how many uses they could come up with as a group and that the total score would be counted up at the end of the session and revealed to the group.

All participants were told that it was the quantity, not the quality, of ideas that was important. Participants in the collective condition were also told that it was okay if they happened to generate some of the same uses as their coworker because both uses would be added to the group total. To ensure that the task was perceived as meaningful, participants were told that a recent theory suggested that rapid thinking is highly correlated with intelligence, so it was extremely important that they come up with as many uses as they possibly could. The experimenter also told participants that their individual or group scores would be compared with those of other individuals or groups that had been in similar research studies at other universities. Participants in the collective condition were told that, after their uses had been counted, they would be discarded and that this would prevent the experimenter from knowing any person's individual score. Finally, participants were told that they would listen to music when thinking of ideas (to prevent participants from talking and monitoring each others' writing speeds during the task).

Participants were then asked to select which messages they would like to send to their partner. The 10 messages, which were identical for both participants, were typed onto separate notecards and placed in envelopes. Envelopes were used so that participants would not expect the experimenter to know which messages were selected. After reading all 10 messages, the participants chose 2 and placed them in an empty envelope, which they handed to the experimenter for "delivery." When transferring the messages, the experimenter unobtrusively switched the participants' envelopes with new envelopes containing two bogus messages. All participants received the message, "This sounds like an interesting experiment," which was meant to increase the chances that the task was perceived as meaningful. The second message varied, depending on coworker ability. Participants in the low-ability condition received, "I'm really bad at this kind of thing. It's hard for me to think of ideas quickly." Participants in the high-ability condition received either, "I'm really good at this kind of thing. It's easy for me to think of ideas quickly," or "I wonder what kind

615 of music they will play."[2]

After participants finished reading the messages, the experimenter asked them to put their headphones on, started the tape, and left the room. Instructions on the tape told participants what object to think of uses
620 for (a knife) and when to start. The tape then played 12 min of new age music at a moderate volume and then asked participants to stop working. After the idea-generation task, participants filled out a questionnaire that probed for suspicion and contained manipulation
625 checks. Participants were then told their individual or group scores and were debriefed and dismissed.

Results and Discussion

Manipulation checks. All questionnaire items used 100-point scales. Participants were asked how well
630 they knew their coworker, how often they expected to interact with their coworker in the future, how much they liked their coworker, and how willing they would be to work with their coworker again in the future. These four items were averaged to produce a cohesive-
635 ness index ($\alpha = .90$). Members of cohesive groups scored significantly higher on the cohesiveness index ($M = 84.51$) than did members of noncohesive groups ($M = 31.30$), $F(1, 156) = 721.38, p < .0001$.

Participants were also asked how much ability they thought their coworker had at the type of task they had
640 just completed. A main effect of coworker ability was found: Participants in the high-ability condition ($M = 76.28$) reported that their coworker had more ability at the task than did participants in the low-ability condition ($M = 55.25$), $F(1, 156) = 57.25, p < .0001$. No
645 other significant effects were found for this question ($Fs < 1$). Thus, differential levels of coworker ability were successfully manipulated within both cohesiveness conditions. In addition, when participants were asked how hard they thought their coworker had tried
650 on the task, there was no main effect of coworker ability ($F < 1$), suggesting that participants did not attribute differential levels of effort to their coworkers on the basis of ability.

Participants were also asked whether the experi-
655 menter was interested in their individual or their group's performance and to what extent they thought

---

[2] Originally, we attempted to manipulate three levels of co-worker ability with the "music" message intended to create a neutral, control condition. Initial analyses of a manipulation check, which was used to assess perceptions of coworker ability, revealed that both the high-ability and control conditions differed significantly from the low-ability condition but did not differ from each other. Thus, it appears that, in the absence of information to the contrary, participants assumed that their coworker had relatively high ability at the task. Analyses of the performance data revealed no significant differences and identical patterns of means for the high-ability and control conditions. Therefore, to clarify and simplify our presentation, we combined these two conditions into a single, high-ability condition.

that the experimenter would be able to tell how well they had performed individually. Participants were more likely to report that the experimenter was inter-
660 ested in their individual performance in the coactive condition (69%) than in the collective condition (4%), $\chi^2(1, N = 164) = 72.95, p < .0001$. Similarly, participants in the coactive condition rated the likelihood that the experimenter would be able to monitor their indi-
665 vidual scores as higher ($M = 77.32$), than did participants in the collective condition ($M = 41.10$), $F(1, 152) = 87.06, p < .0001$.

Performance data. A $2 \times 2 \times 2$ between subjects analysis of variance was performed on the performance
670 data. There was a significant Work Condition × Co-worker Ability interaction, $F(1, 156) = 6.05, p < .02$. Participants in the high-ability condition tended to work harder coactively ($M = 31.53$) than collectively ($M = 28.73$), whereas participants in the low-ability
675 condition worked harder collectively ($M = 30.96$) than coactively ($M = 24.79$).

More important, the predicted three-way interaction was significant, $F(1, 156) = 4.35, p < .04$ (cell means and standard deviations are provided in Table 2).
680 Within the high-ability condition, there was a signifi-cant interaction between work condition and cohesive-ness, $F(1, 105) = 6.02, p < .02$. Members of noncohe-sive groups socially loafed, working harder coactively than collectively, $F(1, 49) = 7.13, p < .02$, whereas
685 members of cohesive groups worked equally hard col-lectively and coactively ($F < 1$). These results both replicate the pattern of findings from Experiment 1 and demonstrate that a significant social loafing effect was eliminated in cohesive groups. These results also sug-
690 gest that, whereas members of noncohesive groups may tend to take advantage of their coworkers' high levels of expected performance and loaf, members of cohesive groups may feel compelled to work hard, even when the group might succeed without their
695 maximum efforts.

Within the low-ability condition, a significant so-cial compensation effect was found, such that partici-pants worked harder collectively ($M = 30.96$) than coactively ($M = 24.79$), $F(1, 51) = 5.70, p < .03$. This
700 finding replicates prior research on social compensa-tion and shows that, under some conditions, individuals actually work harder on a group task than on an indi-vidual task when they expect their coworkers to per-form poorly. Interestingly, simple contrasts reveal that
705 the social compensation effect only reached signifi-cance in the noncohesive condition, $F(1, 24) = 4.83, p < .04$. Thus, contrary to Williams and Karau's (1991) suggestion that members of cohesive groups may be especially willing to increase their collective efforts to
710 compensate for coworkers who perform poorly, mem-bers of cohesive groups in our study did not work sig-nificantly harder collectively than coactively, $F(1, 27) = 1.30, p > .20$.

Table 2
Mean Number of Uses Generated for a Knife as a Function of Coworker Ability, Group Cohesiveness, and Work Condition

Group cohesiveness	Work condition	
	Coactive	Collective
Low coworker ability		
Noncohesive		
M	26.14	34.75
SD	7.86	11.96
n	14	12
Cohesive		
M	23.53	27.71
SD	9.49	10.23
n	15	14
High coworker ability		
Noncohesive		
M	34.00	25.00
SD	13.37	10.46
n	26	25
Cohesive		
M	29.45	32.19
SD	11.19	14.41
n	31	27

Finally, although we were primarily interested in the coactive-collective comparisons (described above) most central to our hypotheses, we also conducted several analyses that shed additional light on the performance data. These analyses suggest that, consistent with the CEM, members of noncohesive groups may have been more attentive to the strategic implications of their efforts than were members of cohesive groups. It also appears that participants tended to match the expected performance levels of their coworkers under certain conditions. Specifically, within noncohesive groups, there was a significant interaction between coworker ability and work condition, $F(1, 73) = 10.24$, $p < .01$, such that participants socially loafed when working with high-ability coworkers but socially compensated when working with low-ability coworkers (as described earlier). In addition, an examination of the low- and high-ability comparisons within this interaction reveals that participants tended to match their coworkers' expected performance when working coactively but tended to mirror their coworkers' expected performance when working collectively. Thus, coactive participants worked harder in the presence of coworkers who were high, rather than low, in ability, $F(1, 38) = 4.05$, $p < .051$, whereas collective participants worked harder with coworkers who were low, rather than high, in ability, $F(1, 35) = 6.42$, $p < .01$. These results suggest that members of noncohesive groups behaved in a strategic fashion that maximized their individual outcomes. Specifically, when working coactively, participants reduced their efforts when their coworker posed little competitive threat but worked very hard when their coworker could make them look bad by comparison. However, when working collectively, participants worked especially hard when they were in danger of being negatively evaluated because of their coworker's poor performance but slacked off when their group was likely to succeed, even without his or her best efforts.

In contrast, members of cohesive groups appeared less strategic in their actions and tended to match their coworkers' expected performance levels, regardless of work condition. Thus, there were no significant differences between coactive and collective conditions ($Fs < 1.50$), but there was a marginally significant main effect of coworker ability, $F(1, 83) = 3.67$, $p < .06$, showing that participants tended to work harder with a high-ability coworker ($M = 30.72$) than with a low-ability coworker ($M = 25.55$). It is possible that members of cohesive groups worked hard, regardless of work condition, and tended to match their coworkers' performance levels due to a reduced emphasis on individualistic concerns and increased attention to group-level factors, including statements made by their coworkers.

General Discussion

Both studies suggest that group cohesiveness may moderate social loafing. Whereas members of noncohesive groups tended to reduce their collective efforts and socially loaf, members of cohesive groups worked just as hard collectively as coactively. Given the paucity of studies on social loafing among naturally occurring groups, these results are especially consequential and raise important, yet neglected, questions as to the generality of social loafing. Consistent with both the CEM and theories of self-evaluation processes in groups, the results of our research suggest that, when working with respected colleagues or friends, individuals may work just as hard collectively as they would individually to maintain a favorable self-evaluation. Even though this evaluation is somewhat indirect because it is derived from a collective rather than individual-level comparison, it still appears to have a significant impact on motivation.

The data from the low-ability conditions in Experiment 2 also provide additional documentation of the phenomenon of social compensation. In contrast to the vast majority of studies demonstrating social loafing, the recent social compensation research demonstrates that certain collective performance settings can actually lead to greater individual effort. These data also suggest that the impact that expectations of coworker performance have on motivation may vary as a function of group cohesiveness. These expectations had a dramatic impact on the effort expended by members of noncohesive groups but had less impact on members of cohesive groups. Therefore, despite our earlier (Williams & Karau, 1991) suggestion that members of cohesive groups might be especially willing to compensate for coworkers who perform poorly, the social compensation effect was not significant in the cohesive condition of our study. Why?

805   First, whereas members of noncohesive groups may seek to maximize their individual outcomes in a strategic fashion, members of cohesive groups may be relatively inattentive to the strategic implications of their actions and may focus instead on collective processes

810 and outcomes. The CEM suggests that individuals are unlikely to systematically process all available information about the task or situation and are instead likely to focus on salient features. Therefore, "some situations may lead individuals to respond automatically to a pre-

815 existing effort script, whereas other situations may lead individuals to strategically increase or decrease their collective effort" (Karau & Williams, 1993, p. 685). When working with strangers, people may be attentive primarily to individualistic concerns, and such attention

820 may be enhanced when coworkers are expected to perform especially well or poorly. When working in cohesive groups, however, people may be far less attentive to individualistic concerns and may simply work hard across work settings because the group and its mem-

825 bers are valued. Stated differently, group cohesiveness may create a "high-effort" heuristic that produces consistently high levels of motivation across settings. Consistent with this reasoning, members of noncohesive groups tended to behave in ways that maximized their

830 individual outcomes—working hard only when such effort was vital to a favorable individual outcome and slacking off otherwise. In contrast, members of cohesive groups tended to work hard across coactive and collective settings, even when such effort was not di-

835 rectly conducive to individualistic outcomes. Future research could test these ideas more directly by manipulating attention to task features within a social compensation paradigm.

Second, coworker statements may serve as a cue for

840 how much effort should be exerted on the task, possibly leading individuals to match their coworkers' expected performance levels under some conditions. Matching could result either from a desire to maintain equity in effort (cf. Jackson & Harkins, 1985) or

845 through social influence processes. Prior research has shown that coworkers' attitudes and work-related statements frequently influence one's own attitudes (for a review, see Zalesny & Ford, 1990) and that social influences on attitudes are typically magnified in

850 cohesive groups (e.g., Festinger, Schachter, & Back, 1950; Lott & Lott, 1965). Therefore, coworker statements might produce a matching tendency that may be enhanced in cohesive groups. Consistent with this reasoning, members of cohesive groups tended to match

855 their coworkers' expected performance levels across work conditions, whereas members of noncohesive groups matched their coworkers' performance only in the coactive condition, where such matching also served a strategic, individualistic purpose. In noncohe-

860 sive groups, the individuals' strategic concerns may have enhanced the coworkers' social influence when working coactively but overwhelmed it when working collectively. Future research could examine these processes more directly by manipulating coworker state-

865 ments specific to productivity norms or task meaningfulness.

Finally, attribution research provides another possible reason why a significant social compensation effect was not found within cohesive groups. This research

870 has typically found that self-serving attributions decrease, whereas group-serving attributions increase, within cohesive groups (e.g., Dion, Miller, & Magnan, 1971; Leary & Forsyth, 1987). Members of cohesive groups may also be more willing to accept individual

875 responsibility for a group failure than would members of noncohesive groups (e.g., Schlenker & Miller, 1977). Thus, friends might be expected to cushion the blow of failure on the task and to refrain from attaching blame or stigma to individual members, thereby re-

880 ducing motivation to compensate for others by making the avoidance of negative social outcomes less contingent on individual action. Future research could test this hypothesis by assessing the impact of expectations of coworker performance on attributional processes

885 within cohesive groups.

With regard to self-evaluation processes, it is intriguing to compare the results of our research with those of Harkins and Szymanski (1989). Findings from both sets of studies suggest that enhancing individuals'

890 concern for self-evaluation vis á vis the performance and evaluation of their group can eliminate social loafing. However, this concern for group-relevant outcomes may be much harder to activate in members of noncohesive groups, who may view such outcomes

895 primarily in terms of individualistic consequences. Harkins and Szymanski eliminated social loafing in noncohesive groups both by creating an expectation that groups' scores would be compared with those of rival groups and by providing a tangible, objective,

900 performance standard. In contrast, in our research, we found that social loafing was eliminated in cohesive groups merely by implying that group-level comparisons would be made, without actually providing a comparison standard. Therefore, consistent with the

905 CEM, group-level outcomes may have special relevance to members of cohesive groups because of their immediate implications for self-evaluation.

In conclusion, any job setting in which peoples' unidentifiable efforts are combined into a single output

910 might be susceptible to social loafing. For this reason, business practices of merely placing people into teams in hopes of increasing group spirit, job satisfaction, and productivity may not necessarily be effective. Work in groups per se may not lead to any of these positive

915 outcomes. Our research raises the intriguing possibility that factors that serve to increase intragroup attraction or commitment, or that serve to activate individuals' concern with collective self-validation, may be helpful in reducing the tendency to engage in social loafing. If

920 these results are found to replicate across settings and tasks, it is possible that the use of team-building exercises, democratic decision-making processes, and even careful selection processes that identify compatible group members, when combined with real or implied
925 group-level comparisons, may reduce the chances of motivation losses.

It will be important for future research to isolate what specific aspects of group cohesiveness motivate high levels of collective effort. Although groups of
930 friends and strangers almost certainly differ in group cohesiveness, the precise nature of these differences is currently unclear. In addition, such groups probably differ in a variety of attributes other than cohesiveness (Lott & Lott, 1965; Zander, 1971). Our research takes
935 the vital first step of documenting differences in the collective effort of members of groups that differ in their levels of cohesiveness and stands in sharp contrast to the bulk of social loafing studies that have examined artificial groups composed of aggregates of strangers.
940 However, before our findings can be applied with confidence to everyday groups, it will be necessary for future research to take the additional step of manipulating discrete aspects of group cohesiveness (e.g., amount of prior acquaintance, commitment to a com-
945 mon goal, liking, attitude similarity, and social identification with important groups and social categories). Some of this work is already underway in our own laboratories and those of other researchers. Future research might also examine the generalizability of group
950 cohesiveness effects or the impact that additional potential moderating variables, such as salient group norms or group goals, perceived responsibility, and identifiability, may have on the relationship between group cohesiveness and individual motivation on col-
955 lective tasks. Finally, future research might also seek to identify the conditions under which group cohesiveness enhances or reduces one's motivation to engage in social compensation.

References

Abrams, D. & Hogg, M. A. (1990). *Social identity theory: Constructive and critical advances*. New York: Springer-Verlag.

Banaji, M. R. & Prentice, D. A. (1994). The self in social contexts. *Annual Review of Psychology, 45*, 297–332.

Baumeister, R. F. & Leary, M. R. (1995). The need to belong: Desire for interpersonal attachments as a fundamental human motivation. *Psychological Bulletin, 117*, 497–529.

Breckler, S. J. & Greenwald, A. G. (1986). Motivational facets of the self. In R. M. Sorrentino & E. T. Higgins (Eds.), *Handbook of motivation and cognition* (Vol. 1, pp. 145–164). New York: Guilford.

Brickner, M. A., Harkins, S. G. & Ostrom, T. M. (1986). Effects of personal involvement: Thought provoking implications for social loafing. *Journal of Personality and Social Psychology, 51*, 763–769.

Caporael, L., Dawes, R., Orbell, J. & van de Kragt, A. (1989). Selfishness examined: Cooperation in the absence of egoistic incentives. *Behavioral and Brain Sciences, 12*, 683–699.

Crocker, J. & Luhtanen, R. (1990). Collective self-esteem and ingroup bias. *Journal of Personality and Social Psychology, 58*, 60–67.

Dion, K. L., Miller, N. & Magnan, M. A. (1971). Cohesiveness and social responsibility as determinants of group risk taking. *Journal of Personality and Social Psychology, 20*, 400–406.

Early, P. C. (1989). Social loafing and collectivism: A comparison of the United States and the People's Republic of China. *Administrative Science Quarterly, 34*, 565–581.

Evans, N. J. & Jarvis, P. A. (1980). Group cohesion: A review and re-

evaluation. *Small Group Behavior, 11*, 359–370.

Festinger, L., Schachter, S. & Back, K. (1950). *Social pressures in informal groups*. New York: Harper.

Gabrenya, W. K., Latané, B. & Wang, Y. (1983). Social loafing in cross-cultural perspective: Chinese in Taiwan. *Journal of Cross-Cultural Psychology, 14*, 368–384.

Gabrenya, W. K., Wang, Y. E. & Latané, B. (1985). Social loafing on an optimizing task: Cross-cultural differences among Chinese and Americans. *Journal of Cross-Cultural Psychology, 16*, 223–242.

Goethals, G. R. & Darley, J. M. (1987). Social comparison theory: Self-evaluation and group life. In B. Mullen & G. R. Goethals (Eds.), *Theories of group behavior* (pp. 21–47). New York: Springer-Verlag.

Hardy, C. J. & Latané, B. (1988). Social loafing in cheerleaders: Effects of team membership and competition. *Journal of Sport and Exercise Psychology, 10*, 109–114.

Harkins, S. G. & Petty, R. E. (1982). Effects of task difficulty and task uniqueness on social loafing. *Journal of Personality and Social Psychology, 43*, 1214–1230.

Harkins, S. G. & Szymanski, K. (1989). Social loafing and group evaluation. *Journal of Personality and Social Psychology, 56*, 939–941.

Hogg, M. A. (1992). *The social psychology of group cohesiveness: From attraction to social identity*. New York: New York University Press.

Jackson, J. M. & Harkins, S. G. (1985). Equity in effort: An explanation of the social loafing effect. *Journal of Personality and Social Psychology, 49*, 1199–1206.

James, K. & Greenberg, J. (1989). In-group salience, intergroup comparison, and individual performance and self-esteem. *Personality and Social Psychology Bulletin, 15*, 604–616.

Karau, S. J. & Williams, K. D. (1993). Social loafing: A meta-analytic review and theoretical integration. *Journal of Personality and Social Psychology, 65*, 681–706.

Leary, M. R. & Forsyth, D. R. (1987). Attributions of responsibility for collective endeavors. *Review of Personality and Social Psychology, 8*, 167–188.

Lott, A. J. & Lott, B. E. (1965). Group cohesiveness as interpersonal attraction: A review of relationships with antecedents and consequent variables. *Psychological Bulletin, 64*, 259–309.

Mullen, B. & Copper, C. (1994). The relation between group cohesiveness and performance: An integration. *Psychological Bulletin, 115*, 210–227.

Schlenker, B. R. & Miller, R. S. (1977). Group cohesiveness as a determinant of egocentric perceptions in cooperative groups. *Human Relations, 30*, 1039–1055.

Shirakashi, S. (1985). Social loafing of Japanese students. *Hiroshima Forum for Psychology, 10*, 35–40.

Szymanski, K. & Harkins, S. G. (1987). Social loafing and self-evaluation with a social standard. *Journal of Personality and Social Psychology, 53*, 891–897.

Triandis, H. C. (1989). The self and social behavior in differing cultural contexts. *Psychological Review, 96*, 506–520.

Tziner, A. (1982). Differential effects of group cohesiveness types: A clarifying overview. *Social Behavior and Personality, 10*, 205–211.

Vroom, V. H. (1964). *Work and motivation*. New York: Wiley.

Williams, K. D. (1981, May). *The effects of group cohesiveness on social loafing*. Paper presented at the annual meeting of the Midwestern Psychological Association, Detroit, MI.

Williams, K. D., Harkins, S. G. & Latané, B. (1981). Identifiability as a deterrent to social loafing: Two cheering experiments. *Journal of Personality and Social Psychology, 40*, 303–311.

Williams, K. D. & Karau, S. J. (1991). Social loafing and social compensation: The effects of expectations of co-worker performance. *Journal of Personality and Social Psychology, 61*, 570–581.

Williams, K. D., Nida, S. A., Baca, L. D. & Latané, B. (1989). Social loafing and swimming: Effects of identifiability on individual and relay performance of intercollegiate swimmers. *Basic and Applied Social Psychology, 10*, 73–81.

Zaccaro, S. J. & McCoy, M. C. (1988). The effects of task and interpersonal cohesiveness on performance of a disjunctive group task. *Journal of Applied Social Psychology, 18*, 837–851.

Zalesny, M. D. & Ford, J. K. (1990). Extending the social information processing perspective: New links to attitudes, behaviors, and perceptions. *Organizational Behavior and Human Decision Processes, 47*, 205–246.

Zander, A. (1971). *Motives and goals in groups*. New York: Academic Press.

Acknowledgments: We thank Anne Avise, Sue Burmont, Tom Daly, Teri Garstka, Richard Heslin, Richard Opie, Dennis Solomon, and Karen Williams for assistance in conducting the experiments. We also thank Martin Bourgeois, Jason Hart, and Mike Markus for providing comments on drafts of this article. Portions of this article were presented at the 1981 convention of the Midwestern Psychological Association in Detroit, MI; the 1990 convention of the American Psychological Society in Dallas, TX; and the 1990 Nags Head Conference on Groups and Organizations in Nags Head, NC.

Address correspondence to: Steven J. Karau, Department of Psychology, Virginia Commonwealth University, Richmond, VA, 23284-2018.

Exercise for Article 10

Factual Questions

1. How did the researchers define *cohesiveness*?

2. In Experiment 1, which group typed the fastest on the average?

3. In which experiment was a task with high personal involvement used?

4. How many participants were eliminated from the final analysis for Experiment 2 because they were suspicious of the note-passing task?

5. In Experiment 2, on what basis were participants assigned to a work condition and a coworker-ability condition?

6. What was the mean number of uses for a knife produced by the low coworker ability group in the collective-noncohesive condition?

7. How many participants were in the high coworker ability group that was assigned to cohesive groups in the collective work condition?

Questions for Discussion

8. In Experiment 1, students were assigned at random to conditions. Is this important? Why? Why not? (See lines 310–312.)

9. The researchers speculate that the students in Experiment 1 who were unexpectedly assigned to nonpreferred groups (nonfriends) may have created the "potential for reactance." Speculate on the meaning of this term. (See lines 450–453.)

10. The researchers attempted to ensure that the task was perceived as meaningful. Do you think they succeeded? Explain. (See lines 576–581 and 605–608.)

11. How important are the data generated by the manipulation checks in Experiment 2? Do they increase your confidence in the results of the experiment? (See lines 627–668.)

12. The researchers mention the use of groups in business. Do you think the results of this study have direct implications for business practices? Explain. (See lines 4–6 and 910–913.)

13. If you were to conduct additional research on this topic, would you use the same tasks (i.e., typing speed and naming uses for a knife) or would you use some other tasks? Explain.

Quality Ratings

Directions: Indicate your level of agreement with each of the following statements by circling a number from 5 for strongly agree (SA) to 1 for strongly disagree (SD). If you believe an item is not applicable to this research article, leave it blank. Be prepared to explain your ratings.

A. The introduction establishes the importance of the study.

SA   5   4   3   2   1   SD

B. The literature review establishes the context for the study.

SA   5   4   3   2   1   SD

C. The research purpose, question, or hypothesis is clearly stated.

SA   5   4   3   2   1   SD

D. The method of sampling is sound.

SA   5   4   3   2   1   SD

E. Relevant demographics (for example, age, gender, and ethnicity) are described.

SA   5   4   3   2   1   SD

F. Measurement procedures are adequate.

SA   5   4   3   2   1   SD

G. All procedures have been described in sufficient detail to permit a replication of the study.

SA   5   4   3   2   1   SD

H. The participants have been adequately protected from potential harm.

SA   5   4   3   2   1   SD

I. The results are clearly described.

SA   5   4   3   2   1   SD

J. The discussion/conclusion is appropriate.

SA   5   4   3   2   1   SD

K. Despite any flaws, the report is worthy of publication.

SA   5   4   3   2   1   SD

Article 11

Assigned Versus Participative Goal Setting and Response Generalization: Managing Injury Control Among Professional Pizza Deliverers

TIMOTHY D. LUDWIG
Appalachian State University

E. SCOTT GELLER
Virginia Polytechnic Institute and State University

ABSTRACT. Safety belt use, turn signal use, and intersection stopping were observed at 3 pizza delivery locations per driver's license plate numbers. After baseline observations, employees at 1 store participated in goal setting targeting complete stops. Employees at the other store were assigned a goal. Over 4 weeks, the group's percentages of complete intersection stopping were posted. Both intervention groups significantly increased their complete intersection stops during the intervention phase. The participative goal-setting group also showed significant increases in turn signal and safety belt use (nontargeted behaviors) concurrent with their increases in intersection stopping (targeted behaviors). Drivers decreased their turn signal and safety belt use concurrent with the assigned goal condition targeting complete stops.

From *Journal of Applied Psychology*, *82*, 253–261. Copyright © 1997 by the American Psychological Association, Inc. Reprinted with permission.

The pizza delivery business has become a particularly dangerous occupation. Indeed, pizza deliverers have a driving accident rate three times the national average (Meagher, 1989). This has resulted in fatalities, personal injuries, and costs amounting to millions of dollars for the communities and corporations involved. Three factors have contributed to the excessive vehicle crashes among pizza deliverers. First, the majority of pizza deliverers are inexperienced drivers ranging in age from 18 to 24, the age where insurance companies compute the most risk into their premiums. Second, pizza delivery businesses have developed the product image of "fast-to-your-door," and, until recently, most had offered time-based guarantees. Finally, pizza deliverers are compensated with commissions that are based on number of pizzas delivered, thereby rewarding fast and convenient driving practices that are often unsafe. The present research compared the impact of two goal-setting procedures designed to improve the driving practices of pizza deliverers.

Assigned Versus Participative Goal Setting

Numerous empirical studies (e.g., Fellner & Sulzer-Azaroff, 1985; Komaki, Barwick, & Scott, 1978) have demonstrated the usefulness of goal setting for improving occupational safety. From their review of nearly 500 studies, Locke and Latham (1990) concluded that the influence of goal-setting interventions on behavior is indeed a robust research finding. They also concluded that the method in which goals are set, either assigned or participative, does not affect subsequent performance (see also meta-analyses by Mento, Steel, & Karren, 1987, and Tubbs, 1986). Observed differences between participative and assigned goal setting are presumably due to differences in mediating variables such as goal difficulty (Latham & Saari, 1979a; Latham, Steele, & Saari, 1982; Kernan & Lord, 1988), information (Latham & Saari, 1979b), experimental support (Latham, Erez, & Locke, 1988), and strategy development (Latham, Winters, & Locke, 1994). When these factors are considered, Locke and Latham (1990) found no appreciable differences in performance between assigned and participatory-set goals. The present research compared the impact of assigned versus participative goal setting. Unlike prior research, however, effects on both targeted and nontargeted behaviors were examined.

Response Generalization

In studies reviewed by Locke and Latham (1990), the impact of goal setting has always been operationally defined as observed changes in a targeted behavior. In the real world, however, there are many behaviors that covary, correlate, or otherwise share a functional similarity to one another. Therefore, when a goal-setting intervention seeks to operate on one behavior, it is possible that behaviors similar to the target behaviors but not directly targeted by the goal-setting intervention may also be affected. If the frequency of a nontargeted behavior is observed to change during an intervention targeting another behavior, *response generalization* has presumably taken place (Ludwig & Geller, 1995).

There is some evidence that response generalization may be a special benefit of intervention programs that promote participant involvement. Ludwig and Geller (1991) observed that after an intervention targeted only safety belt use among pizza deliverers, the use of both

65 safety belts and turn signals increased. For a second intervention study, pizza deliverers promoted safety belt use in the surrounding community. During this intervention, deliverers' safety belt use rose as expected, and turn signal use also increased 20 percent-
70 age points above baseline (Geller & Ludwig, 1991; Ludwig, Geller, & Roberts, 1990). An analogous result was found by Streff, Kalsher, and Geller (1993), who targeted the use of safety glasses in an industrial setting. After the successful intervention, employees also
75 increased their use of safety belts 174% over baseline when leaving the plant parking lots in their personal vehicles.

When driving a vehicle, individuals may refer to personal norms or rules governing their behavior. For
80 example, a personal rule to avoid injury from an automobile crash may be achieved behaviorally through the use of vehicle safety belts, as well as by using turn signals or coming to a complete stop at intersections. From this perspective, these behaviors should correlate
85 (Fricker & Larsen, 1989; Ludwig & Geller, 1991, 1995). Similarly, Locke and Latham (1990) suggested that individuals set implicit goals for themselves in the absence of assigned goals. These implicit goals have been shaped over time and can consist of various be-
90 haviors functionally related to goal achievement.

When individuals participate in goal setting, they undoubtedly refer to their implicit goals in order to provide opinions about the rationale of the goal-setting process. Referring to implicit goals may also influence
95 their consideration of other functionally related behaviors. If there is a strong previous association between nontargeted behaviors functionally related to the behavior targeted by the goal, the effect of the intervention may generalize to these behaviors. On the other
100 hand, if an assigned goal is perceived as being externally controlled, it might not activate implicit goals. Under these circumstances, it is likely that no other behavior than the target behavior will be promoted by the external consequences. Response generalization
105 would not be expected to occur because implicit goals about related but nontargeted behaviors are not activated.

The present study compared the impact of assigned versus participative goal setting in a field setting where
110 three driving behaviors were unobtrusively observed: intersection stopping, turn signal use, and safety belt use. Employees of pizza delivery stores were exposed to an assigned or participative goal-setting and feedback intervention that targeted only complete intersec-
115 tion stops. We hypothesized that response generalization (i.e., concurrent changes in turn signal and safety belt use) would occur as a result of participative goal setting but not as a result of assigned goal setting.

Method

Participants and Settings

Pizza deliverers (N = 324) from three different

120 pizza stores (two intervention sites and one control) were observed departing for and arriving from their deliveries. Employees at the stores consisted mainly of college students nearly identical in age (M = 21) and education (M = 2 years of college). Both intervention
125 stores were owned by the same franchise; however, they were located in separate towns, each servicing a state university. The pizza deliverers at a third store served as a nonintervention control. All employees worked on commission (per total pizzas sold), which
130 averaged approximately $0.58 a delivery plus gratuity. At the time of this study, Virginia had a safety belt use law (BUL) with secondary enforcement and a $25 fine for convicted violators.

All three stores had employee parking lots with en-
135 trances and exits connected to four-lane, two-way streets in city limits with a speed limit of 35 mph. Each store was within a mile of a college or university campus and within 200 meters of a shopping complex. The parking lots of each store were also connected to side
140 streets, which also fed into the main four-lane street.

Observation Procedures and Data Collection

During peak business hours (i.e., 5:00 p.m. to 8:00 p.m.), vehicle observations were unobtrusively recorded from windows of nearby businesses overlooking the store parking lots. Data were collected by
145 trained observers using a checklist format developed over a decade of driver observations and over 2 years of observing pizza deliverers (cf. Ludwig & Geller, 1991). The data collectors recorded whether each pizza deliverer, identified by vehicle license plate, used the
150 available shoulder strap. (Two late-model cars with automatic shoulder straps were identified and excluded from data analysis.) Observers also recorded which direction the deliverer turned and whether the turn signal was used.
155 Observers also recorded the kind of stop the vehicle made while entering the main road at the intersection near each store. One of three types of stops were recorded: (a) a *complete* stop, whereby the vehicles' wheels stopped moving; (b) a *slow rolling* advance,
160 whereby the vehicle slowed to approximately the walking speed of an adult; and (c) a *fast rolling* advance, whereby the vehicle proceeded through the stop with little or no attempt to slow down. At the time of these observations, data collectors also recorded the
165 traffic conditions the driver confronted when entering the main road. More specifically, a simple binary estimate (i.e., yes or no) was made to record whether the oncoming traffic should have affected the deliverer's stopping behavior. It was emphasized that stopping and
170 traffic were, however, mutually exclusive variables (e.g., a deliverer could do a fast rolling advance under traffic conditions in which they should have stopped). This recording method is similar to the extensive measurement of stopping by McKelvie (1986, 1987).
175 Interobserver reliability data were collected on ap-

proximately one-third of the observation sessions. During reliability sessions, two data observers collected data concurrently but independently at a single store. Data collectors were unaware of the scheduling and assignment of the intervention conditions.

Experimental Design

The quasiexperimental design was multiple baseline across settings with a nonequivalent control group. After an initial observation period of 6 weeks (i.e., baseline phase), deliverers in the participative group received an intervention consisting of a discussion-based meeting, participative goal setting, and 4 weeks of group feedback. One week after the participative group's initial meeting, employees in the assigned group received an intervention consisting of a lecture-based meeting, assigned goal setting, and 4 weeks of group feedback. The control site received no intervention. After the group feedback was removed from the stores, approximately 4 to 5 weeks of observations were conducted (i.e., withdraw phase). Thus, after a 7- to 8-week hiatus, field observations continued for 10 to 11 weeks (i.e., follow-up phase).

Experimental Conditions

The participative and assigned interventions were designed to be similar in all aspects except for the participation variable. Both groups attended a 1-hr meeting, received the same information, left with the same behavioral goal, and received identical group feedback displayed at similar locations in the store. Planned differences between the interventions were: (a) the participative group generated the information in a discussion format, whereas the assigned group had the same information lectured to them; (b) the participative group participated in the goal setting, whereas the assigned group had the goal (set by the participative group) assigned to them; and (c) after the group feedback was withdrawn, each group received slightly different signs announcing the end of the intervention.

One week before the intervention meeting, the managers at each store used hand counters to record the occurrence of complete intersection stops. This procedure provided behavioral feedback on complete intersection stops for the intervention meeting and set an ostensive precedent for the group feedback during the 4 weeks following the intervention (i.e., to increase the believability that the store manager collected the feedback data).

Before the intervention meetings, the managers from each store met with the facilitator (i.e., the first author) to receive training on the technique to be used at the meeting. During the actual group meeting, the facilitator and manager served as instructors, either lecturing the material (for the assigned group) or leading discussion and prompting goal setting (for the participative group).

Discussion versus lecture format. For the participative group, issues were presented in the form of questions to facilitate group interaction. During the discussion, the facilitator repeated what was said by an employee or asked for other reactions. The following questions were asked to promote discussion:

1. What are situations in which you should come to a complete stop?
2. What are reasons for coming to a complete stop?
3. What are reasons for not coming to a complete stop?
4. How would you respond to these reasons for not stopping completely (referring to responses from Question 3)?
5. Why should pizza deliverers come to a complete stop?

The entire discussion was recorded on videotape. All the information from the discussion with the participative group was written out in a script for the lecture to give the assigned group 1 week later. The lecture format used with the assigned group did not attempt to solicit employee involvement. Instead, the facilitator lectured the same information discussed in the participative session. No questions were asked of the employees.

A content analysis was completed on the videotapes by independent judges who used a structured checklist. The checklist was compiled to assess the degree of overlap between information solicited from the participative group and the information lectured to the assigned group. The videotapes were first viewed by two assistants who noted all content items during the discussion and lecture. All content items were randomly transcribed onto one checklist that was subsequently used to analyze the videotapes.

Participative versus assigned goal setting. After the discussion, the participative group was asked to come to a consensus about the need to come to a complete stop at intersections. Upon affirmation of group commitment, the manager told the employees they came to a complete stop outside the store 55% of the time over the past week. The facilitator asked what group goal should be set for complete stopping over the next 4 weeks. The goal was stated as: "The percentage of complete stops to remain above _____% for the next 4 weeks." Each member of the group was encouraged to give their opinion on a goal level. After deliberating, the facilitator then asked each employee to vote publicly on the final goal. The participants decided unanimously on a group goal of 75% complete stops.

After the lecture to the assigned group, the manager told the employees their incidence of complete stops had been 55% during the previous week. The manager then announced his decision to increase the incidence of complete stops among the deliverers in his store. The complete stopping goal agreed upon with the participative group (i.e., 75%) was then assigned in the form of a mandate to the assigned group with no discussion or consensus about the goal (a method used by

Kernan & Lord, 1988).

The employees in both intervention groups were shown a poster on which percentages of complete stops would be displayed every 4 days for the following month. The current percentage of complete stops (i.e., ostensively 55%) was marked with a data point and a horizontal line was drawn across the graph at the 75% level.

Postmeeting questionnaire. At the end of the meeting, employees completed a short questionnaire to assess their perceptions of the meeting. Four items on the questionnaire served as a manipulation check. These items assessed perception of participation during the meeting and during goal setting, the perception of the meeting as a discussion or lecture and checked to see if they knew the goal. Other questions were distracters (i.e., questions about driver training) or they assessed the employee's intentions to come to a complete stop.

Group feedback. After the all-employee meeting, the managers at each store continued observing their deliverers' complete intersection stops. Complete stop percentages were graphed every 4 days on the large in-store poster. To assure both intervention stores received the same feedback, the complete stop percentages posted were not a calculation of actual field observations. Instead, the percentages posted every 4 days at each store were randomly chosen from percentages ranging from 78% to 90% with a mean of 83%. The percentages posted for the assigned group were identical to the percentages posted for the participative group 1 week earlier. Feedback was posted for 4 consecutive weeks. After 4 weeks, the feedback posters were replaced by posters appropriate for the intervention condition: "Congratulations, you have exceeded the goal which you have set for yourselves" (participative group) or "Congratulations, you have exceeded the goal which was set for you" (assigned group). After 4 more days, these posters were removed from the stores and follow-up data were collected for 5½ months.

Results

Interobserver Reliability

Interobserver agreement percentages were calculated by dividing the total number of observations agreed upon by two independent data collectors for a particular data category (i.e., complete stops, safety belt use, and turn signal use) by the total number of agreements and disagreements and multiplying the result by 100. The percentages for days when reliability data were collected were then averaged to give overall interobserver reliability estimates.

Reliability data were collected for 104 data collection sessions (i.e., days), representing 25% of all observation sessions. Overall reliability (or percentage agreement) was 86% for observations of complete stops, 91% for observations of safety belt use, and 87% for turn signal use. There were no differences in reliability results across the three experimental sites.

Content Analysis of Intervention Meetings

Two raters viewed the videotapes of the intervention meetings and agreed 85% of the time on specific topics presented at a particular meeting. The two raters reported a 94% and an 86% overlap of information, respectively, between the intervention sessions for the participative and the assigned groups. In addition, raters confirmed that the words *safety belt*, *seat belt*, *turn signal*, or *blinker* were never verbalized by either group leaders or employees throughout both intervention sessions.

The amount of employee participation was also measured. The participative meeting lasted 49 min, 2 s, and the assigned meeting lasted 49 min, 31 s. Employees spoke a total of 13 min, 53 s during the participative meeting and only 5 s during the assigned meeting. Interrater reliability was 100% for each duration (accomplished by using the videoplayer counter).

Manipulation Checks

There was a significant relationship, $\chi^2(1, N = 31) = 10.4, p < .01$, between the type of intervention meeting (i.e., participative or assigned) and whether the meeting was described as a discussion or lecture in the postmeeting questionnaire completed by employees. Furthermore, attendees of the participative meeting felt they "participated in the goal setting" significantly more than did the attendees of the assigned meeting, $t(29) = 2.25, p < .05$. They also felt they participated marginally more during the overall discussion, $t(29) = 1.89, p = .06$. Finally, according to a nonsignificant trend in the data, attendees of the assigned meetings stated they intended to come to a complete stop more than did attendees of the participative meetings, $t(29) = -1.91, p = .06$. No other questions differentiated between the assigned and participative meetings.

Repeated Measures Analysis

The results presented in the repeated measures analysis represent only the data observed from pizza deliverers observed in each of the baseline, intervention, and withdraw phases and also observed at least six times per phase. (Data from the follow-up phase were not used in this data analysis because few participants met the criteria in the follow-up phase ($n = 29$). Percentages observed during the follow-up phase, however, are presented in accompanying figures.)

There were 40 participants whose data conformed to these criteria (participative group, $n = 20$; assigned group, $n = 11$; control group, $n = 9$). Therefore, only about 10% of the 324 different deliverers observed in this study met the criteria and were included in this analysis. However, because these employees were observed most often during the study, the 10% of individuals used in the repeated measures analysis actually represented over 50% of the 28,915 total behavioral observations recorded.

Daily percentages of behavioral data per deliverer were averaged to arrive at a phase percentage. The data points were calculated in each group by averaging individual subject means. Means and standard deviations
400 of behavioral data and manipulation checks are presented in Table 1. The repeated measures analysis using the individual as the level of analysis instead of the treatment setting added precision. It is noteworthy that analyses using all 324 participants yielded essentially
405 the same results as analyses using the 40 participants conforming to the stated criterion.

Complete intersection stops. Figure 1 depicts group means of complete intersection stops over four experimental phases. Participants in both the participative
410 group and the assigned group increased their percentage of complete intersection stops across the intervention phases, showed some maintenance during the withdraw phase, and returned to baseline levels during the follow-up phases. The control site maintained an
415 average of 46% complete intersection stops throughout the study.

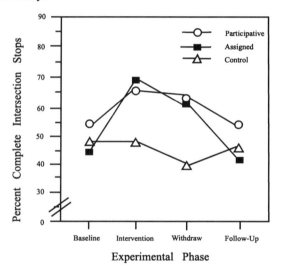

Figure 1. Percentage of complete stops across four experimental phases. Open circles represent the participative goal-setting group, filled squares represent the assigned goal-setting group, and open triangles represent the control group.

Because this data could potentially contain restriction of variance because of the use of percentages as the dependent variable, an arcsine transformation was
420 completed on the data before statistical analysis. A 3 intervention condition (participative, assigned, control) × 3 phase (baseline, intervention, withdraw) repeated measures analysis of variance (ANOVA) on complete stopping did not show a significant interaction between
425 experimental condition and phase, $F(4, 78) = 1.9$, $p = .12$. Separate ANOVAs for the two intervention groups showed significant main effects of phase; participative: $F(2, 38) = 3.12$, $p < .05$; assigned: $F(2, 20) = 3.35$, $p < .05$.
430 *Turn signal use.* Figure 2 depicts group means of

turn signal use over four experimental phases. The participative group showed an increase in turn signal use between the baseline and intervention phases and a continued increase during the withdraw phase. The
435 assigned group showed no prominent changes in turn signal use across phases, although there seems to have been a general decreasing trend. The control site showed no marked changes in turn signal use across phases.

440 An arcsine transformation was completed on the data before analysis. A 3 intervention condition (participative, assigned, control) × 3 phase (baseline, intervention, withdraw) repeated measures ANOVA on turn signal use showed a significant interaction between
445 experimental condition and phase, $F(4, 78) = 3.38$, $p < .05$. A 2 intervention condition × 3 phase repeated measures ANOVA on the participative and assigned groups showed a significant Group × Phase interaction, $F(2, 56) = 5.69$, $p < .05$. Separate one-way repeated
450 measures ANOVAs per intervention group indicated a significant main effect of phase for the participative group, $F(2, 38) = 6.30$, $p < .05$, but not the assigned group, $F(2, 18) = 1.69$, $p = .21$.

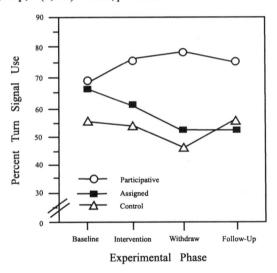

Figure 2. Percentage of turn signal use across four experimental phases. Open circles represent the participative goal-setting group, filled squares represent the assigned goal-setting group, and open triangles represent the control group.

Safety belt use. Figure 3 depicts group means of
455 safety belt use over four experimental phases. The participative group showed an increase between baseline and intervention phases, and maintenance during the withdraw phase. The assigned group showed no changes in safety belt use between baseline, intervention, and withdraw phases. The control site showed
460 minimal variation across the four phases.

An arcsine transformation was completed on the data before analysis. Additionally, 5 subjects (3 from the participative group and 2 from the control group)
465 who had a baseline safety belt use of 100% were re-

Table 1

Means and Standard Deviations for Each Driving Behavior Across Phases and Within Groups, and for the Postmeeting Questionnaire Items

Measure and phase	Overall		Participative		Assigned		Control[a]	
	M	SD	M	SD	M	SD	M	SD
Complete stops (%)								
Baseline	51.4	15.9	54.1	11.6	45.2	23.4	48.7	17.1
Intervention	58.2	21.8	65.9	12.9	68.5	12.8	49.0	31.9
Withdraw	52.5	22.6	60.0	18.5	59.0	18.2	38.6	23.2
Follow-up	48.3	19.5	53.5	18.5	41.8	14.6	46.6	23.9
Turn signal use (%)								
Baseline	64.4	21.5	68.1	17.2	66.3	13.5	56.4	16.4
Intervention	65.1	25.3	76.1	14.6	61.8	21.7	54.6	32.1
Withdraw	63.9	26.3	78.5	19.4	52.7	23.1	47.7	24.2
Follow-up	62.5	23.0	71.6	14.6	51.3	16.5	53.5	30.9
Safety belt use (%)								
Baseline	58.8	38.8	75.4	28.4	57.0	39.8	38.6	43.6
Intervention	62.5	39.9	84.9	21.8	56.2	36.9	31.0	44.7
Withdraw	63.9	34.2	83.8	24.1	58.3	33.0	37.0	31.3
Follow-up	71.7	35.8	88.9	18.5	60.6	44.8	35.8	40.7
Meeting participation[b]	1.65	4.9	1.31	.48	1.92	.28		
Goal participation[c]	3.15	1.31	3.69	1.38	2.61	1.04		
Discussion participation[d]	3.65	0.98	0.40	1.0	3.3	.85		
Intention to stop[e]	4.58	0.76	4.3	.95	4.8	.38		

[a]Did not participate in postmeeting questionnaire.   [b]1 = *no* and 2 = *yes*.   [c]1 = *not at all* and 5 = *very much*.   [d]1 = *not at all* and 5 = *very much*.   [e]1 = *never* and 2 = *every time*.

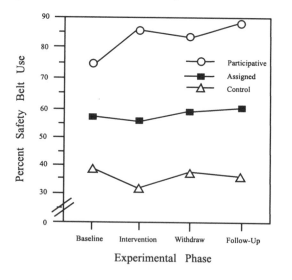

Figure 3. Percentage of safety belt use across four experimental phases. Open circles represent the participative goal-setting group, filled squares represent the assigned goal-setting group, and open triangles represent the control group.

moved from the analysis. A 3 intervention condition (participative, assigned, control) × 3 phase (baseline,
470 intervention, withdraw) repeated measures ANOVA on safety belt use showed a significant interaction between experimental condition and phase, $F(4, 68) = 2.87, p < .05$. A 2 intervention condition × 3 phase repeated measures ANOVA for the two intervention groups
475 showed a trend albeit nonsignificant interaction be-

tween these groups and phase, $F(2, 50) = 1.91, p = .15$. One-way repeated measures ANOVAs per group showed that the participative intervention influenced a significant change in deliverers' safety belt use across
480 phases, $F(2, 32) = 6.10, p < .05$, whereas the assigned goal-setting intervention did not, $F(2, 18) = .23, p = .79$. Finally, a significant difference in baseline safety belt use was found among the three groups. $F(2, 43) = 3.19, p < .05$.

Discussion

485 The data analyses showed that both variations of the goal-setting and feedback intervention increased safe intersection stopping. These findings are consistent with the experimental literature on the efficacy of goal setting as a robust research finding (Locke &
490 Latham, 1990). This study also supported the conclusions of Locke and Latham (1990) and Latham and Lee (1986) in that it provided no evidence that goals set participatively by subjects improved target performance any more than goals that were assigned.

Response Generalization

495 By observing two behaviors in addition to the behavior targeted by the intervention, the current study investigated generalized intervention impact across behaviors (Stokes & Baer, 1977). This type of analysis has seldom been used in goal-setting studies in par-
500 ticular or in applied psychology research in general. This is the case despite the urging of some researchers to take a greater ecological perspective in applied re-

search. For example, Willems (1974, 1977) challenged applied researchers to anticipate and investigate second- and third-order consequences of interventions (see also Eisenberg, 1972; Rogers-Warren & Warren, 1977). Indeed, perspectives on social validity have called for an evaluation of unpredicted side effects (Schwartz & Baer, 1991) or the undesired behaviors which occur concurrent with an intervention program (Geller, 1987, 1991).

Response generalization was operationally defined in this study as a change in a nontargeted behavior (i.e., turn signal and/or safety belt use) during an intervention that targeted another behavior (i.e., complete intersection stopping). Although they were not directly targeted, turn signal and safety belt use were found to increase concurrently with intersection stopping during the participative goal-setting intervention. In contrast, the assigned intervention site showed sustained decreases in these nontargeted behaviors over the same period of time. Whereas increases in safety belt use were sustained after the participative intervention, the percentage of safety belt use dropped below baseline levels after the withdrawal of the assigned intervention.

The functional control (cf. Kazdin, 1973) of the participative goal setting (i.e., targeting complete intersection stops) on each nontarget behavior was evident and implies a causal relationship between the intervention and the nontargeted behaviors. According to statistical analysis, response generalization occurred only at the site which received the participative intervention. These results suggest that a beneficial side effect of the participative intervention was a desirable change in related, nontargeted behaviors, whereas the assigned intervention may have produced undesired side effects in nontargeted behaviors. This finding has provocative implications worthy of substantial follow-up research.

Participative Versus Assigned Goals Revisited

A major contribution of this research was the impact of goal setting on a whole class of behaviors. Most goal-setting research has focused on the efficacy of differential goal-setting strategies to promote a desired change in the behavior targeted by the goal. Not one of the more than 500 studies reviewed by Locke and Latham (1990) examined the effects of goal-setting interventions on nontargeted behaviors. Indeed, Locke and Latham concluded, "Further research on the motivational effects of different goal setting methods would appear to have limited value" (p. 172). It is an unfortunate possibility that if research were to cease on participative goal setting, the nonobvious beneficial side effects could be overlooked.

The generalization of effect in the participative intervention supported our hypotheses. It is possible the participative intervention facilitated the activation of implicit rules, which, in turn, influenced behavior beyond the external consequences of the intervention. Streff et al. (1993) used a similar explanation to inter-

pret their observation of an increase in a nontargeted behavior (i.e., vehicle safety belt use) after a participatory intervention increased workers' use of safety glasses on the job.

In contrast, during the assigned intervention, the deliverer may have been motivated to come to a complete stop by the external contingencies provided by the mandated goal, feedback, and managerial observations. The deliverers in the assigned group may have actively sought to avoid probable undesirable consequences of disobeying their manager. However, some drivers seemingly showed reactance to the overt control by decreasing related safe-driving behaviors not directly associated with the manager's mandate. This is consistent with the theory of psychological reactance (Brehm & Brehm, 1981) and the notion of countercontrol (Skinner, 1953).

As an explanatory mechanism for this phenomenon, the discussion of implicit goals is reminiscent of the research on intrinsic motivation even though it is not consistent to argue that safe driving behaviors are intrinsically motivated. Deci and Ryan (1985) argued that when a previously intrinsically motivated behavior is associated with external contingencies, the behavior becomes extrinsically motivated. This extrinsic motivation undermines or replaces intrinsic motivation. If an individual's implicit goal includes an entire class of behaviors (e.g., safe driving made up of complete intersection stopping, turn signal use, and safety belt use as well as many others such as not exceeding the speed limit and maintaining a safe vehicle following distance), then it is possible an intervention with strong external control (e.g., assigned goals) may replace this implicit goal and no longer activate behaviors not targeted by the intervention.

This study does not provide data to discriminate between potential theoretical mechanisms. Deliverers were not asked about their implicit driving goals before or after the intervention. In fact, Latham et al. (1994) argued the need to measure the strategies developed by participants of the participative and nonparticipative conditions. Such questions were not asked in this study, in order to avoid potentially prompting participants to engage in the nontargeted behaviors. However, we suggest future studies of this type consider inquiring about changes in implicit goals at the conclusion of data collection.

The issue of response generalization has important ramifications for external validity. Too often applied researchers only measure a specific target behavior and thereby fail to investigate the rich information available from a more ecological approach. Behavioral ecology (Rogers-Warren & Warren, 1977) directs the researcher to ask specific questions about the target behavior, related behaviors, and setting events that could naturally support the target behavior. In fact, Wahler and Fox (1981a, 1981b) asserted that prolonged naturalistic observation of behavior and setting events is a must for applied research.

620   Two nontargeted behaviors studied here were found to be related to the targeted behavior of complete intersection stopping. There are undoubtedly more behaviors in this response class that could have been influenced by the intervention process. Vehicle following distance and speed in relation to posted limits come to mind. An understanding of how behaviors fit together

625   under the rubric of response class may move applied research beyond simple demonstration projects or epidemiological surveys to a systematic analysis of intervention effectiveness, response generalization, and natural maintaining contingencies.

630   In summary, this study introduced some new field methodologies and presented noteworthy findings worthy of further investigation. The research exemplified the need to venture beyond short-term demonstration projects, to continue investigating participative

635   goal setting as an applied intervention strategy, and to study response generalization and its implications.

References

Brehm, S., & Brehm, J. W. (1981). *Psychological reactance: A theory of freedom and control.* New York: Academic Press.

Deci, E. L., & Ryan, R. M. (1985). *Intrinsic motivation and self-determination in human behavior.* New York: Plenum.

Eisenberg, L. (1972). The human nature of human nature. *Science, 176,* 123–128.

Erez, M. (1986). The congruence of goal setting strategies with socio-cultural values, and its effect on performance. *Journal of Management, 12,* 585–592.

Erez, M., & Arad, R. (1986). Participative goal setting: Social, motivational, and cognitive factors. *Journal of Applied Psychology, 71,* 591–597.

Fellner, D. J., & Sulzer-Azaroff, B. (1985). Occupational safety: Assessing the impact of adding assigned or participative goal setting. *Journal of Organizational Behavior Management, 7,* 3–24.

Fricker, J. D., & Larsen, R. J. (1989). Safety belts and turn signals: Driver disposition and the law. *Transportation Research Record, 1210,* 47–52.

Geller, E. S. (1987). Environmental psychology and applied behavior analysis: From strange bedfellows to a productive marriage. In D. Stokols & I. Altman (Eds.), *Handbook of environmental psychology* (Vol. 1, pp. 361–380). New York: Wiley.

Geller, E. S. (1991). Where's the validity in social validity? *Journal of Applied Behavior Analysis, 24,* 179–184.

Geller, E. S., Casali, J. G., & Johnson, R. P. (1980). Seat belt usage: A potential target for applied behavior analysts. *Journal of Applied Behavior Analysis, 13,* 669–675.

Geller, E. S., & Ludwig, T. D. (1991). A behavior change taxonomy for improving road safety. *Proceedings of the OCED International Road Safety Symposium, 1,* 41–45.

Kazdin, A. E. (1973). Methodological and assessment considerations in evaluating reinforcement programs in applied settings. *Journal of Applied Behavior Analysis, 6,* 517–531.

Kernan, M. G., & Lord, R. G. (1988). Effects of participative vs. assigned goals and feedback in a multi-trial task. *Motivation and Emotion, 12,* 75–86.

Komaki, J., Barwick, K. D., & Scott, L. R. (1978). A behavioral approach to occupational safety: Pinpointing and reinforcing safe performance in a food manufacturing plant. *Journal of Applied Psychology, 63,* 434–445.

Latham, G. P., Erez, M., & Locke, E. A. (1988). Resolving scientific disputes by the joint design of crucial experiments by the antagonists: Application to the Erez-Latham dispute regarding participation in goal setting [Monograph]. *Journal of Applied Psychology, 73,* 753–772.

Latham, G. P., & Lee, T. W. (1986). Goal setting. In E. A. Locke (Ed.), *Generalizing from laboratory to field settings.* Lexington, MA: Lexington Books.

Latham. G. P., Mitchell, T. R., & Dossett, D. L. (1978). Importance of participative goal setting and anticipated rewards on goal difficulty and job performance. *Journal of Applied Psychology, 63,* 163–171.

Latham, G. P., & Saari, L. M. (1979a). The effects of holding goal difficulty consent on assigned and participatory set goals. *Academy of Management Journal, 22,* 163–168.

Latham, G. P., & Saari, L. M. (1979b). Importance of supportive relationships in goal setting. *Journal of Applied Psychology, 64,* 151–156.

Latham, G. P., Steele, T. P., & Saari, L. M. (1982). The effects of participation and goal difficulty on performance. *Personnel Psychology, 35,* 677–686.

Latham, G. P., Winters, D. W., & Locke. E. A. (1994). Cognitive and motivational effects of participation: A mediator study. *Journal of Organizational Behavior, 15,* 49–63.

Latham, G. P., & Yukl, G. A. (1975). Assigned versus participative goal setting with educated and uneducated woods workers. *Journal of Applied Psychology, 60,* 299–302.

Locke, E. A., & Latham, G. P. (1990) *A theory of goal setting and task performance.* Englewood Cliffs, NJ: Prentice-Hall.

Ludwig, T. D., & Geller, E. S. (1991). Improving the driving practices of pizza deliverers: Potential moderating effects of age and driving record. *Journal of Applied Behavior Analysis, 24,* 31–44.

Ludwig, T D., & Geller, E. S. (1995). *On the necessity of structure in an arbitrary world: Behavioral co-occurrence within and between response classes.* Unpublished manuscript, Virginia Polytechnic Institute and State University, Blacksburg.

Ludwig, T. D., Geller, E. S., & Roberts, D. S. (1990, April). *Intervening to increase safe driving among pizza deliverers: Tests of response generalization.* Paper presented at the Southeastern Psychological Association, Atlanta, GA.

McKelvie, S. J. (1986). An opinion survey and longitudinal study of driver behavior at stop signs. *Canadian Journal of Behavioral Science, 18,* 75–85.

McKelvie, S. J. (1987). Drivers' behavior at stop signs: A deterioration. *Perceptual and Motor Skills, 64,* 252–254.

Meagher, M. (Producer) (1989, February). Death in the delivery zone. *Inside edition.* New York: American Broadcasting Company.

Mento, A. J., Steel, R. P., & Karren, R. J. (1987). A meta-analytic study of the effects of goal setting on task performance: 1966–1984. *Organizational Behavior and Human Decision Processes, 39,* 52–83.

Rogers-Warren, A., & Warren, S. F. (1977). *Ecological perspectives in behavior analysis.* Baltimore: University Park Press.

Schwartz, I. S., & Baer, D. M. (1991). Social validity assessments: Is current practice state of the art? *Journal of Applied Behavior Analysis, 24,* 189–204.

Skinner, B. F. (1953). *Science and human behavior.* New York: Macmillan.

Stokes, R. F., & Baer, D. M. (1977). An implicit technology of generalization. *Journal of Applied Behavior Analysis, 10,* 349–367.

Streff, F. M., Kalsher, M. J., & Geller, E. S. (1993). Developing efficient workplace safety programs: Observations of response covariation. *Journal of Organizational Behavior Management, 13,* 3–14.

Tubbs, M. E (1986). Goal-setting: A meta-analytic examination of the empirical evidence. *Journal of Applied Psychology, 71,* 474–483.

Wahler, R. G., & Fox, J. J. (1981a). Response structure in deviant child-parent relationships: Implications for family therapy. *Nebraska Symposium on Motivation, 21,* 1–46.

Wahler, R. G., & Fox, J. J. (1981b). Setting events in applied behavior analysis: Toward a conceptual and methodological expansion. *Journal of Applied Behavior Analysis, 14,* 327–339.

Willems, E. P. (1974). Behavioral technology and behavioral ecology. *Journal of Applied Behavior Analysis, 7,* 151–165

Willems, E. P. (1977). Steps toward an ecobehavioral technology. In A. Rogers-Warren & S. F. Warren (Eds.), *Ecological perspectives in behavior analysis* (pp. 9–32). Baltimore: University Park Press.

About the authors: Timothy D. Ludwig, Department of Psychology, Appalachian State University; E. Scott Geller, Department of Psychology, Virginia Polytechnic Institute and State University.

Acknowledgments: We acknowledge the significant contribution of research associates within the Center for Applied Behavior Systems at Virginia Polytechnic Institute and State University, as well as Tim and Caroline Bell (i.e., proprietors of the two intervention-based pizza stores). Preparation of this report was supported in part by Grant 1 R01 OHMH03397-01 from the National Institute for Occupational Safety and Health (NIOSH) and by the Centers for Disease Control and Prevention. Portions of this research were presented at the Annual Meeting of the Society for Industrial and Organizational Psychology, Orlando, FL, May 1995.

Address correspondence to: Timothy D. Ludwig, Department of Psychology, Appalachian State University, 114 Smith-Wright Hall, Boone, NC 28608. Electronic mail may be sent via Internet to ludwigtd@conrad.appstate.edu

Exercise for Article 11

Factual Questions

1. According to Locke and Latham's (1990) review of nearly 500 studies, does the method in which goals are set affect subsequent performance?

2. How did the researchers complete this phrase: "We hypothesized that…"?

3. The 75% goal was presented as a "mandate" to which group (*assigned* or *participative*)?

4. How many participants met the criteria to be included in the repeated measures analysis?

5. For the participative group, what was the mean percentage for safety belt use at baseline? What was it at follow-up?

6. How was response generalization "operationally defined" in this study?

7. Behavioral ecology directs researchers to ask questions about what three things?

Questions for Discussion

8. In the Table of Contents of this book, this study is classified as an example of "Quasi-Experimental Research." Why does it have this designation (as opposed to true experimental research)?

9. How important is the information in lines 134–140? Explain.

10. Speculate on why vehicle observations were "unobtrusively recorded." (See lines 141–144.)

11. The researchers use the term "nonequivalent control group" in line 182. What do you think this term means?

12. The feedback percentages that were posted every four days were not real. Instead, they were random numbers chosen from percentages ranging from 78% to 90%. In your opinion was this a good idea? (See lines 310–319.)

13. In your opinion, how important is the information on content analysis in lines 344–360? Explain.

14. The researchers state that their findings are noteworthy and worthy of further investigation. Do you agree? Why? Why not?

Quality Ratings

Directions: Indicate your level of agreement with each of the following statements by circling a number from 5 for strongly agree (SA) to 1 for strongly disagree (SD). If you believe an item is not applicable to this research article, leave it blank. Be prepared to explain your ratings.

A. The introduction establishes the importance of the study.

SA   5   4   3   2   1   SD

B. The literature review establishes the context for the study.

SA   5   4   3   2   1   SD

C. The research purpose, question, or hypothesis is clearly stated.

SA   5   4   3   2   1   SD

D. The method of sampling is sound.

SA   5   4   3   2   1   SD

E. Relevant demographics (for example, age, gender, and ethnicity) are described.

SA   5   4   3   2   1   SD

F. Measurement procedures are adequate.

SA   5   4   3   2   1   SD

G. All procedures have been described in sufficient detail to permit a replication of the study.

SA   5   4   3   2   1   SD

H. The participants have been adequately protected from potential harm.

SA   5   4   3   2   1   SD

I. The results are clearly described.

SA   5   4   3   2   1   SD

J. The discussion/conclusion is appropriate.

SA   5   4   3   2   1   SD

K. Despite any flaws, the report is worthy of publication.

SA   5   4   3   2   1   SD

Article 12

The Influence of Personal Message with Music on Anxiety and Side Effects Associated with Chemotherapy

CAROLYN E. SABO
University of Nevada, Las Vegas

SUSAN RUSH MICHAEL
University of Nevada, Las Vegas

ABSTRACT. The purpose of this pilot study was to evaluate the benefits of a message from a patient's physician audiotaped over music on reducing anxiety and side effects of patients receiving chemotherapy. A convenience sample of 97 adult patients receiving chemotherapy for the first time was assigned to either an experimental or control group. Before beginning the first chemotherapy treatment, all subjects completed a demographic questionnaire and the Spielberger State Anxiety Inventory (SSAI). Participants in the experimental group ($n = 47$) received taped music and a message from their physicians during the next four chemotherapy treatments. Participants in the control group ($n = 50$) received no intervention from the researchers and underwent their next four chemotherapy treatments as prescribed. After the fourth chemotherapy treatment, the SSAI and a side-effects self-assessment evaluation were completed by all subjects. A paired one-tailed t test found a significant difference between pre- and postintervention scores on the state anxiety scale ($p < 0.001$). In addition, anxiety remained the same over time in the control group. There was no significant difference in the severity of side effects experienced between control and experimental groups. These preliminary findings indicate that a simple and cost-effective intervention can decrease a patient's anxiety when receiving chemotherapy.

From *Cancer Nursing*, 19, 283–289. Copyright © 1996 by Lippincott-Raven Publishers, Philadelphia. Reprinted with permission.

For patients with a diagnosis of cancer, chemotherapy can be a traumatic experience fraught with fear and anxiety. Health professionals have long recognized the role that fear and anxiety play in intensifying the
5 physiologic and psychologic impact of receiving chemotherapy. It is the role of the nurse to reassure the patient and to work to diminish the anxiety these people experience during chemotherapy treatment. Furthermore, interventions to minimize the side effects
10 associated with chemotherapy will directly contribute to the patient's comfort and indirectly promote a sense of relaxation and lessened anxiety, particularly in anticipation of subsequent chemotherapy treatments.

Studies have demonstrated the influence of guided
15 imagery and relaxation techniques in reducing the anxiety and side effects associated with chemotherapy and other nursing care situations (1,2). The positive effects of these interventions are well documented. Other alternative therapies have been used to lessen
20 anxiety and side effects associated with treatment interventions, including music therapy, biofeedback, and back massage (3–5). However, there are several limitations to all of these techniques. Significant time commitments on the part of both the nurse and the patient
25 and administration by an expert trained in the particular alternative therapy are required, and the high cost (in terms of both time and money) inhibits widespread use.

The purpose of this study was to evaluate the benefits of an intervention that did not require excessive
30 time commitments from staff or patient or administration by a trained expert and was not accompanied by a significant increase in cost. Researchers believed that a message from the physician conveying *personal* support and compassion to the patient would be beneficial.
35 The benefits from such a message of support and comfort from the patient's personal physician as a component of an overall relaxation and imagery intervention was the topic of interest for this research project.

Literature Review

A review of the literature reflects an increasing in-
40 terest in using behavioral interventions to minimize the impact on patients of receiving chemotherapy (1,3,6–10). Much of the literature has dealt with such techniques as progressive relaxation and guided imagery. Sims (10) reviewed studies conducted from 1979 to
45 1983 in which progressive relaxation or progressive relaxation with guided imagery was used among patients receiving chemotherapy and found that most were single case studies or cited only anecdotal reports of success or that the samples were so small that there
50 was a lack of statistical significance. Mastenbrook and McGovern (8) also reviewed articles from 1979 to 1987, looking at the effectiveness of relaxation techniques in controlling the side effects of chemotherapy. The researchers identified the same limitations as Sims,
55 but also found that it was impossible to determine any differences in effectiveness between various tech-

niques. The researchers raised questions about alternative methods to provide techniques in a cost-effective manner, determining patients' proficiency in using the techniques, and controlling subject groups in studies of the variables of type of cancer and method of chemotherapy.

In addition to relaxation techniques and guided imagery, music therapy has been used as a behavioral intervention for patients receiving chemotherapy (3,7). Cook (7) described the benefits of music therapy: it is readily available and easily affordable and has the potential to make a significant contribution in the context of cancer treatment. Lane (3) reported the use of music therapy at a cancer center for hospitalized patients and its psychological and physiological benefits. Two subject groups of 20 each were randomized to control and experimental groups. The control group participated in normal hospital routines, while the experimental group received 30 min of interactive music therapy. Immunoglobulin A (IgA) levels were measured pre- and postintervention as an indicator of the status of the immune system. Results indicated that there was a significant increase in IgA in the experimental group, reflecting a physiologic effect from the music therapy. Lane suggested that studies need to be done to provide further insight into this phenomenon.

Frank (1) combined the techniques of music therapy and guided imagery and found them to be effective in significantly reducing anxiety and perceived degrees of vomiting, but no significant reduction was seen in perceived nausea. Because the study used a single-group pre- and postintervention design, it is difficult to conclude whether the effect was due to the intervention or to such factors as history, maturation, or testing. The sample was also very small ($n = 15$).

Carey and Burish (6) used three strategies for providing relaxation to cancer chemotherapy patients. The researchers randomly assigned 45 patients to four treatment conditions. The four conditions were progressive muscle-relaxation training (PMRT) and guided relaxation imagery (GI) provided by a professional therapist, PMRT and GI provided by a trained volunteer therapist, PMRT and GI provided by professionally prepared audiotapes, and standard treatment (antiemetic medications only). Results indicated that the professionally administered PMRT and GI were superior to both audiotaped and paraprofessionally administered training in minimizing physiological symptoms of chemotherapy and increasing food intake in patients undergoing chemotherapy. In this study, it is difficult to determine whether the results were due solely to the mode of delivery of the intervention or whether the presence of a therapist contributed to the individual's feeling cared for by a professional. While most would agree that a therapist would be helpful for most anyone experiencing such a life-threatening event, the practicality and cost-effectiveness of using such an individual limits widespread adoption of this intervention.

Research studies indicate that behavioral techniques to decrease anxiety and side effects associated with chemotherapy look promising as a viable intervention to improve the quality of life for cancer patients. However, limitations in these studies have been noted. The purpose of our study was to investigate the influence of a personalized message, placed over background music, on the anxiety and side effects associated with chemotherapy. This study is significant as a step in validating the usefulness of a nurse-prescribed intervention that (a) requires minimal preparation or investment of time by the nurse, (b) can be administered in an outpatient setting, and (c) requires little training of patients and no participant practice for successful implementation. Expanding nursing knowledge and intervention strategies with empirically grounded studies is imperative to further our efforts toward providing a strong scientific basis for nursing practice.

Conceptual Framework

Neuman's Systems Model (11) is an open-systems model viewing the individual as a biopsychosocial spiritual being who is constantly interacting with the environment. Neuman conceptualizes the core of the individual as composed of anything that keeps the system alive, such as the genetic structure, normal temperature range, ego, and organ strength. The core is protected by concentric circles that Neuman refers to as the lines of resistance, the normal lines of defense, and the flexible lines of defense. The three concentric circles function at varying levels to protect the core from the effects of both environmental and internal stressors. Stressors have an impact on the system at any level; the host's reaction is determined by the interaction between the stressor and the lines of defense and resistance. In this study, the stressor is the chemotherapy, and the intervention is aimed at minimizing the reaction to this stressor by strengthening the flexible lines of defense through the intervention of music and a personalized message from the patient's physician during chemotherapy.

Methodology

Human Subject Rights

Before beginning the study, approval was obtained from the University Office of Research Administration Human Subject Rights Review Board. The study proposal was also approved by the physicians whose patients were to become the subject pool for the study. Permission to use the electric harp music of Hillary Stagg (12) as the background music was obtained from the music publisher. Subjects were approached before their first chemotherapy treatment. After explaining the purpose and conduct of the study, the researchers obtained signed consent forms from all participants.

Subjects

The offices of two oncology physician groups were

used for data collection; participants for the experimental group were taken from one office, and participants for the control group were taken from the other. The offices of the two physician groups were adjacent but not adjoining. They were similar in terms of physical environment, the physician's approach to the patient, and scheduling of chemotherapy treatments. Subjects were ≥ 21 years old, spoke and read English, and had no hearing impairment that would interfere with their ability to listen to the taped music.

Both the control and experimental groups were made up of a convenience sample of 50 patients. In all cases, the subjects were receiving chemotherapy for the first time in the physician's office. No limitations were placed on the type of cancer—participants had a wide range of cancer diagnoses. Participation in the study ended when a subject had completed four chemotherapy cycles or treatments. Because chemotherapy is given in intermittent cycles depending upon the drug used, the length of time between beginning and ending participation in the research study varied among subjects from 4 days (four treatments given over 4 consecutive days) to 9 weeks (four treatments given at 3-week intervals).

Instruments

The Spielberger State Anxiety Inventory (SSAI) is a 20-item, self-report likert-type scale. The items are designed to reflect how the subject feels at the time of questioning. Possible scores range from 20 to 80; higher scores are associated with greater anxiety. The SSAI has been used in a number of research studies since 1970. It was revised in 1980 to its current form. Reliability and validity are well established—the tool has been used in over 2,000 research projects, including those studying subjects in the context of health care (13).

The Cancer Chemotherapy and Side-Effects Inventory was developed by the researchers (Table 1). The inventory was given to three oncologists and six oncology nurse specialists for review and revision, thus establishing content validity. The inventory is a self-report scale eliciting the subject's perception of the degree to which he or she has experienced selected side effects commonly associated with chemotherapy. One question related to the perception of quality of life was also included in the inventory for all subjects. Participants in the experimental group were also asked to comment about the tape recording and how it helped or did not help them during their chemotherapy experience.

Procedure

Before the first chemotherapy treatment, all subjects completed a demographic data questionnaire and the SSAI (13). Participants in the experimental group were then given preselected taped music that was played through a headset. The tape began with an introductory statement (added over the background mu-

sic) from the patient's physician encouraging the patient to relax, listen to the music, and imagine the chemotherapy working to accomplish treatment goals. The physician's message was derived from a scripted text created by the researchers; however, the physicians were encouraged to modify the script slightly to make it more individualized. For example, one physician told a few jokes (e.g., "Do as I say, not as I do" and "We will take care of you, like that insurance company holding you in their hands"). After the message, the harp music continued.

Table 1
Cancer chemotherapy and side-effects inventory

Directions:	Please circle the response number that most closely rates your experience with the following problems that may be associated with cancer or chemotherapy. For example, if you experience no leg sores, you would circle the number 1.	
A.	Leg sores[a]	1 2 3 4 5 6 7 8 9 10
1.	Mouth ulcers	1 2 3 4 5 6 7 8 9 10
2.	Loss of hair	1 2 3 4 5 6 7 8 9 10
3.	Fatigue	1 2 3 4 5 6 7 8 9 10
4.	Diarrhea	1 2 3 4 5 6 7 8 9 10
5.	Constipation	1 2 3 4 5 6 7 8 9 10
6.	Low blood counts	1 2 3 4 5 6 7 8 9 10
7.	Skin rash	1 2 3 4 5 6 7 8 9 10
8.	Loss of appetite	1 2 3 4 5 6 7 8 9 10
9.	Sore throat	1 2 3 4 5 6 7 8 9 10
10.	Metallic taste in mouth	1 2 3 4 5 6 7 8 9 10
11.	Nausea	1 2 3 4 5 6 7 8 9 10
12.	Vomiting	1 2 3 4 5 6 7 8 9 10
13.	If you identified nausea as a problem, how long did the nausea last?	
14.	If you identified vomiting as a problem, how long did the vomiting last?	
15.	How would you rate your quality of life today (circle the number that most clearly relates)[b]	1 2 3 4 5 6 7 8 9 10

[a] 1 = none; 10 = severe.
[b] 1 = very bad; 10 = very good.

The participant was given the option of stopping and restarting the music if he or she desired. Those in the experimental group were provided with the intervention tape during their first four chemotherapy treatments. It should be noted that the same tape was used at each of the four sessions. The participants in the control group received no intervention from the researchers and underwent their chemotherapy treatments as prescribed. The two subject groups were treated in different offices to avoid any bias associated with subjects knowing that music intervention was given to some patients and not others.

After the fourth chemotherapy treatment, the SSAI and a chemotherapy side-effects self-assessment questionnaire were completed by all subjects. Subjects in the experimental group were able to continue using the

music for the duration of their chemotherapy treatments if they desired. Subjects in the control group
were advised that they could begin using the taped music with their individual physician's message on completion of the study. This option was taken by approximately three of the subjects who had been in the
control group.

Hypotheses

Hypothesis 1

The intervention of music and a message from the
physician will strengthen the flexible lines of defense
of a patient receiving chemotherapy, as evidenced by a
decrease in anxiety over time. (Specific wording is
appropriate for the conceptual framework identified.)

Hypothesis 2

The intervention of music and a message from the
physician will lessen the impact of the stressor of chemotherapy, as evidenced by a decrease in the severity
of side effects.

Results

The sample consisted of 97 patients—39 men and
58 women, ranging in age from 21 years to >70 years.
Patients were assigned to either the experimental group
or the control group by physician's office grouping.
The two groups were similar in terms of distribution of
age, sex, marital status, and race (Table 2). They were
also similar in terms of the type of primary cancer
identified by the demographic data (Table 3). Data
analysis techniques consisted of descriptive tests and
the use of a paired one-tailed t test to address Hypotheses 1 and 2. A paired one-tailed t test was used for data
analysis, as opposed to analysis of variance (ANOVA),
because the groups were sufficiently small ($n \leq 50$) that
use of ANOVA would have been inappropriate. A
paired one-tailed t test with this group size is a much
more robust test (14).

Hypothesis 1 was supported (Table 4). In the experimental group, anxiety scores before intervention
ranged from 20 to 72, with a mean of 42.51 ($SD =$
12.44), and postintervention anxiety scores ranged
from 20 to 62, with a mean of 36.39 ($SD = 10.58$). A
paired one-tailed t test found a significant difference
between the pre- and postintervention scores on the
SSAI ($t = 3.32$; $df = 46$; $p < 0.001$). In the control
group, scores ranged from 20 to 74 before intervention,
with a mean of 39.00 ($SD = 10.14$), while postintervention scores ranged from 20 to 64 with a mean of
39.94 ($SD = 10.44$). A paired one-tailed t test showed
no significant difference between the scores before and
after intervention on the SSAI ($t = 0.76$; $df = 49$; $p =$
0.227).

A comparison of pretest anxiety sum minus posttest anxiety sum confirmed a significant difference
between the experimental and control groups ($t = 2.19$;
$df = 87.18$; $p < 0.015$) (Table 5). Additionally, anecdotal data from subjects in the experimental group

showed that, for the most part, the audiotaped music
with the physician's message helped them to relax. For
some, it helped them to think about more pleasant
times, and for others, it distracted them from the needles. Subjects said that the tape eased their minds and
relaxed their bodies during treatment, kept their minds
off the problems, and gave them pleasant thoughts.
One patient said that it was "nice to know the doctor
much better, have more respect for him." This individual was referring to having a greater respect for the
physician in terms of his willingness to provide the
message on the tape in an attempt to relax and/or calm
the patient. Other patients commented that they preferred to relax with a book as well as enjoy the message, but they liked a different type of music.

Table 2
Characteristics of the subject population (n = 97)

Characteristics	Control group		Experimental Group	
	n	%	*n*	%
Gender				
Male	21	42	18	38
Female	29	58	29	61
Age				
21–30	1	2	0	0
31–40	5	10	3	6.4
41–50	7	14	7	14.9
51–60	10	20	9	19.1
61–70	19	38	20	42.6
70+	8	16	8	17
Marital status				
Single (never married)	1	2	0	0
Married	33	66	36	76.6
Separated	1	2	0	0
Divorced	7	14	9	19.1
Widowed	8	16	2	4.3
Race				
White (non-Hispanic)	43	86	43	91.5
Black	2	4	3	6.4
Hispanic	1	2	3	6.3
Asian	2	4	0	0
American Indian	1	2	0	0
Other	1	2	1	2.1

Hypothesis 2 was not supported. No significant difference was found in the severity of side effects experienced between the control and experimental groups. A
possible explanation for the lack of difference in side
effects is that there were numerous uncontrolled variables, perhaps the biggest being that so many different
types of cancer were represented in the subject population that there were over 40 different protocols of chemotherapy. With so much variety in the chemotherapy,
there was enormous variation in the number and types
of side effects. Also, because of the significant number
of independent variables incurred with the numerous
different primary cancer types and chemotherapy protocols, data analysis proved to be weak, with unstable

330 results. Therefore, neither additional analysis of this data nor discussion of the results was conducted in terms of the data obtained from the Cancer Chemotherapy and Side-effects Inventory. Furthermore, no record was kept of which patient was receiving treatments
335 besides chemotherapy (such as radiation therapy) that might have influenced the emergence of side effects.

Table 3
Primary cancers of participants

Cancer type	Control group n	Control group %	Experimental group n	Experimental group %
Colon	8	16	3	6.4
Breast	8	16	14	29.3
Lung	13	26	11	23.4
Pancreatic	1	2	1	2.1
Testicular	1	2	0	0
Prostate	1	2	1	2.1
Ovarian	5	10	2	4.3
Leukemia	0	0	2	4.3
Brain	1	2	3	6.4
Lymphoma	3	6	3	6.4
Bladder	1	2	0	0
Other	5	10	5	10.6
Missing	3	6	2	4.3

Discussion

The personalized message over music significantly lessened the level of anxiety for patients receiving chemotherapy in the experimental group. Moreover,
340 anecdotal comments by the patients supported the positive effects of the intervention. The strongest comments related to the feeling that the physician's message provided words of comfort and a degree of distraction from the process of receiving chemotherapy
345 and also to the fact that the physician was willing to take the time to contribute to the audiotape preparation. It may have been that clients felt their physicians really cared about them and understood their apprehension and anxiety in receiving chemotherapy. Listening to
350 the tape, patients may have seen their physicians in a caring role, helping them through a difficult procedure, rather than seeing them only as the director of their treatment. Personalization of the scripted message also allowed the subject to hear the physician's familiar
355 voice using familiar words and phrases, thus contributing to the sense that the physician really was speaking directly. Finally, while anxiety diminished in the experimental group, side effects were of approximately the same severity in both groups. A possible explana-
360 tion for this lack of difference in side effects is that there were numerous uncontrolled variables, as previously discussed.

The cost-effective nature of the intervention is based on the premise that the only real cost would be in
365 the initial purchase of tape recorders and the preparation and duplication of the audiotapes along with the ongoing replacement of batteries. After the initial out-

lay and preparation, the nurse need only offer the tape recorder and audiotapes to the patient for use during
370 administration of the chemotherapy. There is no additional cost associated with nursing time or use of equipment.

Table 4
Spielberger State Anxiety Inventory scores: pre- and post-treatment

Group	n	Mean	SD	t	df	p value
Control						
Pre	50	39.0039	10.145	0.76	49.0	0.227[a]
Post	50	39.9450	10.441			
Experimental						
Pre	49	42.5128	12.441	3.32	46.0	0.001[a]
Post	47	36.3919	10.582			

[a] A paired, one-tailed *t* test was used.

Table 5
Comparison: Pretreatment anxiety sum minus post-treatment anxiety sum (n = 97)

Group	n	Mean	SD	t	df	p value
Control	50	1.0589	9.90	2.19	87.18	0.015
Experimental	47	6.1208	12.631			

[a] A paired, one-tailed *t* test was used.

Five limitations to the study were realized: many different protocols of chemotherapy; small sample size;
375 mixture of message, music, and guided imagery treatments (on one tape); bias introduced by the use of physician's offices for subject selection rather than randomization of all subjects available; and the varied quality of the audiotapes (some participants stated that
380 parts of the audiotapes were difficult to hear). These limitations will be addressed in ongoing studies related to this intervention technique.

This study contributes to the growing body of literature that indicates that a simple intervention can
385 reduce a patient's anxiety when receiving an unpleasant medical treatment such as chemotherapy. In addition, this study introduces a nurse-prescribed and nurse-administered intervention that uses a personal message from the patient's physician, incorporates
390 guided imagery, and does not need to be practiced by the patient at home. While studies have established the benefits of teaching patients guided imagery and then having them practice, not all patients are motivated or desire to learn these techniques. Furthermore, having
395 clients walk in for chemotherapy with an intervention that requires little assistance from a busy office staff increases the likelihood that it will be used and provides additional flexibility for nurses to spend more time with patients who are having difficulties associ-
400 ated with chemotherapy.

Clearly, further research is needed in this area. A replication of this study using a larger sample with

more homogeneity in terms of the type of primary cancer would minimize the variation in chemotherapy
405 regimens given, thus helping determine whether the
tape-recorded message might have physical benefits
(decreased side effects) as well as the psychological
benefit (decreased anxiety) demonstrated in this study.
Although it is not a major factor, a professionally pro-
410 duced audiotape with the physician's message played
over the music would enhance the clarity of the sound.
A professionally produced tape would incur initial additional costs, yet the ongoing intervention would not
result in higher expense.

References

1. Frank JM. The effects of music therapy and guided visual imagery on chemotherapy-induced nausea and vomiting. *Oncol Nurs Forum* 1985; 12(5):47–52.
2. Tiernan PJ. Independent nursing interventions: relaxation and guided imagery in critical care. *Crit Care Nurse* 1994; October: 47–51.
3. Lane D. Music therapy: gaining an edge in oncology management. *J Oncol Manage* 1993(n.–Feb.:42–6.
4. Burish TG, Shartner CD, Lyles JN. Effectiveness of multiple muscle-site EMG biofeedback and relaxation training in reducing the aversiveness of cancer chemotherapy. *Biofeedback Self Regul* 1981;4:65–78.
5. Scott DW, Donahue DC, Mastrovito RC, Hakes TB. The antiemetic effect of clinical relaxation: report of an exploratory pilot study. *J Psychosoc Oncol* 1983;1:71–84.
6. Carey M, Burish T. Providing relaxation training to cancer chemotherapy patients: a comparison of three delivery techniques. *J Consult Clin Psychol* 1987;55(5):732–7.
7. Cook JD. Music as an intervention in the oncology setting. *Cancer Nurs* 1986;9(1):23–8.
8. Mastenbrook I, McGovern L. The effectiveness of relaxation techniques in controlling chemotherapy-induced nausea: a literature review. *Aust Occup Ther J* 1991;38(3):137–42.
9. Morrow G, Morrell C. Behavioral treatment for the anticipatory nausea and vomiting induced by cancer chemotherapy. *N Engl J Med* 1982;307:1476–80.
10. Sims SER. Relaxation training as a technique for helping patients cope with the experience of cancer: a selective review of the literature. *J Adv Nurs* 1987;12:583–91.
11. Neuman B. *The Neuman systems model*, 3rd ed. Norwalk: Appleton & Lange, 1995.
12. Stagg H. *Dream spiral*. Sausalito: Real Music, 1991.
13. Spielberger CD. *Manual for State Trait Anxiety Inventory (form Y)*. Palo Alto, CA: Consulting Psychologists Publishers, 1983.
14. Munroe B, Page EB. *Statistical methods for health care research*, 2nd ed. Philadelphia: JB Lippincott, 1993.

About the authors: Carolyn E. Sabo is an Associate Professor and Interim Dean at the College of Health Sciences, University of Nevada, Las Vegas, Nevada. Susan Rush Michael is an Associate Professor of Nursing at the University of Nevada, Las Vegas, Nevada.

Address correspondence to: Carolyn E. Sabo, R.N., Ed.D., College of Health Sciences, 2842 Brockington Drive, Las Vegas, NV 89120.

Exercise for Article 12

Factual Questions

1. The researchers cite a study by Frank in their literature review. Was there a control group in Frank's study? Explain.

2. Did the researchers use a "convenience sample?"

3. The Spielberger State Anxiety Inventory has been used in how many previous research projects?

4. How was the content validity of the Cancer Chemotherapy and Side-Effects Inventory established?

5. Was there a statistically significant difference between the pretest and posttest means of the control group on the SSAI?

6. Was Hypothesis 2 supported?

7. What is the value of *p* for the *t* test for the difference between the mean change for the control group and the mean change for the experimental group?

Questions for Discussion

8. In the first sentence of the Abstract at the beginning of this article, the researchers refer to this study as a "pilot study." Do you agree that it is a pilot study? Explain.

9. In describing a previous study by Carey and Burish, the researchers state that patients were "randomly assigned" to one of four treatment conditions. Is it important to know that they were randomly assigned? Explain. (See lines 92–101.)

10. In the Table of Contents of this book, this research report is classified as an example of "Quasi-Experimental Research." What would need to be changed in this study to make it an example of "True Experimental Research?"

11. Is the information presented in Table 2 important? Explain.

12. The researchers mention five limitations in lines 373–382. In your opinion, are all five important? Are some more important than others?

Quality Ratings

Directions: Indicate your level of agreement with each of the following statements by circling a number from 5 for strongly agree (SA) to 1 for strongly disagree (SD). If you believe an item is not applicable to this research article, leave it blank. Be prepared to explain your ratings.

A. The introduction establishes the importance of the study.

SA   5   4   3   2   1   SD

B. The literature review establishes the context for the study.

SA   5   4   3   2   1   SD

C. The research purpose, question, or hypothesis is clearly stated.

SA   5   4   3   2   1   SD

D. The method of sampling is sound.

SA   5   4   3   2   1   SD

E. Relevant demographics (for example, age, gender, and ethnicity) are described.

SA   5   4   3   2   1   SD

F. Measurement procedures are adequate.

SA   5   4   3   2   1   SD

G. All procedures have been described in sufficient detail to permit a replication of the study.

SA   5   4   3   2   1   SD

H. The participants have been adequately protected from potential harm.

SA   5   4   3   2   1   SD

I. The results are clearly described.

SA   5   4   3   2   1   SD

J. The discussion/conclusion is appropriate.

SA   5   4   3   2   1   SD

K. Despite any flaws, the report is worthy of publication.

SA   5   4   3   2   1   SD

Article 13

Changing Health Behavior
Via Telecommunications Technology:
Using Interactive Television to Treat Obesity

JEAN HARVEY-BERINO
University of Vermont

ABSTRACT. This study compared a 12-week behavioral weight-control treatment program conducted over interactive television ($N = 133$) to a standard therapist-led (in-person) treatment condition ($N = 33$). Subjects started treatment with an average Body Mass Index (BMI) of 34.9 and lost 7.7 kg over 12 weeks with no difference between conditions noted for weight loss, calorie (–622 calories per day), or exercise changes (+970 calories expended per day). Ratings of the technology were positive and there was no difference in subjects' expectations for change, nor was there any difference by treatment condition in overall attrition. A cost-effectiveness analysis showed that the per-person cost of the interactive technology was higher.

From *Behavior Therapy*, 29, 505–519. Copyright © 1998 by the Association for Advancement of Behavior Therapy. Reprinted with permission.

Obesity is a serious public health problem in the United States, affecting nearly 1 in 3 adults (Flegal, 1996). Obesity significantly contributes to increased morbidity and mortality from a number of chronic dis-
5   eases and costs the health care industry up to $70 billion annually (Stipps, 1995).

Improvements in the physiological risk factors associated with obesity-related diseases have been attributed to weight reduction. Weight loss can reduce blood
10 pressure (Chiang, Perlman, & Epstein, 1969), favorably alter the balance in serum lipids (Thompson, Jeffery, Wing, & Wood, 1979), and improve nearly every index of coronary efficiency (Alexander & Peterson, 1972). Moreover, these improvements can be re-
15 alized with weight losses as small as 2 kg (Kanders & Blackburn, 1992). Currently, the best weight losses to date are achieved with behavioral weight-loss techniques. Behavioral approaches, developed in the late 1960s (Ferster, 1962), govern the treatment of mild to
20 moderate obesity (Brownell & Jeffery, 1987; Kirschenbaum & Fitzgibbon, 1995; Perri, Nezu, Patti, & McCann, 1989). Participation in behavioral weight-control treatments results in lower attrition rates (Volkmar, Stunkard, Woolston, & Bailey, 1981), better
25 maintenance of weight losses achieved during treat-

ment (Bloom, 1988; Brownell & Wadden, 1986), and improvements in a number of psychological parameters (O'Neil & Jarrell, 1992). Thus, behavioral treatments are the weight-loss method of choice for outpatient
30 treatment of mild to moderate obesity (Kirschenbaum & Fitzgibbon, 1995).

Unfortunately, the professional, face-to-face delivery of behavioral weight-loss programs remains an expensive, time-consuming process (Agras, Taylor,
35 Feldman, Losch, & Burnett, 1990; Yates, 1978). Because professionally trained behavioral weight-loss therapists are not widely available and cost is a barrier, high-quality, behavioral weight-control treatment programs are effectively inaccessible to large groups of
40 the population. Low-income individuals and those in rural areas without access to state-of-the-art medical care will be unable to participate in the safest, most reliable method of weight reduction. There is clearly a pressing need to develop cost-effective behavior ther-
45 apy treatments that are accessible to a larger percentage of the population (Agras et al., 1990; Fitzgibbon, Stolley, & Kirschenbaum, 1993; Jeffery & Gerber, 1982).

Earlier research has demonstrated success with behavioral interventions conducted over television.
50 Frankel and colleagues (Frankel, Birkimer, Brown, & Cunningham, 1983) provided an eating behavior intervention over a local morning television broadcast. The authors reported an average weight loss of 0.68 to 0.90 kg per week, results similar to standard in-person
55 weight-loss programs (Brownell & Wadden, 1986). Meyers, Graves, Whelan, and Barclay (1996) tested the effectiveness of face-to-face, therapist-led behavioral weight loss against an identical program delivered over a cable television channel. There were no significant
60 between-group differences noted, with both groups losing approximately 4.3 kg over an 8-week treatment. Thus, these studies suggest that behavioral weight control via televised media can be effective and acceptable to consumers. However, the ability to dupli-
65 cate the methodology of the studies previously cited remains problematic. Both studies took advantage of the goodwill of local television stations to broadcast their interventions and both were televised to a primar-

ily urban audience. The cost of ongoing behavioral
70 weight-control sessions offered only via commercial
television channels would be prohibitively expensive to
sustain long-term. Additionally, local television channels can reach only a local audience, thereby rendering
televised programs inaccessible to consumers outside
75 the local viewing area.

One technological solution to this problem is interactive videoconferencing or interactive television. Interactive television involves the translation of transmis-
sions from video and microphones into digital signals,
80 which are then transported via telephone lines. The use
of telephone lines is affordable, with hourly costs
ranging from $10 to $35 (Attwood & Graham, 1993).
The use of videoconferencing to support telemedicine
is still fairly novel, although it has been growing in
85 popularity (McGee & Tangalos, 1994). Telecommunications technology has been used as a vehicle to support professional training of health care staff, provide
diagnostic and consultative services to practitioners at
distant sites, as well as to support the provision of di-
90 rect services to rural, medically underserved individuals (Hubble, Pahwa, Michalek, Thomas, & Koller,
1993; McGee & Tangalos, 1994). While every indication suggests that this technology holds promise for
reaching rural, medically underserved populations
95 (Allen & Hayes, 1994; Troster, Paolo, Glatt, Hubble, &
Koller, 1995), many questions remain regarding its
effectiveness and acceptability. In a 1994 report on
potential contributions of telecommunications technology, McGee and Tangalos cite the important role tele-
100 communications can play in the delivery of health education to underserved populations. However, they argue that "the starting point must be the consumer—
what is needed and will be used are more important
issues than what is technologically possible" (p. 1133).
105 Currently, there is no report in the literature on the use
of televised telecommunications technology to foster behavior change. Therefore, the objectives of this study
were to determine if interactive video-conferencing is a
feasible, acceptable, effective, and cost-efficient vehi-
110 cle for delivering a behavioral weight-control intervention.

Method

Subjects

Subjects were recruited with newspaper ads placed
in six different locations throughout the state. These
sites were chosen to represent a mix of rural and more
115 urban geographic locations, and all were not within a
reasonable driving distance of the university. Subjects
were required to be over 18 years old, ≥ 20% over ideal
body weight based on Metropolitan Life Insurance
norms (1983), and free of any major medical problems
120 that would contraindicate participation in a weight-loss
program. After subjects were screened by phone, they
were invited to attend an orientation session held in
each location. The study was explained and informed

consent was obtained at this time. Participants at the
125 university site were also informed that they would be
randomized to an interactive television (IT) group or a
standard therapy (ST) group that met in person with a
therapist.

Design

Each group met weekly for 12 consecutive weeks
130 and received an identical behavioral weight-loss treatment program run by a Ph.D.-level, trained behavioral
therapist. Only subjects recruited from the university
site were randomly assigned to attend treatment sessions at the local interactive television studio or in a
135 campus classroom. Assessments were done at baseline
and at Week 12.

Treatment

The treatment program for both groups focused on
the modification of eating and exercise habits through
the use of behavioral strategies and self-management
140 skills. The program was similar to the LEARN Program for Weight Control (Brownell, 1994). Subjects
met weekly for 1 hour and printed lessons were given
out to reinforce the weekly discussion. Subjects were
instructed to reduce their caloric intake to 1,000 to
145 2,500 calories per day, depending on their baseline
body weight. Calorie goals were determined by multiplying baseline weight by 12 (to get an estimate of current calorie consumption) and subtracting 1,000 calories. This method has been used in previous studies and
150 is known to encourage a weight loss of 1 to 2 pounds
per week (Jeffery et al., 1993). The large range in calorie goals was based on the fact that one participant
weighed over 300 pounds at baseline. Over 95% of the
calorie goals ranged between 1,000 and 1,800 calories
155 per day and the proportion of subjects with 1,000,
1,200, 1,500 and 1,800 calorie goals were evenly distributed between groups.

During treatment, subjects were taught the principles of a healthy diet and generally encouraged to fol-
160 low a diet that met the Dietary Guidelines (United
States Department of Agriculture, 1995). The emphasis, however, was on staying below their calorie goal.
Subjects recorded their calorie intake daily throughout
the 12-week program. Their diaries were reviewed and
165 advice was given on strategies for lowering caloric
intake while maintaining a nutritionally balanced diet.
Patients in both groups were taught the benefits of exercise for weight management and other coronary heart
disease risk factors. Graded goals for programmed ac-
170 tivity (i.e., walking) were used throughout the program,
and patients monitored the amount of energy expended
on a daily basis. The importance of lifestyle activity
(e.g., using the stairs instead of the elevator) was also
emphasized, and patients were encouraged to gradually
175 increase lifestyle activity throughout the program.
Subjects were also taught the principles of behavior
modification to enhance self-management of energy
intake and expenditure. Weekly sessions included dis-

180 cussions of stimulus control, problem solving, social skills training, and relapse prevention training.

Subjects were recruited and treated in two cohorts. Four interactive television sites participated in the first 12-week session; three in the second. The IT group site that was closest to the university was used to broadcast
185 the IT sessions for both cohorts. Thus, there were six different IT sites used, with four participating in the first cohort (the university site and three distant sites) and three in the second cohort (the university site and two other distant sites). The group therapist broadcast
190 treatment sessions out of the interactive television studio closest to the university with a live group participating in that studio and two or three additional groups simultaneously participating via distant interactive television sites. All subjects could see and hear the
195 therapist at all times and each participant could be heard by all others by speaking into their own microphone. The audio system activated the video system; thus, participants were always on camera and visible when they were speaking.

200 In order to facilitate communication, each distant site had a site facilitator. Local Extension Educators and one local dietitian served in this capacity. The site facilitator weighed participants before each session, reviewed self-monitoring diaries weekly for partici-
205 pants of their site and generally served as the local contacts for their group. Site facilitators were trained in how to weigh participants and review self-monitoring diaries, but they were not trained behavior therapists and did not deliver any of the weight-loss therapy ses-
210 sions. Generally, site facilitators were trained to give written positive feedback in the self-monitoring diaries to participants regarding their healthy food choices, participation in physical activity, and attempts to successfully meet program goals. The same feedback was
215 given by the therapist for the ST and IT groups run closest to the university.

Measures

Data collection consisted of demographic measures, smoking status, dietary intake, and questionnaire measures of exercise and expectations for change.
220 Subjects were weighed in street clothes on a high-quality floor model scale at baseline and at Week 12. Additionally, IT subjects were asked to rate the interactive television technology.

Diet and exercise. Dietary change was determined
225 by having subjects complete 3-day food records, including 2 weekdays and 1 weekend day. While self-report measures of dietary intake have limitations, 3-day food records are appropriate for measuring changes in group means (Stern, Grivetti, & Castonguay, 1984)
230 while limiting the subject burden associated with monitoring food intake. Subjects were given training in portion size estimation and were encouraged to record all food intake in as much detail as possible. All food diaries were documented for accuracy and complete-

235 ness. Analyses of the food diaries were done by trained coders at the General Clinical Research Center of the University of Vermont using the Food Intake Analysis System, Version 2.1, 1992 (USDA Human Nutrition Information Service, University of Texas Health Sci-
240 ence Center at Houston, TX). All diary analysis was done blinded to subjects' group assignment. Physical activity, as calories expended, was assessed using the Paffenbarger Physical Activity Questionnaire (Paffenbarger, Wing, & Hyde, 1978). The Paffenbarger has
245 shown good test-retest reliability and validity when compared to more objective measures of fitness and energy expenditure (Ainsworth, Leon, Richardson, Jacobs, & Paffenbarger, 1993).

Expectations. Because participants' expectations
250 for change may have been influenced by barriers imposed by the telecommunications technology, expectations for change were assessed both before and after participation in the program. Subjects rated the degree of change expected for 10 mental and physical func-
255 tioning items on a Likert scale ranging from 1 (*no change expected*) to 10 (*extreme improvement expected*). This scale was based on one used previously by King and colleagues (King, Barr-Taylor, & Haskell, 1993) to examine perceived change both during and
260 after an exercise program and has been shown to have adequate test-retest reliability and concurrent and discriminant validity (King, Barr-Taylor, Haskell, & De-Busk, 1989). The items were related specifically to subject expectations for weight loss, eating behavior,
265 well-being, health, appearance, and fitness changes.

Cost-effectiveness. Costs generated for the IT and ST groups were recorded. Costs consisted of postage, interactive television time, materials for the program, and expenses for the behavior therapist and site facili-
270 tators. Site facilitators were paid a set fee per session and for any travel expenses incurred driving to their interactive television site. The therapist time was calculated at an hourly rate based on the base salary of this individual. The total expense for each group was
275 then divided by the number of participants that started treatment in each condition. Additionally, program expenses were divided by the total number of pounds lost in each treatment condition to determine the cost-effectiveness of weight loss produced.
280 *Feasibility and acceptability.* In order to assess acceptability of the technology, subjects in the IT groups were asked to complete a 6-item questionnaire during the 3rd week of treatment that assessed their perceptions regarding the interactive television technology.
285 Participants responded to the following five questions on a 5-point scale (1 = *strongly disagree*, 5 = *strongly agree*): (a) I would prefer being in a non-IT group; (b) I would be more successful if I was not on interactive television; (c) I understand and can follow the class
290 leader over interactive television; (d) Our group would be more successful if we were not on interactive television; and (e) I feel I can communicate effectively over

interactive television. The sixth question asked subjects how satisfied they were with the interactive television system (5 = *very*, 1 = *not at all*). Also examined was attrition from the groups by treatment condition. Finally, to assess feasibility, recruitment numbers were carefully tracked to determine if individuals from rural communities at sites distant from the university were as interested and willing to participate in this type of program as those closer to the university.

Statistical Analysis

Analysis of variance (ANOVA) was used to examine the effect of treatment condition on change in body weight, percent of body weight lost, diet, exercise, and expectations for change. Baseline values were compared with *t* tests. Chi-squared analysis was used to assess differences in the categorical variables.

Results

Subject Characteristics

Characteristics of study participants at baseline are shown in Table 1 by treatment group. Subjects were on average about 45 years old, relatively well educated, almost exclusively white, and approximately three-fourths female. The only significant difference at baseline was in the percent of subjects that were married, with significantly more subjects in the IT groups being married. A majority of subjects had also participated previously in some organized weight-reduction program. Group sizes ranged from 11 in one of the smaller IT sites to 25 in one of the larger. IT group sizes were dictated by the number of seats available in each studio. ST groups ($n = 18$ and $n = 15$ for cohort one and two, respectively) were recruited to be approximately equivalent to the IT group sizes. Preliminary analysis was done comparing the IT groups with a live therapist ($n = 41$) to the distant IT sites ($n = 92$) and also comparing all IT sites ($n = 17, 22, 23, 19, 11, 25, 16$) to each other. There were no differences between groups for any dependent variables; thus, all IT groups were combined into one ($N = 133$) for all subsequent analyses.

Table 1
Baseline Characteristics of Study Participants by Condition

	IT	ST	*p*
N	133	33	
Age (years)[1]	45.8 ± 8.0	44.4 ± 6.6	.38
Non-college graduate (%)	53	39	.38
White (%)	97	100	.68
Married (%)	73	58	.03
Previous weight programs (%)	70	81	.12
Weight (kg)	97.7 ± 18.4	102.1 ± 18.7	.22
BMI (kg/m²)	34.5 ± 5.4	35.4 ± 5.7	.40
Gender (% female)	81	75	.33
Smoker (%)	7.5	9	.88

Note. P values are derived from analysis of variance of continuous values and chi-squared analysis for categorical variables.
[1] ± SD

Feasibility and Acceptability

Subject recruitment for the interactive television groups was limited by the number of seats available in each IT studio. The total number of seats available for IT groups was 168. Five hundred and fifty-eight individuals responded to recruitment ads, and 25% of those were from the geographic area closest to the university. Three hundred and forty-eight individuals were invited to orientation meetings (approximately twice the number of seats available), and, of those attending, 96% signed informed consent. Because the number of eligible, interested participants far exceeded the number we could treat, subjects were randomly chosen from the consented list for each site until the maximum number of IT participants was obtained. Only 79% of subjects ($N = 133$) selected to participate actually began treatment. There was no difference between the percent of selected subjects who began treatment in the IT (78%) versus the ST group (80%). A total of 133 individuals began treatment in an IT group. After treatment began, overall IT group attrition was 22%; this did not differ significantly from attrition in the ST group (18%, $p = .73$).

Subjects' rating of the interactive television technology is presented in Table 2. Overall, subjects' perceptions of the technology were positive, with the majority of participants reporting they would not necessarily prefer to be in a non-IT group (nor did they feel that they or their group would be any more successful if in a non-IT group). Subjects also reported agreeing with the statement, "I can understand and follow the class leader" (84.4%), although they were less likely to report agreeing with the statement, "I feel I can communicate effectively over IT" (47.8%). Finally, 85% of participants reported being very satisfied with the IT system.

Body Weight, Diet, and Exercise

Change in body weight was determined by assessing total weight loss in kilograms as well as percent of initial body weight lost after treatment. Subjects in both conditions lost a significant amount of weight during treatment ($p < .0001$); however, there were no significant differences between treatment conditions in either number of kilograms lost or percent of body weight lost (Table 3). Both ST and IT groups lost an average of 7.8 ± 5.1 and 8.0 ± 4.8% ($p = .85$) of baseline body weight. Similarly, subjects in both conditions experienced significant positive changes in eating and exercise behaviors, with calories decreasing by an average of 622 during treatment, percentage of calories from fat decreasing from 32.3 to 29.5, and calories expended in exercise increasing over the 12 weeks from 970 calories to 1,424 calories. There were no differences between conditions for either the nutrient intake or exer-

Table 2
Subject Rating of Interactive Television (N = 133)

	Strongly Disagree %	Disagree %	Undecided %	Agree %	Strongly Agree %
I would prefer being in a non-IT group.	22.5	35.2	22.5	16.9	2.8
I would be more successful if I were not on IT.	39.4	47.8	12.6	0	0
I can understand and follow the class leader over IT.	4.2	2.8	8.4	46.4	38.0
Our group would be more successful if we were not on IT.	25.3	32.3	32.3	7.0	2.8
I feel I can communicate effectively over IT.	11.2	21.1	19.7	29.5	18.3

cise values.

Expectations

Subjects' reported expectations for change are presented in Table 4. There were no significant differences between groups at baseline in any of the 10 expectations reported, nor were there differences by group in how those expectations changed during treatment.

Table 3
Change in Weight, Diet, and Exercise by Treatment Condition

	IT (n = 103)	ST (n = 27)	p value
Body weight (kg)			
Baseline[1]	97.7 ± 18.4	102.1 ± 18.7	
Week 12	89.9 ± 17.5	92.5 ± 17.9	
Change	−7.6 ± 4.1	−7.9 ± 5.4	.80
Calorie intake			
Baseline	1,959 ± 692	2,176 ± 794	
Week 12	1,386 ± 471	1,497 ± 417	
Change	−607 ± 632	−638 ± 521	.81
Fat intake (% of calories)			
Baseline	32.2 ± 6.3	32.3 ± 6.8	
Week 12	28.3 ± 7.3	29.1 ± 5.6	
Change	−3.4 ± 7.9	−2.1 ± 6.6	.42
Exercise (calories expended)			
Baseline	857 ± 1,174	1,083 ± 1,202	
Week 12	1,519 ± 1,301	1,358 ± 1,289	
Change	664.3 ± 1,346	244.5 ± 943	.13
% Baseline body weight lost	8.0 ± 4.8	7.8 ± 5.1	.85

[1] ± SD

Cost-effectiveness

Total program costs for IT and ST groups were calculated. The total cost for each group was then divided by the number of subjects who began treatment in that condition. The per-patient cost of running the IT groups ($34.71 per subject) was substantially higher than the ST groups ($24.65 per subject). The average price per pound of weight loss for the ST groups was $2.00. The average price per pound of weight loss for the IT groups was $2.56.

Table 4
Responses to "To What Extent Do You Believe You Will..." by Treatment Condition

	IT (n = 103)	ST (n = 27)
...lose weight?		
Baseline[1]	7.6 ± 1.8	7.7 ± 1.7
Week 12	.33 ± 2.1	.51 ± 2.9
...improve your appearance?		
Baseline	7.1 ± 2.1	7.6 ± 1.6
Week 12	.28 ± 2.4	.03 ± 2.3
...be less hungry?		
Baseline	6.1 ± 2.4	5.6 ± 2.5
Week 12	.76 ± 3.0	.37 ± 3.3
...be less tense or stressed?		
Baseline	6.1 ± 2.5	5.7 ± 2.6
Week 12	.42 ± 2.6	.85 ± 3.0
...be less anxious?		
Baseline	5.6 ± 2.5	5.7 ± 2.7
Week 12	.64 ± 2.6	.25 ± 2.6
...have more energy?		
Baseline	7.9 ± 1.6	8.1 ± 1.5
Week 12	.25 ± 2.0	.00 ± 1.9
...be happier?		
Baseline	7.1 ± 2.5	7.5 ± 2.2
Week 12	.34 ± 2.5	.03 ± 2.8
...be more physically fit?		
Baseline	8.0 ± 1.9	8.3 ± 1.5
Week 12	.08 ± 2.0	.11 ± 2.0
...be able to eat less?		
Baseline	7.3 ± 2.2	7.2 ± 2.0
Week 12	.01 ± 2.6	.66 ± 3.2
...be healthier?		
Baseline	8.3 ± 1.8	8.6 ± 1.2
Week 12	.15 ± 2.0	.04 ± 2.1

[1] ± SD

Discussion

This study found that a behavioral weight-control program conducted over interactive television technology was as effective for inducing weight loss as a standard behavior therapy intervention. Subjects in both conditions lost significant and comparable amounts of weight and both groups made significant and comparable positive changes in eating and exercise behaviors.

Additional objectives of this study were to determine if conducting a behavioral intervention via interactive television technology would be feasible and acceptable to participants. Based on recruitment statistics and subject ratings of the technology, we have every indication that the program was not only highly acceptable but highly desired as well. Simple recruitment efforts in different geographic locations throughout the state consistently yielded two to three times the number of eligible participants we could accommodate. Once they were introduced to the program by attending an orientation session, nearly all signed informed consent—an indication of their willingness to experience the interactive television technology. What is surprising is that nearly 21% of the subjects selected to participate in both IT and ST groups never attended even the first group meeting. The majority of these participants reported having work- or family-related commitments that took priority—even though they had been told at orientation meetings when the group meetings would be held. Perhaps the lack of intensive pre-assessment data and the message that not all subjects would be selected for participation led some individuals to consent to participate without being totally committed to following through.

After the program began, ratings of the interactive television technology were better than acceptable, with the majority of participants being very satisfied with the technology. This is most notable for the subjects who attended the IT group close to the university. Theirs was the only group that was randomly assigned to IT or ST conditions. In other words, even knowing they had had a chance at having a therapist to themselves did not change their perceptions of the interactive television technology.

Although the majority of subjects were satisfied with the technology, over 50% were not sure about, or were not satisfied with, their ability to communicate over interactive television. This did prove to be the most difficult feature of the technology. Subjects had to "wait their turn" to speak, speak into a microphone, and speak loudly enough to be heard above someone else who might simultaneously be trying to speak. Because the technology rating was completed during Week 3 of the intervention, it is possible that participants eventually "learned" how to communicate and became more comfortable with this aspect of the technology. Nevertheless, attrition after treatment began was similar between the two groups and was comparable to other behavioral weight-control programs (Wing,

1992), again suggesting that participants were not disproportionately unhappy with their treatment group.

One final indication that the technology was acceptable to participants was the assessment of expectations for change. Subjects had fairly high expectations for both physical and mental health changes at baseline, and these ratings did not differ by condition. This suggests that participants in the IT groups did not start treatment with any negative perceptions regarding their ability to succeed based on the technology. Additionally, for each of the 10 items, subjects in both conditions reported increasing their expectations for improvement after treatment. The degree of this change was not different for the IT versus ST groups. Both groups remained equally confident in their ability to see improvements in physical and mental-health parameters.

Weight losses during treatment were also similar to those reported in the literature for a 12-week behavioral intervention. Subjects lost on average .65 kg per week, consistent with current recommendations of .45–.90 kg per week (Dwyer, 1995) and similar to weight losses experienced in other behavioral interventions (Wadden, 1993; Wing, 1992). While the weight loss differences between the groups were very small, a post-hoc power analysis revealed that we may not have had a large enough sample size to detect significant differences, given the large variability in weight change. One additional study limitation was the lack of follow-up. There is, however, little reason to suspect that weight loss maintenance would be different for the two conditions. Despite these limitations, subjects in both groups lost a clinically significant amount of weight with no apparent differences between treatment conditions.

Although subjects appeared to be equally successful in both treatment groups, the cost-effectiveness analysis was somewhat disappointing. Presumably, an intensive behavioral intervention to so many more individuals via telecommunications technology would be less expensive than a standard intervention with one therapist and a group of 20 to 25 participants. This, however, was not the case. While there are a number of ways to calculate a cost-benefit analysis, the two ways chosen in this study—a per-subject cost and a per-pound cost—yielded the same results: The IT condition was more expensive. The per-subject cost of conducting the IT groups was $7 higher and the per-pound cost was approximately 50 cents more. The difference in cost between the two conditions is explained by the interactive television charge ($50 per hour—$35 per hour for one site and $50 per hour for multiple sites) and the salary and travel paid to the site facilitators. In fact, if the expense of the site facilitators is subtracted from the IT group costs, the two conditions would be comparable in cost: $23.45 per subject for the IT condition versus $24.65 per subject for the ST condition. Site facilitators added a human element to the distant IT sites. They weighed subjects each week, reviewed self-monitoring diaries, and served as the local contact person for IT group participants. While it is certainly theoretically possible to conduct a similar program without site facilitators, it would likely result in a much less supportive environment for group participants and might compromise their continued participation. However, similar research done with a television intervention (Meyers et al., 1996) suggests that subjects can do well on their own with little direct therapist support. While future research in this area should carefully consider efforts to try to improve the cost-effectiveness of the technology, it's important to consider what may have been the greatest benefit of all—the improved access to high-quality treatment for residents living in remote areas of the state. Travel costs and time savings were not calculated for the participants. However, for those who were within driving distance of the university and may have chosen to drive there for treatment, the availability of an IT group in their community was a huge benefit.

In summary, the results of this project have demonstrated that telecommunications technology can be used successfully to induce behavior change. Moreover, while the focus of this project was on determining the feasibility, acceptability, and effectiveness of using this medium for weight loss, there is every reason to believe it would be just as effective for facilitating weight maintenance as a standard intervention. Previous research has shown that continued support is predictive of better weight maintenance (Perri, Shapiro, Ludwig, Twentyman, & McAdoo, 1984). Thus, IT and other telecommunications technology could play an exciting role in the preservation of the client-therapist relationship. Therefore, our results have significant implications for a medium that has previously been used primarily to support clinical teaching, consultation, and teleconferencing. Over one-third of the U.S. population is overweight. While we have developed high-quality, medically appropriate, behaviorally focused obesity treatment interventions, they are not accessible or affordable for large segments of the population. The advent of telecommunications technology provides one possible solution. Future research should continue to focus on innovative applications of this technology to the problems of obesity treatment and prevention.

References

Agras, W. S., Taylor, C. B., Feldman, D. E., Losch, M., & Burnett, K. F. (1990). Developing computer-assisted therapy for the treatment of obesity. *Behavior Therapy; 21,* 99–109.

Ainsworth, B. E., Leon, A. S., Richardson, M T., Jacobs, D. R., & Paffenbarger, R. S. (1993). Accuracy of the College Alumnus Physical Activity Questionnaire. *Journal of Clinical Epidemiology, 46,* 1403–1411.

Alexander, J. L., & Peterson, L. (1972). Cardiovascular effects of weight reduction. *Circulation, 45,* 310–316.

Allen, A., & Hayes, J. (1994). Patient satisfaction with telemedicine in a rural clinic. *American Journal of Public Health, 84,* 1693.

Attwood, R., & Graham, P. (1993). Telemedicine answers the call. *Bulletin from the University of Kansas Medical Center, 43,* 20–25.

Bloom, B. L. (1988). *Health psychology: A psychosocial perspective.* Englewood Cliffs, NJ: Prentice-Hall.

Brownell, K. D. (1994). *The LEARN Program for Weight Control.* Dallas, TX: American Health Publishing Company.

Brownell, K. D., & Jeffery, R. W. (1987). Improving long-term weight loss: Pushing the limits of treatment. *Behavior Therapy, 18,* 353–374.

Brownell, K. D., & Wadden, T. A. (1986). Behavior therapy for obesity: Modern approaches and better results. In K. D. Brownell & J. P. Foreyt (Eds.), *Handbook of eating disorders: Physiology, psychology, and treatment of obesity, anorexia, and bulimia* (pp. 180–212). New York: Basic Books.

Chiang, B. N., Perlman, L. V., & Epstein, F. H. (1969). Overweight and hypertension: A review. *Circulation, 39,* 403–421.

Dwyer, J. (1995). Popular diets. In K. D. Brownell & C. Fairburn (Eds.), *Eating disorders and obesity* (pp. 491–497). New York: Guilford Press.

Ferster, C. B., Nurnberger, J. I., & Levitt, E. B. (1962). The control of eating. *Journal of Mathetics, 1,* 87–109.

Fitzgibbon, M. L., Stolley, M. R., & Kirschenbaum. D. S. (1993). Obese people who seek treatment have different characteristics than those who do not seek treatment. *Health Psychology, 12,* 342–345.

Flegal, K. M. (1996). Trends in body weight and overweight in the US population. *Nutrition Reviews, 54,* S97–S100.

Frankel, A. J., Birkimer, J. C., Brown, J. H., & Cunningham, G. K. (1983). A behavioral diet on network television. *Behavioral Counseling and Community Interventions, 3,* 91–101.

Hubble, J. P., Pahwa, R., Michalek, D. K., Thomas, C., & Koller, W. C. (1993). Interactive videoconferencing: A means of providing interim care to Parkinson's disease patients. *Movement Disorders, 8,* 380–382.

Jeffery, R. W., & Gerber, W. M. (1982). Group and correspondence treatment for weight reduction used in the multiple risk factor intervention trial. *Behavior Therapy, 13,* 24–30.

Jeffery, R. W., Wing, R. R., Thorsen, C., Burton, L. R., Harvey, J. R., & Mullen, M. (1993). Strengthening behavioral interventions for weight loss: A randomized trial for food provision and monetary incentives. *Journal of Consulting and Clinical Psychology, 61,* 1038–1045.

Kanders, B .S., & Blackburn, G. L. (1992). Reducing primary risk factors by therapeutic weight loss. In T. A. Wadden & T. B. VanItallie (Eds.), *Treatment of the seriously obese patient* (pp. 213–230). New York: Guilford Press.

King, A. C., Barr-Taylor, C., & Haskell, W. L. (1993). Effects of differing intensities and formats of 12 months of exercise training on psychological outcomes of older women. *Health Psychology, 12,* 292–300.

King, A. C., Taylor, C. B., Haskell, W. L., & DeBusk, R. F. (1989). Influence of regular aerobic exercise on psychological health: A randomized, controlled trial of healthy middle-aged adults. *Health Psychology, 8,* 305–324.

Kirschenbaum, D. S., & Fitzgibbon, M. L. (1995). Controversy about the treatment of obesity. Criticisms or challenges? *Behavior Therapy, 26,* 43–68.

McGee, R., & Tangalos, E. G. (1994). Delivery of health care to the underserved: Potential contributions of telecommunications technology. *Mayo Clinic Proceedings, 69,* 1131–1136.

Meyers, A. W., Graves, T. J., Whelan, J. P., & Barclay, D. R. (1996). An evaluation of a television delivered behavioral weight loss program: Are the ratings acceptable? *Journal of Consulting and Clinical Psychology, 64,* 172–178.

O'Neil, P. M., & Jarrell, M. P. (1992). Psychological aspects of obesity and dieting. In T. A. Wadden & T. B. VanItallie (Eds.), *Treatment of the seriously obese patient* (pp. 252–272). New York: Guilford Press.

Paffenbarger, R. S., Wing, A. L., & Hyde, R. T. (1978). Physical activity as an indicator of heart attack risk in college alumni. *American Journal of Epidemiology, 108,* 161–175.

Perri, M. G., Nezu, A. M., Patti, E. T., & McCann, K. L. (1989). Effect of length of treatment on weight loss. *Journal of Consulting and Clinical Psychology, 57,* 450–452.

Perri, M. G., Shapiro, R. M., Ludwig, W. W., Twentyman, C. T., & McAdoo, W. G. (1984). Maintenance strategies for the treatment of obesity: An evaluation of relapse prevention training and posttreatment contact by mail and telephone. *Journal of Consulting and Clinical Psychology, 52,* 404–413.

Stern, J. S., Grivetti, L., & Castonguay, T. W. (1984). Energy intake: Uses and misuses. *International Journal of Obesity, 8,* 535–541.

Stipps, A. J. (1995). Cost of obesity and related diseases. *Future, 132,* 167–171.

Thompson, P. D., Jeffery, R. W., Wing, R. R., & Wood, P. D. (1979). Unexpected decrease in plasma high density lipoprotein cholesterol with weight loss. *American Journal of Clinical Nutrition, 32,* 2016–2021.

Troster, A. I., Paolo, A. M., Glatt, S. L., Hubble, J. P., & Koller, W. C. (1995). "Interactive video conferencing" in the provision of neuropsychological services to rural areas. *Journal of Community Psychology, 23,* 85–88.

United States Department of Agriculture. (1995). *Dietary Guidelines for Americans* (4th ed.). Washington, DC: Department of Health and Human Services.

Volkmar, F. R., Stunkard, A. J., Woolston, J., & Bailey, R. (1981). High attrition rates in commercial weight reduction programs. *Archives of Internal Medicine, 141,* 426–428.

Wadden, T. W. (1993). Treatment of obesity by moderate and severe caloric restriction. *Annals of Internal Medicine, 119,* 688–693.

Wing, R. R. (1992). Behavioral treatment of severe obesity. *American Journal of Clinical Nutrition, 55,* 545S–551S.

Yates, B. T. (1978). Improving the cost-effectiveness of obesity programs: Three basic strategies for reducing the cost per pound. *International Journal of Obesity, 2*, 249–267.

Note: Supported by the General Clinical Research Center of Fletcher Allen Health Care (GCRC M01 RR109) and USDA Hatch funds (VT-97-516).

Acknowledgments: The author would like to thank Sara Burczy, Dianne Lamb, Sue Montague, and Marlene Thibault for being site facilitators and Rob Reiber for coordinating the technical aspects of Vermont Interactive Television. We all thank the volunteers for their commitment and participation.

Address correspondence to: Jean Harvey-Berino, Ph.D., RD, Associate Professor, University of Vermont, Department of Nutritional Sciences, Terrill Hall, Burlington, VT 05405-0148; E-mail: jharvey@zoo.uvm.edu

Exercise for Article 13

Factual Questions

1. How were subjects recruited?

2. Were the site facilitators trained behavior therapists?

3. What was the only baseline characteristic in Table 1 on which there was a significant difference between the two groups?

4. Were any of the differences in baseline expectations statistically significant?

5. The IT group had the lowest average at baseline on which expectation in Table 4? What is the value of the average?

6. Did the IT groups *or* the ST groups have a higher average price per pound of weight lost?

Questions for Discussion

7. The researcher states that *only* subjects recruited from the university site were randomly assigned to attend the IT or the ST programs. Would it have been desirable to do this for all subjects? Explain. (See lines 131–135.)

8. In the Table of Contents of this book, this study is classified as a "Quasi-Experiment." Is it? Explain.

9. The researcher states that "self-report measures of dietary intake have limitations." Speculate on what those limitations are. (See lines 225–228.)

10. The researcher states that "all diary analysis was done blinded to subjects' group assignment." Speculate on why the researcher did this.

11. The attrition rates in the two groups were similar. How important is this information? (See lines 347–350.)

12. The researcher states that a limitation of the study was a lack of follow-up. In your opinion, how serious is this limitation? (See lines 480–481.)

13. Do you agree with the last sentence in the research article? Explain. (See lines 553–556.)

Quality Ratings

Directions: Indicate your level of agreement with each of the following statements by circling a number from 5 for strongly agree (SA) to 1 for strongly disagree (SD). If you believe an item is not applicable to this research article, leave it blank. Be prepared to explain your ratings.

A. The introduction establishes the importance of the study.

SA   5   4   3   2   1   SD

B. The literature review establishes the context for the study.

SA   5   4   3   2   1   SD

C. The research purpose, question, or hypothesis is clearly stated.

SA   5   4   3   2   1   SD

D. The method of sampling is sound.

SA   5   4   3   2   1   SD

E. Relevant demographics (for example, age, gender, and ethnicity) are described.

SA   5   4   3   2   1   SD

F. Measurement procedures are adequate.

SA   5   4   3   2   1   SD

G. All procedures have been described in sufficient detail to permit a replication of the study.

SA   5   4   3   2   1   SD

H. The participants have been adequately protected from potential harm.

SA   5   4   3   2   1   SD

I. The results are clearly described.

SA   5   4   3   2   1   SD

J. The discussion/conclusion is appropriate.

SA   5   4   3   2   1   SD

K. Despite any flaws, the report is worthy of publication.

SA   5   4   3   2   1   SD

Article 14

Counselor Prompts to Increase Condom Taking During Treatment for Cocaine Dependence

KIMBERLY C. KIRBY
Temple University

DOUGLAS B. MARLOWE
Allegheny University of the Health Sciences

DANIELLE R. CARRIGAN
Allegheny University of the Health Sciences

JEROME J. PLATT
Allegheny University of the Health Sciences

ABSTRACT. This study examined whether active prompting would increase the number of free condoms taken from dispensers placed in counselors' offices in a cocaine abuse treatment clinic. Using a combined multiple baseline and reversal design, two teams of counselors were instructed to actively prompt and encourage condom taking during some conditions and to avoid commenting on or encouraging condom use in other conditions. To monitor accuracy of implementing the intervention, counselors completed a checklist for every subject they saw in their office during the day. Overall, the number of condoms taken per visit during prompting conditions was almost six times greater than during baseline conditions. However, implementation declined during the study, and all counselors complained about the intervention. Implications for dispensing free condoms to reduce HIV risk in drug abuse treatment clinics are discussed.

From *Behavior Modification*, 22, 29–44. Copyright © 1998 by Sage Publications, Inc. Reprinted with permission.

Drug abusers are a high-risk group for contracting HIV. Although most attention has been directed to intravenous drug users, who increase their risk of HIV infection by sharing needles, use of cocaine also has received attention as a possible correlate of increased risk (e.g., DeHovitz et al., 1994). Intravenous drug users (IVDUs) who are on methadone maintenance are more likely to engage in risky injection practices if they are also using cocaine compared to IVDUs who do not use cocaine. Those using cocaine are also more likely than noncocaine users to exchange sex for money or drugs and are less likely to report condom use (Grella, Anglin, & Wugalter, 1995). HIV infection is also increasing among noninjecting drug users (Des Jarlais et al., 1991). Of particular concern are crack cocaine users, who are more likely to engage in increased sexual activity, to trade sex for money or drugs, or to have sex with multiple partners (Balshem, Oxman, van Rooyen, & Girod, 1992; Hudgins, McCusker, & Stoddard, 1995; Weatherby et al., 1992). These individuals report insufficient condom use to reduce the risk of contracting a sexually transmitted disease or HIV (Edlin et al., 1992; Weatherby et al., 1992).

Although factors related to high risk behaviors are frequently studied, less research has focused on effective methods for reducing high risk behavior. Studies have examined preventive methods using HIV testing and education. It is generally known that proper use of condoms decreases the risk of contracting sexually transmitted diseases and HIV, but health care providers and educators do not necessarily know how to get high risk populations to obtain and use condoms. Watkins, Metzger, Woody, and McLellan (1993) found that knowledge that one is HIV-positive is an important determinant of condom use. In a survey of the attitudes, knowledge, and behavior related to HIV testing of adolescents and young adults in an alcohol and drug treatment facility, 60% reported that they would be more likely to use condoms if found to be HIV positive (Friedman, Strunin, & Hingson, 1993). Among sexually active adolescents in general, education appears to increase the likelihood of obtaining and reporting condom use (Hingson, Strunin, & Berlin, 1990; Rickert, Gottlieb, & Jay, 1992). However, McCusker, Stoddard, Zapka, and Lewis (1993) found that there was no effect on sexual risk behaviors of adult drug users in treatment who had received an informational or enhanced small-group educational intervention.

A promising area of study involves providing free condoms with or without an educational component. Provision of condoms has been studied in a variety of settings, including public health facilities (Glasser, Dennis, Orthoefer, Carter, & Hollander, 1989), bars (Honnen & Kleinke, 1990), and drug and alcohol treatment clinics (Amass, Bickel, Higgins, Budney, & Foerg, 1993; Calsyn, Meinecke, Saxon, & Stanton, 1992; Carrigan, Kirby, & Marlowe, 1995).

Through questionnaires, Glasser et al. (1989) found that free condoms offered at a family planning clinic of the public health department were positively evaluated by males who visited the clinic. Most of the males who completed the questionnaire reported using condoms during sex (although many did not use them regularly) and most returned to the clinic more than once. The authors suggested that counseling and communication might further increase the use of a condom with every sexual encounter.

Honnen and Kleinke (1990) placed a sign directly above the container of free condoms that gave statistics on AIDS deaths and informing bar patrons that condoms reduce the spread of AIDS. Other signs containing information on safe sex practices and indicating where to obtain free condoms were placed throughout the bar. The number of condoms taken by patrons increased by 47%.

In a similar study, Amass et al. (1993) examined the influence of poster prompts and distribution location on the number of free condoms taken in a drug abuse treatment clinic. Over a 6-month period, containers of free condoms were alternately placed in the clinic's private restroom and in a public waiting area, with and without posters that encouraged condom use. Although the presence of posters had no apparent effect on the number of condoms taken, nearly four times more condoms were taken from the private restroom than from the public waiting area. The investigators concluded that private dispenser locations increased condom taking. Calsyn et al. (1992) reported similar results in a study in which jars filled with condoms were placed throughout an outpatient drug abuse treatment clinic that did not previously offer free condoms. A questionnaire regarding sexual behavior and condom acquisition was administered to 103 men who attended the clinic just prior to and 4 months after the beginning of the study. Condoms were primarily taken from the men's restroom (47.8%), followed by the dispensary waiting room (26.6%), the group therapy room (11.3%), staff offices (10.1%), and the women's restroom (4.4%). Of all clients attending the clinic, 60% reported taking condoms, and at follow-up, there was a significant increase in reports of condom use during vaginal intercourse (from 20.3% to 33.7%).

To replicate the findings of Amass et al. (1993) and Calsyn et al. (1992) that private dispenser locations increase condom acquisition, Carrigan et al. (1995) compared the number of free condoms taken when the container was placed in a public day room or waiting area versus private counselors' offices. Participants were five times more likely to take free condoms from the public day room or waiting area than from a counselor's office (3.3 condoms taken per person daily from the day room versus 0.7 in the counselors' offices). Because it is common practice for free condoms to be placed in counselors' offices, the considerably lower rate of condom taking from this location may have important treatment implications. We speculated that the higher rate in the day area might have occurred because of approval or encouragement from clients' peers or that lack of explicit encouragement or comment from the counselors may have suppressed con-

dom taking from the counselors' offices. In the Carrigan et al. study, experimental control required that the counselors avoid actively prompting or encouraging the clients to take condoms from their office. In a usual treatment situation, counselors would be free to actively encourage safe sex practices.

In this study, we attempted to determine if an active counselor intervention could increase the number of free condoms taken from counselors' offices. Using a combination of multiple baseline and reversal designs, counselors were instructed to actively prompt and encourage condom taking during some conditions and to avoid commenting on or encouraging condom use in other conditions.

Method

Participants

The study was conducted at a university medical school-affiliated cocaine research and treatment clinic located in an inner-city setting and included all 88 clients who attended the clinic between October 10, 1994, and April 28, 1995. Research and treatment participants were predominantly unemployed (81%), Black (80%) males (80%) with a mean age of 34 years (range = 19 to 52) who were dependent on cocaine. Almost all of the participants primarily used crack cocaine (99%), and the remainder primarily used cocaine intranasally. All subjects were participants in a larger controlled clinical trial evaluating the benefit of adding adjunct services to a basic cognitive behavioral treatment for cocaine dependence. This treatment provided structured, individual, cognitive behavioral counseling; HIV education; relapse prevention; and a variety of skills training programs in outpatient and day treatment modalities.

Research Design

Four counselors were paired into two teams. Each team consisted of a senior counselor who had more than 2 years of experience at the treatment clinic and a junior counselor who had less than 1 year of experience at the clinic.

The study was conducted over a 29-week period. We employed a multiple baseline design across counselors with reversals. After 5 weeks of monitoring condom taking without any intervention, the first team of counselors was trained on the prompting intervention and began implementing it. The second team of counselors was trained 7 weeks later and began implementing the intervention. All four counselors implemented the intervention for 7 weeks, then a brief reversal was scheduled where all counselors stopped implementing the intervention for 3 weeks. At the end of 3 weeks, all four reinstated the intervention.

We employed two rules for changing study conditions. First, the last three data points of the condition had to show either (a) no clear directional trend or (b) a trend in the direction opposite of the anticipated change. Second, there had to be less than .5 standard deviation variability in the last three points. One violation of these rules occurred in error. The last three data points during the first counselor prompting intervention for Counseling Team 2 violated the second rule; however, overall, no clear trend was present in this condition.

General Procedure

Transparent cookie jars with lids were placed on each of the four counselors' desks in close proximity to where the client would sit during an individual counseling session. The cookie jars were filled with 50 individually wrapped, Lifestyles condoms. One additional condom was taped to the top of the lid on the cookie jar to indicate the contents of the jar. Condoms were replenished daily at clinic closing by research assistants. The maximum number of condoms that could be taken daily from all four offices was 200.

Baseline Conditions

During baseline conditions, condom jars were easily accessible to clients on the counselors' desks but counselors did not prompt or encourage clients to take the free condoms. If a client took condoms from the jar, the counselor made no comment about it and paid no special attention to the client during or afterwards. If a client asked about the condom jar, counselors simply stated, "Help yourself."

Prompting Intervention

Counselors were trained to implement the prompting intervention on the Friday afternoon before the week that they were scheduled to begin implementing it. They were instructed to spend a few minutes discussing the importance of using condoms and telling clients that they would approve if they took the free condoms in the jar. We encouraged them to be supportive and to avoid giving an AIDS education speech or pregnancy speech. They were provided with the following example:

I just would like to let you know that I am concerned for your well being, because people who have used cocaine are at higher risk for HIV infection. We strongly promote the use of condoms at this clinic because this is an effective way for you to reduce your risk. Sometimes people feel uncomfortable taking condoms in front of their counselor but I want you to know that I will be pleased if you take condoms with you, even if it's at every session. In fact, I will encourage you to take care of yourself this way. Please take some.

Counselors were also instructed that on subsequent sessions during the experimental period, just prior to the client leaving the session, they should lift the lid to the condom cookie jar and tell the client to take some condoms. We emphasized that they should make a statement and not merely a suggestion (e.g., "Take some," not "Would you like some?"). The following examples were provided:

Take a few condoms with you.
Grab a handful.
Take some for the road.
Don't leave home without them, take a few.
I want you to be safe, take these with you.

Dependent Variable Monitoring

Condoms were counted daily at clinic closing by research assistants. Accuracy of the condom count was verified by a recount approximately 90% of the time. Subject traffic also was monitored daily by written counselor report. The main dependent measure for the study (average number of condoms taken per client visit) was calculated by dividing the total number of condoms taken by the number of clients visiting the counselor offices.

Intervention Accuracy Monitoring

To assess the implementation accuracy of the prompting intervention, once counselors were trained on the intervention, they were given a checklist to fill out for each subject that they saw in their office during the day. If counselors failed to give the intervention, they were instructed to note this on the checklist. We emphasized that there would be no negative consequences for forgetting to implement the intervention and that filling out the checklists accurately was critical. The checklist asked four questions to verify that the intervention was done correctly: (a) Is this your first session with this client in the intervention period? (If no, jump to Question c); (b) Just prior to ending the session, did you discuss the importance of using condoms and encourage condom taking? (c) Did you lift the lid off the cookie jar and tell the client to take some before she or he left the session? (d) Briefly indicate what you said to the client.

Results

Intervention Accuracy

To determine if counselors were filling out intervention checklists for every client they saw, we compared the number of checklists completed to the number of clients seen. This verified that counselors completed checklists on 93% of the client visits during the intervention.

Table 1 shows the percentage of client visits for which counselors reported having accurately implemented the prompting intervention. Because no counselors had been trained on the intervention, intervention accuracy was not monitored during Weeks 1 through 5. During Weeks 6 through 12, when first implementing the intervention, Counseling Team 1 reported correctly prompting clients to take condoms during 80% of the client sessions. Again, because Counseling Team 2 had not been trained on the intervention, accuracy was not monitored during this time.

During this condition and on all occasions throughout the study, when the intervention was not accurately implemented, it was primarily because the counselors did not implement the intervention at all. Counselors usually indicated that they forgot to implement the intervention, but on 12 (3%) of the 388 opportunities reported during the study, the counselor chose not to implement the intervention because it seemed inappropriate given the content of the counseling session (e.g., the client was suicidal, agitated, or depressed).

Table 1
Percentage of Opportunities Prompting Intervention Implemented

Condition	Weeks	Counseling Team 1	Counseling Team 2
Counseling Team 1 only	6–12	80	NA
Counseling Team 1 and 2	13–19	77	70
Baseline	20–22	7	5
Counseling Team 1 and 2	23–28	86	54

During Weeks 13 through 19, when beginning to implement the intervention, Counseling Team 2 reported moderate accuracy, correctly prompting clients to take condoms during 70% of client sessions. During this period, Counseling Team 1 continued to implement the intervention with 77% accuracy.

In the next condition, Weeks 20 through 23, a return to baseline was scheduled and both counseling teams were instructed to stop conducting the prompting intervention. Table 1 shows that the counseling intervention was implemented on only 7% and 5% of the occasions by Counseling Teams 1 and 2, respectively. One counselor on each team mistakenly implemented the intervention with the first client seen after the condition change was scheduled. After this, all counselors stopped prompting for the remainder of the condition.

Finally, during the last experimental condition (Weeks 23 through 28), all counselors were instructed to begin implementing the intervention again. Counseling Team 1 successfully reintroduced the intervention, prompting clients to take condoms on 86% of the opportunities; however, Counseling Team 2 prompted on only 54% of the opportunities during this condition. This reduction in intervention accuracy for Counseling Team 2 was detected and all counselors were again instructed on the proper intervention and reminded to implement it consistently at the end of Week 26 of the study. Prior to reminding the counselors to conduct the prompting intervention (Weeks 23 through 26), Counseling Team 1 averaged 83% accuracy, whereas Counseling Team 2 averaged only 45% accuracy. After reminding them, accuracy increased for both teams to 94% and 72%, respectively.

Condom Taking

During the initial 5-week baseline, clients took very few condoms. Figure 1 shows that the average number of condoms taken from the offices of Counseling Team 1 ranged from 0 to .88 condoms per person, averaging

.34 (± .33) condoms taken per person weekly. The average number taken from the offices of Counseling Team 2 was slightly lower, ranging from 0 to .90 condoms per person and averaging .25 (± .38) condoms taken per client visit.

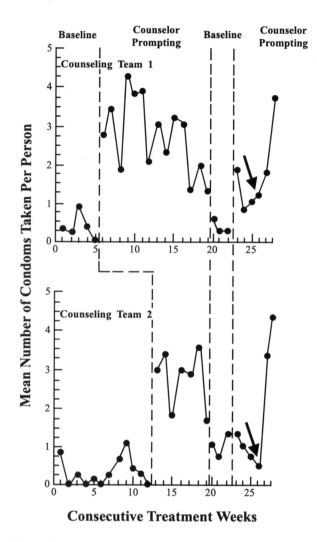

Figure 1. Mean rate of condom taking from dispensers placed in counselors' offices during baseline and counselor prompting conditions. The arrow indicates when counselors were reminded to implement the prompting intervention consistently.

During Week 6, when Counseling Team 1 began prompting and encouraging condom taking, the average number of condoms taken per person dramatically increased to 2.73 condoms per person. In contrast, no condoms were taken from the offices of Counseling Team 2 (who had not yet been trained in the prompting intervention). Over the full 7 weeks of this condition, the number of condoms taken from the offices of Counseling Team 1 ranged from 1.88 to 3.90 per person, averaging 3.17 (± .95) condoms taken per client visit. In contrast, the number of condoms taken from the offices of Counseling Team 2 ranged from 0 to 1.07

per person, averaging .31 (± .37) condoms taken per client visit.

During Week 13, Counseling Team 2 began implementing the prompting intervention. As Figure 1 shows, there was an immediate increase in condom taking, with an average of 3.04 condoms taken from Counseling Team 2 offices during this week. Over the full 7 weeks of this condition, the number of condoms taken from Counseling Team 2 offices ranged from 1.71 to 3.55 per person, averaging 2.78 (± .74) condoms taken per client visit. The number of condoms taken from Counseling Team 1 offices decreased slightly to 2.33 (± .85) during the second 7 weeks of their prompting intervention but still remained well above the original baseline. Over the entire 14 weeks during which Counseling Team 1 conducted the prompting intervention, 2.75 (± .97) condoms were taken on average per client visit.

Beginning at Week 20, all counselors were instructed to stop prompting and encouraging condom taking. During this 3-week baseline condition, there was a complete reversal in condom taking for Counseling Team 1. Their clients averaged only .36 (± .19) condoms taken per client visit—a number virtually identical to that of the original baseline. The number of condoms taken for Counseling Team 2 also declined considerably to 1.09 (± .27); however, this level is slightly higher than the original baseline average (.31 ± .37) and therefore does not represent a complete return to baseline.

In the final condition, when counselors reinstated prompting and encouragement, the average number of condoms taken per client visit for Counseling Team 1 increased modestly to levels similar to those seen during the last few weeks of the previous prompting intervention (i.e., Weeks 17–19). Generally, Team 1 clients averaged .97 to 1.83 condoms taken per client visit until the last week of the intervention. During the last week of the study, there was an increase in condoms taken and Counseling Team 1 clients averaged 3.93 condoms per client visit, for a condition average of 1.75 (± 1.02). Counseling Team 2 clients initially showed no increase in average number of condoms taken. For the first 4 weeks of this condition, the average number of condoms taken per client visit ranged from .57 to 1.32. This period corresponds to the report of low intervention accuracy for Counseling Team 2 (prompting on only 54% of the opportunities). Once retraining occurred and Counseling Team 2 increased prompting to 72% of the opportunities, an increase in condom taking emerged, with 3.37 and 4.40 condoms taken per client visit, respectively. For the entire condition, Counseling Team 2 clients averaged 1.66 (± 1.61) condoms taken per client visit.

Over the entire 28-week period, clients took an average of .43 condoms per visit during baseline conditions, compared to an average of 2.45 condoms per visit during counselor prompting conditions. The difference in condom taking between baseline and prompting conditions was statistically significant, $t(55) = 7.53, p < .001$.

Discussion

This study demonstrates that having counselors prompt and encourage condom taking can increase the number of condoms taken from free dispensers placed in their offices. Overall, the programmed multiple baselines and reversals appeared to show good experimental control and effectiveness of the counselor prompting intervention until the final condition when reinstatement of the intervention did not result in a clear increase in condom taking. This reduction in the efficacy of the intervention corresponded to the deterioration in the counselors' accuracy of implementing the intervention. Once counselors were reminded to implement the intervention consistently, accuracy of implementing the intervention increased and, correspondingly, the number of condoms taken per client visit increased.

Over the entire 28-week period, clients took an average of .43 condoms per visit during baseline conditions, compared to an average of 2.45 condoms per visit during counselor prompting conditions. This represents nearly a sixfold increase, which is similar to the magnitude of increase that we noted in our previous study (Carrigan et al., 1995). In that study, we had placed condom dispensers either in the counselors' offices or in a day room. Counselors did not prompt condom taking in either setting. Clients were five times more likely to take condoms from the day room (3.3 condoms taken per person daily) than from the counselors' offices (0.7 condoms taken per person daily). These results, combined with those of the present study, suggest that cocaine treatment programs that dispense free condoms from counselors' offices may increase the number of condoms taken by either having counselors prompt condom taking or by moving the condom dispenser to a day room or waiting area.

Although the counselor prompting intervention was as effective in increasing the number of condoms taken as was placing the dispenser in the day room or waiting area, our experience in implementing the counselor prompting intervention suggests to us that it is not as practical as other alternatives. Deterioration in the accuracy of intervention implementation was accompanied by complaints from counselors that they did not like the intervention. They complained that it was disruptive to their interactions with clients and that clients began refusing to take condoms. These complaints emerged slowly, only after counselors had implemented the prompting intervention for about 7 weeks or more. Because similar levels of condom taking can be produced by placing the condom dispenser in a day room (Carrigan et al., 1995) or private restroom (Amass et al., 1993), it would seem that placing condom dispensers in strategic places is a simpler intervention than relying on counselors to prompt condom taking.

One limitation of this study is that we measured only condom taking. Although some research suggests that drug abuse patients who take condoms report using them (Calsyn et al., 1992), future research should consider including measures to verify condom use. Although similar research with non-drug-abusing populations has polled clients' spouses or partners to verify self-reports, among crack cocaine abusing populations, these measures are likely to be limited to self-reports by the clients. Because behaviors that put these users at higher risk for HIV infection include exchanging sex for money or drugs and sex with multiple partners, verification of condom use with an identified spouse or partner would not capture the range of relevant high risk behaviors. Verification by multiple partners is very difficult because clients are understandably reluctant to cooperate, and in many cases they are not able to provide enough information to allow location of sexual contacts.

Despite our conclusion that the counselor prompting intervention is not the ideal method for increasing condom taking from a drug treatment clinic, we believe that this study makes some important points. First, it confirms the argument that if counselors prompt and encourage clients to take condoms from dispensers placed in their office, they can increase condom taking by their clients. For counselors who are comfortable implementing this intervention, dispensing free condoms from their offices is a viable option. However, because all four counselors in our clinic found the intervention aversive and did not maintain it reliably without close monitoring by their supervisor, it seems prudent to suggest that clinic directors be wary about relying on counselors to dispense condoms from this location. Instead, we advise clinics to explore several locations for dispensing condoms and to stay with the locations in their clinic that appear to produce the highest rates of condom taking.

References

Amass, L., Bickel, W. K., Higgins, S. T., Budney, A. J., & Foerg, F. E. (1993). The taking of free condoms in a drug abuse treatment clinic: The effects of location and posters. *American Journal of Public Health, 83,* 1466–1468.

Balshem, M., Oxman, G., van Rooyen, D., & Girod, K. (1992). Syphilis, sex and crack cocaine: Images of risk and morality. *Social Science and Medicine, 35*(2), 147–160.

Calsyn, D. A., Meinecke, C., Saxon, A. J., & Stanton, V. (1992). Risk reduction in sexual behavior: A condom giveaway program in a drug abuse treatment clinic. *American Journal of Public Health, 82*(11), 1536–1538.

Carrigan, D. R., Kirby, K. C., & Marlowe, D. B. (1995). Effect of dispenser location on taking free condoms in an outpatient cocaine abuse treatment clinic. *Journal of Applied Behavior Analysis, 28,* 465–466.

DeHovitz, J. A., Kelly, P., Feldman, J., Sierra, M. F., Clarke, L., Bromberg, J., Wan, J. Y., Vermund, S. H., & Landesman, S. (1994). Sexually transmitted diseases, sexual behavior, and cocaine use in inner-city women. *American Journal of Epidemiology, 140,* 1125–1134.

Des Jarlais, D. C., Abdul-Quader, A., Minkoff, H., Hoegsberg, B., Landesman, S., & Tross, S. (1991). Crack use and multiple AIDS risk behaviors. *Journal of Acquired Immune Deficiency Syndrome, 4,* 446–447.

Edlin, B. R., Irwin, K. L., Ludwig, D. D., McCoy, H. V., Serrano, Y., Word, C., Bowser, B. P., Faruque, S., McCoy, C. B., Shilling. R. F., & Holmberg, S. D. (1992). High-risk sex behavior among young street-recruited crack co-

caine smokers in three American cities: An interim report. *Journal of Psychoactive Drugs, 24*(4), 363–371.

Friedman, L. S., Strunin, L., & Hingson, R. (1993). A survey of attitudes, knowledge, and behavior related to HIV testing of adolescents and young adults enrolled in alcohol and drug treatment. *Journal of Adolescent Health, 14,* 442–445.

Glasser, M., Dennis, J., Orthoefer, J., Carter, S., & Hollander, E. (1989). Characteristics of males at a public health department contraceptive service. *Journal of Adolescent Health Care, 10,* 115–118.

Grella, C. E., Anglin, M. D., & Wugalter, S. E. (1995). Cocaine and crack use and HIV risk behaviors among high-risk methadone maintenance clients. *Drug and Alcohol Dependence, 37,* 15–21.

Hingson, R., Strunin, L., & Berlin, B. (1990). Acquired immunodeficiency syndrome transmission: Changes in knowledge and behaviors among teenagers, Massachusetts Statewide Survey, 1986 to 1988. *Pediatrics, 85,* 24–29.

Honnen, T. A., & Kleinke, C. L. (1990). Prompting bar patrons with signs to take free condoms. *Journal of Applied Behavior Analysis, 23,* 215–217.

Hudgins, R., McCusker, J., & Stoddard, A. (1995). Cocaine use and risky injection and sexual behaviors. *Drug and Alcohol Dependence, 37,* 7–14.

McCusker, J., Stoddard, A. M., Zapka, J. G., & Lewis, B. F. (1993). Behavioral outcomes of AIDS educational interventions for drug users in short-term treatment. *American Journal of Public Health, 83*(10), 1463–1466.

Rickert, V. I., Gottlieb, A. A., & Jay, M. S. (1992). Is AIDS education related to condom acquisition? *Clinical Pediatrics, 31*(4), 205–210.

Watkins, K. E., Metzger, D., Woody, G., & McLellan, A. T. (1993). Determinants of condom use among intravenous drug users. *AIDS, 7,* 719–723.

Weatherby, N. L., Shultz, J. M., Chitwood, D. D., McCoy, H. V., McCoy, C. B., Ludwig, D. D., & Edlin, B. R. (1992). Crack cocaine and sexual activity in Miami, Florida. *Journal of Psychoactive Drugs, 24*(4), 373–380.

About the authors: Kimberly C. Kirby, Ph.D., is an associate professor of psychological studies at Temple University. Her research addresses pharmacological and behavioral aspects of drug addiction and focuses on development and evaluation of behavioral treatments for heroin and cocaine addiction. She has published numerous journal articles, abstracts, and book chapters in behavior analysis and substance abuse. Recently, she has begun investigating the effects of drug abuse on families.

Douglas B. Marlowe, J.D., Ph.D., is an assistant professor of psychiatry and public health at Allegheny University of the Health Sciences. His research addresses psychiatric comorbidity and other behavioral aspects of drug addiction. Recently, he began investigating coercion in drug abuse treatment and the social policy and legal implications of coerced psychological care in general. He has published numerous articles, abstracts, and book chapters in both psychological and legal journals.

Danielle R. Carrigan, B.A., received her bachelors degree in psychology from Rutgers University in 1990. She was a research assistant with Allegheny University of the Health Sciences, Division of Addiction Research and Treatment. She has previously published research and presented data at professional meetings.

Jerome J. Platt, Ph.D., is a professor of psychiatry and the director of the Division of Addiction Research and Treatment at Allegheny University of the Health Sciences. His major areas of interest are drug abuse treatment program development, treatment evaluation research, and social skills training for substance abusers. He has published numerous articles, abstracts, and papers and has authored or edited 12 books. He recently received funding from the Office of National Drug Control Policy to examine drug abuse treatments for adolescent offenders.

Authors' note: We thank Randy Alexander, Lynda Bonieski, Shelley Braunstein, and Shelley Evans for their assistance in conducting this study.

Address correspondence to: Dr. Kimberly C. Kirby, Counseling Psychology Program, Temple University, Weiss Hall (265-63), 1701 N. 13th St., Philadelphia, PA 19122-6085.

Exercise for Article 14

Factual Questions

1. The reversal in which all counselors stopped implementing the intervention lasted for how many weeks?

2. Did counselors encourage clients to take free condoms during the baseline condition?

3. What was the "main dependent measure?"

4. The checklist was used to assess what?

5. What was the main reason counselors gave for failing to implement the intervention?

6. Over the entire period, clients took an average of .43 condoms per visit during baseline conditions. What was the average per visit during counselor prompting conditions?

7. What test was used to determine the significance of the difference between the two averages referred to in question 6?

Questions for Discussion

8. The researchers used a "multiple baseline," with one team starting to prompt at week 5 while the other team did not start until week 12. (See Figure 1 and lines 160–166.) Speculate on why they used two baselines instead of having all counselors begin to prompt on the same date.

9. If you had planned this study, would you have planned to check whether the counselors were actually prompting the clients (as was done in this study) or would you have merely assumed that the counselors would comply with the directions to prompt? Explain.

10. Are you surprised that the counselors did not like the intervention and complained about it? Explain. (See lines 442–450.)

11. Beginning in line 457, the authors discuss a limitation of their study. In your opinion, how important is this limitation? Explain.

12. If you were to conduct a similar study, what changes in the research methodology, if any, would you make?

13. To what population(s), if any, would you be willing to generalize the results of this study (i.e., with what other groups would you expect the results of this study to apply)?

Quality Ratings

Directions: Indicate your level of agreement with each of the following statements by circling a number from 5 for strongly agree (SA) to 1 for strongly disagree (SD). If you believe an item is not applicable to this research article, leave it blank. Be prepared to explain your ratings.

A. The introduction establishes the importance of the study.

SA   5   4   3   2   1   SD

B. The literature review establishes the context for the study.

SA   5   4   3   2   1   SD

C. The research purpose, question, or hypothesis is clearly stated.

SA   5   4   3   2   1   SD

D. The method of sampling is sound.

SA   5   4   3   2   1   SD

E. Relevant demographics (for example, age, gender, and ethnicity) are described.

SA   5   4   3   2   1   SD

F. Measurement procedures are adequate.

SA   5   4   3   2   1   SD

G. All procedures have been described in sufficient detail to permit a replication of the study.

SA   5   4   3   2   1   SD

H. The participants have been adequately protected from potential harm.

SA   5   4   3   2   1   SD

I. The results are clearly described.

SA   5   4   3   2   1   SD

J. The discussion/conclusion is appropriate.

SA   5   4   3   2   1   SD

K. Despite any flaws, the report is worthy of publication.

SA   5   4   3   2   1   SD

Article 15

Successful Interdisciplinary Intervention with an Initially Treatment-Resistant Social Phobic

LOUIS B. LAGUNA
University of Nebraska-Lincoln

E. CHARLES HEALEY
University of Nebraska-Lincoln

DEBRA A. HOPE
University of Nebraska-Lincoln

ABSTRACT. Despite very successful treatments for social phobia, with many studies reporting as many as 75% of social phobics making clinically significant gains with 3 months of treatment or less, some social phobics fail to respond to treatment. This case presents a woman with social phobia who received several trials of treatment for severe public-speaking fears but failed to improve, as demonstrated by persistent reports of fear and avoidance equal to those before treatment. With the assistance of a speech language pathologist, this client received combined therapy that included cognitive-behavioral therapy to treat her public-speaking fear and avoidance and voice therapy to treat excessive muscle contractions in the respiratory and phonatory systems. Overall, the combined treatment was successful, with the client's self-reported levels of fear and avoidance of public speaking decreasing dramatically. Specific improvements during voice therapy and implications for the treatment of social phobia are also discussed.

From *Behavior Modification*, 22, 358–371. Copyright © 1998 by Sage Publications, Inc. Reprinted with permission.

Although once termed the *neglected anxiety disorder* (Liebowitz, Gorman, Fyer, & Klein, 1985), social phobia has received considerable attention from researchers in the last decade. A substantial portion of that research effort has addressed the development and evaluation of both psychosocial and pharmacological interventions (see Heimberg & Juster, 1995, and Potts & Davidson, 1995, for their respective reviews). It appears that social phobia is quite treatable, with many studies reporting as many as 75% of social phobics making clinically significant gains with 3 months of treatment or less. In fact, this success suggests that it is time to more closely examine the individuals with social phobia who fail to progress in the standard treatments and to begin to develop interventions that may be more effective for this subgroup.

Fear of negative evaluation by others is the hallmark of social phobia (*DSM-IV;* American Psychiatric Association, 1994), and many social phobics are particularly fearful that signs of their anxiety (e.g., voice or hand tremors, blushing) will be visible to others (McEwan & Devins, 1983; Warner, Hope, & Herbert, 1995). In typical cognitive-behavioral interventions for social phobia, fear of others seeing one's anxiety symptoms is addressed both directly and indirectly. For example, the fear may be addressed directly through cognitive restructuring based on a series of questions:

- Do you know for certain the symptom is visible to others?
- If the symptom is visible, will others necessarily draw a negative conclusion about you?
- Even if the symptom is visible and others evaluate you negatively because of it, how bad is that?

As an alternate approach, the fear of a visible anxiety symptom may be addressed only indirectly on the assumption that reduction of anxiety will make it less likely that the symptom occurs and, consequently, less likely that the fear of the visible symptom will be evoked. However, as will be seen in the case presented below, some social phobics fail to respond to these types of interventions and continue to be excessively concerned about a particular anxiety symptom. In such cases, it may be appropriate to attempt to directly relieve the symptom.

Recent advances in computer technology have presented sophisticated methods for treating voice disorders (Boone & McFarlane, 1988). For voice disorders that involve excessive muscle contraction in the respiratory and phonatory systems, a problem often exacerbated by extreme anxiety, combined management by a psychologist and a speech-language pathologist may be indicated. In one recent study (Sime & Healey, 1993), remediation of a voice disorder involving phonatory systems was attributed to collaborative treatment by a voice specialist and a counseling psychologist using a combination of voice therapy, cognitive-behavioral therapy, and biofeedback training.

The case below presents a woman with social phobia who received several trials of treatment for severe public-speaking fears but who failed to improve. After completing a group-treatment program, she reported levels of fear and avoidance equal to those before treatment. The client reported embarrassment about her voice quality when she was speaking to an audience. As the client became anxious, the combination of vocal tremors, dysphonia, and occasional spasmodic closure of her vocal folds caused noticeable impairment in her voice fluency, resulting in anxious preoccupation and subsequent avoidance of public-speaking situations.

Method

Participant

70 The participant was a 51-year-old White woman who first sought treatment in response to public-service announcements about free treatment for social phobia in exchange for participation in psychopathology re-search. She was interviewed using the Anxiety Disor-
75 ders Interview Schedule-Revised (ADIS-R) (DiNardo & Barlow, 1988) and met *DSM-III-R* criteria for social phobia, generalized type. (A post hoc review of her case indicates that she would meet the same diagnosis under *DSM-IV* criteria.) The social phobia was judged
80 to be very severe based on a rating of 7 on the 0 to 8 clinician's severity rating included in the ADIS-R. The participant also met criteria for a secondary diagnosis of posttraumatic stress disorder (in partial remission).

The client reported a physically and psychologi-
85 cally abusive childhood and a long history of psycho-logical distress. She appeared to have made significant progress in various psychotherapies as well as antide-pressant and anxiolytic medication trials over two dec-ades. At the time of the initial psychological assess-
90 ment, she was generally functioning as well as she had during her adult life. She indicated that social phobia was her primary concern because it prevented her from completing her graduate degree and interfered with her ability to speak in public, which was part of her free-
95 lance occupation. Her primary goal in treatment was to reduce her fear of speaking in front of people.

Assessment Measures

As part of the research-assessment battery, the cli-ent completed the Social Phobia and Anxiety Inventory (SPAI) (Turner, Beidel, Dancu, & Stanley, 1989). The
100 SPAI uses a Likert-scale (1–7) format that includes 45 items, 32 comprising a Social-Phobia subscale and 13 comprising an Agoraphobia subscale. Turner et al. rec-ommend using a difference score (Social-Phobia sub-scale score minus the Agoraphobia subscale score)
105 when assessing social phobia. Although there is no proposed cutoff score to identify presence or absence of social phobia, previous research (Beidel, Turner, & Cooley, 1993) found a mean SPAI difference score of 103.3 ($SD = 28.08$) for social phobics.
110 With the assistance of a cognitive-behavioral clini-cian, the client developed a fear and avoidance hierar-chy that included 10 interpersonal situations rank or-dered in terms of anxiety-evoking potential. The 10 situations were rated on 0 to 100 scales for both fear
115 and behavioral avoidance, with higher numbers indi-cating greater distress or avoidance. Traditionally, cli-ents do not tend to report 10 distinct functionally unre-lated situations; rather, they report variations on two or three situations (Hope, 1993). Thus, the client's most
120 severe fear, formal speaking in front of several people, was used to index her progress, and only fear and

avoidance ratings from that situation will be reported here.

Voice assessment. A voice evaluation was per-
125 formed by the second author, a speech-language pa-thologist and professor who specializes in the evalua-tion and treatment of voice disorders at the University of Nebraska at Lincoln. During the initial evaluation, the client was perceived to have a slight degree of vo-
130 cal tremor, tense phonations, and breathiness, which resulted in reduced vocal intensity. Muscle tension was present by direct observation and palpation. The vocal symptoms occurred consistently throughout the evaluation during conversation and oral reading. The
135 client was diagnosed as having a muscle tension dys-phonia (MTD).

MTD is a common clinical voice syndrome among voice-disordered individuals. Most MTD clients have problems coping with stress. Vocal symptoms of MTD
140 clients include excessive laryngeal tension and insuffi-cient control of the breathstream for phonation. The client stated that she felt a great deal of muscle tension in her face and neck area. She also reported that talking about her voice problem seemed to make the facial and
145 neck tension worse. The client reported having an oc-casional choking feeling (an indirect evidence of ex-treme laryngeal tension) during the evaluation. Toward the end of the evaluation session, the client indicated that the focus and discussion of her speaking difficul-
150 ties brought about the same levels of muscle tension and voicing problems that she experienced on a daily basis.

Psychological Interventions

Cognitive-behavioral group therapy. The client participated in 12 weeks of cognitive-behavioral group
155 therapy (CBGT) for social phobia that included cogni-tive restructuring, in-session exposure to feared situa-tions, and homework for *in vivo* exposure (Heimberg, 1991; Hope, 1993). Consistent with CBGT protocol (Heimberg, 1991), the client's CBGT group included
160 six other clients and two experienced therapists (the third author and an advanced doctoral student). The first two sessions of CBGT consist of establishing the group rules, orienting group members to the rationale behind the intervention, and initial training in cognitive
165 restructuring (e.g., identification, analysis, and dispu-tation of irrational/dysfunctional thoughts). Behavioral exposure to feared situations begins in Session 3 of CBGT. Exposures involve role playing of feared situa-tions in the context of the group, using therapists and
170 other group members as role-play partners. Role plays proceed in a graduated fashion, with progressively more anxiety-provoking situations enacted as the group progresses from Session 3 to 12. Cognitive restructur-ing is integrated around role-played exposure. Early in
175 treatment, homework assignments focus on cognitive-restructuring skills. Later assignments require group members to enter previously feared or avoided situa-

tions in their daily lives while using cognitive skills to help cope with their anxiety.

180   The client attended all 12 weeks of CBGT and completed homework as requested. By the end of the intervention, she completed five in-session exposures ranging from talking about herself to the group while seated to formal presentations similar to the ones that
185   she avoided in graduate school. However, as noted below, the client failed to progress with her treatment goals in CBGT, so she was referred to the in-house clinic for further treatment.

Nondirective psychotherapy. Following CBGT, the
190   client attended 22 sessions of nondirective individual psychotherapy (10 sessions with the doctoral student who had served as one of her CBGT therapists, then 12 sessions with the first author). Although both therapists occasionally referred back to some of the cognitive-
195   restructuring skills gained in the group, most sessions consisted primarily of supportive psychotherapy regarding a range of topics (e.g., issues related to family of origin and spouse).

Individual cognitive-behavioral therapy (CBT).
200   After approximately 22 sessions of nondirective psychotherapy, the client indicated that she would like to begin focusing on her public-speaking fears, as she believed that unless she would be able to present her master's research to a large audience—a requirement
205   of her program—she would be unable to complete her degree. During the next 8 weeks, the client received CBT closely based on CBGT with the first author and supervised by the third author. The client completed six exposures involving public-speaking scenarios. Three
210   of these exposures involved an audience of at least eight people.

Although the client reported slight reductions in her anxiety during in-session exposures, it was readily apparent to both her and the therapist that individual CBT
215   was no more effective than CBGT had been, despite the highly intensive treatment. She consistently reported that her main concern when addressing an audience was that her voice would shake while she spoke and that she would not be able to breathe properly. She
220   felt convinced that the audience would observe these symptoms and notice that she was "ready to fall apart." Because the client's symptoms actually were noticeable to observers, it was difficult to negate her concerns that these symptoms would have some degree of
225   impact on audience perceptions. According to the client, it was her belief that until she learned to speak without vocal tremors, she would not be able to successfully give a public presentation. Given these circumstances, the first author contacted the second
230   author, who agreed to meet with the client to assess whether voice tremors and breathing difficulties may be related to a particular voice disorder potentially impeding improvement.

Voice Therapy

After the voice assessment described above, the cli-
235   ent participated in voice therapy with the second author for 21 sessions over a 5-month period. Voice therapy focused directly on normal voice physiology by having the client use increased respiratory support for phonation as well as having her initiate and sustain smooth,
240   relaxed phonations and reductions in neck and facial tension. Implementation of these goals was facilitated through the use of Computer-Aided Fluency Establishment Training (CAFET). The CAFET system (Goebel, 1986) runs on an Apple IIe computer and
245   provides integration and visual feedback of various respiratory and phonatory behaviors. Respiratory and phonatory performance related to inadequate breathing patterns for speech and ease of voicing onsets are monitored by devices that the client wears over cloth-
250   ing. Movements of the abdominal musculature and voicing patterns are transduced and shown on the computer screen. Errors in respiratory and phonatory patterns based on a specified criterion-based performance level are also displayed on the screen for client feed-
255   back. Clients are taught target speech skills of inhalation/exhalation patterns without phonation, easy onsets of phonation, and continuous phonation patterns, with accompanying gradual increases in vocal intensity. The majority of each treatment session was spent on the
260   CAFET system. Most of the client's initial breathing patterns were associated with tense, irregular inhalation/exhalation patterns that could easily be seen with the CAFET system. Treatment also focused on eliciting easy breathing and voicing patterns in linguistically
265   simple and emotionally neutral speech contexts. As success was achieved, the clinician gradually increased the length and linguistic complexity of utterances produced by the client. Topics that increased the client's emotional levels were gradually introduced into each
270   session.

During this 20-week period of voice therapy, the client concurrently participated in additional individual CBT that included approximately nine exposures to feared public-speaking situations.

Procedure

275   The client participated in the following interventions in the order listed: CBGT (12 sessions), nondirective psychotherapy (22 sessions), individual CBT (8 sessions), and individual CBT (12 sessions) combined with voice therapy (21 sessions). Because this case was
280   not treated in the context of a research protocol, order of the treatments was not randomized. Rather, the case reflects treatment as it occurs in clinical practice in which the standard, empirically validated intervention is first used. Then, if the client fails to progress, other
285   treatments are employed based on the changing conceptualization of the problem.

Results of therapy were evaluated on the basis of (a) the client's subjective ratings of fear and avoidance

of public speaking, which were completed at six as-
290 sessment points: before CBGT, between CBGT and
nondirective psychotherapy, before, during, and after
the combined individual CBT and voice therapy, and at
a 7-month follow-up; (b) the client's SPAI administered prior to CBGT, just after combined treatment
295 began, then again 7 months after treatment was completed; and (c) the client's subjective report of degree
of vocal strain as well as a record of respiratory and
phonatory signals (e.g., CAFET) evaluated on a ses-
sion-by-session basis during voice therapy.

Results

300 As illustrated in Figure 1, the client's pre-CBGT
hierarchy ratings for fear and avoidance related to presenting in front of a large group were 100 and 75, respectively. Following CBGT, she rated her fear at 100
(indicating no change from pretreatment) and her
305 avoidance at 100 (indicating an increase of 25 from her
pretreatment rating of 75). At the beginning of individual CBT, the client's fear and avoidance were both
rated as 100. Twelve weeks into combined therapy, her
ratings decreased moderately (from 100 to 85) for fear
310 and substantially (from 100 to 50) for avoidance. Post-
combined-treatment ratings taken about 1 week after
voice therapy ended indicate a significant reduction in
fear (from 100 to 25) and avoidance (from 100 to 25).
A 7-month follow-up revealed that these posttreatment
315 gains were maintained.

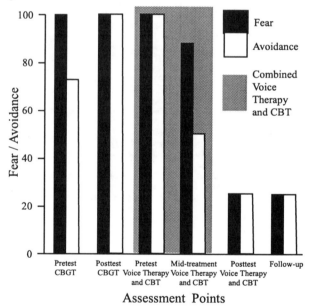

Figure 1. Fear and avoidance related to public speaking at
multiple assessment points during treatment.
Note: CBGT = Cognitive-behavioral group therapy, CBT =
Cognitive-behavioral therapy.

The client's SPAI difference scores at pre-CBGT,
pre-combined therapy, and 7-month follow-up were
reported as 104, 109.7, and 53.6, respectively. SPAI
difference scores prior to CBGT and again prior to the
320 initiation of combined therapy were virtually the same,

indicating significant social anxiety; however, 7
months after the completion of combined therapy, the
client's SPAI difference score decreased significantly
and was within the normal range (Beidel et al., 1993).
325 As presented in Figure 2, results of the voice-
therapy program revealed that the client gradually became more proficient in producing the target respiratory and phonatory skills. The client's management of
the respiratory and phonatory target behaviors during
330 short utterances led to success with appropriate phrase-
length utterances 70% to 80% of the time compared to
baseline measures. By the end of the voice-treatment
program, the client was producing relaxed phonations
and normal-sounding speech on a consistent basis.

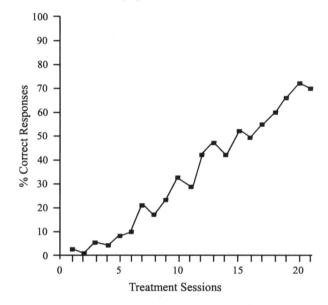

Figure 2. Percentage of correct responses for client's respiratory and phonatory target behaviors as measured by the
Computer-Aided Fluency Establishment Training (CAFET)
system.

Discussion

335 This case involved a woman with social phobia
who failed to improve in the standard cognitive-
behavioral interventions. Because the client reported
being embarrassed about her voice when she was
speaking to an audience due to vocal tremors and dys-
340 phonia, a voice specialist was contacted for consultation. Only when this client was treated by a voice specialist for these specific difficulties in combination
with cognitive-behavior therapy did she make significant improvements.

345 Although treatment of social phobia has been demonstrated to be quite successful, some clients simply do
not improve. Several factors ranging from a client's
lack of motivation to possible severe comorbid disorders can often be identified as factors partially respon-
350 sible for lack of improvement. However, the case described in this article presents an unanticipated treatment failure. That is, the client did not demonstrate
comorbid psychopathology to the degree that it was

355 expected to interfere with treatment and did not suffer from a lack of motivation during treatment. In fact, this client attended every session and adhered strictly to the treatment protocol. An important finding in this study that helped to illuminate potential reasons for this client's lack of improvement is that she suffered from a
360 very real voice disorder that negatively affected her performance when addressing an audience. Despite efforts to help the client habituate to anxiety associated with public speaking and thus reduce vocal tremors, severity of this specific symptom prohibited the ac-
365 complishment of this task. It was only after recognizing that her vocal tremors may have been exacerbated by a voice disorder that treatment could be adjusted to include voice therapy.

With regard to the client's reported gains, she indi-
370 cated that muscle-tension levels in the neck and face areas were significantly less than they were at the beginning of voice therapy. The client also stated that respiratory skill training for supporting phonation had a significant impact on her vocal quality inside and out-
375 side of therapy, because focusing on breath control for speech allowed her to focus on her voice quality rather than on the anxiety that she was experiencing prior to treatment. During the final week of voice therapy, the client participated in an oral presentation related to her
380 graduate work. Success with this activity prompted her to consider participating in an invited panel discussion. According to the client, she "finally felt ready to face a public audience." When questioned about the utility of the combined treatment, the client indicated that she
385 felt that both components of treatment were important in her anxiety reduction. Without voice therapy, the client felt that she would have been unable to learn exercises to treat the problem. Additionally, without the CBT, she felt that she would have never initiated
390 the kinds of interactions that enabled her to overcome her anxiety. That is, by recognizing that she had more control over her voice tremors and breathing, she was able to successfully habituate to her anxiety over public speaking.
395 Considering that MTD is a common clinical voice syndrome and that many MTD clients have difficulty coping with stress, it seems likely that therapists treating social phobia will encounter individuals who may be affected by MTD. This is particularly true for clients
400 with fears unique to public speaking. This case study presents the first known collaborative treatment of a social phobic using cognitive-behavior therapy combined with voice therapy. Because this case was not planned as a research protocol, much of these data re-
405 flect different treatment strategies that were employed in an attempt to alleviate the client's public-speaking fears. Consequently, inferences that can be drawn from these results are obviously limited, as threats to internal and external validity were not controlled. Without in-
410 dependent corroboration, a single client's subjective reports should not be accepted uncritically (Kazdin,

1992). Because CBT and voice therapy were used concurrently, it is difficult to identify those elements of the treatment(s) responsible for the client's improvement.
415 However, because CBT closely followed the protocol for CBGT and the client failed to respond to CBGT, it seems likely that voice therapy was effective. Whether voice therapy alone would have had the same results remains a question for future research. Although only
420 self-report measures were used to assess the client throughout treatment, it should be noted that both standardized and idiographic observations were consistent with these self-reports. Despite these inherent shortcomings, significant decreases in self-reported levels of
425 fear and avoidance, changes in SPAI difference scores from pretreatment to follow-up, and improvements in voice quality as demonstrated by the CAFET system during combined therapy are encouraging. Future research should focus on conducting a controlled study
430 of individuals who are diagnosed with social phobia and MTD, offering combined therapy. Specifically, systematic examination of each of the treatment modalities individually as well as combined will be important.
435 The unique clinical problem presented in this case study provides an illustration of how collaboration between professionals in very different, yet overlapping, professions can be quite beneficial for a client.

References

American Psychiatric Association. (1994). *Diagnostic and statistical manual of mental disorders* (4th ed.). Washington, DC: Author.

Beidel, D. C., Turner, S. M., & Cooley, M. R. (1993). Assessing reliable and clinically significant change in social phobia: Validity of the Social Phobia and Anxiety Inventory. *Behavior Research and Therapy, 31,* 331–337.

Boone, D., & McFarlane, S. (1988). *The voice and voice therapy* (4th ed.). Englewood Cliffs, NJ: Prentice-Hall.

DiNardo, P. A., & Barlow, D. H. (1988). *Anxiety Disorders Interview Schedule-Revised (ADIS-R).* Albany, NY: Phobia and Anxiety Disorders Clinic, State University of New York.

Goebel, M. (1986). *A computer-aided fluency establishment trainer (CAFET).* Falls Church, VA: Annadale Fluency Clinic.

Heimberg, R. G. (1991). *Cognitive behavioral treatment of social phobia in a group setting: A treatment manual* (2nd ed.). (Available from Social Phobia Program, Weiss Hall, Department of Psychology, Temple University, Philadelphia, PA 19122-6085.)

Heimberg, R. G., & Juster, H. R. (1995). Cognitive-behavioral treatments: Literature review. In R. G. Heimberg, M. R. Liebowitz, D. A. Hope, & F. R. Schneier (Eds.), *Social phobia: Diagnosis, assessment, and treatment.* New York: Guilford.

Hope, D. A. (1993). Conducting exposure-based treatments with social phobics. *The Behavior Therapist, 16,* 7–12.

Kazdin, A. E. (1992). *Research design in clinical psychology* (2nd ed.). Boston: Allyn and Bacon.

Liebowitz, M. R., Gorman, J. M., Fyer, M. J., & Klein, D. F. (1985). Social Phobia: Review of a neglected anxiety disorder. *Archives of General Psychiatry, 42,* 729–736.

McEwan, K. L., & Devins, G. M. (1983). Is increased arousal in social anxiety noticed by others? *Journal of Abnormal Psychology, 92,* 417–421.

Potts, N. L. S., & Davidson, R. T. (1995). Pharmacological treatments: Literature review. In R. G. Heimberg, M. R. Liebowitz, D. A. Hope, & F. R. Schneier (Eds.), *Social phobia: Diagnosis, assessment, and treatment.* New York: Guilford.

Sime, W. E., & Healey, E. C. (1993). An interdisciplinary approach to the treatment of hyperfunctional voice disorder. *Biofeedback and Self-Regulation, 18,* 281–287.

Turner, S. M., Beidel, D. C., Dancu, C. V., & Stanley, M. A. (1989). An empirically derived inventory to measure social fears and anxiety: The Social Phobia and Anxiety Inventory. *Psychological Assessment, 1,* 35–40.

Warner, M. D., Hope, D. A., & Herbert, J. D. (1995, November). *Content analysis of automatic thoughts elicited before therapeutic exposures among social phobics: Further findings.* Paper presented at the annual meeting of the Association for Advancement of Behavior Therapy, Washington, DC.

Authors' note: Completion of this manuscript was supported in part by Grant No. MH 48751 to the third author from the National Institute of Mental Health. No author has financial interests in the company that produces the CAFET system or has been compensated in any way for the use of the CAFET system.

About the authors: Louis B. Laguna is a doctoral student in the clinical psychology program at the University of Nebraska, Lincoln. E. Charles Healey is an associate professor at the University of Nebraska, Lincoln. Currently, he is associate editor for *Journal of Speech and Hearing Research* and is an editorial consultant for *Journal of Fluency Disorder* and *American Journal of Speech-Language Pathology*. He has published many research articles as well as a book of readings on stuttering. During the past 18 years, he has presented a number of workshops for school clinicians and organizations around the country on the clinical management of children and adults who stutter.

Debra A. Hope, Ph.D., is associate professor at the University of Nebraska, Lincoln. She has published widely on the psychopathology, assessment, and treatment of social phobia and related topics. Dr. Hope also serves as director of the Psychological Consultation Center, the training clinic for the UNL clinical psychology training program.

Address correspondence to: Debra A. Hope, Ph.D., Department of Psychology, University of Nebraska, Lincoln, NE 68588-0308; e-mail: dhope@unlinfo.unl.edu

Exercise for Article 15

Factual Questions

1. What is identified as "the hallmark" of social phobia?

2. How old was the participant in this study?

3. CBGT stands for what words?

4. Was the individual cognitive-behavioral therapy more effective than the CBTG had been?

5. The participant received voice therapy for how many weeks?

6. Before CBGT, the participant rated her avoidance at 75. What was her avoidance rating at the end of CBGT?

7. Did the researchers consider the participant to be motivated?

Questions for Discussion

8. In your opinion, is this research interesting and informative even though there was only one participant? Explain.

9. The researchers note that the order of the treatments was not randomized. Do you think it would be desirable to randomize it in future studies on this topic? Explain. (See lines 279–286.)

10. How important is a follow-up in a study of this type? Explain. (See lines 314–315.)

11. The researchers state that "because CBT and voice therapy were used concurrently, it is difficult to identify those elements of the treatment(s) responsible for the client's improvement." Is this an important consideration when interpreting the results of this study? Explain.

Quality Ratings

Directions: Indicate your level of agreement with each of the following statements by circling a number from 5 for strongly agree (SA) to 1 for strongly disagree (SD). If you believe an item is not applicable to this research article, leave it blank. Be prepared to explain your ratings.

A. The introduction establishes the importance of the study.

SA   5   4   3   2   1   SD

B. The literature review establishes the context for the study.

SA   5   4   3   2   1   SD

C. The research purpose, question, or hypothesis is clearly stated.

SA   5   4   3   2   1   SD

D. The method of sampling is sound.

SA   5   4   3   2   1   SD

E. Relevant demographics (for example, age, gender, and ethnicity) are described.

SA   5   4   3   2   1   SD

F. Measurement procedures are adequate.

SA   5   4   3   2   1   SD

G. All procedures have been described in sufficient detail to permit a replication of the study.

SA   5   4   3   2   1   SD

H. The participants have been adequately protected from potential harm.

SA   5   4   3   2   1   SD

I. The results are clearly described.

SA   5   4   3   2   1   SD

J. The discussion/conclusion is appropriate.

SA   5   4   3   2   1   SD

K. Despite any flaws, the report is worthy of publication.

SA   5   4   3   2   1   SD

Article 16

Birth Order and Sexual Orientation in Women

ANTHONY F. BOGAERT
Brock University

ABSTRACT. One of the world's largest databases on human sexuality was used to investigate whether lesbians, like homosexual men, have a later birth order relative to heterosexual comparisons. The women ($N >$ 5,000) were interviewed by investigators at the Kinsey Institute for Sex and Reproduction from 1938 to 1963. The women were dichotomously classified as lesbian (n = 257) or heterosexual (n = 5,008). No significant birth order effect was observed. Results support theories of gender-specific mechanisms in the development of sexual orientation in women and men.

From *Behavioral Neuroscience, 111*, 1395–1397. Copyright © 1997 by the American Psychological Association, Inc. Reprinted with permission.

Research has established that homosexual men have, on average, a later birth order than population norms or comparable groups of heterosexual men (Blanchard & Bogaert, 1996a, 1996b, 1997; Blanchard & Sheridan, 1992; Blanchard & Zucker, 1994; Blanchard, Zucker, Bradley, & Hume, 1995; Blanchard, Zucker, Cohen-Kettenis, Gooren, & Bailey, 1996; Bogaert, Bezeau, Kuban, & Blanchard, 1997; Hare & Moran, 1979; Slater, 1962; Zucker & Blanchard, 1994). Recently, this difference has been demonstrated to be primarily the result of homosexual men being born later among their brothers, relative to heterosexual men (Blanchard & Bogaert, 1996a, 1996b, 1997; Bogaert et al., 1997). A number of theories can be forwarded to account for the birth order effect among brothers, including the conditioning-of-arousal to same-sex activity/fantasy, and a maternal immune response, where a mother develops antibodies to a male-related factor (e.g., H-Y antigen) over successive male pregnancies (Blanchard & Bogaert, 1996b; Blanchard & Klassen, 1997).

Birth order and sexual orientation in women has been less studied and results are inconsistent. Two early studies are contradictory, with one indicating that lesbians are later born relative to the general population (Slater, 1962) and another indicating that lesbians are earlier born relative to heterosexual comparisons (Saghir & Robins, 1973). Five additional research teams reported no clear difference between lesbians and comparable heterosexuals (Bell, Weinberg, & Hammersmith, 1981; Blanchard & Sheridan, 1992; Gundlach & Reiss, 1976; Hare & Moran, 1979;

Siegelman, 1973). Most of the above-mentioned studies had samples that were small, not all reported statistical significance tests, and none tested the more specific question of whether a possible birth order effect occurs among sisters or brothers. Thus, new research on a large sample would help clarify this relation.

The present study used information from the Kinsey Institute for Research in Sex and Reproduction, one of the world's largest databases on human sexuality, to investigate the relationship between sexual orientation and birth order in women.

Method

From 1938 to 1963, 18,216 case histories were recorded by the Kinsey Institute for Sex Research using the interview schedule devised by Alfred Kinsey (Gebhard & Johnson, 1979). The computer data files containing adult white and nonwhite women with no convictions for felonies or misdemeanors (other than traffic violations) make up 5,954 cases. To minimize unreliable data, 225 individuals having incomplete sibship information or who at some point resided in a foster home or institution before age 18 were eliminated. The remaining 5,729 cases were the database for the present investigation.

Women were classified as lesbian if they reported "extensive" homosexual experience, defined by Gebhard and Johnson (1979) as more than 20 female sexual partners or more than 50 homosexual experiences (with one or more partners). Women were classified as heterosexual if they reported either "no" or "rare" homosexual experience, the latter defined by Gebhard and Johnson as 1 female sexual partner or 1–5 homosexual experiences, *and* they did not respond that they experienced "much" or "some" arousal to questions about sexual arousal from seeing and thinking of females. Using these criteria, 464 individuals could not be classified as either heterosexual or homosexual. Of the remaining 5,265 cases, 257 were classified as lesbian and 5,008 were classified as heterosexual.

Birth order was derived from the proband's number of older brothers, older sisters, younger brothers, and younger sisters. Unfortunately, as part of the original interview/coding protocol, sibling numbers over 8 were collapsed into one category, 8+; thus, a proband with 9 or more older sisters was given the same score as a proband with 8 older sisters, and so on. In addition, there was no way to distinguish full, half, and step sib-

Table 1
Demographic Comparisons of Lesbian and Heterosexual Women

| | Score | | | | | |
| | Lesbians (n = 257)[a] | | Heterosexuals (n = 5008)[a] | | | |
Variable	M	SD	M	SD	t	p
Age	34.05	10.12	28.73	11.06	7.55	< .001
Year of birth	1913.12	10.44	1916.86	10.58	5.53	< .001
Father's age at proband's birth	32.62	8.39	32.51	7.00	0.20	.575
Mother's age at proband's birth	28.13	6.84	28.25	5.90	0.27	.790
No. of sisters	1.14	1.42	1.08	1.25	0.69	.487
No. of brothers	1.11	1.32	1.15	1.26	0.52	.600
Parental SES[b]	4.78	1.57	4.94	1.34	1.54	.125

[a]Sample size may vary for some variables because of missing cases. [b]Parental socioeconomic status (SES) varies from 1 (extreme poverty) to 8 (extreme wealth).

lings in the computerized data. Deceased siblings were recorded, however, and twins were not counted in the totals.

Also assessed were age, year of birth, biological parents' age at proband's birth, number of brothers and sisters, and parental socioeconomic status. Education was not used as a social class measure because many probands were still in school when interviewed and their current education would not reflect their ultimate education.

Results

Birth order was quantified using Berglin's (1982) index, (older siblings + 0.5)/(total siblings + 1), a metric that controls for family size. This index expresses birth order as a quantity between 0 and 1, with higher values indicating a later birth order. Berglin's index for heterosexual women, 0.486 (SD = 0.250), did not differ significantly from that for lesbians, 0.487 (SD = 0.250), $t(5263) = 0.11$, $p = .911$. Note that this and all remaining statistical tests are two-tailed.

To evaluate possible birth order effects among brothers or sisters, two new indices, a fraternal index and a sororal index, were calculated. The fraternal index quantifies a proband's birth order relative to his or her brothers as (older brothers + 0.5)/(total brothers + 1) and, like Berglin's index, ranges between 0 and 1, where a higher value indicates a later birth order among brothers. The sororal index similarly quantifies a proband's birth order relative to his or her sisters as (older sisters + 0.5)/(total sisters + 1). The fraternal index for the heterosexual women was 0.493 (SD = 0.212); for the lesbians, it was 0.505 (SD = 0.209). The sororal index for the heterosexual women was 0.493 (SD = 0.205); for the lesbians, it was 0.476 (SD = 0.207). No significant differences occurred on these indices, $t(5263) = 0.88$, $p = .379$ and $t(5263) = 1.30$, $p = .193$, respectively.

The two groups differed on age and year of birth (see Table 1). Because a proband's expected birth order depends upon demographic trends operative around the time of his or her birth, any between-group differences in year of birth represent a potential artifact in birth order comparisons (Hare & Price, 1969). Thus, in additional birth order comparisons, year of birth trends were controlled using analyses of covariance (ANCOVAs). All results remained nonsignificant.

Finally, the two groups were assessed for their sibling sex ratios, that is, the proportion of brothers to sisters collectively reported by a given group of probands, and these values were compared with the known human sex ratio, .5146, using the z approximation to the binomial test. Unlike birth order, the human sex ratio is resistant to perturbation by demographic variables (James, 1987). Neither the lesbians' nor the heterosexuals' sex ratio (.4931 and .5150, respectively) differed significantly (both $ps > .300$) from the expected value.

Discussion

One of the world's largest databases on human sexuality was used to investigate whether lesbians, like homosexual men, have a later birth order relative to heterosexual comparisons. No relationship was found. These null results are noteworthy given the large sample size and the resulting power to detect very small effects.

The results have implications for the etiology of sexual orientation in both women and men. Not only do these results suggest that birth order does not affect women's sexual orientation, they also suggest that a gender-specific mechanism accounts for the relation between (fraternal) birth order and sexual orientation in men. The maternal immune response hypothesis involves a gender-specific mechanism and thus is consistent with these results. This hypothesis is partly based on the argument that a woman's immune system would appear to be the most capable of "remembering" the number of male (but not female) fetuses she has previously carried and of progressively altering its response to the next fetus according to the current tally of preceding males. If the immune hypothesis is correct, then the connection between the mother's immune reaction and the child's future sexual orientation would likely be some effect of maternal antibodies on the sexual differentiation of the fetal brain. Various lines of indirect support for male-specific Y-linked H-Y antigen as the relevant fetal antigen (Blanchard & Bogaert, 1996b; Blanchard & Klassen, 1997) include evidence that H-Y antigen may be responsible for the greater antigenicity of male (versus female) fetuses (see Gaultieri & Hicks, 1985), and findings that male mice whose mothers were immunized to H-Y prior to pregnancy are less likely to mate with receptive females (Singh & Verma, 1987).

Other explanations, such as same-sex fantasy/activity mechanisms, have been proposed to account for the birth order effect in men. One hypothesis is that a large number of older brothers increases the likelihood of sex fantasy/activity among brothers, the assumption being that such experiences produce a stronger learning/conditioning effect on the younger of the siblings involved. Similarly, Sulloway (1996, pp. 433–434, 488) hypothesized that the birth order phenomenon reflects later borns' greater openness to experience, which predisposes them to experiment sexually, including same-sex activity. These psychosocial explanations are not eliminated by the present data, but an additional question is now raised about why an increased number of older siblings, including same-sex siblings (and the resulting opportunity for increased same-sex fantasy/activity), increases the likelihood of same-sex attraction in men but not in women.

References

Bell, A. P., Weinberg, M. S., & Hammersmith, S. K. (1981). *Sexual preference: Its development in men and women.* Bloomington: Indiana University Press.

Berglin, C. G. (1982). Birth order as a quantitative expression of date of birth. *Journal of Epidemiology and Community Health, 36*, 298–302.

Blanchard, R., & Bogaert, A. F. (1996a). Biodemographic comparisons of homosexual and heterosexual men in the Kinsey interview data. *Archives of Sexual Behavior, 25*, 551–579.

Blanchard, R., & Bogaert, A. F. (1996b). Male homosexuality and number of older brothers. *American Journal of Psychiatry, 153*, 27–31.

Blanchard, R., & Bogaert, A. F. (1997). Additive effects of older brothers and homosexual brothers in the prediction of marriage and cohabitation. *Behavior Genetics, 27*, 45–54.

Blanchard, R., & Klassen, P. (1997). H-Y antigen and homosexuality in men. *Journal of Theoretical Biology, 185*, 373–378.

Blanchard, R., & Sheridan, P. M. (1992). Sibship size, sibling sex ratio, birth order, and parental age in homosexual and nonhomosexual gender dysphorics. *Journal of Nervous and Mental Disease, 180*, 40–47.

Blanchard, R., & Zucker, K. J. (1994). Reanalysis of Bell, Weinberg, and Hammersmith's data on birth order, sibling sex ratio, and parental age in homosexual men. *American Journal of Psychiatry, 151*, 1375–1376.

Blanchard, R., Zucker, K. J., Bradley, S. J., & Hume, C. S. (1995). Birth order and sibling sex ratio in homosexual male adolescents and probably prehomosexual feminine boys. *Developmental Psychology, 31*, 22–30.

Blanchard, R., Zucker, K. J., Cohen-Kettenis, P. T., Gooren, L. J. G., & Bailey, J. M. (1996). Birth order and sibling sex ratio in two samples of Dutch gender-dysphoric homosexual males. *Archives of Sexual Behavior, 25*, 495–514.

Bogaert, A. F., Bezeau, S., Kuban, M., & Blanchard, R. (1997). Pedophilia, sexual orientation, and birth order. *Journal of Abnormal Psychology, 106*, 331–335.

Gebhard, P. H., & Johnson, A. B. (1979). *The Kinsey data: Marginal tabulations of the 1938–1963 interviews conducted by the Institute for Sex Research.* Philadelphia, PA: Saunders.

Gaultieri, T., & Hicks, R. E. (1985). An immunoreactive theory of selective male affliction. *Behavioral and Brain Sciences, 8*, 427–441.

Gundlach, R. H., & Reiss, B. F. (1967). Birth order and sex of siblings in a sample of lesbians and non-lesbians. *Psychological Reports, 20*, 61–62.

Hare, E. H., & Moran, P. A. P. (1979). Parental age and birth order in homosexual patients: A replication of Slater's study. *British Journal of Psychiatry, 134*, 178–182.

Hare, E. H., & Price, J. S. (1969). Birth order and family size: Bias caused by changes in birth rate. *British Journal of Psychiatry, 134*, 178–182.

James, W. H. (1987). The human sex ratio. Part 1: A review of the literature. *Human Biology, 59*, 721–752.

Saghir, M. T., & Robins, E. (1973). *Male and female homosexuality: A comprehensive study.* Baltimore: Williams & Wilkins.

Siegelman, M. (1973). Birth order and family size of homosexual men and women. *Journal of Consulting and Clinical Psychology, 41*, 164.

Singh, J., & Verma, I. C. (1987). Influence of major histo(in)compatibility complex on reproduction. *American Journal of Reproductive Immunology and Microbiology, 15*, 150–152.

Slater, E. (1962). Birth order and maternal age among homosexuals. *Lancet, 1*, 178–182.

Sulloway, F. J. (1996). *Born to rebel: Birth order, family dynamics, and creative lives.* New York: Pantheon Books.

Zucker, K. J., & Blanchard, R. (1994). Reanalysis of Bieber et al.'s 1962 data on sibling sex ratio and birth order in male homosexuals. *Journal of Nervous and Mental Disease, 182*, 528–530.

Acknowledgments: I thank Thomas G. Albright for running the statistical analyses, Ray Blanchard for suggestions regarding analyses, Caroline Rougier-Chapman for helping with a literature search, Carolyn L. Hafer for comments on an earlier draft of this article, and the Kinsey Institute for allowing access to these data.

Address correspondence to: Anthony F. Bogaert, Department of Psychology, Brock University, St. Catherines, Ontario, L2S 3A1 Canada. Electronic mail: tbogaert@spartan.ac.brocku.ca

Exercise for Article 16

Factual Questions

1. According to the researcher, "research has established" what?

2. Of the 5,729 cases, how many could not be classified as either heterosexual or homosexual using the criteria suggested by Gebhard and Johnson?

3. Do higher values on Berglin's index indicate *a later birth order* or *an earlier birth order*?

4. The mean parental SES for the lesbians is 4.78. What is the corresponding mean for the heterosexuals?

5. Which group has greater variability in their ages?

6. What has Sulloway (1996) hypothesized?

Questions for Discussion

7. What is your opinion of the definitions of "lesbian" and "heterosexual" used in this study? (See lines 56–70.)

8. The interviews that gathered the data for this study were conducted from 1938 to 1963. Is the lack of current interviews a weakness of this study? Explain.

9. Was the difference between the two means for parental SES in Table 1 statistically significant? Explain how you arrived at your answer.

10. How important are the demographic comparisons presented in Table 1? Would the study be weaker if they had been omitted from the research report? Explain.

11. The researcher cites a study involving male mice. In your opinion, is animal research relevant to the research problem considered in this article? Explain. (See lines 166–169.)

12. Do you think that more research is needed on this topic? Why? Why not?

Quality Ratings

Directions: Indicate your level of agreement with each of the following statements by circling a number from 5 for strongly agree (SA) to 1 for strongly disagree (SD). If you believe an item is not applicable to this research article, leave it blank. Be prepared to explain your ratings.

A. The introduction establishes the importance of the study.

SA   5   4   3   2   1   SD

B. The literature review establishes the context for the study.

SA   5   4   3   2   1   SD

C. The research purpose, question, or hypothesis is clearly stated.

SA   5   4   3   2   1   SD

D. The method of sampling is sound.

SA   5   4   3   2   1   SD

E. Relevant demographics (for example, age, gender, and ethnicity) are described.

SA   5   4   3   2   1   SD

F. Measurement procedures are adequate.

SA   5   4   3   2   1   SD

G. All procedures have been described in sufficient detail to permit a replication of the study.

SA   5   4   3   2   1   SD

H. The participants have been adequately protected from potential harm.

SA   5   4   3   2   1   SD

I. The results are clearly described.

SA   5   4   3   2   1   SD

J. The discussion/conclusion is appropriate.

SA   5   4   3   2   1   SD

K. Despite any flaws, the report is worthy of publication.

SA   5   4   3   2   1   SD

Article 17

Parental Bonding and Current Psychological Functioning Among Childhood Sexual Abuse Survivors

ROXANNE SCHREIBER
University of Southern Mississippi

WILLIAM J. LYDDON
University of Southern Mississippi

ABSTRACT. The relation between perceived parental bonding to maternal and paternal primary caregivers and current psychological functioning was examined among an adult female sample (*n* = 78) of child sexual abuse survivors (CSASs). Although CSASs revealed significantly poorer psychological adjustment than non-CSASs, high paternal care was significantly associated with better psychological functioning among CSASs. These data are discussed in the context of attachment theory.

From *Journal of Counseling Psychology, 45*, 358–362. Copyright © 1998 by the American Psychological Association, Inc. Reprinted with permission.

During the last two decades, there has been an increasing awareness and concern about childhood sexual abuse. Current prevalence rates range anywhere from 20% to 45% of the female population (Morrow &
5　Smith, 1995), with some researchers suggesting that these figures are underestimates (Geffner, 1992). Along with this growing concern is the recognition of the often serious and damaging psychological sequelae associated with childhood sexual abuse, including de-
10　pression, anxiety, relationship difficulties, low self-esteem, suicidal behavior, substance abuse, sexual dysfunction, and personality disorders (Cole & Putnam, 1992).

Although research on childhood sexual abuse has
15　led to improved knowledge of this phenomenon, there is concern about the lack of a viable theoretical framework from which to interpret research findings and direct future exploration (Morrow & Smith, 1995). As a result, researchers have almost exclusively taken a
20　*symptom* approach (Briere, 1989) to the study of sexual abuse (see also Courtois, 1988; Russell, 1983), portraying the consequences of sexual abuse in lengthy lists of symptoms (Cole & Putnam, 1992). This approach has left the field with a wide range of associated
25　symptoms and no clear explanations as to why these symptoms occur in some cases and do not occur in others (Morrow & Smith, 1995). Furthermore, the differences in severity and type of reported psychological sequelae associated with childhood sexual abuse are

30　also a notable source of confusion. Some sexual abuse survivors report profound traumatization, whereas others report only mild or transient symptoms resulting from the abuse (Finkelhor, 1990; Green, 1993). Thus, the symptom approach has failed to identify a specific
35　childhood sexual abuse syndrome with predictable psychological consequences (Cole & Putnam, 1992; Green, 1993).

Briere (1989), arguing against a symptom approach, advocated a theory-based perspective for un-
40　derstanding sexual abuse. More recently, Morrow and Smith (1995) also suggested that a theory-driven, construct-oriented approach might provide some meaningful order to the "chaos of symptomology" (p. 24) that currently characterizes this field. In response to this
45　call for a theory-based approach, we propose the application of Bowlby's (1973, 1977, 1980) attachment theory to the study of childhood sexual abuse. What follows is a brief review of Bowlby's attachment theory, including a model formulated by Parker, Tupling, and
50　Brown (1979) that assesses the influence and interaction of two primary dimensions of attachment or bonding: care and overprotection. The rationale for the potential relevance of parental bonding to the study of sexual abuse is also discussed.

Attachment Theory

55　Attachment theory is based on the notion that there are individual differences in the way infants become emotionally attached to their primary caregivers and that these differences influence a child's perceptions of self, others, and resources for emotional self-regulation
60　in times of crisis (Bowlby, 1977). According to Bowlby, attachment security depends largely on the caretaker's response to the infant's needs and distress. If the caretaker is warm and responsive on a consistent basis, then the relationship is characterized as a *secure*
65　attachment. *Insecure* attachment, on the other hand, is characterized by caretaker inconsistency or rejection of the infant's bids for attention and care. Attachment theorists further contend that through continued interaction, a child develops *internal working models*, or
70　beliefs and expectations about (a) the caretaker's trustworthiness and responsiveness and (b) his or her own

personal sense of being worthy of care and attention. These formative working models of self and others are thought to influence subsequent relationships and how the child will perceive and react to others (Bowlby, 1973; Sroufe & Fleeson, 1986). For example, securely attached infants have been found to exhibit greater competence with peers, more ego resiliency, and more popularity than their insecurely attached counterparts (Sroufe, 1983).

Although attachment researchers have focused on childhood and infancy, Bowlby (1973, 1977, 1980) emphasized that working models of attachment persist throughout the life span. Studies of adult attachment have found results comparable to that of the attachment research with children. For example, securely attached adults have been found to be more comfortable with a wide range of emotions in romantic relationships (Haft & Slade, 1989) and more self-confident and trusting of other adults (Feeney & Noller, 1990; Hazan & Shaver, 1987) than insecurely attached adults. Insecurely attached adults also have been described as uncomfortable with intimacy, clingy, dependent, jealous, and overly expressive in relationships with other adults (Brennan & Shaver, 1991; Feeney & Noller, 1990).

In assessing attachment in adults, Parker et al. (1979) developed the Parental Bonding Instrument, which assesses two dimensions of parental characteristics that are thought to contribute to the quality of attachment or bonding: care and overprotection (or psychological control). Parker et al. suggested that four types of bonding or attachment may be assessed when considering the interaction of these dimensions: (a) high care–low overprotection, conceptualized as *optimal bonding*; (b) low care–low overprotection, conceptualized as *absent or weak bonding*; (c) high care–high overprotection, conceptualized as *affectionate constraint*; and (d) low care–high overprotection, conceptualized as *affectionless control*. Several studies have used these classifications to identify and compare secure and insecure parental bonding groups (Mackinnon, Henderson, & Andrews, 1993; Parker, 1979, 1983).

Integration and Purpose of the Present Study

As early as 1943, Anna Freud wrote about the influence of parent–child relationships on the psychological functioning of children after a trauma (Freud & Burlington, 1943). Since that time, researchers have suggested that affective support from a child's parents serves as an important protective mechanism that helps the child cope with trauma (Werner & Smith, 1982). This notion is particularly important in the context of Bowlby's (1977) attachment theory. In attachment terms, a threat of crisis such as abuse will tend to elicit stronger attachment behaviors. If the primary caretaker responds in a negative way, such as being cold or rejecting, the child's ability to cope may be limited (Everson, Hunter, Runyon, Edelsohn, & Coulter, 1989).

Some researchers suggest that long-term psychological sequelae of childhood sexual abuse also may be determined more by family relationships, especially parental warmth and support, than by actual abuse variables, such as duration of abuse, severity of abuse, and type of perpetrator (Alexander, 1992). Friedrich, Beilke, and Urquiza (1987), for example, found that family environments characterized by conflict or lack of family cohesion accounted for more of the problems that survivors reported than specific abuse variables. Although these studies suggest a relation between parental behaviors and adjustment after the experience of abuse, they do not provide direct evidence in the framework of attachment theory. As a result, the primary purpose of this study is to explore childhood sexual abuse in the context of Bowlby's (1973) attachment theory. In particular, we wanted to determine if the dimensions of parental bonding (care and overprotection) would be associated with differences in psychological functioning among a sample of child sexual abuse survivors (CSASs). We hypothesized that CSASs reporting optimal bonding (high care–low overprotection) would exhibit significantly better psychological functioning than CSASs reporting parental bonding characterized as either absent, affectionate constraint, or affectionless control.

Method

Participants

Seventy-eight of the participants reported an unwanted sexual experience in childhood. They ranged in age from 18 to 55 years ($M = 26.87$ years, $SD = 8.51$). Seventy-three percent of these participants were Caucasian, 17% were African American, 3% were Native American, 1% were Hispanic, and 6% did not report racial–ethnic information. Forty percent reported incest, 54% reported extrafamilial abuse, and 6% did not report the type of abuse experienced. Seventy-eight percent indicated abuse by one perpetrator, 18% indicated two to three perpetrators, 2% indicated four or more perpetrators, and 2% did not report the number of perpetrators.

The remaining participants, who did not meet the definition for childhood sexual abuse, were used as a comparison group for certain statistical analyses. The final number of participants not meeting the definition of childhood sexual abuse was 221, ranging in age from 17 to 55 years ($M = 23.13$ years, $SD = 7.19$). Of these participants, 64% were Caucasian, 29% were African American, 1% were Hispanic, 1% were Native American, 2% indicated "other" for race–ethnicity, and 3% did not report racial–ethnic information. All participants were undergraduate female psychology students from a small public university in the southeastern United States, who received experimental credit for their participation.

Measures

Parental Bonding Instrument (PBI). The PBI (Parker et al., 1979) is a 25-item self-report measure designed to assess persons' perceptions of parental or primary caretaker behavior during the first 16 years of life. PBI items are anchored on a 4-point Likert-type scale, ranging from 0 (*very much like my mother/father/primary caretaker*) to 3 (*very unlike my mother/father/primary caretaker*). The PBI consists of two subscales: Care and Overprotection. The Care subscale contains 12 items that measure "care/involvement versus indifference/rejection" (Parker et al., 1979, pp. 2–3). The Overprotection subscale contains 13 items that measure "control/over-protection versus encouragement of independence" (Parker et al., 1979, p. 3). Adequate reliability and validity (predictive and concurrent) for the PBI have been demonstrated in several studies, with significant correlations between participants' reports of parental bonding and those of siblings, as well as those of judges who interviewed mothers (Parker, 1979, 1983; Parker & Lipscombe, 1981).

For this study, a grid was formed based on the intersection of the Care and Overprotection means obtained from large normative groups (Parker, 1977). Maternal Care and Overprotection means were 27.0 and 13.5, respectively. Paternal Care and Overprotection means were 24.0 and 12.5, respectively. All participants were classified into the four quadrants based on whether their scores on the two PBI dimensions fell above or below the normative means of each subscale. This classification was done twice, once on the basis of participants' maternal bonding scores and once on the basis of paternal bonding scores.

Symptom Checklist—90 (SCL–90). SCL–90 (Derogatis, 1977) is a 90-item measure designed to assess current psychological functioning and symptoms of distress in adult populations. The SCL–90 consists of nine subscales, which measure specific symptom constructs: Somatization, Obsessive–Compulsive, Interpersonal Sensitivity, Depression, Anxiety, Hostility, Phobic Anxiety, Paranoid Ideation, and Psychoticism. Participants indicate how much they have been bothered recently by each symptom, on a Likert-type scale ranging from 0 (*not at all*) to 4 (*extremely*). Summing across all 90 items produces the Global Symptomatic Index (GSI). The total Cronbach's alpha internal consistency coefficient has been reported as .98 (Hoffman & Overall, 1978). The total score also has been shown to be reliable across populations, with psychiatric populations scoring significantly higher on psychological problems than the general nonclinical populations (Hoffman & Overall, 1978).

Sexual Abuse Questionnaire. For this study, *sexual abuse* was defined as an unwanted sexual experience before the age of 16 perpetrated by someone older or more powerful. Information about the participant's relationship to the person who committed the unwanted sexual experience, the number of people with whom unwanted sexual experiences occurred, the age of the participant when the sexual experience began and ended, the frequency of the unwanted sexual experiences, the availability of outside support, and the availability of parental support in dealing with the experiences was also obtained. *Incest* was defined as an unwanted sexual experience with a sibling, mother, father, stepfather, stepmother, grandfather, uncle, aunt, or parental figure with whom the victim lived. *Extrafamilial abuse* was defined as an unwanted sexual experience with a person who was not a close blood relative, stepparent, or live-in parental figure.

Procedure

All participants completed the research protocol in small groups. The protocol included a short demographic form, the 15-item Sexual Abuse Questionnaire, the PBI, and the SCL–90. Because of the sensitive nature of the study, participants were told of the nature of the study before they began to read the protocols. The opportunity to leave or stop at any time without penalty was stressed. Participants signed release forms before beginning the study, but the release forms in no way obligated them to complete the questionnaires. The release forms with the respondents' signatures were not traceable to the completed questionnaires in any way.

Due to the possibility that the nature of this study might bring up uncomfortable feelings related to sexual abuse, telephone numbers of the university counseling clinics, a local mental health center, and the community rape crisis center also were distributed separately with the questionnaires. The investigator's name and telephone number as well the name and number of a university licensed psychologist were given to the participants in the event that they had any questions or concerns.

Results

Between-Group Comparisons

We conducted an analysis of variance to compare the abused group and comparison group on their GSIs [derived from the SCL-90]. The abused group ($M = 1.03$, $SD = 0.73$) scored significantly higher than the comparison group ($M = 0.77$, $SD = 0.65$), $F(1, 295) = 9.09$, $p = .003$.

Within-Group Comparisons

We conducted two 2×2 analyses of covariance (one for maternal bonding and one for paternal bonding), with CSASs' maternal Care and Overprotection scores (high vs. low) and paternal Care and Overprotection scores (high vs. low) serving as the independent variables and their GSIs serving as the dependent variable. The variables paternal perpetrator and type of abuse (incest vs. extrafamilial) were included as covariates, to control for the possible confounding effects of the perpetrator being the paternal caregiver and for the possible confounding effects of type of abuse. There was a significant main effect for the paternal

Care score, with CSASs reporting low care scoring significantly higher [on the dependent variable], indicating more psychological difficulties ($M = 1.17$, $SD = 0.74$ for low care; $M = 0.78$, $SD = 0.66$ for high care); $F(1, 77) = 5.05$, $p = .03$. There was no significant main effect for paternal Overprotection scores, $F(1, 77) = 2.08$, $p = .15$, nor was there a significant interaction between the two paternal bonding dimensions, $F(1, 77) = 2.39$, $p = .13$. There were no significant main effects for maternal Care and Overprotection scores, $F(1, 77) = 0.64$, $p = .43$; $F(1, 77) = 1.23$, $p = .27$, respectively. There was also no significant interaction between the two maternal bonding dimensions, $F(1, 77) = 0.64$, $p = .43$. Neither of the covariates contributed significantly to CSASs' psychological functioning: $F(1, 77) = 0.27$, $p = .61$ (paternal perpetrator) and $F(1, 77) = 0.01$, $p = .96$ (type of abuse), when examining paternal bonding; $F(1, 77) = 0.29$, $p = .59$ (paternal perpetrator), and $F(1, 77) = 0.01$, $p = .96$ (type of abuse), when examining maternal bonding.

Discussion

Our results suggest that attachment theory may be a viable conceptual framework for understanding childhood sexual abuse. For example, although there was not a significant interaction between the Care and Overprotection scales, high paternal care was significantly associated with better psychological functioning in our CSAS sample. Because researchers have indicated that sexual abuse is primarily perpetrated by males (Green, 1993), it stands to reason that the type of paternal bonding might hold important significance for the way a child incorporates the experience of being abused by a male into her existing framework of self and others. Furthermore, because a child's working models of self and others are thought to be self-confirming and increasingly self-perpetuating over time (Bowlby, 1977), there are at least two distinct ways in which this incorporation of the abusive experience may take place. If the child has experienced high levels of care from a paternal figure and then experiences abuse by a male, she may be less likely to characterize all males as bad and untrustworthy and may be more likely to conclude that the specific male that abused her was bad and untrustworthy. Experiencing high levels of paternal care is also likely to preserve a working model of self as worthy of love and protection. In contrast, if the child has experienced low levels of care from a paternal figure, subsequent abuse by a male would more likely confirm and further strengthen her working models of males as bad and untrustworthy, as well as to potentially perpetuate a view of self as unworthy of love and protection.

Our findings about the role of paternal care in CSAS adjustment may hold important implications for counseling adult CSASs also. First, a thorough assessment of a CSAS's working models of paternal bonding may be important to a fuller understanding of how she

has incorporated the experience of being abused by a male into her existing cognitive framework. Second, because of the self-confirmatory nature of working models, helping the CSAS client first identify and then actively test existing working models, especially of males, may be an important counseling strategy. In regard to the counseling relationship, a CSAS who has low levels of paternal care may have initial difficulty trusting a male counselor. However, from an interpersonal perspective (Teyber, 1997), forming a working alliance with a male counselor may be a particularly powerful way of facilitating a shift in negative working models that may be organized along gender lines. For example, Lopez, Melendez, Sauer, Berger, and Wyssmann (1998) pointed out the importance of identifying and addressing "potentially problematic expectancies regarding the counselor's trustworthiness and dependability that may be part of the client's more general, internalized working models of others" (p. 83).

Other findings from our study are consistent with past research and underscore the wide prevalence of unwanted sexual experiences in childhood as well as the negative consequences associated with such abuse. Twenty-six percent of the college women in this study reported an unwanted sexual experience before the age of 16 that they believed to be associated with at least moderate trauma in their lives. This number is consistent with other research in college settings examining child sexual abuse (Finkelhor, 1984). Also consistent with past literature is the significantly poorer psychological functioning reported by CSASs when compared with our nonabused sample.

Only 1% of the current sample reported the abuse to authorities, and only 29% reported the experience to their parents. Twenty-one percent reported receiving parental support after the abuse. These numbers suggest that feelings of fear, shame, and stigmatization from the abuse may leave many abused young women with few perceived sources of support.

One of the limitations of this study is that the variables examined were all assessed at one point in time. Therefore, any conclusions about how the variables may be causally linked are not possible. With regard to external validity, our relatively homogeneous sample of college female undergraduates may not be representative of women in general. However, this sample may be representative of college women, in a nonclinical population, who have had an unwanted sexual experience in childhood that represents a significant trauma in their life.

In conclusion, we support Morrow and Smith's (1995) suggestion that a theory-driven approach is needed to provide a semblance of order to the "chaos of symptomology" (p. 24) that currently characterizes the field of child sexual abuse. On the basis of our findings, we suggest that attachment theory may be a viable framework from which to examine the experi-

405 ence and potential consequences of sexual abuse in the adult survivor.

References

Alexander, P. C. (1992). Application of attachment theory to the study of sexual abuse. *Journal of Consulting and Clinical Psychology, 60,* 185–195.

Bowlby, J. (1973). *Attachment and loss: Vol. 2. Separation, anxiety, and anger.* New York: Basic Books.

Bowlby, J. (1977). The making and breaking of affectional bonds. *British Journal of Psychiatry, 130,* 201–210.

Bowlby, J. (1980). *Attachment and loss: Vol. 3. Loss.* New York: Basic Books.

Brennan, K. A., & Shaver, P. R. (1991). Dimensions of adult attachment and the dynamics of romantic relationships. *Personality and Social Psychology Bulletin, 99,* 66–77.

Briere, J. (1989). *Therapy for adults molested as children: Beyond survival.* New York: Springer.

Cole, P. M., & Putnam, F. W. (1992). Effect of incest on self and social functioning: A developmental psychopathology perspective. *Journal of Consulting and Clinical Psychology, 60,* 174–184.

Courtois, C. A. (1988). *Healing the incest wound: Adult survivors in therapy.* New York: Norton.

Derogatis, L. R. (1977). *SCL–90 administration, scoring and procedures manual—1.* Baltimore: Johns Hopkins University Press.

Everson, M. D., Hunter, W. M., Runyon, D. K., Edelsohn, G. A., & Coulter, M. L. (1989). Maternal support following disclosure of incest. *American Journal of Orthopsychiatry, 59,* 197–207.

Feeney, J. A., & Noller, P. (1990). Attachment style as a predictor of adult romantic relationships. *Journal of Personality and Social Psychology, 58,* 281–291.

Finkelhor, D. (1984). *Child sexual abuse: New theory and research.* New York: Free Press.

Finkelhor, D. (1990). Early & long term effects of child sexual abuse: An update. *Professional Psychology: Research and Practice, 21,* 325–330.

Freud, A., & Burlington, D. (1943). *War and children.* London: Medical War Books.

Friedrich, W. N., Beilke, R., & Urquiza, A. J. (1987). Children from sexually abusive families: A behavioral comparison. *Journal of Interpersonal Violence, 2,* 391–402.

Geffner, R. (1992). Current issues and future directions in child sexual abuse. *Journal of Child Sexual Abuse, 1*(1), 1–13.

Green, A. H. (1993). Child sexual abuse: Immediate and long-term effects and intervention. *Journal of the American Academy of Child and Adolescent Psychiatry, 32,* 890–902.

Haft, W. L., & Slade, A. (1989). Affect attunement and maternal attachment: A pilot study. *Infant Mental Health Journal, 10,* 157–172.

Hazan, C., & Shaver, P. (1987). Romantic love conceptualized as an attachment process. *Journal of Personality and Social Psychology, 52,* 511–524.

Hoffman, N. G., & Overall, P. B. (1978). Factor structure of the SCL–90 in a psychiatric population. *Journal of Consulting and Clinical Psychology, 46,* 1187–1191.

Lopez, F. G., Melendez, M. C., Sauer, E. M., Berger, E., & Wyssmann, J. (1998). Internal working models, self-reported problems, and help-seeking attitudes among college students. *Journal of Counseling Psychology, 45,* 79–83.

Mackinnon, A., Henderson, A. S., & Andrews, G. (1993). Parental "affectionless control" as an antecedent to adult depression: A risk factor refined. *Psychological Medicine, 23,* 135.

Morrow, S. L., & Smith, M. L. (1995). Constructions of survival and coping by women who have survived childhood sexual abuse. *Journal of Counseling Psychology, 42,* 24–33.

Parker, G. (1977). *Parental antecedents to depression.* Unpublished master's thesis, University of New South Wales, Sydney, New South Wales, Australia.

Parker, G. (1979). Parental characteristics in relation to depressive disorders. *British Journal of Psychiatry, 134,* 138–147.

Parker, G. (1983). Parental "affectionless control" as an antecedent to adult depression. *Archives of General Psychiatry, 40,* 956–960.

Parker, G., & Lipscombe, P. (1981). Influences on maternal overprotection. *British Journal of Psychiatry, 138,* 303–311.

Parker, G., Tupling, H., & Brown, L. B. (1979). A parental bonding instrument. *British Journal of Medical Psychology, 52,* 1–10.

Russell, D. E. (1983). The incidence and prevalence of intrafamilial and extrafamilial sexual abuse of female children. *Child Abuse and Neglect, 7,* 133–146.

Sroufe, L. A. (1983). Individual patterns of adaptation from infancy to preschool. In M. Perlmutter (Ed.), *Minnesota Symposium on Child Psychology* (Vol. 16, pp. 41–85). Minneapolis: University of Minnesota Press.

Sroufe, L. A., & Fleeson, J. (1986). Attachment and the construction of relationships. In W. Hartup & Z. Rubin (Eds.), *Relationships and development* (pp. 51–71). Hillsdale, NJ: Erlbaum.

Teyber, E. (1997). *Interpersonal process in psychotherapy* (3rd ed.). Pacific Grove, CA: Brooks/Cole.

Werner, E., & Smith, R. (1982). *Vulnerable but invincible: A study of resilient children.* New York: McGraw-Hill.

Address correspondence to: Roxanne Schreiber or William J. Lyddon, Department of Psychology, Box 5025, University of Southern Mississippi, Hattiesburg, MS 39406-5025. Electronic mail may be sent to rschreib@whale.st.usm.edu

Exercise for Article 17

Factual Questions

1. What does the symptom approach "portray?"

2. How is "optimal bonding" defined?

3. "GSI" stands for what words?

4. What was the dependent variable?

5. Did the *abused group* or the *comparison group* have significantly higher GSI scores?

6. The researchers report that CSASs with low paternal care scores scored significantly higher than CSASs with high paternal care scores on the GSI. This difference is statistically significant at what probability level?

7. What percentage of the sample in this study reported the abuse experience to their parents?

Questions for Discussion

8. To what extent did the discussion of attachment theory assist you in understanding and interpreting this study?

9. For interpreting this study, how important is it to know that both groups were similar in age? (See lines 156–157 and 172–173.)

10. The researchers suggest that this study does not identify causal links. Do you agree? Why? Why not? (See lines 386–389.)

11. Do you agree with the researchers' assessment of the external validity of the study? Explain. (See lines 389–396.)

12. Do you agree that based on the findings in this report, "attachment theory may be a viable framework from which to examine the experience and potential consequences of sexual abuse in the adult survivor?" Explain.

13. If you were planning research on this topic, what changes, if any, would you make in the research methodology?

Quality Ratings

Directions: Indicate your level of agreement with each of the following statements by circling a number from 5 for strongly agree (SA) to 1 for strongly disagree (SD). If you believe an item is not applicable to this research article, leave it blank. Be prepared to explain your ratings.

A. The introduction establishes the importance of the study.

SA   5   4   3   2   1   SD

B. The literature review establishes the context for the study.

SA   5   4   3   2   1   SD

C. The research purpose, question, or hypothesis is clearly stated.

SA   5   4   3   2   1   SD

D. The method of sampling is sound.

SA   5   4   3   2   1   SD

E. Relevant demographics (for example, age, gender, and ethnicity) are described.

SA   5   4   3   2   1   SD

F. Measurement procedures are adequate.

SA   5   4   3   2   1   SD

G. All procedures have been described in sufficient detail to permit a replication of the study.

SA   5   4   3   2   1   SD

H. The participants have been adequately protected from potential harm.

SA   5   4   3   2   1   SD

I. The results are clearly described.

SA   5   4   3   2   1   SD

J. The discussion/conclusion is appropriate.

SA   5   4   3   2   1   SD

K. Despite any flaws, the report is worthy of publication.

SA   5   4   3   2   1   SD

Article 18

The Influence of a Big Brothers Program on the Adjustment of Boys in Single-Parent Families

DOUGLAS A. ABBOTT
University of Nebraska–Lincoln

WILLIAM H. MEREDITH
University of Nebraska–Lincoln

ROLEE SELF-KELLY
Big Brothers–Big Sisters of the Midlands

M. ELIZABETH DAVIS
University of Nebraska at Omaha

ABSTRACT. This study is an evaluation of the self-competence, academic performance, behavioral problems, and parent–child relations of boys who had been raised in single-parent families headed by their mothers and who had weekly contact with an adult friend or companion through a midwestern affiliate of the Big Brothers/Big Sisters of America. Results indicated that participation in such a program was not related to changes in the areas investigated. These findings are not consistent with the social support literature suggesting that an adult companion or friend may benefit children in single-parent families. Further study with a larger sample, over a longer time frame, is recommended.

From *The Journal of Psychology*, *131*, 143–156. Copyright © 1997 by Heldref Publications, 1319 Eighteenth St., N.W., Washington, DC 20036-1802. Reprinted with permission from the Helen Dwight Reid Educational Foundation.

Professionals in the field of marriage and the family are increasingly concerned about the fragmentation of the American family and its effects on children (Children's Defense Fund, 1988). The divorce rate remains high, and it is estimated that over 50% of the marriages of those now in their 20s will end in divorce (Norton & Moorman, 1987). Over 1,000,000 children will experience the trauma of their parents' divorce or separation each year (Spanier, 1989). The rate of out-of-wedlock pregnancy also continues to increase, and currently 27% of all live births are to unwed women, which leaves another 1,000,000 children per year in single-parent families (Edwards, 1987).

Children in single-parent families may be at greater risk than children of two-parent families (Amato & Keith, 1991a, 1991b; Bahr, 1989; Bilge & Kaufman, 1983; Booth, Brinkerhoff, & White, 1984; Booth & Edwards, 1989; Bumpass, 1990; McLanahan & Booth, 1989; Glenn & Kramer, 1985, 1987; Krein, 1986; Lauer & Lauer, 1991; Mackinnon, Brody, & Stoneman, 1982; Mueller & Cooper, 1986). Amato (1993) suggested that single parenthood is problematic for children's socialization because many children with one parent receive less economic and emotional support, practical assistance, information, guidance, and supervision, and less role modeling for adult interpersonal interaction than children in two-parent families.

Wallerstein has studied children from families disrupted by divorce across three generations and concluded that such children "lose something fundamental to their development—family structure, the scaffolding upon which children mount successive developmental stages, which supports their psychological, physical and emotional ascent into maturity" (Wallerstein & Blakeslee, 1990, p. 64). Lamb (1987) concluded: "Suffice it to say the boys growing up without fathers seemed to have problems in the areas of sex-role and gender-identity development, school performance, psychological adjustment, and perhaps, in the control of aggression" (p. 14).

As a result of the increasing numbers of children in single-parent families, programs have been established that pair an adult volunteer with a child who may benefit from adult companionship. The largest and most prominent of these programs in America is the Big Brothers/Big Sisters organization. The purpose of this study was to evaluate the influence of a Big Brothers program on the academic, psychological, and social development of boys. Knowledge acquired from this type of research may improve the effectiveness of intervention programs that seek to support children in single-parent families.

Potential Benefits of Social Support for Children of Single Parents

If we accept the premise that, on average, children in single-parent families are more likely to experience difficulties, then the question becomes, what can we do to assist and support these children? Amato (1993) presents some evidence that such children may experience a higher level of well-being if another adult is available to provide the role functions of the absent parent (see also Dornbusch et al., 1985). Santrock and Warshak (1979) found that contact with adult caretakers other than the custodial mother was associated with positive behavior among children of divorced parents. Cochran, Larner, Riley, Gunnarsson, and Henderson

65 (1990) reported that among boys in families with only the mother as the parent, school success was associated with the amount of task-orientated interaction with adult male relatives.

70 Guidubaldi, Cleminshaw, Perry, and McLaughin (1983) found that a child's positive relationships with adult caretakers predicted positive social adjustment. Sandler, Miller, Short, and Wolchik (1989) suggested that positive interaction with caring adults can enhance the self-esteem of children experiencing stressful life 75 events like divorce (see also Sandler, Wolchik, & Brower, 1987). These studies suggest that an adult friend or companion who provides some caretaking functions may have a beneficial impact on a child in a single-parent family. Thus, one therapeutic option is to 80 provide the child with regular contact with an adult friend who shows a consistent interest and concern in the child's welfare.

Child–adult companion programs such as Big Brothers/Big Sisters are one type of intervention that 85 may help to support a child in a single-parent family. The Big Brothers/Big Sisters program is a national, nonprofit organization that recruits adults who volunteer to spend some time each week with a child from a single-parent family whose custodial parent has re-90 quested this service. The organization was started in 1907 and now has 502 affiliate programs distributed in all 50 states. There are approximately 50,000 boys and girls being served by Big Brothers/Big Sisters. Volunteers are carefully screened and then matched with a 95 same-sex child. The volunteer meets with the child each week for a visit and/or activity.

In spite of the growing number of volunteer programs, we found no published studies on the value of or effectiveness of adult companions on the emotional 100 or social development of children from single-parent families. There is some research on how contact and involvement by the noncustodial father influences a child's adjustment to divorce, but these studies were not considered equivalent to the influence of a nonre-105 lative adult companion on a child's development (Guidubaldi, 1986).

Theory and Hypothesis

An adult companion program such as Big Brothers/Big Sisters may provide a positive influence on a child's development. This assumption rests on two 110 theoretical foundations: modeling theory and social support theory (Bandura, 1977; Lee, 1979; Wolchik, Ruehlman, Braver, & Sandler, 1989). Modeling theory stresses the importance of the relationship between the observer (e.g., the child) and the model (e.g., the Big 115 Brother) in eliciting imitative behavior. The child is more likely to model adult action and personality if the adult is seen as important, powerful, warm and nurturant (Bandura & Walters, 1963). The Big Brother or Big Sister volunteer serves as a positive role model for 120 the child in a variety of vocational, psychological, and social ways.

One aspect of social support theory suggests that an individual or family is more likely to cope with stressful or difficult life circumstances (e.g., low-income 125 single parenting) if supported by family, friends, and helping professionals or organizations (Boss, 1988; Milardo, 1988; Perlman & Rook, 1987; Unger & Powell, 1980). The Big Brothers/Big Sisters agency personnel provide institutional support to the single parent 130 through frequent interviews (every 2 to 3 months), counseling, and referral to other community resources. This type of social support may buffer the child against the stressful life events so often experienced by poor children in single-parent families (Cohen & Willis, 135 1985).

Supported by these theoretical assumptions, our program evaluation was guided by the major goals of the local Big Brothers/Big Sisters program, which were to (a) improve the child's feelings of self-competence, 140 (b) encourage the child's achievement in school, (c) monitor the child's psychosocial problems, and (d) encourage a positive parent–child relationship. Given these goals, we posited that regular adult companionship over many months could have many beneficial 145 general effects on a child's development. A child's feelings of self-competence may be enhanced by regular, long-term contact with an adult companion. The special attention and the weekly activities with an attentive and interested adult may help the child feel 150 better about himself or herself.

In addition, an adult volunteer who frequently shares facts and feelings about work and careers and helps the child with homework and school projects may encourage the child's school performance. Ideally, 155 with enhanced self-competence and improved school performance, the child may be less likely to display behavioral problems. Finally, the parent–child relationship may be indirectly affected by the combined effect of all these factors. A child who is more self-160 competent, who is doing better in school, and who displays fewer behavior problems, may engender more positive relations with his mother. The Big Brother or Big Sister may also directly encourage the child to work out conflicts and problems with his mother.

165 Our major purpose in this study was to evaluate whether a child's participation in a companionship program was related to changes in the child's (a) self-competence, (b) school performance, (c) emotional and social problems, and (d) parent–child relationship. 170 Based on the previous rationale, we hypothesized that boys with a Big Brother would evidence greater improvement over time in self-competence, in school performance, in reducing emotional and social problems, and in the quality of the parent–child relationship 175 than boys without a Big Brother.

Method

Participants

We selected the children from single-parent families and the adult companions from a midwestern affiliate of the Big Brothers/Big Sisters of America, a nationally known and well-respected adult-companion program. Because the great majority of clients at this chapter of Big Brothers/Big Sisters were boys, only boys 8–14 years of age were selected for the study. All children came from mother-headed, single-parent households. None of the boys had been diagnosed with any mental or physical disabilities.

About 120 boys began the study, approximately 40 in the intervention group (those who received a Big Brother) and 80 in the comparison group (those on the waiting list who had not yet received a Big Brother). Out of the comparison group (at the end of the study), those boys who matched most closely the demographics of the intervention groups were selected for the final sample. Over the 2-year span of the study, about 60% of the boys dropped out of the program because of relocation or loss of contact with the organization.

The final sample consisted of 44 boys: 22 in the intervention group, who had had at least weekly contact with a Big Brother for 12–18 months, and 22 in the comparison group, who had been on the waiting list for 12–18 months and had not yet received an adult companion. The boys were matched on several variables such as age, race, number of siblings, mother's education and income, reason for single-parent status (e.g., divorced/separated, widowed, or unwed motherhood), the child's age when the father left home, and the extent of the child's contact with the noncustodial father. No significant differences were found between the intervention and comparison groups on any of these variables (see Table 1).

Design and Procedure

A pretest–posttest longitudinal design was used. Boys with Big Brothers were compared with boys on the waiting list on the outcome measures at the beginning of the study and then 12–18 months later. We obtained permission from both parents and children by using adult and child consent forms. Big Brothers case managers administered the self-report questionnaires to the parents and children during a regularly scheduled visit required by the program. The surveys were administered to the intervention group when the children were matched with an adult volunteer and then 12–18 months after the match. The comparison group was surveyed when they were put on the waiting list and then 12–18 months later if they had not yet been assigned a Big Brother.

Instruments and Measures

To measure the child's level of self-competence and personal competence, we administered Harter's (1985) Self-Perception Profile. This scale measures six domains of competence: scholastic, social, athletic, physical, behavioral conduct, and global self-competence. Harter's scale is generally accepted as a valid and reliable measure of various components of self-competence (Stigler, Smith, & Mao, 1985).

Table 1
Demographic Characteristics of Boys with and without a Big Brother

Characteristic	With a Big Brother (n = 22)		Without a Big Brother (n = 22)	
	M	SD	M	SD
Child's age	9.7	3.5	10.7	1.6
Mother's age	36.3	4.5	36.1	5.1
Mother's education	14 yrs	3.5	13 yrs	3.1
Siblings	1.3	0.7	1.6	1.2
Age when father left home	4.5	3.7	3.6	3.3
Mother's average income	$11,000–20,000		$11,000–20,000	
Father living	75%		76%	
Reason for single parent				
Divorce	71%		80%	
Unmarried	19%		10%	
Widowed	10%		10%	
Father visitation	Once a year or less		Once a year or less	

The Harter instrument uses a structured alternative format. The child is first asked to decide which kind of child is most like him or her, and then whether this is *sort of true* or *really true* for him or her. Items are scored from 1 to 4, with 1 indicating low perceived competence. Each of the six subscales contained six items. Reliabilities for all subscales based on Cronbach's alpha ranged from .71 to .86 on four samples as reported by Harter (1985). Two test–retest evaluations were completed after 3 months and correlated at .80 and .83 (Harter, 1985). Cronbach's alpha reliability for this study was .85.

The children's school performance was evaluated by obtaining the child's school grades after receiving written permission from the parents. Grades were based on a 5-point scale with a 1 indicating superior performance or a grade of A.

To measure the child's relationship with his mother, we developed the Family Feelings scales, consisting of two forms, one for the child to complete and one for the mother to complete. The items on both scales were similar in content but worded for a child to evaluate his relationship with his mother (e.g., "Mom and I fight about the same things over and over"), or for the mother to evaluate her relationship with her son (e.g., "My son and I fight about the same things over and over"). We developed the scales after a review of items from the Parent-Adolescent Communication Scale (Barnes & Olson, 1985), the Family Satisfaction Scale (Olson & Wilson, 1985), the Family Environment Scale (Moos & Moos, 1981), and the Inventory of Family Feelings (Lowman, 1981).

Our scale was evaluated for content validity and age appropriateness by 15 family professionals in child development, social work, psychology, and sociology. Two professors in teacher education determined that the reading level of the scale was suitable for young children. The scale was composed of 28 items. A high score on the Family Feelings Scale indicates more positive parent–child relations. For this study, the mean on the child version of family feelings was 63.4 ($SD =$ 8.0) and Cronbach's alpha was .78. For the parent version, the mean was 63.3 ($SD = 7.9$) and Cronbach's alpha was .85.

To measure the child's social and emotional problems, we had the mothers complete the Revised Behavior Problem Checklist (Quay & Peterson, 1987). The RBPC consists of 89 items scored on a 3-point scale: *no problem* (0), *mild problem* (1), *severe problem* (2). It is appropriate to use the total score of all 89 items and/or the individual subscale scores.

The checklist is divided into six subscales: Conduct Disorder (e.g., gets into fights); Socialized Aggression (e.g. belongs to a gang); Immaturity (e.g., is irresponsible and undependable); Anxiety–Withdrawal (e.g., feels inferior); Psychotic Behavior (e.g., expresses strange ideas); Motor Excess (e.g., is restless, unable to sit still). The instrument is rated at the fifth-grade reading level and takes approximately 15 minutes to complete. Quay and Peterson (1987) provide substantial reliability and validity information, including 2-month test–retest correlations of .61–.83 with various samples of children. The RBPC has strong correlations with measures of similar content including the Child Behavior Checklist (Achenbach & Edelbrock, 1983) and Conner's Revised Parent Rating Scale (Conners, 1970). For this sample, the mean score for behavior problems was 46.6 ($SD = 29.9$) and Cronbach's alpha was .96.

Results

Significant correlations among dependent variables would indicate that multivariate statistics should be used, whereas a lack of significant associations would indicate multiple ANOVAs should be computed (Huberty & Morris, 1989). Because there were no significant correlations between grade point average or quality of parent–child relationship as perceived by the parent and the child, we computed three 2 (group: boys with Big Brothers vs. boys without) × 2 (time: Time 1, Time 2) repeated measures ANOVAs on each of these three dependent variables.

The other two dependent measures were Harter's Self-Competence subscales and Quay's Behavior Problem subscales. Because the Harter subscales are interrelated, and Quay's subscales are interrelated, two 2 (group) × 2 (time) MANOVAs were done to assess differences on these measures between boys with and

without Big Brothers. Because of the exploratory nature of these analyses, an alpha level of $p < .10$ was used.

The major research question of this study was whether the boys, who over a sustained period of time, had regular companionship of a Big Brother differed from a matched sample of boys without a Big Brother in the areas of self-concept, school grades, emotional relationships with their mothers, and frequency of behavioral problems. The t tests revealed no pretest group differences between the boys with Big Brothers and the boys without Big Brothers on any dependent measures.

The results of the overall MANOVA revealed no significant Group × Time interaction and no group or time main effects on the set of self-competence subscales between boys with and without Big Brothers. There were no significant Group × Time interactions and no group or time main effects on any of the behavior problem subscales between boys with and without Big Brothers.

There was a significant Group × Time interaction related to grade point average, $F(1, 39) = 3.6, p < .07$; contrary to our hypothesis, analysis of simple effects indicated that performance in school of boys with a Big Brother *decreased* from Time 1 ($M = 2.13$) to Time 2 ($M = 2.43$), $F(1, 39) = 3.0, p < .09$ (1 = high GPA, 5 = low GPA). The boys *without* a Big Brother showed no significant change in grade point average from Time 1 ($M = 2.71$) to Time 2 ($M = 2.56$).

There was a significant Group × Time interaction on parent's perceptions of the parent–child relationship, $F(1, 42) = 3.3, p < .08$. Analysis of simple effects indicated that the mothers of boys without a Big Brother reported improvement in the parent–child relationship from Time 1 ($M = 62.5$) to Time 2 ($M = 67.1$), $F(1, 42) = 5.53, p < .02$. Mothers of boys with Big Brothers reported no significant change in their parent–child relationship from Time 1 ($M = 64.0$) to Time 2 ($M = 63.5$).

With regard to the children's perceptions of the parent–child relationship, there was no Group × Time interaction, and there was no group main effect. A time main effect, $F(1, 42) = 2.7, p < .06$, indicated that all the boys in both groups reported improved parent–child relationships from Time 1 ($M = 63.3$) to Time 2 ($M = 65.6$).

Table 2 contains the statistics related to a comparison of boys with and without a Big Brother on the major dependent variables.

Discussion

In general, the results of this research indicate that the weekly companionship of an adult volunteer was not related to positive changes in certain developmental outcomes for boys participating in the Big Brothers program. These findings are not consistent with the social support literature that suggests that children in nonnuclear families often benefit from the companion-

Table 2

A Comparison of Boys with and without a Big Brother on Major Dependent Variables

| | With a Big Brother (*n* = 22) | | | | Without a Big Brother (*n* = 22) | | | |
| | Pretest | | Posttest | | Pretest | | Posttest | |
Variable	*M*	*SD*	*M*	*SD*	*M*	*SD*	*M*	*SD*
Child feeling	64.7	8.2	65.5	5.6	62.0	8.2	65.6	5.6
Parent feeling	64.0	7.6	63.5	9.4	62.5	8.1	67.1	9.7
Grade point average	2.13	1.0	2.43	1.1	2.71	1.1	2.56	1.2
Self-perceived competence								
Scholastic	18.5	3.8	17.6	4.2	16.5	4.9	16.4	3.0
Social	16.4	4.5	17.5	4.1	16.7	5.1	17.1	4.1
Athletic	16.4	4.4	18.5	3.8	17.1	5.7	16.9	3.9
Appearance	17.6	4.3	17.5	3.2	16.2	3.8	16.1	5.4
Behavior	18.5	2.6	17.8	5.4	16.9	5.1	15.9	3.9
Global	19.3	3.7	18.7	4.3	18.1	4.3	18.3	3.1
Behavior problems								
Conduct	16.7	11.0	17.3	11.1	21.0	11.6	20.4	11.8
Aggression	3.2	3.7	2.6	3.6	3.6	4.3	3.2	5.0
Immaturity	8.6	5.9	8.5	6.2	10.6	7.3	11.0	9.6
Anxiety	8.5	4.4	7.4	4.6	9.1	5.0	8.0	5.1
Psychotic	1.5	1.9	2.0	2.8	1.6	2.3	1.8	2.6
Motor	2.0	2.1	2.1	2.5	3.5	3.1	2.8	2.9

375 ship and active involvement of an adult friend (Cochran et al., 1990; Ihinger-Tallman, 1986; Lamb, 1982). Other researchers have also suggested that adult companions/friends may help children buffer stressful life events, enhance their self-esteem, and reduce deviant 380 behaviors (Dornbush et al., 1985; Sandler et al., 1989).

Our results, however, should be viewed with caution. One year may not be long enough to register changes in our particular dependent measures, especially with our small sample. Our measures (grade 385 point average, behavioral problems, self-competence, and the quality of parent–child relations) may have shown changes if the study had been extended over a longer period of time.

We were surprised that the school grades of boys 390 with a Big Brother showed no improvement over the boys without a Big Brother. This result was unexpected because the case workers at Big Brothers told us repeatedly that an adult companion frequently asks questions about the child's school performance and encour- 395 ages the child's attendance and achievement in school. Many volunteers help with the child's homework and school projects. Some Big Brothers go to the child's school open house, or may accompany the child's parent to parent–teacher conferences. Furthermore, the 400 Big Brother, who is usually college educated and employed, may serve as a school/work role model for the male child, thus indirectly encouraging the child to succeed in school.

There were no significant changes in behavioral 405 problems for the boys with and without a Big Brother across the time period of this study. One explanation for this may be that their scores at the beginning and end of this study were already high. The subscale

means on conduct disorder, socialized aggression, and 410 anxiety withdrawal for boys with *and* without Big Brothers were one to two standard deviations above Quay's norms for normal children, and similar to Quay's norms for his clinical samples of inpatients and outpatients at psychiatric facilities (Quay & Peterson, 415 1983).

Modest gains in the quality of the parent–child relationship, as reported by all the boys, are difficult to explain. Improvement may be the natural result of time and the continued adjustment of the child and parent to 420 a single-parent family situation. On the other hand, gains may be related to the mother and child's involvement in the Big Brothers organization.

Again, caution is warranted in evaluating these findings. The results could be an artifact of the small 425 sample. In addition, the magnitude of the differences on the dependent measures between the boys with and without a Big Brother are small. This may indicate that the intervention of a volunteer companion, in and of itself, has only a limited impact on the development of 430 boys in single-parent households. On the other hand, it may also indicate that the mothers of the control boys, motivated to have their sons placed with a Big Brother, may have attempted to accomplish this goal in other ways, that is, by giving more personal attention to their 435 sons or finding other adult friends for them. A third explanation for these findings may suggest that the variables we studied and the method of measuring these concepts were less than adequate to identify change in development over a 1-year period.

440 Given these limitations, suggestions for improvements of this study are warranted. The impact of such a program might have been more readily assessed if a

larger pool of boys had been evaluated. Multisite samples could be pooled together from several cities across the country. Also, the time frame of the project could have been extended to 2 or 3 years if more resources had been available. However, given the mobility of Big Brothers/Big Sisters clients and volunteers, the evaluation of a larger sample over a longer time period may be difficult to accomplish. One solution might be to use different developmental measures that are more sensitive to change over a shorter period of time. In addition, any child on a waiting list may need more regular contact with the organization to prevent dropouts. Program staff could provide occasional activities, such as a field trip, a swimming party, or a parent–child activity for the families on the waiting list.

Arrangements with the various Big Brothers/Big Sisters programs could be worked out so that the researchers have more direct access to the participants. For this study, we were not allowed to contact the participants directly. We could only remind the case managers of when to do the assessments and hope they would follow through and collect the data on time. On several occasions, however, because of staff turnover or work overload, data were not collected or were obtained too late to be of use in the study.

Implications for Practice

In this study, program goals were not clearly and concisely articulated and we (the research team) may have missed some of the important outcomes or benefits of this program. Thus, the first implication of this study is a pragmatic one. When doing program evaluation, program staff, and the external evaluation team if one is used, should make a concerted effort to identify and specify as concretely as possible the program goals and expected behavioral outcomes (Posavac & Carey, 1985; Rutman, 1977). Research methods could then be more easily designed and used to evaluate performance objectives. For example, if the goal of the program is improved parent–child communication, then specific assessments of communication, using a variety of instruments, can be done.

A second advantage to ongoing evaluation is that it may remind program staff of program goals, and this may encourage accomplishment of those goals. Ongoing evaluation may also serve to motivate program staff to carry out their responsibilities by providing them with periodic progress reports on the children and adults they serve (Theobald, 1985).

Another suggestion for improving program evaluation would be the use of some qualitative measures in the evaluation (Gilgun, 1992; Rossi & Freeman, 1989). The results of our quantitative study may have limited our understanding of how such programs benefit children. In this study, structured interviews with mothers and sons, asking them directly to talk about any perceived effects of participation in the program, may have yielded relevant data that are not easily obtained through quantitative global variables such as our measures of self-competence or grade point average.

In programs like Big Brothers/Big Sisters, where an adult has direct and intensive interaction with a child, the quality of that child–adult relationship may be a key variable in predicting improvement in child outcomes. This relationship variable should be evaluated and monitored closely. If practitioners examined specific aspects of the child–adult relationship and the processes of relationship development, it may be possible to understand how or why the relationship flourishes or fails and how this is related to program goals.

Another implication of this study is that children who have chosen to participate in such adult-helper programs may be at high risk for social and emotional difficulties. Program staff may want to administer more thorough intake evaluations of these children to gain a better understanding of the nature of their clients. If some children are rated as high risk, then more selective matching with adult helpers could be done. An adult volunteer could be chosen (or recruited) who has the knowledge and skills to deal with a more disturbed or difficult child. These adults could also be provided with special training by the sponsoring organization.

Although this study does not provide evidence that a volunteer program like Big Brothers/Big Sisters has a significant positive influence on the development of male children in homes headed by the mother, this does not mean that such programs are not effective. Additional research is needed in order to understand how such a program may benefit a child and what can be done to improve the effectiveness of such programs. If current trends in divorce and unwed parenthood continue, the numbers of children from single-parent homes will only increase, and understanding their challenges and developing strategies to assist them should be a high priority for social service professionals.

References

Achenbach, T. M., & Edelbrock, C. (1983). *Manual for the Child Behavior Checklist.* Burlington, VT: Dept. of Psychiatry, University of Vermont.

Amato, P. R. (1993). Children's adjustment to divorce: Theories, hypotheses, and empirical support. *Journal of Marriage and the Family, 55,* 23–38.

Amato, P., & Keith, B. (1991a). Parental divorce and adult well-being: A meta-analysis. *Journal of Marriage and the Family, 53,* 43–58.

Amato, P., & Keith, B. (1991b). Parental divorce and the well-being of children: A meta-analysis. *Psychological Bulletin, 110,* 26–46.

Bahr, S. (1989). *Family interaction* (pp. 178–180). New York: Macmillan.

Bandura, A. (1977). *Social learning theory.* Englewood Cliffs, NJ: Prentice-Hall.

Bandura, A., & Walters, R. (1963). *Social learning and personality development.* New York: Holt, Rinehart & Winston.

Barnes, H., & Olson, D. H. (1985). Parent-adolescent communication. In D. H. Olson & Associates (Eds.), *Family inventories.* St. Paul, MN: Family Social Science, University of Minnesota.

Bilge, B., & Kaufman, G. (1983). Children of divorce and one-parent families: Cross-cultural perspectives. *Family Relations, 32,* 59–71.

Booth, A., Brinkerhoff, D., & White, L. (1984). The impact of parental divorce on courtship. *Journal of Marriage and the Family, 46,* 85–94.

Booth, A., & Edwards, J. (1989). Transmission of marital and family quality over the generations: The effect of parental divorce and unhappiness. *Journal of Divorce, 14,* 41–58.

Boss, P. (1988). *Family stress management.* Newbury Park, CA: Sage.

Bumpass, L. (1990). Children's experience in single-parent families: Implications of cohabitation and marital transitions. *Family Planning Perspectives,*

113

21, 256–260.

Children's Defense Fund. (1988). *A briefing book on the status of American children in 1988.* Washington, DC: Author.

Cochran, M., Larner, M., Riley, D., Gunnarsson, L., & Henderson, C. (1990). *Extending families: The social networks of parents and their children.* Cambridge. MA: Cambridge University Press.

Cohen, S., & Willis, T. (1985). Stress, social support, and the buffering hypothesis. *Psychological Bulletin, 98,* 310–317.

Conners, C. (1970). Symptom patterns in hyperkinetic, neurotic, and normal children. *Child Development, 41,* 667–682.

Dornbush, S., Carlsmith, J., Bushwall, S., Ritter, P., Leiderman, H., Hastort, A. H., & Gross, R. T. (1985). Single parents, extended households, and the control of adolescents. *Child Development, 56,* 326–341.

Edwards, J. N. (1987). Changing family structure and youthful well-being: Assessing the future. *Journal of Family Issues, 8,* 355–371.

Gilgun, J. (1992). *Qualitative methods in family research.* Newbury Park, CA: Sage.

Glenn, N. D., & Kramer, K. (1985). The psychological well-being of adult children of divorce. *Journal of Marriage and the Family, 47,* 905–912.

Glenn, N. D., & Kramer, K. B. (1987). The marriages and divorces of the children of divorce. *Journal of Marriage and the Family, 49,* 811–825.

Guidubaldi, J. (1986). The role of selected family environmental factors in children's post-divorce adjustment. *Family Relations, 35,* 141–142.

Guidubaldi, J., Cleminshaw, H., Perry, J., & McLaughin. (1983). The impact of parental divorce on children: Report of a national NAP study. *School Psychology Review, 12,* 300–323.

Harter, S. (1985). *Manual for the Self-Perception Profile for Children.* Denver, CO: University of Denver Press.

Huberty, C. J., & Morris, J. D. (1989). Multivariate analysis versus multiple univariate analyses. *Psychological Bulletin, 105,* 302–308.

Ihinger-Tallman, M. (1986). Member adjustment in single-parent families: Theory building. *Family Relations, 35,* 215–222.

Krein, S. F. (1986). Growing up in a single-parent family: The effect of education and earnings on young men. *Family Relations, 35,* 161–168.

Lamb, M. E. (1982). *Nontraditional families: Parenting and child development.* Hillsdale, NJ: Erlbaum.

Lamb, M. E. (1987). *The father's role in child development: Cross-cultural perspectives.* Hillsdale, NJ: Erlbaum.

Lauer, R., & Lauer, J. (1991). The long-term relational consequences of problematic family backgrounds, *Family Relations, 40,* 286–290.

Lee, G. R. (1979). Effects of social networks on the family. In W. Burr, R. Hill, F. Nye, & I. Reiss (Eds.), *Contemporary theories about the family* (pp. 27–56). New York: The Free Press.

Lowman, J. (1981). Love, hate, and the family: Measures of emotion. In E. E. Filsinger & R. Lewis (Eds.), *Assessing marriage: New behavioral approaches* (pp. 55–73). Beverly Hills, CA: Sage.

Mackinnon, C. E., Brody, G. H., & Stoneman, Z. (1982). The effects of divorce and maternal employment on the home environment of preschool children. *Child Development, 53,* 1392–1399.

McLanahan, S., & Booth, K. (1989). Mother-only families: Problems, prospects and politics. *Journal of Marriage and the Family, 51,* 557–588.

Milardo, R. (1988). *Families and social networks.* Newbury Park, CA: Sage.

Moos, R. H., & Moos, B. S. (1981). *Family Environment Scale manual.* Palo Alto, CA: Consulting Psychologists Press.

Mueller, D. P., & Cooper, P. W. (1986). Children of single-parent families: How they fare as young adults. *Family Relations, 35,* 169–176.

Norton, A. J., & Moorman. J. E. (1987). Current trends in marriage and divorce among American women. *Journal of Marriage and the Family, 49,* 3–14.

Olson, D. H., & Wilson, M. (1985). In D. H. Olson & Associates (Eds.), *Family inventories.* St. Paul, MN: Family Social Science, University of Minnesota.

Perlman, D., & Rook, K. (1987). Social support, social deficits, and the family. In S. Oskamp (Ed.), *Family process and problems: Social psychological aspects.* Newbury Park, CA: Sage.

Posavac, E., & Carey, R. (1985). *Program evaluation: Methods and case studies.* Englewood Cliffs, NJ: Prentice-Hall.

Quay, H. C., & Peterson, D. (1983). A dimensional approach to behavior disorder: The Revised Behavior Problem Checklist. *School Psychology Review, 12,* 244–249.

Quay, H. C., & Peterson, D. (1987). *Manual for the Revised Behavior Problem Checklist.* Coral Gables, FL: Herbert C. Quay.

Rossi, P., & Freeman, H. (1989). *Evaluation: A systematic approach.* Newbury Park, CA: Sage.

Rutman, L. (1977). *Evaluation research methods: A basic guide.* Beverly Hills, CA: Sage.

Sandler, I., Miller, P., Short, J., & Wolchik, W. (1989). Social support as a protective factor for children in stress. In D. Belle (Ed.), *Children's social networks and social support* (pp. 277–307). New York: Wiley.

Sandler, I., Wolchik, S., & Brower, S. (1987). Social support and children of divorce. In I. G. Sarason (Ed.), *Social support: Theory, research and application* (pp. 371–391). New York: Wiley.

Santrock, J., & Warshak, R. (1979). Father custody and social development in boys and girls. *Journal of Social Issues, 35,* 112–125.

Spanier, G. B. (1989). Bequeathing family continuity. *Journal of Marriage and the Family, 51,* 3–13.

Stigler, J., Smith, S., & Mao, L. (1985). The self-perception of competence by Chinese children. *Child Development, 56,* 1259–1270.

Theobald, W. (1985). *The evaluation of human service programs.* Champaign, IL: Management Learning Laboratories.

Unger, D., & Powell, D. (1980). Supporting families under stress: The role of social networks. *Family Relations, 29,* 566–574.

Wallerstein, J. S., & Blakeslee, S. (1990). *Second chances: Men, women and children a decade after divorce.* New York: Ticknor & Fields.

Wolchik, S., Ruehlman, L., Braver, S., & Sandler, I. (1989). Social support of children of divorce: Direct and stress-buffering effects. *American Journal of Community Psychology, 17,* 485–501.

Address correspondence to: William H. Meredith, University of Nebraska–Lincoln, Arts and Sciences Hall 108, Omaha Campus, 60th and Dodge, Omaha, NE 68182-0214.

Exercise for Article 18

Factual Questions

1. Nationally, the Big Brothers/Big Sisters program serves approximately how many boys and girls?

2. In which lines do the researchers explicitly state what they "hypothesized?"

3. Grades were expressed on a scale from 1 to 5. Which score (a *1* or a *5*) indicates superior performance (i.e., a grade of A)?

4. How was the Family Feeling Scale evaluated for content validity and age appropriateness?

5. What was the mean grade point average for the boys with a Big Brother at Time 1? What was their mean at Time 2?

6. On the pretest, what was the mean Conduct score for the boys with a Big Brother? What was it for the boys without a Big Brother?

7. What result do the researchers describe as "unexpected?"

Questions for Discussion

8. How important is it to know that the boys in the two groups were closely matched? Explain. (See lines 196–209 and Table 1.)

9. The researchers state that "one year may not be long enough." Do you agree? Why? Why not? (See lines 382–388.)

10. The researchers suggest that the control boys may have been influenced by "motivated" mothers. In your opinion, is this a serious threat to this study? Explain.

11. The researchers suggest the possible use of some qualitative measures in evaluation. Do you agree? Why? Why not? (See lines 490–500.)

12. Do you agree that "additional research is needed?" Explain. (See lines 528–536.) If so, what changes, if any, would you recommend to future researchers?

13. Were you surprised by the results of this study? Explain.

Quality Ratings

Directions: Indicate your level of agreement with each of the following statements by circling a number from 5 for strongly agree (SA) to 1 for strongly disagree (SD). If you believe an item is not applicable to this research article, leave it blank. Be prepared to explain your ratings.

A. The introduction establishes the importance of the study.

SA   5   4   3   2   1   SD

B. The literature review establishes the context for the study.

SA   5   4   3   2   1   SD

C. The research purpose, question, or hypothesis is clearly stated.

SA   5   4   3   2   1   SD

D. The method of sampling is sound.

SA   5   4   3   2   1   SD

E. Relevant demographics (for example, age, gender, and ethnicity) are described.

SA   5   4   3   2   1   SD

F. Measurement procedures are adequate.

SA   5   4   3   2   1   SD

G. All procedures have been described in sufficient detail to permit a replication of the study.

SA   5   4   3   2   1   SD

H. The participants have been adequately protected from potential harm.

SA   5   4   3   2   1   SD

I. The results are clearly described.

SA   5   4   3   2   1   SD

J. The discussion/conclusion is appropriate.

SA   5   4   3   2   1   SD

K. Despite any flaws, the report is worthy of publication.

SA   5   4   3   2   1   SD

Article 19

A Cautionary Study: Unwarranted Interpretations of the Draw-A-Person Test

DAVID SMITH
McGill University

FRANK DUMONT
McGill University

ABSTRACT. Therapists have numerous psychodiagnostic instruments at their disposal for use in assessing patients, although no one can achieve competency in more than a small minority of them. The issues addressed here bear on the penchant of some otherwise competent professional psychologists to use such specialized instruments (a) for which they have not received adequate formal training, (b) without compliance with canons of sound interpretation presented in the research literature as well as the relevant manual, and (c) for which sufficient evidence of validity is lacking. In this descriptive study, use of the Draw-A-Person Test (K. Machover, 1949) by a sample ($N = 36$) of clinicians provides grounds for these concerns. Some reasons that might dispose psychologists to such practice are proffered, and some implications for clinical praxis as well as for training programs are examined.

From *Professional Psychology: Research and Practice, 26,* 298–303. Copyright © 1995 by the American Psychological Association, Inc. Reprinted with permission.

The use of a diagnostic instrument with which one has little familiarity but that bears some similarity to instruments of another type with which one has had extensive experience evokes a number of issues that bear on practice as well as training. Similarly, using an instrument whose validity has not been rigorously demonstrated but in the administration of which one has become competent raises some related issues. This article addresses several of these issues.

The application of techniques that are not strongly validated or in which one has not received thorough training is proscribed by the American Psychological Association's (APA's; 1992) "Ethical Principles of Psychologists and Code of Conduct." This code, which has as its primary goal "the welfare and protection of individuals and groups with whom psychologists work" (p. 1599), refers to psychologists' obligation to work solely within the boundaries of their competence. Article 1.04 of the General Principles of the code unambiguously requires that "psychologists provide services, teach, and conduct research only within the boundaries of their competence, based on their education, supervised experience, or appropriate professional experience" (p. 1600).

Creating a satisfactory definition of professional competence is a complex matter that is not fully satisfied by the current practice of credentialing that requires that candidates meet certain standards of education and supervised training. A major problem with this system is that it does not distinguish between the many subcategories of clinical expertise that exist. A licensed psychologist who is authorized (by a paragovernmental body, say) to conduct neuropsychological assessments, biofeedback, and hypnosis may have little or no competence in any of these areas (Pope & Vasquez, 1991, pp. 54–55). Reservations have been cogently articulated about credentialing procedures on the grounds that they yield an invalid judgment of competence (Koocher, 1979). In an effort to flesh out the concept of competence, Weiner (1989) delineated two obligations of the clinician that bear on competence and ethicality in psychodiagnostic assessment. The first, which refers to one component of competence, is that clinicians must know what their tests can do. The second obligation, which refers to ethicality, is that clinicians must act accordingly (that is, in a manner consistent with the limitations of the test) by expressing judgments (and levels of confidence therein) that are warranted by the established validity of the instrument. His argument is reinforced by article 2.04 of the latest ethics code (APA, 1992), Use of Assessment in General and With Special Populations, which requires that

(a) Psychologists who perform interventions or administer, score, interpret, or use assessment techniques [be] familiar with the reliability, validation, and related standardization or outcome studies of, and proper applications and uses of, the techniques they use.

(b) Psychologists recognize limits to the certainty with which diagnoses, judgments, or predictions can be made about individuals. (p. 1603)

Weiner argued that, although one can be competent yet unethical, one cannot be ethical while acting incompetently. "Competence is prerequisite for ethicality, and psychologists who practice or teach psychodiagnosis without being fully informed concerning what tests can and cannot do are behaving unethically" (Weiner, 1989, p. 829).

There is a relative scarcity of studies bearing on competency issues in the area of psychodiagnostics, although there is an ample and expanding literature on a number of ethical matters bearing on the therapist-client relationship in other areas (for example, the conditions and variables that influence client-therapist sexual conduct [Gabbard, 1991; Schoener & Gonsiorek, 1990; Twemlow & Gabbard, 1989] and the harmful consequences of this behavior on client-victims [Bouhoutsos, Holroyd, Lerman, Forer, & Greenberg, 1983; Feldman-Summers & Jones, 1984; Pope & Bouhoutsos, 1986]). Such studies in psychodiagnostics appear to be needed. A recent report of the APA's Ethics Committee (1991) has shown that practicing outside one's area of competence is the second most frequent complaint made to the committee (following complaints involving dual relationships and sexual misconduct), comprising 14% and 16% of all new cases opened in 1989 and 1990, respectively (see Hall & Hare-Mustin, 1983, pp.718–719, for descriptions of actual cases adjudicated by the Ethics Committee). There is evidence that the area of practice in which incompetence is most salient is that of assessment. Pope and Vetter (1992), for example, surveyed members of the APA and asked, among other things, that they furnish examples of ethical dilemmas that they had encountered in their daily practice. Seven percent of the respondents reported examples of incompetent clinical practices that they and their colleagues chose or felt pressured to undertake. More than half (57%) of these ethical breeches involved psychodiagnostic assessment.

A recent example of the problem has been reported by Fine (1992). She presented a school file of an 11-year-old child who had been referred for treatment for behavioral disorders to 24 clinicians (generalists), of whom 12 were interns and 12 were highly experienced professionals with an average of over 12 years of psychotherapeutic experience. In that file were the results of a Draw-A-Person Test (DAP; Machover, 1949). Although the majority of the novices and many of the experts in her sample had had little or no formal training in the use of projectives, with few exceptions they freely commented on the features of the figure such as the rigidity of the mouth or the relative size of body members and the clinical meanings of these features. These findings suggest that a substantial proportion of psychologists make use of any information that comes to hand about a client, especially if the information is presented in an official file. It appears that they would do this even if they themselves would not seek such information, or even if they had not been trained to analyze such information. We decided to look at this again (within the context of a larger study), examining a client file that originated in a different institutional setting.

The Draw-A-Person Test

Question of Validity

The use of projective instruments by psychologists is of special interest given the paucity of evidence of validity for their generality. The classic studies of the Chapmans (Chapman & Chapman, 1967, 1969) demonstrated that highly experienced and expert clinicians found the same correlations between features of 45 DAP drawings and symptoms of pathology as did introductory psychology students who had been given the same drawings to examine. Nisbett and Ross (1980) asked,

How could practicing clinicians, bright and scientifically sophisticated as most of them are, persist in reporting observed associations between certain projective test responses and particular clinical symptoms, when innumerable validation studies have found those presumed associations to be devoid of any empirical basis? For example, objective assessments of the Draw-a-Person test (DAP) reveal that the test has virtually no validity.... Objective assessment of the Rorschach test similarly reveals that the great majority (although not all) of the sign-symptom associations frequently reported by clinicians...are not supported by validation data. (p. 94)

The DAP was originally developed to assess children's intelligence, but its utility was later expanded to include the assessment of personality and psychopathology. Machover (1949) summarized the rationale for using the DAP in this kind of assessment as follows:

The human figure drawn by an individual who is directed to "draw a person" relates intimately to the impulses, anxieties, conflicts, and compensations characteristic of the individual. In some sense, the figure drawn is the person, and the paper corresponds to the environment. (p. 35)

However, research spanning four decades has failed to provide any compelling evidence in support of the validity of human figure drawings in assessing personality, behavior, emotion, or intelligence (for reviews, see Kahill, 1984; Klopfer & Taulbee, 1976; Motta, Little, & Tobin, 1993; Roback, 1968; Swenson, 1968). In spite of these findings, it has remained one of the most popular assessment techniques used by clinicians (Kahill, 1984; Klopfer & Taulbee, 1976).

Interpretive Guidelines

Of the various relationships between drawings and diagnostic criteria that have been researched, only the relationship between global measures (i.e., rating schemes that consider the drawing as a whole or a set of specific features in the drawing) and diagnoses of gross maladjustment has reached levels of statistical significance with some consistency (Swenson, 1968). The clinical significance of this finding is much less impressive, however, as the amount of improvement that such measures have provided beyond chance levels is very slight (Kahill, 1984). The research has also clearly shown that specific signs in human figure drawings, including structural (e.g., placement of drawing on page, shading, erasures, etc.) and content variables (e.g., the rendering of a specific body part), are invalid indicators of personality or pathology. In her review of 15 years of research on the human figure drawing as an assessment device, Kahill (1984) concluded that "the evidence regarding both the content and the structural and formal aspects of drawings fails to support the majority of Machover's hypotheses or is contradictory. Only two of the 30 indices [reviewed] were supported" (p. 288).

Foremost among its problems is that DAP-based inferences are confounded by the quality of the drawing, such that it is impossible to know to what degree a drawing is a product of artistic ability, both innate and cultivated, rather than a product of covert psychodynamics and the drawer's characterological qualities (Kahill, 1984; Klopfer & Taulbee, 1976; Roback, 1968; Swenson, 1968). Environmental factors have also been shown to significantly affect outcomes (Kahill, 1984; Klopfer & Taulbee, 1976), and, again, there is no way to control for their effects.

We proceeded to examine how clinicians dealt with a projective device that had been inserted into a case file they had been requested to examine. Our questions, among others, were these: (a) Do clinicians, novices as well as the experienced, within a simulated clinical situation engage in the diagnostic interpretation of case file material in which they have had no training or very little training and (b) To what extent do clinicians evidence concern for validity issues in the use of such a device?

Method

Participants

Clinical psychologists (*n* = 18) and counseling psychologists (*n* = 18) in a large Canadian city were recruited by phone and by posted announcement in mental health settings (rehabilitation centers, clinics, hospitals) and clinical training institutions. Exactly half of each disciplinary group were experienced psychotherapists with at least 5 years of full-time experience; the modal length of practice was about 11 years. The other half were novices enrolled in either the doctoral program in clinical psychology or the doctoral or master's program in counseling psychology, all three of which require at minimum an undergraduate major in psychology and may routinely lead to paragovernmental accreditation as a psychotherapist. All novices had progressed to approximately the same level in their respective programs: one full year of academic study and one integral practicum experience. Almost all of the counseling psychology students had had no training in projectives—it is not offered in their program—and they so reported. Almost half of the experienced clinicians (both counseling and clinical psychologists) had had no more training in projectives than an episodic workshop or seminar. Each participant was remuner-

ated by check with a stipend for one session that took from 35 to 55 min.

Stimulus Materials

A segmented (dormant) case file of a middle-aged man who had been (in the 1980s) in an outpatient clinic of a local hospital and had been diagnosed as suffering from passive-aggressive personality disorder (301.84 in the revised third edition of the *Diagnostic and Statistical Manual of Mental Disorders* [*DSM-III-R*; American Psychiatric Association, 1987]), but with elements of borderline personality, was edited into 63 segments, each containing one to three sentences that could be presented in serial fashion to the participants. The segments, of which there were four to a page, were widely separated on each page to minimize the influence of the succeeding segment on the interpretation of the segment just read. Material in one version of the case file was rearranged to allow for examination of order effects on problem formulation. A drawing of a male figure (done by someone other then the person described in the case file) was placed at the end of the case file.

Procedure

The experimental procedure was conducted by two doctoral students who were thoroughly familiar with the think-aloud methodology (Ericsson & Simon, 1984) used in the study. Participants were treated individually either in their own office (in the case of practicing professionals) or in a university laboratory office (in the case of novices). The experimenter first read the standardized instructions to the participants and then led them through three practice tasks to familiarize them with the think-aloud procedure used in this study. The participants were presented with a case file that they were asked to read aloud, segment by segment. In addition, they were asked to articulate viva voce whatever thoughts they had bearing on each specific segment and on their evolving understanding of the client's problem or problems. The last page of the case file contained the drawing of the male figure. Participants were told (should they have asked) that it was the product of a DAP and that they were free to make anything of it that they saw fit. The experimenter tape-recorded the participants' voiced thoughts as they reflected on the segments that they were reading. The procedure concluded with three questions in which participants were asked to summarize their assessment of the patient's problem and its putative causes and to indicate the information in the case file on which their judgments were based. Finally, participants completed a questionnaire in writing that sought information about their educational and professional experience and posed several questions relative to the case file. The questionnaire requested information bearing on the participant's formal training in the interpretation of projective tests. The entire audiotaped procedure was later transcribed.

Results

Competence in Test Interpretation

Of the 36 participants involved in this study, 21 (58%) reported that they had had formal training in the use of projective tests; 15 (42%) reported the lack of such training. If we collapse across the factors, level of experience as well as discipline, the following results appear: Of those participants who reported that they had had some training in the use of projectives, 17 used the DAP contained in the case file, whereas only 4 did not. Only 1 of the 36 participants mentioned the validational problems associated with this instrument. Of the 4 who had received training in projectives and chose not to comment on the instrument, none invoked reservations bearing on the validity of the instrument.

Of the 15 participants who reported that they had had no training in the use of projective instruments, 5 chose to interpret the results of the DAP. Five other participants, however, mused that, as they did not know anything about this instrument, they did not care to make any comments about the drawing. Verbatim examples of feature-related and specific diagnostic statements made by participants with no training in the DAP are the following:

- The fingers are…pronounced, which is always or can be indicative of physical abuse. [Experienced clinician]
- He drew a few hairs on the head but then he attempted to draw a beard, and it may be his attempt to want to portray himself…as virile, strong, but he's not. Or he doesn't feel he is. [Novice clinician]

Compliance with Interpretive Guidelines

There are some sound and conservative guidelines for the interpretation of the DAP. As reported previously, there is some empirical support for the use of global measures to diagnose gross maladjustment (Kahill, 1984: Swenson, 1968). Seven participants (2 experts with training, 4 novices with training, and 1 novice without training) made clinical inferences of this type. In other words, in these inferences they did not link any aspect of size of figure, position of drawing (relative to edge of page), clothing, or anatomical feature to specific characterological features of the case file patient. Following are some examples of such interpretations.

- I don't see in this (drawing) any sign of pathology.
- I would have expected to see a drawing where there wouldn't have been as many straight lines if he had [nervous disorder] symptoms.… It doesn't look like a drawing from a person with a neurological problem.
- The drawing is organized; it's got all the parts where they are. No psychosis.
- It's well conceptualized, form level is adequate.… It doesn't look like the kind of thing you get from a schizophrenic.

According to the research literature, specific signs in human figure drawings, including structural variables, on the one hand (e.g., placement of drawing on the page, shading, erasures, etc.) and content variables, on the other hand (e.g., the rendering of a specific body part, such as a foot or a hand) are not reliable indicators of either specific personality traits or pathologies (Kahill, 1984; Roback, 1968; Swenson, 1968). In spite of Swenson's (still operative) proscription—that is, that one-to-one correlations between specific features of the drawing and character traits, whether normal or pathological, are unwarranted—the participants of this study in large measure acted in violation of it. Of the 22 who used the DAP to make clinical inferences, 20 based their judgments on a specific feature of the drawing. (Among the 7 who were noted previously as having made appropriate judgments, 5 are numbered here among those who also made inferences that were feature-specific.) On that basis, they proceeded to either confirm previously stated diagnostic hypotheses or to confect new ones.

We list now an illustrative sampling of interpretive comments about the DAP in question that are as representative of the experienced clinicians in our sample as they are of the novices, for there appeared to be little difference in the character of their interpretations.

- I find [the drawing] very much put to the top of the page with a lot left at the bottom.… There's a little bit of lack of anchoring in reality and more tendency to work in the fantasy world. [Expert with training]
- The only thing to me that's curious is how broad the shoulders are, which indicates that he feels he's carrying a terrible and heavy load. [Expert with training]
- I see big shoulders. He must carry a heavy load. A big, heavy cross. [Novice with no training]
- So what it suggests to me again is the identification with a powerful father figure that has a tremendous negative component to it and a lot of anxiety. [Expert with training]
- Well it's a rather big man with a lot of anxiety. Short hands that are stiffly held down, I would say an inadequate, anxiously depressed person with identity problems. [Expert with training]
- There are indications for dependency, lots of buttons and buckles. [Expert with training]
- As I look at this [drawing] I think immediately of the homosexuality hypothesis, the fact that he may be homosexual and not have admitted it to himself. And I remember at some point reading that a focus on the mid-line is indicative of possible homosexual tendencies and of course we have the focus on the belt buckle and the fly and the buttons. [Novice with training]

119

- Looks [like] a bit of transparency there. Belt with a buckle, buttons: dependency. There seems to be some sexual problems, certainly that's what the manual would say. [Expert with training]
- I see aggressivity in here because the fingers are squared off.... The beard and the broad shoulders would make me think that he's sort of compensating maybe very masculine traits. Could be related to questions about sexual orientation. [Novice with training]
- I get the sense in this picture that he's frightened, the eyes look frightened, and the sketchy drawings would suggest that he's anxious. [Novice with training]
- Large, big shoulders: somebody who stands firm. But [he] has his head [inclined] like maybe a child or somebody who is not social. [Expert with training]
- His eyes are strange and overemphasized. I think he may have problems with men, with some paranoid suspiciousness.... The belt buckle would tend to fit in with my suspicions that he's not comfortable in his role as a man. [Expert with training]
- [He] just looks aggressive: Edges are square on the hands and the feet, tight belt, very wide shoulders, a beard. The eyes look a little paranoid. [Novice with no training]

The inferences drawn about this patient's character by the participants of our study, many of whom had many years of professional experience working with troubled children and adults, lead us to question the principles that govern the use of case file material by a significant number of mental health professionals. We now address this issue.

Discussion

Test-Specific Training

A substantial proportion of participants (14%) who had no formal training in the use of projective tests freely used the DAP information contained in the case file to generate diagnostic and etiological hypotheses or to confirm inferences that they had made in earlier parts of the protocol. That they clearly went beyond their competence in this matter seems evident. We need to note, however, that they did this in an ecologically compromised situation, namely, in an experiment that is a rather remote analogue of a true clinical session. Furthermore, we cannot conclude that any one of them would have administered a DAP either with a client such as the patient who was presented for their professional assessment in this case file or, indeed, with any other client. Moreover it can be alleged that the covert demand characteristics of this experiment evoked responses that normally would not have been emitted. It is plausible to suspect that all the participants felt some constraints imposed by a task for which they were being monetarily remunerated. That they may have felt

impelled to "perform" by saying something "insightful" about a diagnostic instrument that they might otherwise not have used is a possible extenuating factor.

On the other hand, it is quite probable that these same participants will from time to time find themselves in a case conference, or in a consultation, in which they will be asked to assess clinical material such as that which we presented to them. The demand characteristics of such professional situations would be no less coercive than those they experienced in this experiment. Indeed, they would seem to be greater, as there would be livelihood and broader career considerations at stake. In any event, the commendable reaction of the untrained participants to the presentation of such material would have been to indicate to the experimenter that they did not feel justified making judgments in matters in which they had received little or no instruction.

The argument has been made by Glaser and Chi (1988) that "there is little evidence that a person highly skilled in one domain can transfer the skill to another domain" (p. xvii). Psychotherapists with psychometric expertise and test-giving skills may argue that diagnostic assessment constitutes a single domain and that transferability of skills developed in the use of one genre of instrumentation can be made with greater or lesser facility to those of another genre. As Dumont (1991) has stated, "There is no doubt a generalization gradient of skill application [for varying tasks] that is determined by the degree of similarity of the skills needed" to accomplish such tasks. The more the unfamiliar task resembles the familiar one, the greater the transferability of skills—and the more competently and easily the unfamiliar one can be addressed. It remains to be proven, however, that skills in objective testing have a sufficient level of transferability to projective testing to justify the latter activity when one's training in it is minimal, if not nonexistent.

Test-Specific Competence

What is equally important (and troubling) in the results reported here is that 20 participants (87% of those who used the DAP for diagnostic purposes) proffered inferences from their examination of a projective test that finds little justification in the research literature. The correlation, for example, between belts and buckles and homosexuality is a dubious one at best. In addition, the literature is replete with warnings not to make judgments of a personological type by reference to the size of the eyes or the shape of the mouth or any other anatomical feature—which some of our participants did. Typically, those participants who used the drawing for problem formulation cited a particular feature of the drawing and then proceeded to either confirm previously stated diagnostic hypotheses or produce new ones in reference to it. At times they would assimilate the presumed characterological meaning of a feature of the drawing to a diagnosis they had already formulated. Having, for example, hypothesized "pent-up anger," hostility, and paranoia, they seemed to scan the DAP for features that, on the basis of a "representativeness heuristic" (cf. Nisbett & Ross, 1980, pp. 93–97), could be construed to support their hypothesis. Consider this example from the protocol of a novice with training in projectives: "The first thing I notice is the flimsy, sketchy lines: insecurity.... The eyes are just crazy. Eye emphasis is paranoia. It fits right in with his projection of hostility." This skein of inferences bespeaks a popular psychology that has less to do with the instruction that students receive in graduate training than with notions that they assimilated from a journalistic literature prior to training. This is serious enough in itself. That there is evidence that a significant proportion of practicing clinicians may perseverate long beyond graduate training in using such preprofessional, lay schemas is a problem that needs to be addressed by such professional agencies as are empowered to remediate it.

Ethicality and Determining Test Validity

As we noted previously, the DAP is one of the most poorly validated psychometric instruments in the psychotherapeutics armory. Nevertheless, only 1 of the 36 participants expressed a reservation about the validity of this instrument. If we accept the criteria for competence and ethicality articulated by Weiner, namely, that clinicians must know what their tests can do, and that they must act accordingly by expressing judgments (with varying levels of confidence) that are warranted by the validity of the instruments they are using, then the results of a contemporary study such as this provide grounds for concern.

An unquestioning acceptance and use of well-researched and more strongly validated instruments presents, of course, fewer hazards to veridical psycho-diagnosis than does such an attitude toward poorly validated instruments. In addition, it may not even occur to a clinician to entertain a concern about an instrument such as, say, the Minnesota Multiphasic Personality Inventory—2. However, the popularity and long-term usage of a psychometric instrument do not in themselves justify a presumption of validity—on the contrary. Proceeding with caution is imperative—and with far greater reason—where one has relatively little training in the use of an instrument and, furthermore, one is not familiar with the recent research bearing on its validity and reliability.

Conclusion

The gravity of the clinical consequences to clients of a casual use of poorly validated instruments should not be exaggerated. It would seem that therapists tend to find in projectives that they use whatever they are already disposed to find, with greater or lesser accuracy, through other means. They use them to buttress interpretations made on the basis of referral information, intake interviews, and the initial client data elic-

ited through the "art of conversational inquiry." The confirmatory bias that is expressed in anchoring errors (cf., e.g., Dumont, 1993; Ellis, Robbins, Schult, Ladany, & Banker, 1990) disposes clinicians to find support for initial diagnoses in whatever material is at hand—and what therapists are disposed to find has a number of other determinants, not least, their theoretical orientation, but also the results of other tests as well as the parataxic distortions and projections evoked by their client. Nevertheless, the results of this and other studies point to a broader concern that requires vigilance, namely, the seeming penchant of a significant proportion of therapists to use assessment instruments whose usefulness has not been well established, but whose results are determinative in part of the treatment that will be provided to a client. This is a concern, we think, that should generate further, more broadly based studies on the matter on the one hand, and exact increased attention in our training programs on the other hand.

References

American Psychiatric Association. (1987). *Diagnostic and statistical manual of mental disorders* (3rd ed., rev.). Washington, DC: Author.

American Psychological Association. (1992). Ethical principles of psychologists and code of conduct. *American Psychologist, 47*, 1597–1611.

American Psychological Association Ethics Committee. (1991). Report of the Ethics Committee. *American Psychologist, 46*, 750–757.

Bouhoutsos, J., Holroyd, J., Lerman, H., Forer, B., & Greenberg, M. (1983). Sexual intimacy between psychotherapists and patients. *Professional Psychology: Research and Practice, 14*, 185–196.

Chapman, L. J., & Chapman, J. P. (1967). Genesis of popular but erroneous diagnostic observations. *Journal of Abnormal Psychology, 72*, 193–204.

Chapman, L. J., & Chapman, J. P. (1969). Illusory correlation as an obstacle to the use of valid psychodiagnostic signs. *Journal of Abnormal Psychology, 74*, 271–280.

Dumont, F. (1991). Expertise in psychotherapy: Inherent liabilities of becoming experienced. *Psychotherapy, 28*, 422–428.

Dumont, F. (1993). Inferential heuristics in clinical problem formulation: Selective review of their strengths and weaknesses. *Professional Psychology: Research and Practice, 24*, 196–205.

Ellis, M. V., Robbins, E. S., Schult, D., Ladany, M., & Banker, J. (1990). Anchoring errors in clinical judgment: Type I errors, adjustment or mitigation. *Journal of Counseling Psychology, 37*, 343–351.

Ericsson, K. A., & Simon, H. A. (1984). *Protocol analysis: Verbal reports as data.* Cambridge, MA: MIT Press.

Feldman-Summers, S., & Jones, G. (1984). Psychological impacts of sexual contact between therapists or other health care providers and their clients. *Journal of Consulting and Clinical Psychology, 52*, 1054–1061.

Fine, E. (1992). *An investigation of the psycho-educational assessment process: The influence of assessors' theoretical orientation and previous experience on their interpretations of a student's case-file.* Unpublished doctoral dissertation. McGill University, Montreal, Quebec, Canada.

Gabbard, G. (1991). Psychodynamics of sexual boundary violations. *Psychiatric Annals, 21*, 651–655.

Glaser, R., & Chi, M. H. (1988). Overview. In M. H. Chi, R. Glaser, & M. J. Farr (Eds.), *The nature of expertise* (pp. i–xxiii). Hillsdale, NJ: Erlbaum.

Hall, J., & Hare-Mustin, R. (1983). Sanctions and the diversity of ethical complaints against psychologists. *American Psychologist, 38*, 714–723.

Kahill, S. (1984). Human figure drawing in adults: An update of the empirical evidence, 1967–1982. *Canadian Psychology, 25*, 269–292.

Klopfer, W., & Taulbee, E. (1976). Projective tests. *Annual Review of Psychology, 27*, 543–567.

Koocher, G. (1979). Credentialing in psychology: Close encounters with competence. *American Psychologist, 34*, 696–702.

Machover, K. (1949). *Personality projection in the drawing of the human figure.* Springfield, IL: Charles C. Thomas.

Motta, R., Little, S., & Tobin, M. (1993). The use and abuse of human figure drawings. *School Psychology Quarterly, 8*, 162–169.

Nisbett, R., & Ross, L. (1980). *Human inference: Strategies and shortcomings of social judgment.* Englewood Cliffs, NJ: Prentice-Hall.

Pope, K., & Bouhoutsos, J. (1986). *Sexual intimacies between therapists and patients.* New York: Praeger.

Pope, K., & Vasquez, M. (1991). *Ethics in psychotherapy and counseling.* San

Francisco: Jossey-Bass.

Pope, K., & Vetter, V. (1992). Ethical dilemmas encountered by members of the American Psychological Association. *American Psychologist, 47*, 397–411.

Roback, H. (1968). Human figure drawings: Their utility in the clinical psychologist's armamentarium for personality assessment. *Psychological Bulletin, 70*, 1–19.

Schoener, G., & Gonsiorek, J. (1990). Assessment and development of rehabilitation plans for the therapist. In G. Schoener, J. Milgrom, & J. Gonsiorek (Eds.), *Psychotherapists' sexual involvement with clients: Intervention and prevention* (pp. 401–420). Minneapolis, MN: Walk-In Counseling Center.

Swenson, C. (1968). Empirical evaluations of human figure drawings: 1957–1966. *Psychological Bulletin, 70*, 20–44.

Twemlow, S., & Gabbard, G. (1989). The love-sick therapist. In G. Gabbard (Ed.), *Sexual exploitation in professional relationships* (pp. 71–87). Washington, DC: American Psychiatric Press.

Weiner, I. (1989). On competence and ethicality in psychodiagnostic assessment. *Journal of Personality Assessment, 53*, 827–831.

About the authors: David Smith is a doctoral candidate in the PhD program in counseling psychology in the Department of Educational and Counselling Psychology, McGill University. He is currently doing his internship in Camp Hill Medical Center, Halifax Infirmary Hospital, Halifax, Nova Scotia. Frank Dumont received his EdD from the University of Massachusetts, Amherst, in 1971. He is currently the director of the Counselling Psychology Program in the Department of Educational and Counselling Psychology, McGill University.

Address correspondence to: Frank Dumont, Department of Educational and Counselling Psychology, McGill University, 3700 McTavish Street, Montreal, Quebec, Canada H3A 1Y2.

Exercise for Article 19

Factual Questions

1. According to Weiner (1989), what is a prerequisite for ethicality?

2. The DAP was originally developed to assess what trait?

3. How many of the participants were novices?

4. What percentage of the participants reported a lack of formal training in the use of projective tests?

5. How many of the participants based their clinical judgments (inferences) on a specific feature of the drawing?

6. According to the researchers, "confirmatory bias" disposes clinicians to find what?

Questions for Discussion

7. What is your opinion on the procedure used to recruit participants? (See lines 210-214.)

8. Would you like to know more about the drawing placed at the end of the case file? Explain.

9. Have the researchers convinced you that some of the participants made unwarranted interpretations? Explain.

10. The researchers note that there is no evidence that the participants in this study would actually administer the DAP to a client. Is this an important consideration when interpreting this study?

11. In your opinion, are "covert demand characteristics" a threat to the interpretation of this study? (See lines 445-468.)

Quality Ratings

Directions: Indicate your level of agreement with each of the following statements by circling a number from 5 for strongly agree (SA) to 1 for strongly disagree (SD). If you believe an item is not applicable to this research article, leave it blank. Be prepared to explain your ratings.

A. The introduction establishes the importance of the study.

SA   5   4   3   2   1   SD

B. The literature review establishes the context for the study.

SA   5   4   3   2   1   SD

C. The research purpose, question, or hypothesis is clearly stated.

SA   5   4   3   2   1   SD

D. The method of sampling is sound.

SA   5   4   3   2   1   SD

E. Relevant demographics (for example, age, gender, and ethnicity) are described.

SA   5   4   3   2   1   SD

F. Measurement procedures are adequate.

SA   5   4   3   2   1   SD

G. All procedures have been described in sufficient detail to permit a replication of the study.

SA   5   4   3   2   1   SD

H. The participants have been adequately protected from potential harm.

SA   5   4   3   2   1   SD

I. The results are clearly described.

SA   5   4   3   2   1   SD

J. The discussion/conclusion is appropriate.

SA   5   4   3   2   1   SD

K. Despite any flaws, the report is worthy of publication.

SA   5   4   3   2   1   SD

Article 20

Chapman-Cook Speed of Reading Test: Performance of College Students

ROEE HOLTZER
State University of New York
at Binghamton

LYNANNE M. MCGUIRE
State University of New York
at Binghamton

RICHARD G. BURRIGHT
State University of New York
at Binghamton

PETER J. DONOVICK
State University of New York
at Binghamton

ABSTRACT. The performance of 116 college students on the Chapman-Cook Speed of Reading Test on three different occasions was investigated. Descriptive statistics, test-retest reliability measures, and correlations with other tests of reading and verbal ability are provided. Analyses suggest that the Chapman-Cook test provides some information not available from tests currently used to assess reading and verbal ability.

From *Perceptual and Motor Skills*, *86*, 687–690. Copyright © 1998 by Perceptual and Motor Skills. Reprinted with permission.

This report provides descriptive statistics (mean, mode, median, range, and standard deviation) and reliability estimates for the Chapman-Cook Speed of Reading Test obtained from college students. Also, correlations between scores on the Chapman-Cook test and four other measures of reading and verbal ability are reported.

The Chapman-Cook test is a timed test of 25 short paragraphs, each containing one word that is discordant with the paragraph's meaning. Test takers are instructed to find as many disconcordant words as possible in 2.5 min. Chapman and Cook (1923) suggested that the test may assess both comprehension and speed of reading. At the present, psychometric and normative data are not available. A literature review indicated that only two studies, Muncer and Jandreau (1984), and Giroux, Salame, Bedard, and Bellavance (1992) have employed this test for research purposes, evaluating the effect of text presentation on reading and cognitive abilities.

The Chapman-Cook test was administered to 116 college students (63 women, 53 men, M_{age} = 18 years) on three different occasions at 2-wk. intervals. The mean, mode, median, range, and standard deviations obtained for the three test administrations are summarized in Table 1. Analysis of frequencies of correct responses indicates that 37 subjects at Time 1 accurately identified all disconcordant words in the 25 paragraphs, compared with 76 and 90 subjects at Times 2 and 3, respectively. These results suggest a strong practice effect. A ceiling effect was apparent at Time 1 which limits the test for discriminating reading ability in college students. Test-retest reliability between Times 1 and 2, Times 1 and 3, and Times 2 and 3 yielded correlations of .82, .63, and .69, respectively.

To assess the relation between scores on the Chapman-Cook test and other measures of reading ability and intellectual functioning, a different group of 22 college students (11 women, 11 men, M_{age} = 19 yr.) were administered five tests. Scores of each subject on the two administrations over a 2-wk. interval of the Chapman-Cook test were averaged and then correlated with scores on the other four tests.

Table 1
Descriptive Statistics for the Chapman-Cook Speed of Reading Test (N = 116)

Statistics	Test 1	Test 2	Test 3
M	20	23	24
Mdn	22	25	25
Mode	25	25	25
Range	0–25	0–25	12–25
SD	5.6	4.3	2.0

The Shipley Institute of Living Scale has been used to estimate general intellectual functioning in adults and adolescents and to assist in detecting cognitive impairments in individuals with normal premorbid intelligence (Zachary, 1992). The scale consists of two subtests, a 40-item vocabulary test and a 20-item test of abstract thinking. For normative data including reliability and validity indices refer to Zachary (1992).

The Gray Oral Reading Test measures reading speed, accuracy, and comprehension. It consists of two alternate, equivalent forms, each containing 13 increasingly difficult passages that are followed by five comprehension testing questions. Normative data for those 7 to 18 years of age, including reliability and

Table 2

Pearson Correlations for Number Correct Responses on the Chapman-Cook Test and Other Measures of Reading and Verbal Abilities

	r			Kaufman Brief Intelligence Test: Composite IQ		
Measure	2	3	4	Full Scale	Matrices	Verbal Scale
1. Chapman-Cook Test	.60	.55	.60	.60	.23	.53
2. Gray Oral Reading Test: Quotient		.37	.58	.62	.33	.63
3. National Adult Reading Test Revised: Estimated Full Scale IQ			.24	.50	.11	.70
4. Shipley Institute of Living Scale: Estimated Full Scale IQ				.51	.14	.61

validity indices, are given by Wiederholt and Bryant (1992).

60 The Kaufman Brief Intelligence Test is a brief, individually administered measure of intelligence used primarily for screening and related purposes (e.g., Donovick, Burright, Burg, Davino, Gronedyke, Klimczak, Mathews, and Sardo, 1996). The subtests,
65 Vocabulary and Matrices, respectively measure crystallized and fluid intelligence. For normative data, including reliability and validity indices, refer to Kaufman and Kaufman (1990).

The National Adult Reading Test Revised has been
70 used to estimate verbal skills of premorbid cognitive functioning (Berry, Carpenter, Campbell, & Schmit, 1994). It consists of a list of 61 words which the test taker is required to read aloud. Points are given for correct pronunciation of words of increasing difficulty.

75 Pearson correlations between scores on the Chapman-Cook test with those on the four tests are listed in Table 2. The indices employed for the correlations in Table 2 are Number of Correct Responses for the Chapman-Cook test, Oral Reading Quotient for the
80 Gray Oral Reading Test, Estimated Full Scale IQ for The National Adult Reading Test Revised, Estimated IQ for the Shipley, and Verbal Standard score, Matrices Standard score, and the Composite IQ score for The Kaufman Brief Intelligence Test. With the excep-
85 tion of the Matrices subtest in the Kaufman Brief Intelligence Test, correlations between the Chapman-Cook test and the other measures of reading ability and intellectual functioning ranged from .53 to .60. These results suggest that about 25% to 30% of the variance
90 in these scores can be predicted by scores on the Chapman-Cook test. Therefore, some information not available from tests currently used in assessment of reading and verbal intelligence may be provided by the Chapman-Cook test. The results also suggest that the
95 Chapman-Cook test may not be considered as a substitute for the currently used reading tests but as an additional source of information about reading ability. The short administration time of the Chapman-Cook test makes it attractive for quick screening of reading.
100 Research aimed at assessing psychometric properties

and obtaining normative data for this test is warranted.

References

BERRY, D. T-R., CARPENTER, G. S., CAMPBELL, D. A., SCHMIT, F. A., HELTON, K., & LIPKE-MOLBY, T. (1994). The New Adult Reading Test Revised: Accuracy in estimating WAIS-R IQ scores obtained 3.5 years earlier from normal older persons. *Archives of Clinical Neuropsychology, 9,* 239–250.

CHAPMAN, J. C., & COOK, S. (1923). A principle of the single variable in a speed of reading cross-out test. *Journal of Educational Research, 8,* 389–396.

DONOVICK, P. J., BURRIGHT, R. G., BURG, J. S., DAVINO, S., GRONE-DYKE, J., KLIMCZAK, N., MATHEWS, A., & SARDO, J. (1996). The K-BIT: A screen for IQ in six diverse populations. *Journal of Clinical Psychology in Medical Settings, 3,* 131–139.

GIROUX, L., SALAME, R., BEDARD, M., & BELLAVANCE, A. (1992). Performances neuropsychologiques de personnes âgées normales en fonction de l'âge, de la scolarité et de la profession. *Reveu Quebecoise de Psychologie, 13,* 3–27.

KAUFMAN, A. S., & KAUFMAN, N. L. (1990). *Kaufman Brief Intelligence Test.* Minneapolis, MN: American Guidance Service.

MUNCER, S. J., & JANDREAU, S. (1984). Morphemes and syllables, words and reading. *Perceptual and Motor Skills, 59,* 14.

WIEDERHOLT, J. L., & BRYANT, B. R. (1992). *Gray Oral Reading Tests* (3rd ed.). Austin, TX: Pro-Ed.

ZACHARY, R. A. (1992). *Shipley Institute of Living Scale–Revised, Manual.* Los Angeles, CA: Western Psychological Services.

About the authors: Roee Holtzer, Environmental Neuropsychology Laboratory, State University of New York at Binghamton. Lynanne M. McGuire, Environmental Neuropsychology Laboratory, State University of New York at Binghamton. Richard G. Burright, Environmental Neuropsychology Laboratory, State University of New York at Binghamton. Peter J. Donovick, Environmental Neuropsychology Laboratory, State University of New York at Binghamton, and Department of Psychology & Neurosciences, United Health Services Hospitals, Johnson City, New York.

Address correspondence to: Peter J. Donovick, Ph.D., Environmental Neuropsychology Laboratory, Department of Psychology, State University of New York at Binghamton, Binghamton, NY 13902-6000, USA or e-mail (bg4473@bingvmb.cc.binghamton.edu).

Exercise for Article 20

Factual Questions

1. What is the time limit for the Chapman-Cook Test?

2. How many college students participated in the part of the study in which Chapman-Cook Test scores were correlated with other measures of reading ability and intellectual functioning?

3. Based on the information in Table 1, the distribution of scores on which test administration (Test 1, Test 2, or Test 3) has the least variability? Explain the basis for your answer.

4. For Test 1 in Table 1, which measure of central tendency (i.e., average) has the highest value?

5. What is the value of the correlation coefficient for the relationship between the Chapman-Cook test and the Shipley Institute of Living Scale?

6. The weakest correlation coefficient in Table 2 has what value?

Questions for Discussion

7. Would you be interested in knowing more about why the Chapman-Cook test was selected for examination in this study? Explain.

8. Explain in your own words what the researchers probably mean by the term "practice effect." (See lines 30-31.)

9. Explain in your own words what the researchers probably mean by the term "ceiling effect." (See lines 31-33.)

10. Would you characterize the relationship between the Chapman-Cook Test and the Gray Oral Reading Test as "very weak?" If no, how would you characterize it?

11. Do you think that it would be desirable to conduct a replication of this study? Why? Why not?

Quality Ratings

Directions: Indicate your level of agreement with each of the following statements by circling a number from 5 for strongly agree (SA) to 1 for strongly disagree (SD). If you believe an item is not applicable to this research article, leave it blank. Be prepared to explain your ratings.

A. The introduction establishes the importance of the study.

SA   5   4   3   2   1   SD

B. The literature review establishes the context for the study.

SA   5   4   3   2   1   SD

C. The research purpose, question, or hypothesis is clearly stated.

SA   5   4   3   2   1   SD

D. The method of sampling is sound.

SA   5   4   3   2   1   SD

E. Relevant demographics (for example, age, gender, and ethnicity) are described.

SA   5   4   3   2   1   SD

F. Measurement procedures are adequate.

SA   5   4   3   2   1   SD

G. All procedures have been described in sufficient detail to permit a replication of the study.

SA   5   4   3   2   1   SD

H. The participants have been adequately protected from potential harm.

SA   5   4   3   2   1   SD

I. The results are clearly described.

SA   5   4   3   2   1   SD

J. The discussion/conclusion is appropriate.

SA   5   4   3   2   1   SD

K. Despite any flaws, the report is worthy of publication.

SA   5   4   3   2   1   SD

Article 21

A Qualitative Analysis of Client Perceptions of the Effects of Helpful Therapist Self-Disclosure in Long-Term Therapy

SARAH KNOX
University of Maryland, College Park

SHIRLEY A. HESS
University of Maryland, College Park

DAVID A. PETERSEN
University of Maryland, College Park

CLARA E. HILL
University of Maryland, College Park

ABSTRACT. Thirteen adult psychotherapy clients currently in long-term therapy were interviewed twice, with semistructured protocols, about their experiences with helpful instances of therapist self-disclosure. Data were analyzed with a qualitative methodology. Results indicated that helpful therapist self-disclosures (a) occurred when these clients were discussing important personal issues, (b) were perceived as being intended by therapists to normalize or reassure the clients, and (c) consisted of a disclosure of personal nonimmediate information about the therapists. The therapist self-disclosures resulted in positive consequences for these clients that included insight or a new perspective from which to make changes, an improved or more equalized therapeutic relationship, normalization, and reassurance. Implications for psychotherapy are discussed.

From *Journal of Counseling Psychology*, *44*, 274–283. Copyright © 1997 by the American Psychological Association, Inc. Reprinted with permission.

The use of therapist self-disclosure in psychotherapy is controversial. In the psychodynamic tradition, therapists often severely limit their self-disclosure for fear of diluting transference (Basescu, 1990; Kaslow,
5   Cooper, & Linsenberg, 1979; Mathews, 1988). Those with humanistic, existential, and eclectic orientations, on the other hand, claim to use this intervention more freely, equating realness with a fully open, honest, genuine, and personally involved stance (Simon, 1988)
10 and viewing therapist self-disclosure as a means of demystifiying the psychotherapy process (Kaslow et al., 1979).

Although therapist self-disclosure has been studied frequently (cf. Watkins, 1990), this research has most
15 often used volunteer (nonclient) participants in single, contrived sessions. This existing research (e.g., Fox, Strum, & Walters, 1984; Mahrer, Fellers, Durak, Gervaize, & Brown, 1981; Mathews, 1988; Nilsson, Strassberg, & Bannon, 1979; Robitschek & McCarthy,
20 1991; Rosie, 1980) thus does not capture actual client

internal experience of the dynamics of therapist self-disclosure in genuine therapy settings, nor does it give information about the perceived consequences, if any, of this intervention on clients in long-term psychother-
25 apy.

Hill et al. (1988), in one of the few studies of actual therapy, found that although therapist self-disclosures occurred only 1% of the time, they received the highest client helpfulness ratings. This study is useful in illu-
30 minating the potentially profound impact of this rare intervention, but it again does not capture qualitatively the inner perceptions of clients in long-term therapy. Thus, our understanding of how clients internally experience this intervention remains limited. We do not, for
35 instance, know what clients perceive as the effects of therapist self-disclosure on themselves, on the therapy, or on their relationships with their therapists. Such information would illuminate both the process and outcome of therapy. If therapists gained a deeper under-
40 standing of how clients experience self-disclosure, they might more effectively use self-disclosure in their work with clients.

We were interested in studying three potential consequences of therapist self-disclosure for long-term
45 clients that seemed reasonable on the basis of the literature. First, therapist self-disclosures could influence the "real relationship" in that clients might see their therapists as more human or more as persons. The real relationship, according to Gelso and Carter (1994), is
50 that portion of the total relationship that is essentially nontransferential. The real relationship consists of genuineness, or the ability and willingness to be what one truly is in the relationship, and realistic perceptions, or those uncontaminated by transference distor-
55 tions and other defenses. Theoretical statements have been proposed regarding the effects of therapist self-disclosure on the balance of power or control in the therapy, an aspect of the real relationship. It has been suggested, for example, that therapists' revelations of
60 negative information would not result in loss of status

(Chelune, 1979), that therapists' openness with clients about past and present secrets would lead to a balance of power in the relationship (Lander & Nahon, 1992), and that therapist self-disclosure would encourage an
65 equal and balanced alliance between client and therapist (Kaslow et al., 1979). These theoretical propositions, however, have been the focus of minimal, if any, actual research.

A second potential consequence that has been ex-
70 plored is the effect of therapist self-disclosure on feelings of universality. Clients often feel most distressed at the thought that they suffer alone (Yalom, 1975). Therapist self-disclosure, however, might alleviate this despair, for such an intervention might give clients a
75 sense of shared experience or universality, normalizing their ordeals and reassuring them that they are not alone (Chelune, 1979). Mathews (1988) posited that therapist self-disclosure makes clients feel less alone, less crazy, and more hopeful.

80 A third potential consequence is modeling. Mann and Murphy (1975) suggested that when therapists display disclosing behavior, the clients learn through imitation to do the same. Kaslow et al. (1979) noted that therapists serve as a model of form or process, in
85 this case the form or process of disclosure in therapy. Clients might also see therapists as models of content—that is, as examples of individuals who demonstrate thoughts, emotions, or behaviors clients seek to adopt. Therapists could thus serve as broad and en-
90 compassing models of disclosure within the therapy sessions. On the basis of the content of therapist self-disclosure, then, clients might alter their thoughts, feelings, or behaviors, both within and beyond the session itself. Simon (1988) addressed this possibility and
95 found that modeling of adult behavior as a demonstration of problem-solving skills, coping skills, self-acceptance, or assertiveness was the predominant reason therapists cited for self-disclosure. She based her assumptions not on research with clients, however, but
100 on interviews with experienced clinicians. Although this perspective is useful and valuable, it does not lead to any conclusions that are based on clients' internal experiences in therapy sessions. We were open to other possible consequences that might emerge from clients'
105 responses and considered the three mentioned above merely as a good place to start, but surely not to finish.

Prior to being able to investigate therapist self-disclosure, however, we faced a major definitional problem. Previous studies have used widely discrepant
110 definitions of therapist self-disclosure, which makes it difficult to generalize across studies. Weiner (1983), for example, described therapist self-disclosure as occurring when the therapist gives more than just professional expertise or when the therapist is purposely
115 more open and genuine with the client. This openness could take the form of the therapist's revealing such things as his or her feelings, attitudes, opinions, associations, fantasies, experiences, or history. Others have

defined self-disclosure as intrapersonal (therapist re-
120 veals information about his or her personal life outside of counseling) and interpersonal (therapist reveals feelings about the client's problems or the counseling relationship; Nilsson et al., 1979). Still another definition describes self-disclosure in terms of intrapersonal
125 past (therapist reveals information about his or her own past history), intrapersonal present (therapist reveals information about his or her present personal experiences), and self-involving statements (therapist expresses feelings about or reactions to statements or
130 behaviors of the client; Cherbosque, 1987). Yet other researchers define this intervention along different lines, subdividing therapist self-disclosure into positive or negative, personal or demographic, similar or dissimilar, past or present, and self-involving (Watkins,
135 1990) or describing it as consisting of self-involving and self-disclosing self-referent statements, whether positive or negative (Andersen & Anderson, 1985; Robitschek & McCarthy, 1991). Still others have defined self-disclosure as the therapist's revealing factual in-
140 formation about his or her life, revealing feelings he or she has experienced in his or her life, or revealing feelings he or she experiences regarding the client (Mathews, 1989), a system of classification echoed by Wachtel (1993), who discussed disclosure of within-
145 session reactions versus disclosure of other characteristics of the therapist. Finally, Palombo (1987) introduced the concept of spontaneous therapist self-disclosure, which he defined as an intervention that is not intentional or a conscious part of the treatment
150 strategy.

Out of these various definitions, a trend can be discerned: There is generally a distinction between information that therapists reveal about themselves as individuals and information that therapists reveal about
155 their experiences of and with the client in the session as it occurs. In this vein, Hill, Mahalik, and Thompson (1989) studied self-disclosing and self-involving therapist statements but considered both types as forms of therapist self-disclosure. Similarly, Watkins (1990)
160 stated that "although self-involving statements are often contrasted with self-disclosing statements, self-involving statements are still regarded as a form of self-disclosure" (pp. 478–479).

Given such definitional complexity, we used a
165 global conceptualization of therapist self-disclosure, following the lead of Hill et al. (1989) and Watkins (1990), and we included in our study both self-involving and self-disclosing therapist statements. Because this was an exploratory study and a first attempt
170 to qualitatively capture actual clients' inner experience of this intervention, we considered it wiser to examine as many data as possible about the broader phenomenon of therapist self-disclosure. For this study, then, we defined therapist self-disclosure for clients as "an inter-
175 action in which the therapist reveals personal information about him/herself and/or reveals reactions and

responses to the client as they arise in the session."

A qualitative approach seemed appropriate for this exploratory stage of inquiry because it allows the probing of inner experiences without predetermining the responses. We used the consensual qualitative research (CQR) methodology developed by Hill, Thompson, and Williams (in press) and used by Rhodes, Hill, Thompson, and Elliott (1994) and Hill, Nutt-Williams, Heaton, Thompson, and Rhodes (1996). According to Hill et al. (in press), the key features of this approach are the following: (a) The method relies on words to describe phenomena rather than using numbers; (b) a small number of cases is studied intensively; (c) the context of the whole case is used to understand parts of the experience; (d) the process is inductive, with theory being built from observations of the data rather than a structure or theory being imposed on the data ahead of time; (e) the process involves dividing responses to open-ended questions from questionnaires or interviews into domains (i.e., topic areas), constructing core ideas (i.e., abstracts or brief summaries) for all the material within each domain for each individual case, and developing categories to describe the themes in the core ideas within domains across cases (cross-analyses). In the CQR process, all judgments are made by a primary team of from three to five judges so that a variety of opinions is available about each decision; consensus is used to ensure that the "best" construction is developed that considers all of the data. One or two auditors are used to check the consensus judgments in order to ensure that the primary team does not overlook important data. Finally, the primary team continually goes back to the raw data to check to make sure that their interpretations and conclusions are accurate and based on the data.

Hence, our purpose in this study was to use a qualitative approach to examine the antecedents, events, and consequences of helpful examples of therapist self-disclosure as identified by clients.

Method

Participants

Clients. Thirteen clients (9 women and 4 men, all European American) who were currently in long-term therapy participated in the study. These clients ranged in age from 26 to 50 years ($M = 37.69$, $SD = 6.94$), had been in therapy with their therapists from 5 to 192 months ($M = 60.62$, $SD = 61.41$), and were in long-term individual psychotherapy with no planned termination in sight. The number of times clients had been in therapy prior to the present relationship ranged from 0 to 14 ($M = 2.23$, $SD = 2.61$). Clients identified the following presenting problems (not mutually exclusive): depression ($n = 8$), anxiety ($n = 3$), sexuality issues ($n = 3$), drug–alcohol rehabilitation ($n = 1$), borderline personality disorder ($n = 1$), dealing with sudden disability ($n = 1$), eating disorder ($n = 1$), anger ($n = 1$), relationship issues ($n = 1$), dealing with elderly parents

($n = 1$), and life skills ($n = 1$). Clients were seen in the therapists' private practice.

Therapists. As indicated by clients' perceptions, the 5 female and 8 male therapists were all European American and ranged in age at the time of the study from 36 years to older than 51 years. Clients' assessments of their therapists' orientations (not mutually exclusive) were as follows: behavioral–cognitive–behavioral ($n = 5$), psychoanalytic–psychodynamic ($n = 4$), eclectic ($n = 3$), and humanistic–experiential ($n = 2$). Clients reported the frequency of their therapists' self-disclosures as equally balanced between "often" ($n = 4$), "occasionally" ($n = 4$), and "rarely" ($n = 5$).

Judges and interviewer. Three European American graduate students (2 women and 1 man aged 34–42 years) in a doctoral program in counseling psychology participated in this project as the primary research team and served as judges (Sarah Knox, Shirley A. Hess, and David A. Petersen). A European American, 47-year-old female professor who helped to develop the qualitative method (Clara E. Hill) served as the auditor. Sarah Knox, who also served as one of the judges, conducted all of the interviews. In terms of theoretical orientations, Sarah Knox's is humanistic–psychodynamic, Shirley A. Hess and David A. Petersen's are psychodynamic–humanistic, and Clara E. Hill's is humanistic–psychodynamic.

Measures

Demographic form. This form asked for basic demographic information about the participant: age, gender, and race of both participant and therapist, therapy history, and current therapy information (age when client began current therapy, months in current therapy, number of sessions in current therapy, approximate number of sessions anticipated yet to occur in current therapy, and reason or reasons client sought current therapy). The form also asked the participant to indicate the therapist's theoretical orientation by checking the appropriate label. Finally, the form asked for a first name and phone number for further contact.

First interview. The first interview began with a "grand tour" question about the early therapeutic relationship; this question was used to encourage the participant to reenter his or her experiences in the therapy. A second question asked the participant to estimate the frequency of the therapist self-disclosure she or he experienced (per session, per every other session, etc.) and how often therapist self-disclosure had any perceived impact. Clients were asked to describe the general nature of the disclosures their therapists gave. From there, the focus moved to a request for a specific example of a helpful therapist self-disclosure (as determined by the client, following the definition of therapist self-disclosure given in the packet and at the start of the interview) and for a description of its immediate effects on the participant, on the therapy, and on the therapy relationship. Although going into the study, we had postulated possible effects of therapist self-disclosure on the real relationship, on universality, and on modeling, the interviewer was careful to probe for whatever emerged and to follow the clients' lead in order to reduce the possible influence of interviewer bias. Thus, all client comments were probed as part of the interview process. The next question asked the participant to discuss a specific unhelpful therapist self-disclosure (as determined by the client, following the definition of therapist self-disclosure given in the packet and at the start of the interview) and likewise asked about its immediate effects on the participant, on the therapy, and on the therapy relationship. The interviewer next asked about the current therapeutic relationship in order to assess changes over the course of therapy. Finally, the interviewer gave the interviewee a chance to make any final comments and established a time for the follow-up interview.

Follow-up interview. The follow-up interview gave both researcher and participant a chance to ask further questions, to clarify issues, and to amend previous comments. In addition, the interviewer asked the participant if she or he was willing to receive and then correct or amend the transcripts of the two interviews. Finally, the interview concluded with a short debriefing paragraph that once more informed the participant of the study's focus on clients' perceptions of the effects of therapist self-disclosure.

Procedures

Recruiting clients. Twenty-one experienced therapists, all PhD psychologists known to or by the counseling psychology faculty at a large mid-Atlantic U.S. university, were contacted by phone and asked to invite their clients to participate. They were informed that the study would examine clients' perceptions of the effects of therapist self-disclosure. The 14 who agreed to participate were asked to give a research packet to no more than 5 of their adult (at least 18 years old) long-term clients. These clients must have already had at least 10 sessions with the therapist, must have had no planned termination in sight, and must have otherwise been appropriate for participation as determined by their therapist. Each therapist received between two and five packets, for a total of 57 packets. Of these 57, therapists reported that they actually distributed 40 packets.

The first contact between the primary researcher (Sarah Knox) and the potential participants occurred through the research packet, which was distributed by the therapists to those clients who met the above criteria. The packet included a letter to the client containing information about the nature of the study and assuring confidentiality, the client consent form, a demographic form, and a list of the questions that would be asked in the first interview. Clients were informed in the letter that the study was examining clients' inner experience of therapist self-disclosure in psychotherapy, and they were provided with the definition of therapist self-disclosure used in this study as well as examples of therapist self-disclosure. They were told that their consent meant that they would be volunteering to participate in two audiotaped phone interviews and that their therapist would know of their participation only if they chose to tell him or her. Potential participants were then asked to choose whether to continue their participation. For those who refused, their involvement was at an end. Those who agreed to participate completed and returned the consent form and the demographic form. Materials were returned by 20 clients, who were then scheduled for an interview.

Interviewing. The primary researcher interviewed the 20 clients using the interview protocols, which included a restatement of the definition of therapist self-disclosure. At the end of each interview, the researcher made brief field notes indicating how long the interview took, the participant's mood, and the interviewer's ability to develop rapport with the participant. To determine what needed to be clarified in the second interview, the interviewer reviewed the tape of the first interview prior to the second interview, which occurred approximately 2 weeks later. Initial interviews ranged in length from 25 to 60 min ($M = 43.46$, $SD = 8.14$); follow-up interviews ranged in length from 10 to 40 min ($M = 27.31$, $SD = 9.49$).

Transcripts. The interviews were transcribed verbatim (except for minimal encouragers, silences, and stutters) for each participant by undergraduate research assistants. All identifying information was removed from the transcripts, and each participant was assigned a code number to maintain his or her confidentiality. All clients were given the option to review their transcripts, but only 4 clients chose to do so, and the changes they suggested (only 2 of the 4 suggested any changes) were minimal and were typically of a grammatical nature.

Selection of cases. Because our recruiting was so successful, we had more cases than we needed. Qualitative research typically includes 8–15 cases, which is usually adequate for reaching some stability of results. Hence, we decided to select 13 cases, balancing as much as possible across client and therapist gender, therapist theoretical orientation, and when the interview was conducted. Initial analyses were done on these 13 cases, and then a 14th case was examined to determine whether it contributed anything new to the categories. The judges determined that no new data were added, so the categories were considered stable. Only the 13 analyzed cases were considered as part of the final sample.

Selection of data. As we began the analyses, we realized that the data generated from the question on general self-disclosure were too diffuse to be useful because of the wide variations in the responses. In addition, when analyzing clients' experience of unhelpful therapist self-disclosures, we discovered that several clients had no unhelpful examples and so responded with less helpful examples that were not distinguishable from the helpful examples. Hence, we dropped both the general and unhelpful therapist self-disclosures from the analyses.

Bracketing biases. Prior to coding data, all three judges and the auditor explored their expectations–biases by responding to each interview protocol as they expected participants to respond. Thus, for each interview question, the judges and auditor individually wrote responses they felt would be typical of clients who chose to participate in the study. The judges and auditor were then asked to bracket, or set aside, their suppositions and to approach the data with as much objectivity as possible.

Sarah Knox believed that the helpful disclosures would make the clients feel more comfortable in some way, would provoke the clients to think about something from a new perspective, would change the clients' view of themselves, and would also positively affect the therapy relationship. Shirley A. Hess felt that helpful therapist self-disclosures would make clients think more about how they were coming across and would also enable the clients to see the therapists as more real. She felt that clients would consider these disclosures as intended to make the clients become more aware of the effects of their actions and to help the clients understand why they respond as they do. David A. Petersen felt that helpful disclosures would serve to normalize clients' problems, with clients feeling a stronger bond with their therapist as a result of the disclosure. Clara E. Hill (the auditor) expected that therapist self-disclosures of experiences similar to what the clients were going through would have a positive effect because the clients would feel a sense of universality, an increase in the real relationship between therapists and clients, and a desire to model the therapists. Furthermore, she thought clients would be able to use the disclosures, perhaps as models for encouraging "self-talk" when facing challenging situations.

Procedures for Analyzing Data

Consensus. The heart of this type of qualitative research is arriving at consensus about the meaning, significance, and categorization of the data. Consensus is accomplished through team members' discussing their individual conceptualizations and then agreeing on a final interpretation that is satisfactory to all. Initial disagreement is the norm and is then followed by eventual agreement (consensus) on the analysis of the data. Because the three members of the primary team were all graduate students at the same level of training and because they were friends and respectful of each other, power dynamics were not a problem and could be discussed openly.

Determination of domains. Domains (topic areas) were initially developed out of the first few interview cases, were refined by going through additional cases,

and were continually modified to fit the emerging data. The final domains included the following: early relationship between therapist and client, later relationship between therapist and client, antecedent of the self-disclosure, client's perception of therapist's intention for the self-disclosure, the self-disclosure event, and consequences of the self-disclosure.

Assignment to domains. The three judges independently assigned each block of data (one complete thought consisting of a phrase or several sentences related to the same topic, e.g., "client thinks that therapist is not able to understand her struggle with drugs, so client asks him if he's ever tried street drugs"; "therapist disclosed that he had a family member who died of AIDS"; "client senses universality of her problem") from each case into one or more domains. The judges discussed the assignment of these blocks to domains until they reached consensus.

Core ideas. Each judge independently read all data within each domain for a specific case and wrote what he or she considered to be the core ideas that expressed the general ideas in more concise and abstract terms (e.g., "clients perceived their early and later relationships with their therapists as a mixture of positive and negative attributes"). Judges discussed the wording of each core idea until they reached consensus. A consensus version for each case was then developed, which consisted of the core ideas and the raw data for each of the domains.

Audit. The auditor examined the consensus version of each case and evaluated the accuracy of both the domain coding and the wording of the core ideas. The judges then discussed the auditor's comments and made those changes agreed upon by consensus judgment. The judges thus again reached consensus for domains and wording of the core ideas in the revised consensus version. The auditor then reviewed these changes and suggested further modifications, which the judges similarly considered for another revised consensus version.

Cross-analysis. The purpose of cross-analysis was to compare the core ideas within domains across cases. After listing the core ideas of each domain for each case, the judges examined each domain and looked for similarities in core ideas across cases. They then placed these core ideas into coherent themes or categories, seeking to reach a small number of categories within each domain. Although the number of categories varied from domain to domain, the judges and auditor sought to identify those categories that most efficiently and most clearly captured the essence of the domain. For example, several categories were formulated under consequences of helpful therapist self-disclosure: "gave client insight or new perspective to make changes," "allowed client to view therapist as more real and more human," "normalized or universalized client's struggles," and "enabled client to use therapist as model."

After this initial set of categories was developed, the judges returned to the consensus version of each case to determine whether the case contained evidence not previously coded for any of the categories. If such evidence was discerned (as determined by a consensus judgment of the primary team), the consensus version of the case was altered accordingly to reflect this category, and the core idea was added to the appropriate category in the cross-analysis.

The auditor then reviewed the cross-analysis along with the revised consensus version for each case. Suggestions made by the auditor were considered by the primary team and incorporated if agreed upon by consensus judgment. Once again, the auditor suggested additional changes, which the team discussed.

Results

All 13 cases described an example of a helpful therapist self-disclosure. Following the CQR methodology, we considered categories in each domain to be general if they applied to all cases, typical if they applied to at least half but not all cases, and variant if they applied to at least 3 but fewer than half of the cases. In all domains, categories that were applicable to only 1 or 2 cases were dropped from further consideration, because such infrequently occurring categories were considered less typical. Table 1 contains the summary of findings that emerged from the cross-analyses.

Therapeutic Relationship

The early relationship was typically described as having a mixture of positive and negative attributes. For example, 1 client had difficulty trusting her therapist but also saw him as open, patient, and reliable; another client censored what she said yet felt that her therapist's consistency and persistence made her feel comfortable; a 3rd client became disappointed that the therapist did not "fix" everything, yet she also looked forward to her sessions as her "Friday night date."

Like the early relationship, the later relationship was typically described as having a mixture of positive and negative characteristics. For example, 1 client felt the relationship was more comfortable but admitted that the increased closeness occasionally made her feel scared; another said that although she was more comfortable with the process of therapy and felt that her therapist was helpful, caring, and insightful, she occasionally still felt anxious and nervous; a 3rd acknowledged that although she felt more mature in her present relationship and saw this relationship as more real and more equal, she still questioned at times whether her therapist cared for her.

Antecedents

The helpful therapist self-disclosures typically involved the same antecedent: Clients were discussing important personal issues. There was a wide variety in the content of what clients were discussing, but the common factor was that clients reported that they were discussing topics of concern to them. For example, 1 client was questioning whether her therapist would be able to understand her struggles with drugs because she thought he had never tried street drugs, another client was discussing her difficult adolescent experiences, and a 3rd client was discussing her depression.

Table 1

Summary of General, Typical, and Variant Categories of Helpful Therapist Self-Disclosures

Domain	Category	Frequency
Relationship	Mixture of positive and negative attributes	Typical
Antecedent	Client discusses important personal issues	Typical
Intent	Normalize or reassure	Typical
	Help client make constructive change to deal with an issue	Variant
	Client unsure about intention	Variant
Event	Therapist disclosed personal nonimmediate information	General
	(a) Family	Variant
	(b) Leisure	Variant
	(c) Similar experience	Variant
Consequences	Positive	Typical
	(a) Gave client insight or perspective to make changes	Typical
	(b) Therapist seen as more real or relationship seen as improved or equalized	Typical
	(c) Normalized or reassured	Typical
	(d) Client used therapist as model	Variant
	Negative feelings or reactions; negative influence on therapy or therapy relationship	Variant
	Neutral	Variant

Note. $N = 13$. General = category applied to all cases; typical = category applied to at least half of the cases; variant = category applied to fewer than half of the cases. Categories represented by only one or two cases were dropped.

Intent

Clients typically believed that their therapists disclosed to normalize their experiences or to reassure them. For instance, 1 client felt that her therapist disclosed to show her understanding, as a mother, of what the client was feeling about her daughter. Another client believed that her therapist disclosed to ease the client's feelings about upcoming medical tests. Two variant categories also emerged. First, some clients were unsure of their therapists' intentions. One client, for instance, had thought about it quite a bit but remained unsure about why her therapist self-disclosed; another client was uncertain of his therapist's intention. Second, a few clients felt that their therapists disclosed to help clients make constructive changes to deal with issues. For example, 1 client stated that she thought her therapist's disclosure was intended to reduce her self-imposed pressure to resolve difficulties perfectly and immediately; another client felt the disclosure was given to encourage her to confront her issues.

Event

In all 13 helpful therapist self-disclosure examples, therapists disclosed personal nonimmediate information. These disclosures were often from the past, and none were immediate to the therapy relationship, despite instructions to clients that encompassed both self-disclosing and self-involving therapist statements. Variant subcategories within this larger category of personal nonimmediate information were (a) disclosures about family (e.g., 1 therapist discussed spending time at the shore during his childhood, another disclosed having a young son), (b) disclosures about leisure activities (e.g., 1 disclosed about having tried street drugs, another about his hobby of fly-fishing), and (c) disclosures of similar difficult experiences (e.g., 1 disclosed her difficulty arranging transportation because of a disability, another how her coming out as a lesbian affected her relationships with her family).

Consequences

One broad typical category emerged for the consequences of the helpful therapist self-disclosures: They resulted in positive consequences. Within this larger category of positive consequences, four more specific subcategories also emerged. First, clients typically gained insight or a new perspective to make changes (e.g., 1 client began to see solutions to her problems; another client was able to recall good times in her childhood and see her parents as sick instead of evil; a 3rd client was able to use the perspective gained through the therapist self-disclosure to communicate with her partner about the struggles she faced in relationships with her family). Second, clients typically were able to see their therapists as more real, human, or imperfect, which was associated with an improved or equalized therapeutic relationship (e.g., 1 client viewed her therapist as more human and the relationship as more balanced; a 2nd client sensed her therapist as a kindred spirit; a 3rd client stated that the disclosure made his therapist seem more real and more human and showed that his therapist had flaws like all others and did not have all the answers). Third, the disclosures typically normalized or reassured clients, making them feel better (e.g., 1 client sensed the universality of her problem and felt less anxious about her situation; another client felt less alone and less crazy; and a 3rd was able to be more accepting of his own feelings). Fourth, a few clients used therapists as models to make positive changes in themselves or to increase client self-disclosure (e.g., 1 client stated that the disclosure facilitated her own openness and honesty in the therapy, allowing her to feel less protective, whereas another

client used her image of how her therapist would respond to situations to guide her as she interacted with others).

The helpful therapist self-disclosures also occasionally evoked negative effects in the form of negative feelings, reactions, or negative influences on the therapy or therapy relationship. Thus, even within disclosures that clients perceived as a whole as helpful, negative effects were also experienced. One client, for instance, was wary about therapy boundaries and questioned what she was supposed to know as a result of the disclosure, and another client feared the closeness engendered by the disclosure and wanted to push it away.

Finally, a few clients also reported neutral consequences of the therapist self-disclosure. One client stated that the disclosure did not change her views about herself or the therapy process; another said that the disclosure may have been a helpful example of people learning to cope with problems but that it did not add much to his ability to cope with his problems.

Narrative Account of a Helpful Therapist Self-Disclosure

The examples of helpful therapist self-disclosure followed a typical pattern (involving all categories for which we found general or typical results). At the time of the disclosure, clients were discussing important personal issues. They surmised that the therapists disclosed in order to normalize their feelings or to reassure them. The disclosure itself concerned nonimmediate personal information about the therapist. The revelation of the therapist self-disclosure led to positive consequences in the clients in the form of insight, realness or equalization of the relationship, and normalization or reassurance.

Illustrative Example of a Helpful Therapist Self-Disclosure

An example of a helpful disclosure is from a 33-year-old female client who had been seeing her male therapist for 11 years at the time of the interview. She had struggled with drug addiction and chronic depression and was later diagnosed with borderline personality disorder. She described her therapist's theoretical orientation as a combination of behavioral–cognitive–behavioral and humanistic–experiential and indicated that he often disclosed. In their early relationship, this client had difficulty trusting her therapist and thus encountered difficulty in opening up to him. She expressed confusion about what the relationship should be and often tested her therapist to see if he would be trustworthy. At times, she needed him to be responsive, and he was not. She did, however, view him as patient, open, and reliable and stated that she felt comfortable with him right away. At the time of the disclosure, she thought that he would not be able to understand her struggle with drugs, so she asked him if he had ever tried street drugs. She believed he thought that he had no other recourse and needed to stop the argument, so he disclosed to her that he had tried street drugs. This disclosure shocked the client ("It stopped the argument cold"), made her rethink her assumptions and stereotypes, enabled her to recognize the benefits of healthy disagreement, and allowed her to use the therapy relationship as a learning ground for other relationships in her life. She thus became more assertive in expressing her needs and opinions rationally. This disclosure also changed her perspective of her therapist, making him more human and more similar to her, thereby increasing her respect for him, making her feel closer to him, and balancing the relationship. She said, "It snapped me right out of that self-righteous thing, you know, that 'How would you know?'...like I was different than him. At that moment it made him a lot more human than I was feeling at the time...and changed the whole perspective immediately...it made him sort of a kindred spirit in a way."

Discussion

In looking globally at these experiences of specific helpful therapist self-disclosures in long-term therapy, we found that clients perceived self-disclosures to be important events in their therapies. Clients were indeed affected by these revelations, an affirmation of the potency of therapist self-disclosure that is consistent with earlier research (e.g., Hill et al., 1988).

To set the context for these results more completely, we note that the early and later relationships for all cases were described as a mixture of positive and negative attributes. These clients characterized their relationships neither as purely "good" nor as purely "bad" but instead reflected perhaps a more realistic view of their connections to their therapists. Perhaps the presence of at least some positive features in the early relationship allowed the clients the safety and comfort necessary to continue in therapy. Were the negative characteristics not offset by positive elements, these clients may not have remained in therapy and thus may not have been eligible for participation in this study. The negative traits did not seem to drive them from therapy in the beginning, nor did they apparently impede the progress or work of therapy at its later stages. Perhaps the good attributes were indeed strong enough, and thus the relationship itself strong enough, to survive the inevitable difficulties of therapy. These participants, then, represent those who have weathered the potentially tumultuous seasons of the therapy relationship.

These clients typically perceived that immediately preceding the disclosure, they were discussing important personal issues such as relationship difficulties, personal struggles with physical disabilities or substance abuse, or upsetting events with family members. After such antecedents, these clients perceived their therapists as having a clear intention for the disclosure: They saw their therapists as seeking to normalize or reassure them through the disclosure. This reassurance sometimes took the form of letting the client know that things often do work out, of demonstrating the therapist's understanding of the client's struggle, or of letting the client know that his or her feelings were neither unusual nor unexpected. The perception of such positive intentions may have contributed to the clients' experience of these disclosures as helpful.

All of the helpful therapist self-disclosures cited by these clients were of personal nonimmediate information, whether about family, leisure activities, or similar experiences between clients and therapists. Although this information was personal, it was largely historical rather than immediate. Despite instructions that permitted clients to describe either self-disclosing or self-involving therapist statements, these clients cited only the former. These qualitative findings thus differ from the suggestions of other literature that the most helpful self-referent responses are immediate and reassuring (i.e., depict present-tense, direct communications to the client of the therapists' feelings or cognitions regarding the client or the therapy and reveal the therapists' support for, reinforcement for, or legitimization of the clients' perspective, way of thinking, feeling, or behaving; e.g., Hoffman & Spencer, 1977; Hoffman-Graff, 1977; McCarthy & Betz, 1978). This self-involving type of therapist statement was never cited by these clients as an example of a helpful therapist self-disclosure, much less a most helpful therapist self-disclosure. Perhaps clients were better able to recall the distinct historical disclosures, whereas any immediate disclosures that may have occurred were more rapidly forgotten or subsumed under the client's general impression of the therapeutic relationship. Perhaps these clients found the historical disclosures more interesting in providing them with a fuller view of the therapist, whereas the self-involving therapist statements remained less memorable or less helpful because they lacked such revelation. Perhaps also the immediate disclosures were perceived as too intimate or threatening and therefore were not viewed as helpful, whereas the more historical or autobiographical statements enabled these clients to learn more about their therapists and thus feel a greater sense of safety and comfort. Several potential explanations for these clients' citing only self-disclosing therapist statements as examples of helpful therapist self-disclosure are surely possible, but the fact that none of these clients referred to a self-involving therapist statement as an example of a helpful therapist self-disclosure is intriguing, especially because the definition with which they were provided encompassed both types of statement.

In terms of consequences these clients perceived as arising from the disclosures, the helpful self-disclosures resulted in both positive and negative consequences, although there were more positive than negative consequences. One positive consequence was the client's perception of the therapist as more human

810 and more real and of the relationship as more balanced. Thus, therapist self-disclosure did seem to affect the real relationship between these therapists and clients. It is interesting that this increased realness did not, how-
815 ever, appear to result in any loss of status for the therapist, a possibility raised by Andersen and Anderson (1985). Although the clients did not explicitly state that no loss of status occurred, neither did they describe a diminishment of the therapist's status. In addition, the
820 disclosures appeared to equalize the power in the relationship, as suggested by Chelune (1979), Kaslow et al. (1979), Lander and Nahon (1992), and Robitschek and McCarthy (1991). The revelations of the therapist self-disclosures evidently contributed to a more balanced distribution of power in the therapeutic relationship,
825 perhaps again because the clients were able to see their therapists as human and real. These clients seemed to appreciate the realness of their therapists and did not experience this realness as a threat to the therapists' stature. In fact, they described such realness as en-
830 hancing the connection between therapists and clients, thus fostering the therapeutic work.

An unexpected positive consequence was that these therapist self-disclosures resulted in client insights or new perspectives. The clients were apparently able to
835 learn, to understand something new about themselves or their experiences, and to view things from a new point of view. They were encouraged to rethink old assumptions about themselves or about others, were able to see solutions to their problems, acquired a bet-
840 ter sense of a developmental process with which they were struggling, and were able to translate these into interpersonal or intrapersonal changes.

In addition, positive effects appeared to emerge in the helpful instances of therapist self-disclosure
845 through these clients' feeling reassured, feeling that their struggles were normalized, or acquiring a sense of universality. As suggested by Chelune (1979), Mathews (1988), Robitschek and McCarthy (1991), and Yalom (1975), this sense of not being alone in their
850 struggles confirmed the clients' essential connection with others and thus made them feel better.

Another apparent positive consequence was that these clients used therapists as models to make changes in themselves. As suggested in the literature (Egan,
855 1990; Kaslow et al., 1979; Simon, 1988; Watkins, 1990), such modeling may help clients with the basic act of disclosure in that clients are encouraged by the therapists' disclosing to increase their own disclosure in their sessions. Some clients in this study cited just
860 such a consequence, for they seemed to use their therapists' disclosure to spur them on to disclose more themselves. Modeling may also occur when clients use their therapists' disclosed traits, characteristics, or modes of behaving as a guide for themselves outside of
865 therapy. This, too, appeared to occur here, for clients remarked that they internalized attributes demonstrated by their therapists in their own interactions and consid-

ered such internalization a positive change in themselves. These clients seemed to use the helpful disclo-
870 sures, then, as a guide for their own thoughts, feelings, and behaviors, both inside and outside of therapy. In their therapists, they perceived traits they sought in themselves, and then they altered their own interactions by incorporating the therapist as a model.

875 Some negative consequences also occurred, though these were clearly, and expectedly, not the primary consequences of these interventions. A few clients reported negative effects either in terms of feelings and reactions or in terms of the influence on therapy or the
880 therapy relationship. Apparently, even helpful therapist self-disclosures have the potential for some negative impact.

Limitations

The small sample size brings into question the potential representativeness of these participants. All cli-
885 ents and therapists were European American and from one geographical region and thus may not represent the experiences of individuals from other cultures and locations. In addition, all were seen in private practice and may represent only those people who are able to
890 afford long-term psychotherapy.

Furthermore, bias is always a concern in qualitative research. We tried to address this potential limitation by using three individuals on the primary team as well as an auditor. Each of us bracketed our expectations
895 and then tried to set them aside. In addition, we tried to stay very close to the data, typically using the clients' own words in developing the core ideas. At the data analysis stage, Clara E. Hill's function was solely as an auditor, which provided her with even greater objec-
900 tivity in scrutinizing the work of the primary team.

Another limitation was that the definition of therapist self-disclosure used here was broad and encompassing. In the future, researchers should consider using a more limited definition, perhaps one that distin-
905 guishes between self-involving and self-disclosing self-referent statements. In addition, no distinctions were made between the degree of intimacy or risk level of the therapists' self-disclosures. Disclosures of having tried street drugs may have a different effect than
910 revelations of enjoying fly-fishing.

Client characteristics, as well, may have created limitations for this project. As explicated by Nisbett and Wilson (1977), people have varying abilities to recall their internal experiences. Some encounter great
915 difficulty in describing their mental processes when a situation is ambiguous (when the client is unaware of the stimuli that trigger such responses). This may have affected clients' perceptions and responses, especially because we did not know how distal or proximal the
920 cited disclosures were.

Furthermore, clients who agreed to participate may have differed from those who did not, which suggests the possibility of self-selection. We also interviewed only clients who were still in therapy and thus do not have the perspective of those who had already terminated. Clients who have terminated may have left for a variety of reasons, one of which could have been the nature of their experiences with therapist self-disclosure. In addition, therapists might have asked only certain types of clients (e.g., the most compliant or successful) to participate.

The therapists who participated were also a sample of convenience and thus were perhaps not truly representative. Their affiliation with the counseling psychology faculty at a large, mid-Atlantic university, as well, may have influenced their desire to participate. In addition, we investigated only the clients' views of the experience of therapist self-disclosure, which might differ from the therapists' perspectives. Given these limitations, one should exercise caution when attempting to generalize from these results.

Implications

This study enabled an examination of the client's experiences of helpful therapist self-disclosure. We learned more about these clients' actual feelings about therapists and therapy through an "inside view" provided by this qualitative design, a view often inaccessible or even hidden from the therapist in the sessions themselves. By learning about the effects of therapist self-disclosure on these clients, therapists may be able to make more appropriate decisions regarding this intervention with their own clients. Self-disclosing therapist statements seem useful in long-term therapy because they evoke positive consequences within clients. For example, clients often acquired insight or a change in perspective, were able to see their therapist as more human and more real, and felt reassured as a result of therapist self-disclosure. Such consequences are certainly worthy of attention when therapists consider making self-disclosures.

Although there were not enough data for us to investigate this fact more fully, different types of clients seemed to react differently to therapist self-disclosure. Some of these clients were voracious in their desire for therapist self-disclosure, wishing their therapists had disclosed more often or even arranging to meet with another client of the same therapist to share information about the therapist. These clients seemed to want to merge in some way with their therapists. Other clients, however, were less desirous of disclosures, worrying at times that the disclosures blurred the boundaries of the relationship or distinctly stating that self-disclosures were inappropriate because they removed the focus from the client and were unprofessional in their revelations about the therapist. This contrast between those clients who sought therapist self-disclosure and those who preferred more distance from their therapists is worthy of further investigation because it may provide information about how client factors influence whether therapist self-disclosure is seen as an appropriate intervention and, if so, what types of self-disclosure are considered appropriate.

In addition, our understanding of how therapist self-disclosure is experienced by clients may be enhanced by further research into the differential effects of various types of disclosure (i.e., self-involving vs. self-disclosing). As an exploratory investigation, this study qualitatively examined clients' internal experiences of therapist self-disclosure as broadly defined. Similarly designed research into how clients perceive and experience the different types of therapist self-disclosure, however, could prove informative.

Future research into the therapists' perspective regarding therapist self-disclosure would also be instructive in determining whether their perceptions are similar to clients'. We chose not to interview these clients' therapists in this initial study, but comparing therapists' perspectives would be important in future studies.

Finally, given the results suggesting that therapist self-disclosure affects the real relationship between therapist and client, the clients' sense of universality, the clients' ability to use the therapist as a model, and the clients' acquisition of insight, it would be useful to develop ways to assess these effects more concretely and quantitatively. For example, a self-report measure of the effects of therapist self-disclosure could be developed that could be administered after therapy sessions. Furthermore, investigation into whether other therapeutic interventions (e.g., interpretation, reflection of feeling) yield these same effects would also be informative.

References

Andersen, B. & Anderson, W. (1985). Client perceptions of counselors using positive and negative self-involving statements. *Journal of Counseling Psychology, 32,* 462–465.

Basescu, S. (1990). Tools of the trade: The use of self in psychotherapy. *Group, 14,* 157–165.

Chelune, G. J. (1979). *Self-disclosure: Origins, patterns, and implications of openness in interpersonal relationships.* San Francisco: Jossey-Bass.

Cherbosque, J. (1987). Differential effects of counselor self-disclosure statements on perception of the counselor and willingness to disclose: A cross-cultural study. *Psychotherapy, 24,* 434–437.

Egan, G. (1990). *The skilled helper: A systematic approach to effective helping.* Pacific Grove, CA: Brooks/Cole.

Fox, S. G., Strum, C. A. & Walters, H. A. (1984). Perceptions of therapist disclosure of previous experience as a client. *Journal of Clinical Psychology, 40,* 496–498.

Gelso, C. J. & Carter, J. A. (1994). Components of the psychotherapy relationship: Their interaction and unfolding during treatment. *Journal of Counseling Psychology, 41,* 296–306.

Hill, C. E., Helms, J. E., Tichenor, V., Spiegel, S. B., O'Grady, K. E. & Perry, E. S. (1988). Effects of therapist response modes in brief psychotherapy. *Journal of Counseling Psychology, 35,* 222–233.

Hill, C. E., Mahalik, J. R. & Thompson, B. J. (1989). Therapist self-disclosure. *Psychotherapy: Theory, Research, and Practice, 26,* 290–295.

Hill, C. E., Nutt-Williams, E., Heaton, K. J., Thompson, B. J. & Rhodes, R. H. (1996). Therapist retrospective recall of impasses in long-term psychotherapy: A qualitative analysis. *Journal of Counseling Psychology, 43,* 207–217.

Hill, C. E., Thompson, B. J. & Williams, E. (in press). *The Counseling Psychologist.*

Hoffman, M. A. & Spencer, G. P. (1977). Effect of interviewer self-disclosure and interviewer–subject sex pairing on perceived and actual subject behavior. *Journal of Counseling Psychology, 24,* 383–390.

Hoffman-Graff, M. A. (1977). Interviewer use of positive and negative self-disclosure and interviewer–subject sex pairing. *Journal of Counseling Psychology, 24,* 184–190.

Kaslow, F., Cooper, B. & Linsenberg, M. (1979). Family therapist authenticity as a key factor in outcome. *International Journal of Family Therapy, 1,* 194–

199.

Lander, N. R. & Nahon, D. (1992). Betrayed within the therapeutic relationship: An integrity therapy perspective. *Psychotherapy Patient, 8,* 113–125.

Mahrer, A. R., Fellers, G. L., Durak, G. M., Gervaize, P. A. & Brown, S. D. (1981). When does the counsellor self-disclose and what are the in-counseling consequences? *Canadian Counsellor, 15,* 175–179.

Mann, B. & Murphy, K. C. (1975). Timing of self-disclosure, reciprocity of self-disclosure, and reactions to an initial interview. *Journal of Counseling Psychology, 22,* 304–308.

Mathews, B. (1988). The role of therapist self-disclosure in psychotherapy: A survey of therapists. *American Journal of Psychotherapy, 42,* 521–531.

Mathews, B. (1989). The use of therapist self-disclosure and its potential impact on the therapeutic process. *Journal of Human Behavior and Learning, 6,* 25–29.

McCarthy, P. R. & Betz, N. E. (1978). Differential effects of self-disclosing versus self-involving counselor statements. *Journal of Counseling Psychology, 25,* 251–256.

Nilsson, D. E., Strassberg, D. S. & Bannon, J. (1979). Perceptions of counselor self-disclosure: An analogue study. *Journal of Counseling Psychology, 26,* 399–404.

Nisbett, R. E. & Wilson, T. D. (1977). Telling more than we can know. *Psychological Review, 84,* 231–259.

Palombo, J. (1987). Spontaneous self disclosures in psychotherapy. *Clinical Social Work Journal, 15,* 107–120.

Rhodes, R. H., Hill, C. E., Thompson, B. J. & Elliott, R. (1994). Client retrospective recall of resolved and unresolved misunderstanding events. *Journal of Counseling Psychology, 41,* 473–483.

Robitschek, C. G. & McCarthy, P. R. (1991). Prevalence of counselor self-reference in the therapeutic dyad. *Journal of Counseling and Development, 69,* 218–221.

Rosie, J. S. (1980). The therapist's self-disclosure in individual psychotherapy: Research and psychoanalytic theory. *Canadian Journal of Psychiatry, 25,* 469–472.

Simon, J. C. (1988). Criteria for therapist self-disclosure. *American Journal of Psychotherapy, 42,* 404–415.

Wachtel, P. L. (1993). *Therapeutic communication: Principles and effective practice.* New York: Guilford Press.

Watkins, C. E. (1990). The effects of counselor self-disclosure: A research review. *The Counseling Psychologist, 18,* 477–500.

Weiner, M. F. (1983). *Therapist disclosure: The use of self in psychotherapy* (2nd ed.). Baltimore: University Park Press.

Yalom, I. D. (1975). *Theory and practice of group psychotherapy* (2nd ed.). New York: Basic Books.

Authors' note: This study, based on a master's thesis by Sarah Knox completed under the direction of Clara E. Hill, was supported in part by the Graduate School and the Department of Psychology at the University of Maryland College Park. A version of this article was presented in June 1996 at the 27th Annual Meeting of the Society for Psychotherapy Research in Amelia Island, Florida.

Acknowledgments: We express our appreciation to Charles Gelso and Mary Ann Hoffman for serving on the thesis committee. We also express our thanks to Paula Alarid, Samantha Erskine, Julie Hudnall, Craig McManus, Rhonda Rose, Susanna Tipermus, Amy Venema, Maggie Weil, and Mike Wood for their assistance with transcription.

Address correspondence to: Sarah Knox, Department of Psychology, University of Maryland, College Park, MD, 20742-4411. Electronic mail may be sent to sarahk@umd5.umd.edu

Exercise for Article 21

Factual Questions

1. How did the researchers define "self-disclosure" for this study?

2. In the CQR process, why are all judgments made by three to five judges?

3. On the average, the 13 clients had been in therapy with their therapists for how many months?

4. Who served as the auditor in this study?

5. What did the second question in the first interview ask the clients to estimate?

6. According to the researchers, qualitative research *typically* includes about how many cases?

7. The researchers considered categories to the "general" if they applied to how many cases?

8. What was an "unexpected" positive consequence of therapist self-disclosures?

Questions for Discussion

9. In lines 178–181, the researchers state that a qualitative approach seemed appropriate for their research. Do you agree? Do you think that a quantitative study would have been as useful? Explain.

10. Twenty-one therapists were contacted for possible participation, but only 14 agreed to do so. Could this have affected the results of the study? Explain.

11. What is your opinion on the bracketing technique (i.e., having the researchers write down their expectations of the results and then mentally setting them aside so that the data can be viewed objectively)? (See lines 407–441.)

12. The researchers name a number of limitations. In your opinion, is it appropriate for researchers to explicitly state their limitations in a research report? Explain. (See lines 883–941.)

13. In your opinion, are some of the limitations discussed in lines 883–941 more important than others? Explain.

14. In your opinion, are the results of this study valid even though there are few statistics and no tests of statistical significance? Explain.

Quality Ratings

Directions: Indicate your level of agreement with each of the following statements by circling a number from 5 for strongly agree (SA) to 1 for strongly disagree (SD). If you believe an item is not applicable to this research article, leave it blank. Be prepared to explain your ratings.

A. The introduction establishes the importance of the study.

       SA 5 4 3 2 1 SD

B. The literature review establishes the context for the study.

       SA 5 4 3 2 1 SD

C. The research purpose, question, or hypothesis is clearly stated.

       SA 5 4 3 2 1 SD

D. The method of sampling is sound.

       SA 5 4 3 2 1 SD

E. Relevant demographics (for example, age, gender, and ethnicity) are described.

       SA 5 4 3 2 1 SD

F. Measurement procedures are adequate.

       SA 5 4 3 2 1 SD

G. All procedures have been described in sufficient detail to permit a replication of the study.

       SA 5 4 3 2 1 SD

H. The participants have been adequately protected from potential harm.

       SA 5 4 3 2 1 SD

I. The results are clearly described.

       SA 5 4 3 2 1 SD

J. The discussion/conclusion is appropriate.

       SA 5 4 3 2 1 SD

K. Despite any flaws, the report is worthy of publication.

       SA 5 4 3 2 1 SD

Article 22

Black Men's Perceptions of Divorce-Related Stressors and Strategies for Coping with Divorce

ERMA JEAN LAWSON
University of Kentucky

AARON THOMPSON
University of Missouri

ABSTRACT. The divorce rate among Blacks in the United States has increased significantly in recent years. Consequently, an increasing number of Black men confront problems associated with adjusting to divorce. Using data from in-depth interviews, we identify factors that working middle-class Black men perceive to cause significant stress following divorce and we examine strategies that they use to reestablish their lives. The results show that Black men confront the following divorce-related stressors: (a) financial strain, (b) noncustodial parenting, (c) child-support stressors, and (d) psychological as well as physiological distress. The findings suggest that divorced Black men experience profound postdivorce psychological distress. The data further indicate that Black men employ the following strategies to cope with the stress of marital dissolution: (a) reliance on family and friends, (b) involvement in church-related activities, (c) participation in social activities, and (d) establishment of intimate heterosexual relationships one year after divorce. These findings indicate that postdivorce adjustment should be scrutinized within relevant social-cultural contexts.

From *Journal of Family Issues*, *17*, 249-273. Copyright © 1996 by Sage Publications, Inc. Reprinted with permission. All rights reserved.

In the past 30 years, there have been significant changes in the Black family structure (Cherlin, 1992; Farley & Allen, 1987). One dramatic change has been the increased rate of divorce (Cherlin, 1992). For ex-
5 ample, two of three Black marriages end in divorce (Staples, 1985). In 1970, 68% of Black families had both husband and wife present, compared to 50% by 1990. This represents an 18% decrease in 20 years, compared to a 6% decrease of comparable White fami-
10 lies (Pinkney, 1993). Consequently, a large proportion of Blacks are coping with the consequences of divorce.

Despite the high rate of marital dissolution among Blacks, there is an absence of studies that have examined Black men's divorce experience. This lack of re-
15 search is surprising because marital dissolution has been characterized as a particularly stressful process for Black men (Albrecht, 1980; Gove & Shin, 1989). For example, divorce involves the severance of complex marital bonds, negotiation of custody arrange-
20 ments, establishment of a new lifestyle, and often ad-

justment from custodial to noncustodial parenting (Hetherington, Stanley-Hogan, & Anderson, 1976; Tschann, Johnston, & Wallerstein, 1989; Wright & Price, 1986). Divorce has continuing stressful conse-
25 quences (Kitson & Morgan, 1990).

Although health problems may predate divorce, irrespective of race, divorced men exhibit higher rates of automobile accidents, alcohol abuse, diabetes, heart disease, and mental illness compared to their married
30 male counterparts (Bloom, Asher, & White, 1978; Gove & Shin, 1989; Reissman, 1990; Rosengren, Wedel, & Wilhelmsen, 1989; Umberson, 1987). Additionally, fathers who live separately from their children are more likely than fathers who live with their chil-
35 dren to engage in health-compromising behaviors (Umberson, 1987). The decline in health status following divorce is especially significant for Black men because they experience the poorest health status among all racial and gender groups (Billingsley, 1992;
40 Gary, 1981; Staples, 1985; Wilkinson, 1977).

This article identifies factors that working-class/ middle-class Black men, including noncustodial fathers, perceive as divorce-related stressors, and it examines the strategies they used to reestablish their
45 lives. Specifically, we suggest that the mere existence of a divorce-related stressor is an inadequate measure of postdivorce adjustment; it is the individual's perception of stressors that influences postdivorce adjustment. An examination of divorced Black men's per-
50 ceptions is a particularly salient issue given the high rate of marital termination among Blacks and the paucity of research on divorced Black men.

Divorce-Related Stressors

Economic Stressors

A change in economics precipitated by divorce is a major stressor (Albrecht, 1980; Kitson & Holmes,
55 1992; Weitzman, 1985). The immediate impact for women following divorce is downward economic mobility (Albrecht, 1980; Peterson, 1989; Reissman, 1990; Weitzman, 1985). For example, predivorce women who are unemployed experience difficulty re-
60 entering the job market and often discover that their wages are too low to support a family (Albrecht, 1980; Weitzman, 1985). Despite court orders, noncustodial

138

fathers fail to pay $4 billion in child support each year (U.S. Bureau of the Census, 1987). Approximately 53% of women who are due child support do not receive court-ordered support (U.S. Bureau of the Census, 1987). As a result of their limited earning power and their low level of child support, divorced mothers and their children often experience a sharp decline in their standard of living (Albrecht, Bahr, & Goodman, 1983; Kitson & Holmes, 1992; Wallerstein, 1986; Weitzman, 1985).

Although the economic consequences of divorce for women vary based on sociodemographic characteristics, similar information is unavailable for divorced men (Kitson & Morgan, 1990). According to Garfinkel & Oellerich (1989), previous research has assumed that the economic situations of divorced men are nonproblematic. Relatively little attention also has been paid to the relationship between financial stress and the postdivorce adjustment of Black men.

Noncustodial Parenting

In the majority of divorces, mothers are granted custody of the children and fathers are granted visitation (Weitzman, 1985). It is difficult to maintain true joint legal custody of children when one parent has sole physical custody (Clark, Whitney, & Beck, 1988). Thus noncustodial parenting has been reported as a significant source of postdivorce emotional turmoil. First, noncustodial visitation with children is typically superficial (Seltzer, 1991). Second, fathers are often ambivalent about their role as disciplinarian versus weekend friend because there are no established norms for noncustodial fathering (Clingempeel & Reppucci, 1982; Umberson, 1987). Some noncustodial fathers spend more time with children while others decrease the frequency of visits to their children (Cooney & Uhlenberg, 1990; Reissman, 1990; Umberson, 1987).

Psychosocial Stressors

Numerous psychological responses have been associated with divorce, including anger, depression, and ambivalence (Albrecht, 1980; Weiss, 1975; Zeiss, Zeiss, & Johnson, 1980). However, some persons experience little distress following divorce (Albrecht, 1980). Research also indicates that divorced men experience greater emotional distress and report more suicidal thoughts than do women (Reissman & Gerstel, 1985; Rosengren et al., 1989; Wallerstein & Kelly, 1980). According to Kitson and Morgan (1990), there are "his" and "her" responses to divorce. Few studies have examined the type of stressors that exacerbate adjustment problems of Black divorced men.

Moderators of Divorce Distress

Social Support

A variety of psychosocial factors influence postdivorce adjustment. For example, formal and informal social support, religious affiliation, and social participation are correlated with lower distress and better postdivorce adjustment (Furstenberg & Spanier, 1984; Gerstel, 1988). Studies show that women seem better able to draw on supportive networks than are men, thereby minimizing postdivorce psychological distress (Chiriboga & Culter, 1977; Reissman, 1990). Because divorced men are often socially isolated compared to women, their psychological distress intensifies after divorce (Reissman, 1990).

The initiation of divorce has been associated with less postdivorce distress (Kurdek & Blisk, 1983; Wallerstein, 1986). Because women are more likely to initiate divorce, research suggests that women experience fewer postdivorce psychological problems compared to men (Reissman, 1990; Wallerstein, 1986; Wymard, 1994). Perhaps women who initiate divorce have begun the detachment process earlier than men. For example, men are often unaware of the possibility of divorce prior to the divorce decision (Petti & Bloom, 1984). Thus noninitiation of divorce may further inhibit the postdivorce adjustment of men. Additionally, compared to women, men report greater feelings of attachment to their former spouses and assert a greater desire to reconcile, which may also increase postdivorce distress (Bloom & Kindle, 1985). It is unknown whether these findings can be generalized to Blacks in general or Black men in particular.

Heterosexual Relationships

There is evidence that high dating activity moderates postdivorce distress. Spanier and Casto (1979) report that respondents who dated regularly, lived with someone of the opposite sex, or remarried experienced fewer adjustment problems. On the other hand, those who had minimal or no heterosexual activity experienced major postdivorce adjustment problems. Although research suggests that dating a variety of people is as effective as forming a very close relationship, Raschke (1977) found that dating decreases postdivorce distress for males and not for females. There is an absence of research on the potential stress produced by dating for divorced men in general and for Black men in particular.

Race

Blacks and Whites differ in their responses to divorce (Gove & Shin, 1989). Black divorced females adjust more positively to living in single-parent families compared to their White counterparts (Brown, Perry, & Harberg, 1977; Menaghan & Lieberman, 1986). The literature provides inconsistent results on the postdivorce adjustment of Black men. Although Gove and Shin (1989) found no racial differences in the adjustment of Black males after divorce, studies have also reported that divorced Black males experience lower anxiety following divorce compared to their White counterparts (Thoits, 1986).

Previous studies of divorce adjustment have failed to (a) exclusively focus on the adjustment of Black men, (b) include Black divorced fathers, and (c) ade-

170 quately explain reasons for the different racial patterns of postdivorce adjustment.

This study focuses on the following questions: (a) What stressors are perceived by Black working-class/middle-class men to have caused significant
175 stress following divorce? (b) What strategies did Black men use to cope with divorce?

Methods

Sample Selection

A convenience sample of 30 divorced Black men who lived in the North Central region of the United States was recruited with the assistance of directors
180 from the Urban League and the National Association for the Advancement of Colored People. Recruitment was restricted to (a) men who were currently divorced and had not remarried, (b) men who were currently in the labor force (the purpose of selecting men in the
185 labor force was to eliminate psychological distress associated with unemployment), (c) men who had experienced only one divorce, and (d) men who had been married at least 2 years.

The research was described as an investigation into
190 the stressors Black men experience during divorce and what coping strategies they use to cope with marital failure. The men were informed of the study through phone calls, and appointments were made for the interviews. All respondents who were asked agreed to par-
195 ticipate, stating, "It is time that the voices of divorced Black men are heard." The men interviewed acted as referrals for other divorced Black men. Referrals increased the likelihood that the referred men would be of similar social class to the referral's source. A phone
200 call was made to each new, potential participant.

Interviews

Data were collected through face-to-face interviews that were conducted in the setting of the man's choice, most often his home ($n = 27$) or place of employment ($n = 3$). The researchers received permission from each
205 man to tape-record his interview.

The respondents were asked to be informal and spontaneous in telling a story that included "the quality of marital life preceding the separation and postdivorce, the experience during the divorce and postdi-
210 vorce, and the social support received and the coping strategies used postdivorce." Using a semistructured questionnaire, we had a list of probes that were addressed to the respondent if he did not cover a specific topic of interest to us in his answer. Examples of our
215 open-ended questions include: What was the most stressful factor during your divorce? What strategies did you use to cope with divorce? What advice would you give to a man who is coping with divorce? These questions enabled men to describe in their own words
220 divorce-related stressors and their strategies for coping with psychological distress generated by divorce. Discussions on these topics elicited detailed information about the stressors associated with divorce and how those stressors affected men's mental and physical
225 health.

The length of the interviews ranged from 2 to 4 hours, and all interviews were conducted together by the authors, one Black male and one Black female. The tapes were transcribed verbatim with the length of tran-
230 scriptions ranging from 30 to 40 single-spaced typed pages. Following the interviews, respondents also completed a sociodemographic questionnaire including age, length of marriage, income, and education. The most frequent themes that emerged from the prelimi-
235 nary sorting of the data were used to construct initial categories. Data analysis followed the principles described by Glaser (1978), Strauss (1986), and Marshall & Rossman (1989). A list of divorce-related stressors was identified based on the frequency of appearance in
240 the interviews, thus themes were derived from the data. As shown in Table 1, the following themes emerge as significant issues that created stress following a divorce: (a) financial strain, (b) child-support stressors, (c) noncustodial parenting, and (d) psychological dis-
245 tress. These themes were identified based on the number of interviews in which they appeared.

Several themes grouping coping techniques were identified: (a) reliance on family and friends, (b) involvement in church-related activities, (c) increased
250 social participation, and (d) establishment of intimate heterosexual relationships 1 year after divorce (see Table 2).

Table 1
Frequency of Divorce-Related Stressors as Perceived by Respondents

Divorce-Related Stressors	Number of Respondents ($N = 30$)
Financial strain	30
Noncustodial parenting	29
Child-support issues	29
Psychological distress (i.e., anxiety, insomnia, erratic behavioral patterns, alcohol and illicit drug use)	28
Physiological symptoms (i.e., migraine headaches, hypertension, ulcers, heart attack, and weight loss)	27

Note: Conflict with former spouse and loneliness were mentioned by fewer than 15 respondents.

Participant Observation

The authors conducted participant observations over a 2-year period to explore the social world of
255 Black divorced men. Participant observer methodology is defined as direct observation of behavior in everyday life to understand social relationships within natural settings (Bogden, 1972; Denzen, 1970). Because there is an absence of research on divorced Black men, we
260 decided that participant observations would increase knowledge of the everyday lives of Black divorced men. The men interviewed were asked to provide a list

of the places in which they socially participated and frequently visited. The researchers visited these places to observe the natural interaction of respondents, including church activities, Black lodges, fraternity meetings, community meetings, and social events. The purpose of the participant observations was to validate or invalidate information gathered by the interviews.

Table 2
Frequency of Divorce-Related Coping Strategies as Perceived by Respondents

Divorce-Related Strategies	Number of Respondents ($N = 30$)
Reliance on family and friends	30
Church-related activities	26
Increased social participation	24
Establishment of intimate heterosexual relationships 1 year postdivorce	22

Table 3
Demographic Characteristics of the Sample ($N = 30$)

	Percentage
Age	
35–39	10.0
40–45	75.0
46–50	15.0
Education	
0–12 years	10.0
1–2 years of college	80.0
4 or more years of college	10.0
Income	
$20,000–$29,999	5.0
$30,000–$39,999	70.0
$40,000–$49,999	10.0
$50,000 or more	15.0
Length of divorce	
0–1 years	5.0
2–3 years	80.0
4–9 years	10.0
10 years or more	5.0
Length of marriage	
1–5 years	10.0
6–9 years	80.0
10 or more years	10.0
Biological children	
1–2 children	90.0
3 or more children	10.0
Family of origin	
Two-parent family	40.0
Mother only	50.0
Extended family only	10.0
Married women with children	
Wife had no children	30.0
Wife had one child	45.0
Wife had two children	20.0
Wife had three or more children	5.0
Children before marriage	
0 children	90.0
1–2 children	10.0

Results

Sample Characteristics

As shown in Table 3, demographic characteristics of the sample are as follows: Approximately 75% were between the ages of 40 and 44 years, 80% had 1 or 2 years of college education, 70% reported an annual income between $30,000 and $50,000, 40% were raised by two parents, and 45% of the respondents married women who had children prior to the marriage. A large percentage of the respondents were parents (90%), had been married between 6 and 12 years (80%), and had been divorced between 2 and 3 years (80%). With the exception of one man, all mothers gained custody of the children. Overall, the sample consisted of first-divorced, middle-aged, working-class/middle-class Black men who were recently divorced.

Financial Strain

The study participants were asked, what was the major stressor during your divorce? Without exception, the respondents reported that financial strain was a major stressor. These problems included responsibility for tremendous debt accumulated during the marriage, the payment of legal and counseling bills that occurred during the separation, and the maintenance of two households. As a consequence of reduced income, the men in this study experienced a drastic decrease in their standard of living. Jim, a 36-year-old electrician, summarized his postdivorce economic situation: "The main stressor after my divorce was financial since I paid for the divorce, paid the bills my ex-wife created, and supported my ex-wife's cousin. I'm still recovering financially after 3 years." In agreement with Jim, Lennie, a 36-year-old nursing assistant who had been divorced for 1 year, commented:

It's hard to find an average Black man in the United States to live comfortable after a divorce. I have two households that depend on my salary. I am also supporting my mother who is living on Social Security. I am also paying off the bills from the marriage and divorce. I cut the nonessentials like replacing tires on my car, 'cause there isn't enough money.

Finally, Bill reported, "The lack of money was my greatest stressor because I felt like I should be the person to start all over. I tried to put the welfare of my kids first."

The respondents' financial strain was exacerbated because they believed that former spouses should receive all common marital assets. Approximately 83% of the men in this study relinquished to former wives houses, furnishings, and cars because the wives were appointed custody of the children. For example, Carl, aged 44, a psychiatric social worker, recalled his experience of leaving marital assets to his former spouse:

I walked out of the house and gave my ex-wife everything. I viewed it as giving to my son. I believe my needs should come last and the needs of my children should come first. So, I told the judge I did not want any marital assets.

James, a 32-year-old factory worker, echoed similar comments:

I had been married for 7 years and left with two suitcases. I did not go over, "this is mine and this yours." I left things for the children, like the car, television sets, and the stereo.

Fred, a 36-year-old fireman, lived in his car and the fire station until he was financially able to afford an apartment. He explained an obligation to make sacrifices for his children:

I suffered so my children could live in the house 'cause I did not want my children to grow up on welfare. I felt the responsibility to bear the brunt financially and to start all over again 'cause my former spouse had custody of my son and daughter. I told my ex-wife to take it all 'cause I looked at it as giving to my children. I told my former spouse to take the car, take it all—I walked 4 miles to work each morning 'cause I gave her the car for the children.

Fred also noted:

My children did not ask to come here, so when I was homeless, I blocked it out of my mind and told myself this was for my kids. The sacrifice I made for my kids helped me to deal with financial difficulties. I felt like I could cope with anything 'cause I knew where my children were and that their lives were not too disrupted by the divorce. They are living in the same neighborhood with the same friends.

The men reported that the prevention of former wives from seeking public assistance was a major factor for relinquishing all common marital property. "I don't want my children to grow up on welfare 'cause I've seen children tore up by a system that mistreats and labels them. I want them to have what they need" was a representative comment. Indeed, child-support payments have been found to be a major determinant in whether a woman applies for public assistance (Weitzman, 1985). Approximately 38% of women who do not receive child support apply for public assistance income, compared to only 13% of women who receive child support (Freed & Walker, 1988).

Child-Support Stressors

The respondents identified periodic court attendance to approve child support increases as a profound stressor. They questioned the circumstances required to warrant child support increases and reported that increased child support created extreme economic hardships. For example, Ben, a 39-year-old state employee, described the frustration and humiliation he experienced with the reevaluation of child-support payments:

I went back and forth to court, that is losing time from work and paid child-support the best I could. Even when I did not have enough money for myself, I paid child support. Then, after working two jobs to buy a car, I was back in court again. The judge took the money that I budgeted for the car payment; I only had $150.00 a month for myself.

Chris, a 40-year-old bus driver who had been divorced for 5 years, also recounted the frustration he experienced with the court system:

For 2 years I went back and forth to court for reevaluation of child support. Even though I gave my ex-wife everything, gave my kids money for school activities, and lunch money, the judge still increased my child-support payments. I'm very upset at the way the court system works 'cause it leaves the man with nothing.

Although Chris and other respondents reported they regularly paid child support, they complained that periodic increases of support payments created severe financial hardships that exacerbated emotional turmoil after divorce.

Child support payments were stressful because the men believed that racial biases exist in the amount of child-support payments. They emphasized that judges were more likely to enforce compliance of child support by attaching wages and withholding tax refunds of Black compared to White men. Bill, a 44-year-old engineer, claimed that judges were excessively lenient and were more apt to excuse money owed for past child support by White men than by Black men.

I talked with several of my White male friends who pay a fraction of what I'm paying. These men earn the same amount of money as I do and have the same number of children. I feel that judges punish Blacks to send the message that nonsupport of Black children will not be tolerated.

Tony, a 33-year-old apartment manager, reiterated:

Many Black men are jobless or work in minimum wage jobs. Judges base their child-support payments on their potential earnings, rather than their current financial situation. For White men, judges usually consider their current economic status and excuse past neglect of child support payments.

According to Carl, judges provided numerous opportunities for his White friends to make payments before imprisonment, whereas his Black friends were imprisoned immediately for failure to pay child support.

Although divorced men rarely pay more than one-third of their net income for child support, the men in this study believed that judges require Black men to pay more of their income in child support. In fact, the percentage of a husband's income awarded in child support varies based on the husband's income level, with lower-income men typically being required to pay a greater proportion of their incomes in child support (Weitzman, 1985). Because the respondents had friends and family members who were overrepresented in the lower income levels, they perceived that Black men paid higher child support.

Noncustodial Parenting Stressors

Without exception, fathers reported extreme psy-

435 chological distress because courts automatically assume that women should be awarded custody of children. A case in point was Joe, a 47-year-old high
school teacher, who described his reaction when the
judge awarded maternal custody. He complained:

440 I wanted joint custody, and the judge said because I had
been separated from my spouse for 1 year, my daughter
should live with my ex-wife. I was sick to my stomach
for months, I couldn't sleep or eat for weeks 'cause I am a
better parent than my former wife.

445 Danny, aged 43, a construction worker, also voiced the
pain he felt when his ex-wife was awarded custody of
their sons:

The court believed I was an unfit father since I had been
unemployed for 1 year. My ex-wife was granted sole
450 custody of my sons.... I hurt so badly that I cried deep
racking tears when the decision was made. I'm a responsible parent and I can provide as much love and caring to
my sons as my ex-wife. In fact, I'm a better parent than
my ex-wife.

455 Lawrence, a 46-year-old city employee, remarked:

My ex-wife don't want me to have any interaction with
my daughter and son except during the summer when I
pay $1,000 airfare for their visit. I don't mind paying
child support, but I miss how they are growing up on a
460 daily basis.

In response to the question, "What would you say to
your ex-wife if she were present?" without exception,
fathers reported that they would request sole custody of
their children.

465   One reason that maternal sole custody was stressful
for the respondents related to their lack of daily contact
with children. The men reported extreme difficulty in
adjusting to the reduced involvement in their children's
lives. For example, Greg, a 34-year-old state employee,
470 was exuberant at the birth of his daughter. He pointed
out the stress of noncustodial parenting:

I was involved as much as possible with my daughter
from birth. 'Cause I had experienced little warmth from
my father, I wanted to be the opposite of him. I attended
475 prenatal appointments and childbirthing classes with my
ex-wife. I bonded with my daughter prenatally and was in
the delivery room when she was born. When I cut the
umbilical cord, I experienced the greatest moment of my
life.

480   Greg's daughter was 2 years old when he divorced.
He emphasized the following: "I regret not being part
of my daughter's life on a daily basis. Anything that
reminds me of her makes me cry, even a child on TV
commercials." Tim, aged 40, a journalist, also men-
485 tioned, "The greatest stressor is not being there when
my daughter returns from dates. Since I want her to
marry a man like me, I want to meet her dates and be
there when she returns." During the interview, Tim
struggled through tears to express the grief he felt at
490 leaving his daughter and thought about buying a home
"where my daughter would live when she reaches aged

18." He even coached his daughter's basketball team to
spend time with her and expressed considerable pain at
seeing his daughter only intermittently.

495   For the respondents, their absence from the home
was particularly stressful given the high rate of gangs,
homicides, adolescent pregnancies, and illicit drug use
among Black youth. For example, they became anxious
at indications their children were succumbing to a
500 negative teen subculture. Although the respondents
reported that they saw their children in accordance with
the divorce decree, they underscored that these visits
reminded them that they were losing influence over
their children.

505   The respondents also reported numerous difficulties
at maintaining contact with teenage children. Gene,
aged 43, an accountant, expressed the intense frustration of failed attempts to contact his daughter. "When I
call my 16-year-old daughter she's too busy to talk.
510 She's busy with friends, at a dance class, or at the
mall." He also indicated that he felt abandoned when
his daughter failed to acknowledge a birthday or a
holiday. Gene tearfully stated: "My daughter didn't call
to wish me happy birthday, nor did she wish me happy
515 Father's Day. It's like she hates me. I keep telling my
ex-wife to tell my daughter to call me."

Men who were in interracial marriages reported
particular stress of noncustodial parenting. Michael, a
39-year-old electrician, who was married for 7 years
520 and divorced for 4 years, agonized over being unavailable to his son who lived in another state. He explained: "My son is biracial and is struggling with
identity issues, and I am the only one who can help him
with this. He doesn't even know who he is, and he is
525 very angry." Steve, a 40-year-old postal worker, also
voiced profound frustration at being separated from his
biracial daughter. He stated: "My daughter is 16 years
old, and when I see her during the summer months, I
see how confused she is.... I feel so guilty 'cause I
530 can't help her sort out who she is. I have no control
over her life, and that hurts." Steve was convinced that
his daughter should live with him because his ex-wife
was engaged to a man who had concerns about raising
a biracial teenager.

535   Stepfathers also reported frustration over the lack of
daily contact with stepchildren. Don, a 38-year-old
horse trainer, explained, "I raised my 16-year-old stepdaughter from the age of 2. She was like my own
daughter, and I miss her deeply. She was so devastated
540 by the divorce that she failed all her courses in school."
According to stepfathers, their stepchildren wanted to
live with them. As a result, most stepfathers were dissatisfied with the custody arrangement of their stepchildren. In fact, Jessie, a 43-year-old high school
545 coach, waged a court battle with his ex-wife for joint
custody of his stepdaughter. He reported, "My stepdaughter has always been with me. Her father died, so I
feel like I have as much right to her as her mother."

Approximately 85% of fathers coped with noncus-

143

todial parenting by increasing their involvement with their children. Paul, a 35-year-old contractor, moved three blocks from his ex-wife and her husband to be near his son. He asserted that biweekly he participates in activities with his son, including attending church and seeing movies. Fred reported that weekly he takes his children to visit family members and to eat pizza. He declared, "I do things with my children so that they will remember when they are older." Finally, Ben revealed his philosophy of maintaining contact with his children: "My children spend every weekend with me. I take them to doctor's appointments, to get haircuts, to swimming lessons, and wash their laundry. I make sure I spend time with my sons, because I divorced my wife, not my children."

For the majority of men in this study, spending time with children was a priority for the following reasons. First, they were committed to raising their children. Comments such as, "There is absolutely nothing I would not do for my children. I want them to have a better life than I had," were made frequently. Second, they often received encouragement from family members to sustain contact with children. For example, Lennie and other men remarked, "My mother and sister insist that they see my children every week." Third, children often increased the respondents' self-esteem. As Greg proclaimed, "When my daughter tells me I am a great father and when she smiles upon seeing me, I feel 10 feet tall in a society where I am often treated as a second-class citizen."

Psychosocial Stressors

Studies have reported that divorce prompts self-destructive behavioral patterns (Bloom, Asher, & White, 1983; Kitson & Holmes, 1992; Reissman, 1990). Lennie is a representative case. He had been married for 7 years and divorced for 4 years, and had a 7-year-old son and 3-year-old daughter. The following comments revealed his response to the divorce:

I loved my ex-wife and still loved what she once was. I was hurt every minute during the first year of the divorce and wanted it to be a nightmare 'cause I love the married life. I went wild to dull the pain, smoking pot, drinking, and engaging in self-destructive behavior.

Jim's comments also illustrate the initial impact of the divorce. He had been divorced for 2 years and was married for 10 years. He explained:

At the time I married, I was really in love. My ex-wife seemed like the perfect woman to marry. When I signed the divorce papers, I started to drink and hung out at bars. I did not care about myself. I got into the wild life. I smoked marijuana. I punished myself and felt like I was getting ready to shut down—a nervous breakdown.

Consistent with previous research, the men initially used alcohol and drugs to cope with the impact of divorce. They indicated that alcohol and illicit drugs created a sense of well-being enabling them to avoid the negative feelings of divorce. Studies have shown that men typically repudiate feelings of loss by engaging in self-destructive behavior that conforms to the traditional images of masculinity (Reissman, 1990; Rubin, 1983; Wymard, 1994). Paradoxically, while substance abuse relieved the respondents' emotional pain, it simultaneously resulted in adverse consequences, including illnesses and family conflicts.

The respondents also reported such psychological symptoms as loss of appetite, anxiety, insomnia, and impulsive behavioral patterns immediately following divorce. James verbalized tearfully numerous experiences of erratic behavior: "After the divorce, I would catch myself driving past my old home three times daily and stared at the house." He described his reaction to the divorce:

It was a sickening feeling and my nerves fell apart. I developed stomach ulcers, lost weight, and felt really depressed. It was such a depression. I felt lower than the ground I walk on. I had difficulty facing the morning. I sat in my apartment for months and felt sorry for myself and cried. I had to cry to release the pressure 'cause I believe that behind every successful man, there is a woman pushing and supporting him. I have been through some upsetting times.

James could not understand what happened to his marriage. He revealed, "I was a good provider. I was a pretty good guy, never cheated on my wife, and I always paid the bills. I gave my heart and did what I had to do." Other men also reported physiological reactions following the divorce, including stomach problems, migraine headaches, dental problems, eyesight and hearing difficulties, and hypertension resulting in a hospitalization or a visit to the emergency room.

In part, the respondents' psychological and physiological reaction to the divorce was associated with their belief in the permanence of marriage. Fred, a 48-year-old restaurant manager who spent 3 years separated from his wife before the divorce, characterized his situation in this manner: "I may not have lived with my former spouse for 20 years, but I would not have divorced her. I believe that when I make a commitment, I like to keep it until I die." Similarly, Bill, aged 51, remained in a conflictual marriage until his wife finally filed for a divorce. He noted, "Even though I found my former spouse with another man and was miserable in my marriage, I would have never divorced her 'cause I believe that marriage is a life-long commitment." For Bill and others, divorce was traumatic because it subverted their absolute commitment to marriage. Thus marital termination was morally inexcusable. This obligation to marital vows, in turn, led to increased postdivorce distress. In fact, only two men in the study initiated the divorce.

The respondent's emotional distress was intensified by a belief that their marriages eventually would be salvaged. For example, John, a 46-year-old auto mechanic, consulted a marriage therapist to help him confront the termination of his marriage:

665 I didn't believe my marriage was really over 'cause I thought we could regenerate the marriage. So, it was painful when the therapist told me that I needed to realize that the marriage was over and to let go and move on.

Gary, a 48-year-old photographer, echoed similar feelings:

670 I eventually thought that my ex-wife and I would get back together sooner or later, even if we were 70 years old. Even though we probably would not have lived together, I never would have divorced her 'cause there was always a chance of getting back together.

675 John, Gary, Carl, and other men admitted that they fantasized about returning to former spouses months after the divorce had been finalized, and they recalled a number of friends who remained separated for years, established other intimate relationships, but refused to 680 divorce.

In part, the men's reluctance to admit that their marriages had ended was a response to cultural stereotyping. They perceived that a stable marriage counteracted the cultural stereotypes that Black men often ab-685 dicate family responsibilities. A case in point was Travis, a 36-year-old business executive who progressed from a ghetto of Harlem to earning $50,000 annually by cultivating a proper image. He trained himself to speak distinctively and to dress for success. 690 Travis perceived that a stable marriage elevated his social identity and contradicted negative images of Black men. He explained, "A stable marriage is a plus for Black men 'cause few people expect it. Most of my business colleagues believe that Black men don't care 695 about their families. To counteract this image, I denied that my marriage was over." Similarly, Jack, a 40-year-old hospital personnel supervisor, agreed, "It was hard for me to accept that my marriage had ended 'cause I did not want to be viewed as a Black male with little 700 commitment to my family—the image most Whites adopt about Black men." Richard, Dwayne, and Harold, who were in the military during their divorces, reported, "I did not want to admit the marriage failed and separated off and on for 1 year because so many 705 people in the military think Black men don't care about their families." Ironically, although the denial of marital termination counteracted the negative images of Black men and elevated the respondents' perceived social identities, it also led to increased emotional tur-710 moil because their marriages were subsequently terminated.

Approximately 16% of the respondents acknowledged that divorce was beneficial because they had been in an emotionally draining marriage. Tom, a 49-715 year-old computer programmer, disclosed:

Since I had been unhappy for a while, I told my wife that I was leaving. So, I left out of there. I had already worked out in my mind that I would not hurt anymore. I cried and moved on.

720 Roy, a 45-year-old city planner, reiterated, "When I signed the divorce papers I felt relieved, like the weight of the world was lifted off me."

A sense of failure also characterized the postdivorce experience of men who reported that a divorce 725 was beneficial. "Although the divorce was for the best, on some level I felt like a failure 'cause I am not the type of person who wants to give up on anything," is representative of a frequent comment.

Although some respondents expressed relief at the 730 termination of their marriages, they were unprepared for the psychological and physiological symptoms postdivorce. Charles was a representative case. He was a 34-year-old educator who aspired to a middle-class income, an attractive home, two children, and two cars. 735 He achieved all his goals, except one. When his former wife, Jean, refused to become pregnant the second time and had her tubes tied, Charles was devastated. He marked this incident as the beginning of the end of their marriage. His trust in Jean eroded for not involv-740 ing him in the decision. Following frequent arguments, Charles moved out of the house. Six months later he suffered a heart attack and had bypass surgery. The following comments describe his feelings: "The divorce was a mutual decision. Even though I initiated 745 the divorce, I was unprepared for my anger and how my body reacted. I had dental problems, migraine headaches, and was diagnosed with high blood pressure." Charles mourned the loss of the marriage and summarized his view of divorce: "A lot of people say 750 divorce is painless, especially for Blacks. There are no painless divorces—divorce is a hurting thing." Other men also reported a lack of preparation for the psychological and physiological symptoms and for a pervasive sense of failure, even though they believe that 755 the divorce was beneficial.

Strategies to Cope with Divorce

Family and Friend Support

In contrast with previous research with White male samples (i.e., Albrecht, 1980; White & Bloom, 1981), men in this study requested and relied on support from friends and family members to cope with the psycho-760 logical stress of divorce. Without exception, the respondents reported that friends and family members were sources of emotional support postdivorce. Specifically, the respondents reported that their mothers provided emotional and tangible support. Harold re-765 called, "My mother helped me by providing emotional support, and she took care of the kids until I returned from work." John emphasized the financial support he received from his mother: "My mother got me a lawyer, the best lawyer in town, and paid for the divorce." 770 Fred underscored the moral support he received from his mother: "My mother gave me so much emotional support that helped me to cope with the divorce. She understood that I was losing a wife and that it would be painful. That helped a lot." Participant observation 775 revealed that the respondents' sisters volunteered to take children to parks, to sport activities, and to church.

The respondents also formed their own support groups of friends for emotional support. Carl revealed, "I hand-picked my support group from friends who had been in a similar situation. These friends were open-minded and saw both sides of the situation." Dwayne described a common bond that existed between his divorced friends who met weekly to discuss their common experiences. Bill explained, "My friends saw me sitting alone in the dark and encouraged me to get out." Tony noted, "My best friend came and helped me move to another state." Chris stated, "I talked to my friends about the situation and that helped me to cope." Other men mentioned the tangible support of friends such as providing housing, supplying financial support, and assisting with weekend child care. Previous research has shown that friends provide distinctive types of social support (Gerstel, 1988).

Church-Related Activities

Approximately 87% (*n* = 26) of the respondents reported that increased involvement in church activities and a religious community helps them to cope with divorce. James explained, "I pulled myself together and started going to church. The church community helped me to cope." Tim emphasized the assistance from a pastor of a church. He reported:

After the divorce I did not have reason to live, because my wife and daughter were the best things that ever happened in my life. I started to walk in front of cars to kill myself. Then, I went inside a church and talked to the pastor. He encouraged me to seek professional counseling. I checked in an in-patient psychiatric program, and the pastor visited regularly and provided emotional support.

Michael explained, "I wanted to kill my ex-wife, and the church pastor showed me if you have God in your life you can conquer anything." Other men reported that church pastors, members, and activities, as well as prayer, provided emotional support postdivorce.

Increased Social Participation

Consistent with previous studies, 80% (*n* = 24) of the men in this study also coped with the divorce by increasing their time commitment to work and engaging in self-improvement activities. For example, Bill, Harold, and Travis worked overtime; Gene and Wayne worked a part-time job; Chris, Tony, and Danny worked evening full-time jobs. Carl enrolled in a weight-lifting course, Gene and Joe learned to play golf, James coached a basketball team, and Michael biked cross-country.

The respondents increased their involvement in social activities, including Black fraternity events and political functions. Participant observation revealed that Lawrence, Charles, and Chris joined community committees that opposed school busing. Fred, Travis, and Harold formed a group that resisted the closing of parks in Black neighborhoods. The respondents reported other activities that moderate postdivorce distress, including attending movies, visiting museums, collecting Black art, and enrolling in college courses.

Heterosexual Relationships

One of the most difficult tasks for divorced persons is forming new heterosexual relationships (Hetherington et al., 1976; Wymard, 1994; Zeiss et al., 1980). Hetherington et al. (1976) reported that 1-year postdivorce males showed a steady increase in dating and social encounters at bars. In our study, a majority of the respondents did not engage in "frenzy dating activity." Instead, approximately 73% (*n* = 22) of respondents became involved in a close relationship 1 year postdivorce, which often resulted in cohabitation. Although the men recognized that cohabitation was a major commitment, it seemed to happen casually. Jim recalled, "It took about 1 year for me to even want to talk to another woman again. I went back to church and met this wonderful lady who loved me as me, and we started living together." Ben stated:

It took about a year to want to meet women, 'cause I had trouble trusting women. I don't believe in meeting women in bars. A friend introduced me to this woman with three children and we moved in together. So, I went from living alone to adjusting to living with three small children.

Chris revealed, "After about a year, I was ready to become involved with a woman. We had a serious relationship for 5 years 'cause I hate the shallowness of the single scene." In fact, not one respondent expressed positive views about living a single life, but only one man was engaged to be married.

The desire for a stable family life appeared to underlie the reason the men yearned for an intense emotional investment. "I enjoy the family life, that is, having one special person in my life rather than dating a number of women," represents a recurrent comment. Some men also became involved with women who had children, because it provided them with a sense of belonging and served as a substitute for missing their own children. Gene explained, "I live with my girlfriend and her daughter, since I can't raise my own daughter, I can protect and provide security for my girlfriend's daughter." Danny mentioned, "I always wanted to raise a daughter, so my girlfriend and her 2-year-old daughter live with me."

There was no single and uncomplicated explanation that the men expressed for not engaging in a frenzy of dating activity. The need to belong, to be loved, and to raise children were the primary reasons for desiring an intimate relationship.

Discussion and Conclusions

This study identifies factors Black men perceived as significant stressors following divorce and explores strategies they used to adjust to marital termination. The results show that the following are significant

146

885 stressors for men in this study: (a) financial strain, (b) child-support stressors, (c) noncustodial parenting, and (d) psychological and physiological symptoms associated with the impact of the divorce. Exacerbating these stressors was the respondents' belief of racial biases in 890 the determination of court-ordered child-support payments, the perception of losing control of children, the belief in the permanence of marriage, and a reluctance to admit to marital termination. The present study suggests that divorced Black men experience profound 895 psychological stress associated with divorce. Although this has been an accepted conclusion in White samples, it has been largely ignored in studies that identify Black men at risk for psychological and behavioral disorders.

900 The sources of parental role stress identified by fathers of minor stepchildren and biracial children suggest that these children might experience increased difficulty in adjusting to divorce. It is quite likely that behavioral difficulties identified by stepfathers and 905 fathers of biracial children might affect these children in later life. Future research should assess the frequency of divorce-related distress experienced by stepchildren and biracial children. Additionally, according to Umberson (1992), the parental role and its effect on 910 fathers have been neglected areas of research. The findings from this research suggest that this is an important topic for future research on divorced Black men.

The findings suggest that Black men used the following strategies to cope with divorce: (a) reliance on 915 family and friends, (b) involvement in church-related activities, (c) increased social participation, and (d) establishment of intimate heterosexual relationships 1 year postdivorce. The findings are consistent with research that suggests marital termination and divorce 920 should be scrutinized within relevant social-cultural contexts. Future research should consider the mediating role of the Black family, specifically Black mothers and sisters; church activities; and male peer groups as moderators of psychological distress for Black di-925 vorced men. The results suggest a need to sharpen conceptual schemes guiding research on adjustment following divorce. One important component of this conceptual sharpening will be to incorporate a systematic understanding of the way in which social-cultural fac-930 tors, including belief systems, and racial stereotyping affect postdivorce adjustment. Future work also can expand knowledge of postdivorce adjustment and coping strategies of Black men by describing how changes such as remarriage, attachment to former 935 spouses, and relations with former in-laws affect postdivorce adjustment.

The limitations of this study should be noted. First, qualitative methods and cross-sectional data identified 940 perceived stressors and coping strategies of divorced Black men. It would be useful to modify existing quantitative postdivorce adjustment scales to measure such stressors as financial strain, child support issues, and racial biases within the court system. Longitudinal 945 data and random samples are needed to address the issue of causal order, coping responses, and long-term health outcomes in Black divorced male populations. Second, the sample size of this study was small and findings can be generalized only to Black working-950 class/middle-class divorced men. However, the sample is large enough to understand factors that may create significant stress and the coping strategies that Black men use to manage such stressors.

References

Albrecht, S. L. (1980). Reactions and adjustments to divorce: Differences in the experiences of males and females. *Family Relations, 29,* 59–68.

Albrecht, S. L., Bahr, H., & Goodman, K. (1983). *Divorce and remarriage: Problems, adaptations and adjustments.* Westport, CT: Greenwood.

Billingsley, A. (1992). *Climbing Jacob's ladder: The enduring legacy of African-American families.* New York: Simon & Schuster.

Bloom, B., Asher, S. J., & White, S. W. (1978). Marital disruption as a stressor: A review and analysis. *Psychological Bulletin, 85,* 867–894.

Bloom, B. L., & Kindle, K. R. (1985). Demographic factors in the continuing relationship between former spouses. *Family Relations, 34,* 375–381.

Bogden, R. (1972). *Participant observation in organizational settings.* Syracuse, NY: Syracuse University Press.

Brown, P., Perry, L., & Harberg, E. (1977). Sex role attitudes and psychological outcomes for Black and White women experiencing marital dissolution. *Journal of Marriage and the Family, 39,* 549–561.

Cherlin, A. J. (1992). *Marriage, divorce, remarriage* (Rev. ed.). Cambridge, MA: Harvard University Press.

Chiriboga, D. A., & Culter, L. (1977). Stress responses among divorcing men and women. *Journal of Divorce, 1,* 95–105.

Clark, S. C., Whitney, R. A., & Beck, J. C. (1988). Discrepancies between custodial awards and custodial practices: De jure and de facto custody. *Journal of Divorce, 11,* 219–228.

Clingempeel, G. W., & Reppucci, D. N. (1982). Joint custody after divorce: Major issues and goals for research. *Psychological Bulletin, 91,* 102–127.

Cooney, T. M., & Uhlenberg, P. (1990). The role of divorce in men's relations with their adult children after mid-life. *Journal of Marriage and the Family, 52,* 677–688.

Denzen, N. K. (1970). *The research act: A theoretical introduction to sociological methods.* Chicago: Adline.

Farley, R., & Allen, W. R. (1987). *The color line and the quality of life in America.* New York: Russell Sage.

Freed, D. J., & Walker, T. B. (1988). Family law in fifty states: An overview. *Family Law Quarterly, 21,* 417–573.

Furstenberg, F., Jr., & Spanier, G. B. (1984). *Recycling the family: Remarriage after divorce.* Beverly Hills, CA: Sage.

Garfinkel, I., & Oellerich, D. (1989). Noncustodial fathers' ability to pay child support. *Demography, 26,* 219–233.

Gary, L. (1981). *Black Men.* Beverly Hills, CA: Sage.

Gerstel, N. (1988). Divorce and kin ties: The importance of gender. *Journal of Marriage and the Family, 50,* 209–219.

Glaser, B. G. (1978). *Theoretical sensitivity.* Mill Valley, CA: Sociology Press.

Gove, W. R., & Shin, H. (1989). The psychological well-being of divorced and widowed men and women: An empirical analysis. *Journal of Family Issues, 10,* 122–144.

Hetherington, M. E., Stanley-Hogan, M., & Anderson, E. R. (1976). Marital transitions: A child's perspective. *American Psychologist, 44,* 303–312.

Kitson, G. C., & Holmes, O. (1992). *Portrait of divorce: Adjustment to marital breakdown.* New York: Guilford.

Kitson, G. C., & Morgan, L. A. (1990). The multiple consequences of divorce: A decade of review. *Journal of Marriage and the Family, 52,* 913–924.

Kurdek, L. & Blisk, D. (1983). Dimensions and correlates of mothers' divorce experiences. *Journal of Divorce, 6,* 1–24.

Marshall, C., & Rossman, G. B. (1989). *Designing qualitative research.* Newbury Park: CA; Sage.

Menaghan, E. G., & Lieberman, M. A. (1986). Changes in depression following divorce: A panel study. *Journal of Marriage and the Family, 48,* 319–328.

Peterson, R. T. (1989). *Women, work, and divorce.* Albany: State University of New York Press.

Petti, E. J., & Bloom, B. L. (1984). Whose decision was it? The effects of initiator status on adjustment to marital disruption. *Journal of Marriage and the Family, 4,* 587–595.

Pinkney, A. (1993). *Black Americans* (4th ed.). Englewood Cliffs, NJ: Prentice Hall.

Raschke, H. J. (1977). The role of social participation in post-separation and post-divorce adjustment. *Journal of Divorce, 1*, 129–140.

Reissman, C. (1990). *Divorce talk: Women and men make sense of personal relationships*. New Brunswick, NJ: Rutgers University Press.

Reissman, C. K., & Gerstel, N. (1985). Marital dissolution and health: Do males or females have greater risk? *Social Science and Medicine, 20*, 627–635.

Rosengren, A., Wedel, H., & Wilhelmsen, L. (1989). Marital status and morality in middle-aged Swedish men. *American Journal of Epidemiology, 129*, 54–64.

Rubin, L. (1983). *Intimate strangers*. New York: Harper & Row.

Seltzer, J. A. (1991). Relationships between fathers and children who live apart: The father's role after separation. *Journal of Marriage and the Family, 53*, 79–101.

Spanier, G. B., & Casto, R. (1979). Adjustment to separation and divorce: An analysis of 50 case studies. *Journal of Divorce, 2*, 241–253.

Staples, R. (1985). *Black masculinity: The Black male's role in American society*. San Francisco: Black Scholar Press.

Strauss, A. L. (1986). *Qualitative analysis*. Cambridge: Cambridge University Press.

Thoits, P. A. (1986). Social support as coping assistance. *Journal of Consulting and Clinical Psychology, 54*, 416–423.

Tschann, J. M., Johnston, J. R., & Wallerstein, J. S. (1989). Resources, stresses, and attachment as predictors of adult adjustment after divorce: A longitudinal study. *Journal of Marriage and the Family, 51*, 1033–1046.

Umberson, D. (1987). Family status and health behaviors: Social control as a dimension of social integration. *Journal of Health and Social Behavior, 28*, 306–319.

Umberson, D. (1992). Gender, marital status, and the social control of health behavior. *Social Science and Medicine, 34*, 907–917.

U.S. Bureau of the Census (1987). *Child support and alimony: 1985* (Current Population Report, Series P-23, No. 152). Washington, DC: U.S. Government Printing Office.

Wallerstein, J. (1986). Women after divorce: Preliminary report from a ten-year follow-up. *American Journal of Orthopsychiatry, 56*, 65–77.

Wallerstein J., & Kelly, J. (1980). *Surviving the breakup: How children and parents cope with divorce*. New York Basic: Books.

Weiss, R. S. (1975). *Marital separation*. New York Basic Books.

Weitzman, L. (1985). *The divorce revolution*. New York: Free Press.

White, S. W., & Bloom, B. L. (1981). Factors related to the adjustment of divorcing men. *Family Relations, 30*, 349–360.

Wilkinson, D. (1977). The stigmatization process: The politicization of Black male's identity. In D. Wilkinson & R. Taylor (Eds.), *The Black male in America* (pp. 145–158). Chicago: Nelson-Hall.

Wright, D. W., & Price, S. J. (1986). Court ordered child support payment: The effect of the former spouse relationship on compliance. *Journal of Marriage and the Family, 48*, 869–874.

Wymard, E. (1994). *Men on divorce*. Carson, CA: Hay House.

Zeiss, A. M., Zeiss, R. H., & Johnson S. M. (1980). Sex differences in initiation and adjustment to divorce. *Journal of Divorce, 4*, 21–33.

Acknowledgments: We thank Kerry Robertson for editorial assistance. This research was partially funded by a faculty development grant from the University of Missouri Alumni Association and a grant from the College of Human Environmental Sciences, The Margaret Mangel Catalyst Fund, University of Missouri, Columbia.

Exercise for Article 22

Factual Questions

1. According to the research literature cited in the introduction, are women *or* men more likely to initiate divorce?

2. What was the purpose of including in the sample only men who are in the labor force?

3. Were the majority of the men interviewed in their homes or at their places of employment?

4. How is "participant observer methodology" defined?

5. How many of the men identified "reliance on family and friends" as a divorce-related strategy?

6. Did a majority of the respondents engage in "frenzy dating activity?"

7. The researchers explicitly state two "limitations" of their research. What is the second one?

Questions for Discussion

8. In the literature review, there are numerous references to research on Whites. In your opinion, is this appropriate? Why? Why not?

9. Consider the recruitment method as described in lines 177–200. If you were conducting another study on the same topic, would you use the same method? Why? Why not?

10. This article is classified as an example of *qualitative* research in the Table of Contents of this book. Do you agree with the classification? If yes, what features of this study make it qualitative?

11. The Results section of this article (lines 270–880) is much longer than the typical results section of other articles in this book. Is such a long results section justifiable for this particular study? Why? Why not?

12. How important are the direct quotations in helping you understand the results of this study?

Quality Ratings

Directions: Indicate your level of agreement with each of the following statements by circling a number from 5 for strongly agree (SA) to 1 for strongly disagree (SD). If you believe an item is not applicable to this research article, leave it blank. Be prepared to explain your ratings.

A. The introduction establishes the importance of the study.

SA   5   4   3   2   1   SD

B. The literature review establishes the context for the study.

SA   5   4   3   2   1   SD

C. The research purpose, question, or hypothesis is clearly stated.

SA   5   4   3   2   1   SD

D. The method of sampling is sound.

SA   5   4   3   2   1   SD

E. Relevant demographics (for example, age, gender, and ethnicity) are described.

SA   5   4   3   2   1   SD

F. Measurement procedures are adequate.

SA   5   4   3   2   1   SD

G. All procedures have been described in sufficient detail to permit a replication of the study.

SA   5   4   3   2   1   SD

H. The participants have been adequately protected from potential harm.

SA   5   4   3   2   1   SD

I. The results are clearly described.

SA   5   4   3   2   1   SD

J. The discussion/conclusion is appropriate.

SA   5   4   3   2   1   SD

K. Despite any flaws, the report is worthy of publication.

SA   5   4   3   2   1   SD

Article 23

Couples Watching Television:
Gender, Power, and the Remote Control

ALEXIS J. WALKER
Oregon State University

ABSTRACT. I sought to confirm that partners in close relationships "do gender" (West & Zimmerman, 1987) and exercise power (Komter, 1989) even in their ordinary everyday behavior and specifically in their selection of television programming via a remote control device (RCD). Individuals in 36 couples (86% heterosexual, 14% gay or lesbian) were interviewed. Men in heterosexual couples use and control the RCD more than women, and their partners find RCD use more frustrating than they do. Heterosexual women also are less able than men to get their partners to watch a desired show. The results confirm that couples create and strengthen stereotypical notions of gender through the exercise of power, even in the mundane, joint, leisure activity of watching television.

From *Journal of Marriage and the Family, 58,* 813–823. Copyright © 1996 by the National Council on Family Relations, 3989 Central Ave. NE, Suite 550, Minneapolis, MN 55421.

Five years ago, my parents bought a second television set because my mother refused to watch television with my father any longer. "I can't stand the way he flips through the channels," she said. Note that my fa-
5   ther actually has the use of the new television, and my mother has been relegated to the den with the older model. Nevertheless, mother now has her own set, and conflicts about the remote control device have been reduced considerably.
10   Several years ago, journalist Ellen Goodman (1993, p. 181) published an essay in which she described the RCD as "the most reactionary implement currently used to undermine equality in modern marriage." Because family scholars rarely study such mundane, eve-
15   ryday life experience, there is little research available to confirm Goodman's sentiments or to assess the prevalence of solutions to television-watching disagreements such as that employed by my parents. RCD use, however, presents a challenging arena in which to
20   examine gender and relationship issues in the experience of daily living.
Over the past 20 years, feminist scholars have shown that ordinary, routine, run-of-the-mill activities that take place inside homes every day bear an uncanny
25   resemblance to the social structure. For example, the distribution of household labor and of child care is gendered in the same way that paid work is gendered: The more boring and less desirable tasks are disproportionately performed by women, and status has a
30   way of reducing men's, but not women's, participation in these tasks. (See Thompson & Walker, 1989, for a review.) Examining television-watching behavior is a way to extend the feminist analysis to couples' leisure.
Despite the fact that television watching is the
35   dominant recreational activity in the United States today (Robinson, 1990), there is little research on this topic in the family studies literature. Indeed, there is little family research on leisure at all (but see Crawford, Geoffrey, & Crouter, 1986; Hill, 1988; Holman &
40   Jacquart, 1988), although scholars often mention that employed wives and mothers have very little of it (e.g., Coverman & Sheley, 1986; Hochschild, 1989; Mederer, 1993). Recently, Firestone and Shelton (1994), using data from the 1981 *Study of Time Use,* confirmed
45   that married women have less overall leisure time than married men. They also demonstrated gender-divergent patterns in the connection between paid work and both domestic (in-home) and out-of-home leisure time. Women who are employed have less out-of-home lei-
50   sure time than men do, but men who are employed have less domestic leisure time than employed women. Specifically, they found that employment hours do not affect the amount of leisure time that married women have at home. To explain this surprising finding,
55   Firestone and Shelton speculated that leisure at home appears to be the same for employed and nonemployed wives because leisure is compatible with household chores and with child care. In other words, women combine family work with leisure activities. For exam-
60   ple, they iron while watching television.
Although there is little research on leisure in family studies, there is considerable literature on gender and leisure in the field of leisure studies. For example, Henderson (1990), predating Firestone and Shelton
65   (1994), described women's leisure as fragmented because much of it takes place at home where it is mingled with domestic labor. In comparison with men, women say that leisure is less of a priority and that they do not deserve it. Some activities that are defined as
70   leisure pursuits, such as family picnics, are actually

150

occasions for women's work, making leisure a possible source of internal conflict for women (Shank, 1986; Shaw, 1985). In fact, Henderson (1994) called for a deconstruction of leisure because the term embodies contradictions for women, contradictions that may be evident particularly in family leisure (Shaw, 1991).

To develop a way to measure couples' television-watching behavior, I sought guidance from the empirical research on television watching, which also is considerable. Here, studies describe various types of RCD use, sometimes referred to as (a) grazing (sometimes called surfing)—progressing through three or more channels with no more than 5 seconds on any one channel for the purpose of seeing what is available; (b) zapping—switching channels to avoid something, usually a commercial; and (c) zipping—fast-forwarding during a prerecorded program, mostly to avoid commercials (Cornwell et al., 1993; Walker & Bellamy, 1991).

Observational, survey, in-depth interview, and ethnographic data from communications researchers using a wide variety of sampling strategies revealed that when heterosexual families with children watch television together, fathers dominate in program selection and in the use of the RCD. Sons are active as well, using the RCD more than either their mothers or their sisters. That gender differences are smaller among younger persons, however, suggests a potential for women and men to be more similar in their remote control behavior in the future, when the RCD-using youth of today are adults (Copeland & Schweitzer, 1993; Cornwell et al., 1993; Eastman & Newton, 1995; Heeter & Greenberg, 1985; Krendl, Troiano, Dawson, & Clark, 1993; Lindlof, Shatzer, & Wilkinson, 1988; Morley, 1988; Perse & Ferguson, 1993). Note that the dominance in RCD use by men and boys in a family context is not evident when individuals are observed alone. In an experimental study, women were no less likely to use the RCD than were men (Bryant & Rockwell, 1993). The authors concluded that a social context is necessary to produce such gendered behavior.

Morley (1988) described fathers as using the RCD for unnegotiated channel switching—that is, changing channels when they want to—without explaining their behavior to or consulting other television watchers. Unemployed fathers, by the way, are less likely than employed fathers to use the RCD in this way, suggesting a possible connection between RCD use and the use of legitimate power—that is, power derived from and supported by societal norms and values (e.g., Farrington & Chertok, 1993).

Why so much channel switching? Men say they change channels to avoid commercials, to see if something better is on, to see what they are missing, to watch news reports, because they like variety, to avoid looking up the printed listings, to annoy others, and, my favorite reason, to watch more than one show at the same time (Perse & Ferguson, 1993). By contrast, women say they change channels to watch a specific program. A frightening finding is that the children of heavy RCD users are also heavy users, suggesting that parents pass on this behavior and that we can anticipate more grazing in the future (Heeter & Greenberg, 1985).

Copeland and Schweitzer (1993) concluded: "Men have usually been viewed as the persons who control program selection, and domination of the remote control seems to make visually explicit what may have previously been implicit" (p. 165). This notion of power, clearly stated in the language of the communications researchers, is missing from the family research on leisure. In their studies, however, the communications researchers have focused almost exclusively on parents watching television with their children. Rarely have they studied couples watching television. Furthermore, students of communication rarely have combined data about television watching and RCD use with questions of primary interest to those of us who study close relationships among adults. For example, are there any ways in which watching television with your partner is frustrating? Would you change the way that you watch television with your partner if you could? How do you influence your partner to watch something that you want to watch?

These questions address issues of power in relationships described by Aafke Komter (1989). She demonstrated that power is evident not only in the direct, observable resolution of conflict between partners, but also in covert or nonobservable events that reflect structural inequality. Direct expression of power reflects manifest power; covert expression reflects latent power. Examples of latent power are the ability to prevent issues from being raised, the anticipation of the desires of the more powerful partner, and resignation to an undesirable situation due to the fear of a negative reaction from the more powerful partner or worry that change might harm the relationship in some way (see also Huston, 1983; McDonald, 1980). In addition to other domains (e.g., family labor and sexual interaction), Komter included leisure in her study, but she focused only on hobbies and interaction with friends.

I chose to wed the focus of communications researchers on television-watching behavior with Komter's (1989) approach to studying power. I expected that heterosexual couples would "do gender" (West & Zimmerman, 1987) even in such a mundane activity as joint television watching. I anticipated that the creation and affirmation of gender would be evident in the (manifest and latent) power men have over their women partners in the domain of leisure activity. Furthermore, I sought to confirm the importance of gender in partner interaction by examining joint television watching behavior in lesbian and gay couples as well (see Kollock, Blumstein, & Schwartz, 1985).

Method

Participants

The sample for this study was characterized by its diversity. Participants were recruited primarily by students enrolled in an upper-division undergraduate course on gender and family relationships. In recruiting respondent pairs, students worked in groups of four to maximize diversity. Couples were chosen so that each group of four students would select a diverse set of pairs. All respondents were in a romantic (i.e., heterosexual married, heterosexual cohabiting, or cohabiting gay or lesbian) relationship in which both individuals were at least 18 years old. All couples had been living together for at least 1 year and had a television set with an RCD. Within each group, however, participants included (a) couples varying in relationship length, from shorter (1 year) to longer (15 years or more); (b) a lesbian or gay couple; (c) at least one married couple; (d) at least one heterosexual, cohabiting, or unmarried couple; (e) couples with and without children; (f) at least one couple in which at least one partner was Asian American, African American, Latino, or of mixed race; and (g) couples in which both partners were employed and couples in which only one partner was employed. Fourteen percent ($n = 5$ pairs) of the 36 couples (72 individuals) were gay or lesbian. Here, and for much of this report, I focus attention on the 31 heterosexual pairs.

Women and men in these heterosexual couples did not differ significantly on sociodemographic characteristics. (Table 1 shows these characteristics for all couples.) The typical respondent was 34 years old ($SD = 12.69$) and had completed 2 years of academic work beyond high school. Most (77%, $n = 48$) were White, although nearly one quarter were either African American, Hispanic, or of mixed race. Nearly three quarters (74%, $n = 48$) were married; one quarter was cohabiting. On average, their relationships had been in existence for 10 years. Most (77%, $n = 48$) respondents were employed, and just over 30% ($n = 19$) were students; only 16% ($n = 10$) of the sample, however, were nonemployed, nonretired students. Heterosexual respondents represented three income groups. Just over one-third earned less than $20,000 annually, one-third reported an annual household income between $20,000 and $39,999, and just under one-third earned $40,000 or more. One-third had children living at home.

Measures

A semistructured interview was administered to each member of the couple. In addition to sociodemographic questions, respondents were asked about the number and location of television sets and videocassette recorders in the home, the frequency with which they and their partners watched television, and other activities they engage in while watching television. They were asked about use of the RCD, in general, while watching with their partner and during the program most recently watched with the partner. They were also asked if their most recent experience was typical of their joint television watching. These questions were quantitative in nature and are similar to the types of questions asked of participants by communications researchers. Additional single-item, quantitative questions were derived from the family studies literature; that is, questions about relationship happiness, happiness with the way things are regarding watching television with the partner, and how much partners enjoy the time they spend together.

Other questions focused on issues of power à la Komter (1989). These questions were open-ended and concerned changed expectations about watching television with the partner over the history of the relationship, how the couple decides on a program to watch together, how partners get each other to watch programs that they want to watch, and their frustrations with watching television with their partner. Respondents were asked if they would like to change anything about the way they watch television together, if they thought they would be successful at making these changes, whether it would be worth it for them to make the changes, and how their partner would react to the changes. In addition, any changes they had already made in their joint television-watching behavior were described.

Procedures

A coin toss was used to determine which partner to interview first. Partners were interviewed separately, usually in their own homes, by trained student interviewers. Interviews were audiotaped and transcribed. SAS was used to analyze the quantitative data, and transcriptions were read and reread for analysis of the open-ended data.

Results

On average, the heterosexual couples had 1.81 television sets ($SD = 0.99$), but some had only 1, and a few had as many as 5. They had 1.30 videocassette recorders ($SD = 0.53$), with a range from 1 to 3. They also had 1.30 RCDs ($SD = 0.68$), with a range from 1 to 3. The typical home had basic cable television (with no extra channels) or a satellite dish.

These individuals watched television quite often— on average almost daily for nearly 3 hours per day ($M = 2.77$, $SD = 1.48$). During the week prior to the interview, they had, on average, watched television together on 4.87 days ($SD = 2.09$). Nearly all, 94% ($n = 29$), of the women and 87% ($n = 27$) of the men reported that, regarding watching television with their partners, they were happy with the way things are. Yet two-thirds of the women and three-fifths of the men reported that there were things about their joint television watching that were frustrating to them. The interview transcripts were revealing about these frustrations. Women complained about their partners' grazing behavior, both during a show and when they first turned on the televi-

Table 1
Characteristics of Respondents in the Sample

Characteristic	Heterosexual Partners ($n = 62$)		Lesbian or Gay Partners ($n = 10$)	
	M or %	*SD* or *n*	*M* or %	*SD* or *n*
Age	34.1	12.69	36.4	7.52
Education level[a]	3.1	1.70	4.1	1.52
Race (% White)	77.4	48	100.0	10
Relationship status (%)				
Cohabiting	25.8	16	100.0	10
First marriage	58.1	36		
Previous marriage	16.1	10	10.0	1
Years in relationship	10.2	11.22	8.1	3.51
Children at home (%)	32.3	20	0.0	0
Employed (%)	77.4	48	90.0	9
Employment hours[b]	2.8	1.41	3.1	0.38
Income[c]	2.2	1.26	2.4	1.13

Note: Within heterosexual couples, there were no significant differences by gender for any of these variables.
[a]Education measured from 0 (*less than high school*) to 6 (*graduate degree*).
[b]Employment hours measured from 0 (*0 to 10 hours per week*) to 4 (*more than 40 hours per week*).
[c]Income measured from 1 (*less than $20,000*) to 5 (*more than $80,000*).

sion set. One woman in a 3-year cohabiting relationship said:

295   I would say that the only thing that's frustrating for me is when we first turn on the TV and he just flips through the channels. It drives me crazy because you can't tell what's on, because he just goes through and goes through and goes through.

300 Another woman, in the 17th year of a first marriage, reported, "[I get frustrated] only if I get hooked into one show and then he flips it to another one. As soon as I get hooked into something else, he flips it to something else." Such reports from women were common.

305 A married man spontaneously agreed: "We don't watch TV a lot together; I would rather do other activities with my wife. Channel switching wasn't a problem until...the remote control." Indeed, many men indicated that their women partners were bothered by this

310 behavior.

In contrast, men reported being frustrated with the quality of the programming or the circumstances of watching, rather than with RCD activity. For example, one husband said, "I wish we had a VCR.... I wish we

315 had one of those TVs where you could watch two things on the screen at once." Another said, "It's sort of frustrating when I want to watch something she doesn't, and she goes into the other room and gets sort of pouty about it." A third reported, "No, [nothing is

320 frustrating], but she does talk a little."

I looked specifically at the RCD; for example, where is the RCD usually located? Men were more likely than women to say that they usually hold the RCD or have it near them, $\chi^2(1, n = 62) = 7.38, p < .01$,

325 and they were less likely than women to say that their partner usually holds it or has it near them, $\chi^2(1, n = 62) = 14.47, p < .001$. In half the couples ($n = 16$), according to both women and men, men have the RCD. In over 80% ($n = 25$) of the couples, according to both

330 the women and the men, the women do not have control of it solely. According to 16% ($n = 5$) of the women and 10% ($n = 3$) of the men, women control the remote. In roughly one-third of the couples, the RCD is in a neutral location, or both take turns holding it. The

335 pattern was the same when respondents were asked about the RCD's location during the most recent television show that they watched together. The RCD was more likely to be located near men than near women or near both members of the couple, $\chi^2(2, n = 59) = 13.12$,

340 $p < .001$. The transcriptions support this general pattern of RCD location, as well. A husband reported, "I usually use the remote because I know how to use it, and it usually sits right in front of me while I am on the couch." A young married woman said, "I had the baby

345 [the RCD] this time. This was a rare occasion." Roger (all names are pseudonyms), a married man, reported:

I frequently have the remote at my side. I won't change the channel until we are ready to look for something else. If there is someone who wants to change the channel at a

350 commercial, it will be Sally [his wife]. I will hand the remote to her, and she will change it to another favorite show, and then back. And that is very typical.

Sally agreed. The last time they watched television together, the RCD was in "Roger's pocket! Either in his

355 shirt pocket or bathrobe pocket." A young, married man reported:

I don't hold [the RCD], but I pretty much have control of it, and if I don't care what's on, then I let her have it. Sometimes we fight over it. Not like fight, but, I mean,

360 it's like, "You always have the remote control."

Women were significantly more likely than men to say that RCD use was frustrating to them, $\chi^2(1, n = 62) = 8.42, p < .01$. Only 10% ($n = 3$) of the men, but 42% ($n = 13$) of the women evidenced such frustration.

365 Furthermore, women ($M = 0.61, SD = 0.79$) reported that significantly more RCD behaviors were frustrating

to them than men reported ($M = 0.15$, $SD = 0.37$) $t(48)$ $= -2.70$, $p < .01$. Yet 30% ($n = 9$) of the women in the sample and 16% ($n = 5$) of the frustrated men reported that they would like to change how the RCD is used during their joint television watching. This difference was not significant.

What was frustrating about RCD use? Respondents reported being frustrated by the amount of grazing, the speed of grazing, heavy use of the RCD, and the partner taking too long to go back to a channel after switching from it during a commercial. A few respondents actually indicated concern about their own frequent RCD use. Women and men, however, reported similar percentages of other television-watching behaviors that were frustrating (e.g., too much time watching television; bothersome behaviors of the partner, such as making fun of a program); 58% ($n = 18$) of the women and 48% ($n = 15$) of the men were frustrated by these other behaviors.

Thus far, I have shown that men control the RCD more than women and that women are more frustrated by RCD behaviors than men are. I also asked about the other activities engaged in while watching television. Two types of activities were mentioned: family work (e.g., child care, cooking, laundry) and pleasurable activities, such as doing nothing (i.e., relaxing), eating, drinking, playing computer games, and so on. When activities within each type were summed, the findings were revealing. When asked about their most recent joint television-watching episode, men ($M = 1.00$, $SD = 0.52$) responded that they were significantly more likely than women ($M = 0.74$, $SD = 0.44$) to engage in pleasurable behaviors while watching television, $t(62)$ $= 2.11$, $p < .04$. Women ($M = 0.36$, $SD = 0.71$) were not more likely than men ($M = 0.13$, $SD = 0.34$) to do family work while they watched television, although the data suggested a trend in this regard, $t(62) = -1.60$, $p < .12$. The small proportion of households with children (32%, $n = 10$) may have contributed to this finding. At least 80% of both women and men described this most recent experience as typical of their joint television watching and of their RCD use. Interestingly, women ($M = 2.84$, $SD = 0.74$) tended more than men ($M = 3.16$, $SD = 0.69$) to describe the particular show they watched as their partner's preference rather than their own, $t(60) = 1.78$, $p < .08$.

Recall that 30% of the women said they would change the use of the RCD during their joint television watching if they could. Only half as many men would make such a change. The open-ended data support these results. For example, a young married woman described her technique of standing in front of the television to interrupt the signal from the RCD. Another young married woman said that her partner used the RCD to watch more than one program at a time. "I should get him one of those TVs with all the little windows so he can watch them all," she said sarcastically. A middle-aged married woman said that she would like to change their television watching so that she would have "control of the remote for half of our viewing time." Of those who would like to make any changes in their television watching, one in five women expected that they would *not* be successful.

Men typically admitted their heavier RCD use. For example, a middle-aged married man said that he switched channels to avoid commercials. "I'm the guilty party," he said. "My [family members] would leave it there and watch the commercial. I just change it because I'd rather not be insulted by commercials."

One of the most provocative questions asked of respondents was "How do you get your partner to watch a show that you want to watch?" The results were enlightening. A cohabiting woman said, "I tell him that would be a good one to watch, and he says, 'No,' and keeps changing [channels]. I whine, and then usually I don't get [my way]." A middle-aged married woman said:

> Let me think here, when does that occur? [Laughing.] If I really want to watch, I'll say, "I want to watch this one."... I'll say, "Come in here and watch this" if he's not in the room, but pretty much we watch the same things a lot, whether or not that's because I let him. He, a lot of the time, turns it on, and I'll come in and join him. But, if it's something I really want to watch, I'll say, "Don't flip the channel; I want to see this."

In contrast, a young married man said that he gets his partner to watch a show he wants to watch in this way:

> I just sneak the remote away from her if she has it, or, if I'm there first, then.... I mean, if there's sports on, that's usually what we watch unless there's something else on. I mean, usually if there's...some kind of sports game on, we usually watch that, but unless there's...another show on that, you know, she can talk me into, deter my interest, or something....

When asked how his partner gets him to watch something that she wants to watch, he reported:

> Oh, I guess, if there's not anything that I'm...real big on watching then I'll let her choose, or if she, you know, she's interested in something.... A bunch of times, we watch TV, and it's like, well, we'll go back, and, well, that's kind of interesting, we go back and forth.

His wife agreed:

> I usually don't have to beg him. I don't know. [Laughing.] I tie him down, and say, "You're watching this." I don't know. He usually just comes over, and if it's not what he wants, then he'll take the remote and try to find sports.

In other words, this couple watches sports when it is available. If there is no sports program on television and if the husband does not have something else he really wants to watch, then the wife may choose a show, but her husband will be looking for a sports program while her show is on, or at least he will go back and forth between her show and others.

A woman who has been married for 18 years was

deliberate in her efforts to watch a particular show:

> I usually start a couple of days ahead of time when I see them advertised, and it is something that I am going to want to watch. I tell him to "get prepared!" I have to be relatively adamant about it. When the time comes up, I have to remind him ahead of time that I told him earlier that I want to watch the program.

When her husband wants to watch a program, however, she said, "He just watches what he wants. He doesn't ask." Finally, a married man reported, "I just say I want to watch something, and if she wants to watch something really bad, I will let her watch what she wants to watch." Ultimately, the authority is his.

The data are much the same when people report on changes they would like to see in the way they watch television together. One man who has been cohabiting with his partner for one year said, "I should probably let her 'drive' sometimes, but [it] would bug me too much not to be able to do it." A woman who has been married for 37 years painted a brighter picture. When asked, "How do you feel about watching TV with your husband? Are you happy with the way things are?" she responded:

> Yes, right now. But see, without the VCR we'd be in trouble because I just tape anything I want to see. Without that, there'd be more conflict…. Buying a second TV has changed the way we watch TV. It's made it easier—less stress, less conflict.

A young married man also was more positive. When asked, "Have you changed the way you watch television together?" he replied, "We take turns watching our programs, and I let her hold the remote during her programs."

Earlier, I mentioned that 14% ($n = 5$) of the couples in this study were gay or lesbian. In these couples, too, one partner usually is more likely than the other to use the RCD. In a gay male couple, one nearly always used the RCD, and the other almost never used it. When the RCD user was asked why they have this typical pattern, he responded: "Why? I don't know. I just like using the remote. I think I'm better at it than he is." In answer to a question regarding whether he used the RCD at all, his partner indicated: "He doesn't let me." In a second gay male couple, one partner again was far more likely to use the remote than the other partner, but both reported using controlling strategies to get their partner to watch a show they wanted to watch. Greg said, "I just tell him I want to watch it, and we do." Rob said, "I just turn it on, and that is what we watch." When asked, "How does your partner get you to watch a program he wants to watch?" Greg replied: "I usually don't watch programs I don't want to watch. If he asked me to watch it with him for a purpose, I would."

In contrast, one partner in a lesbian pair reported, "If we are both here, we try to make sure it's something that we both like." In fact, this couple limited their television viewing to avoid potential problems result-

ing from their different styles of RCD use. They also made it a practice to talk to each other during the commercials, in part, so that the one partner who tended to do so, would not graze. A second lesbian pair reported similar behavior. When asked, "Think back to the beginning of your relationship with [your partner]. Have your expectations about watching television with her changed over time?" she responded:

> In the beginning,…TV watching was something we could do when we didn't know each other very well yet. You know, it was kind of like a sort of a neutral or a little bit less personal activity that we could sit and watch TV together as a shared activity. And it's still a shared activity…. We don't use it to tune each other out, and if someone wants to talk, we just click the mute button or turn it off.

Becky's partner, Mary, used the RCD much more often than Becky did. According to Becky, however, when Mary grazes, "she's perfectly willing, if I say, 'This looks really good,' she'll stop. She doesn't dominate that way." In fact, when Mary grazes, "she'll just say, 'Is this bothering you?'" Mary agreed that she was the one who usually held the RCD, but that they shared, too. "If Becky has a show she really likes, then I give her the remote so I'm sure I don't play with the TV while she's watching her show." Mary does not "let" her partner hold the RCD; she asks her to hold it to keep her own behavior in check. Indeed, Mary's frustration with their joint television watching comes from her own behavior: "Well, I feel self-conscious about how much I change the channels because I know that she doesn't like to change as often or as fast as I do." Although based on a very modest sample, these findings are intriguing and illustrate how couples successfully develop and maintain egalitarian or peer relationships.

Discussion

These data confirm that for women in heterosexual pairs leisure is a source of conflict—conflict between their own enjoyment and the enjoyment of their partners (Shank, 1986; Shaw, 1985, 1991). The data expose the contradictions between the goal and the reality of leisure for women. Support also comes from the findings that men, more than women, combine other pleasurable pursuits with television watching. Others (Coverman & Sheley, 1986; Firestone & Shelton, 1994; Hochschild, 1989; Mederer, 1993) have shown that women more than men dovetail family labor with their leisure activity.

The data also support previous work suggesting that when heterosexual couples watch television together, men dominate in program selection and in the use of the RCD (Copeland & Schweitzer, 1993; Cornwell et al., 1993; Eastman & Newton, 1995; Heeter & Greenberg, 1985; Krendl et al., 1993; Lindlof et al., 1988; Morley, 1988; Perse & Ferguson, 1993). Indeed, unnegotiated channel switching by male partners was a fre-

595 quent occurrence in this sample. Men use the RCD to avoid commercials, to watch more than one show at a time, and to check what else is on (Perse & Ferguson, 1993). And they do so even when their partners are frustrated by these behaviors.

600 The data reveal that men have power over women in heterosexual relationships (Komter, 1989). Men are more likely than women to watch what they want on television and to do so without considering their partner's wishes. Men control the RCD, which gives them

605 the means to watch what they want, when they want, in the way that they want. Men also persist in RCD use that is frustrating to their women partners. These are examples of manifest power. Men make overt attempts to get their way and are successful at doing so. Men's

610 power is evident, as well, in the lesser power of their women partners. For example, women struggle to get their male partners to watch a program they want to watch and are less able than men to do so. Furthermore, women watch a preferred show on a different

615 television set or videotape it so that they can watch it later. These options do not prevent a husband or male partner from watching a show that he wants to watch when he wants to watch it.

Men's latent power over women is evident as well.

620 Even though women rarely control the RCD, fewer than half report that RCD use is frustrating to them, and only 30% say they would like to change their partner's RCD behavior. According to Komter (1989), resignation to the way things are is evidence of latent

625 power. Another illustration of the effect of latent power is anticipation of a negative reaction. Only four women feel they would be successful if they attempted to change the way their partners use the RCD. In the heterosexual sample, women seem less able than men to

630 raise issues of concern to them, they anticipate the struggles they will encounter when and if their own preferences are made known, and they predict a negative reaction to their wishes from their male partners.

Confirmation of men's latent power over their

635 women partners also was demonstrated by a series of auxiliary analyses. I was unable to explain the dependent variables of respondent's relationship happiness or respondent's enjoyment of the time the couple spends together with independent variables such as frustration

640 with remote control use, dominance of the remote control, or desire to change frustrating remote control use. As Komter (1989) suggested, both lesser power and resignation on the part of women contribute to the appearance of balance in these pairs.

645 Joint television watching in heterosexual couples is hardly an egalitarian experience. As is true for my mother, some women use a second television or a videocassette recorder to level the playing field (i.e., so that they are able to watch the shows they want to

650 watch). A second television set, however, reduces joint leisure time among those couples who can afford it, and a VCR means that a woman may have to wait to

watch her show. Even these solutions to conflict around joint television watching demonstrate that cou-

655 ples watching television are not simply passive couch potatoes. They are doing gender, that is, acting in ways consistent with social structures and helping to create and maintain them at the same time.

Everyday couple interaction is hardly mundane and

660 run-of-the-mill. It is a systematic recreation and reinforcement of social patterns. Couples' leisure behavior is gendered in the same way that household labor is gendered: Social status enhances men's leisure activity relative to women's. Thus, leisure activity has gen-

665 dered meanings (Ferree, 1990). Through it, women and men are creating and affirming themselves and each other as separate and unequal (Ferree, 1990; Thompson, 1993). In other words, leisure activity is both an occasion for relaxation and an occasion for doing gen-

670 der (Fenstermaker, West, & Zimmerman, 1991; Shaw, 1991).

As Osmond and Thorne (1993) point out, "Gender relations are basically power relations" (p. 593). Because the power of men in families is legitimate—that

675 is, backed by structural and cultural supports—it constrains the less powerful to act to maintain the social order and the stability of their relationship (Farrington & Chertok, 1993). Few women make demands of their heterosexual partners so that their patterns of television

680 watching change. Instead, they say they are "happy" with their joint television watching. This same pattern is evident when we examine family labor. Most women describe the objectively uneven distribution of household work as fair (Thompson, 1991).

685 Hochschild (1989) argued that women give up leisure as an indirect strategy to bolster a myth of equality. Rather than resenting her male partner's leisure time, a woman uses the time when he is pursuing his own leisure or interests to engage in what she describes

690 as her interests: housework and child care. Overall, she defines their level of involvement at home as equal, a view that can be sustained only if she ignores her own lack of leisure time, as well as the amount of leisure time her partner has. Hochschild also suggested that a

695 woman sees her male partner's leisure time as more valuable than her own because she feels that more of his identity and time than hers are committed to paid work. She concludes, therefore, that he deserves extra relaxation. In Hochschild's view, and in Komter's

700 (1989), women cannot afford to feel resentment in their close relationships.

In a review of the literature, Szinovacz (1987) wrote that there were few studies of how people in families exercise power. She argued that such studies

705 are needed, as are studies on strategies of resisting power. The data reported here suggest that the exercise of power around couples' television watching behavior can be overt and relentless. Men's strategies to control the content and style of viewing are ways in which they

710 do gender. Women's resistance strategies (e.g., getting

a second television set, using the VCR) are also ways of doing gender. They do little to upset the intracouple power dynamics. Indeed, most women whose male partners are excessive grazers do not describe resis-
715 tance strategies at all. Instead, they maintain the status quo (Komter, 1989).

Of interest is that in lesbian and gay couples one person was more likely to be the heavier RCD user, as well. Yet these couples had some unique patterns. The
720 behavior of the lesbian couples, in particular, is suggestive for those of us wishing to establish and maintain egalitarian partnerships. One lesbian woman demonstrated a solution to the conflict between partners when one is distressed by the other's RCD behavior.
725 Asked, "Is there anything else you'd like to tell us?" she responded:

> Well, I think that the most important thing for me is to remember to be sensitive to the fact that she doesn't have the same tastes as me, and I try to think about that. And,
730 if she mentions that she likes something, then I ask her before I change the channel if she's done watching it, or if she's not interested, if I could change the channel.

In this act, she elevates the importance of her partner's wishes to the level of her own. She demonstrates the
735 consideration that her partner desires and deserves (Hochschild, 1989; Thompson, 1991). When asked if it would be important for them to make changes in the way they watch television together, her partner expressed insight into her own behavior. Mary, the RCD
740 user, likes to "veg out" and watch TV, but Becky likes to:

> pretend I'm not going to watch, I'm going to get a magazine or the newspaper,...or I'll bring some desk paper work over to do.... I think, well, I'll just sit there in the
745 living room while Mary watches TV. I'll work on our bills or something.... Then, what happens is I'll look around and think that looks kind of interesting. Although usually by the time I've looked around, she's changed the channel.... I think what happens is that she's more up
750 front about saying, "Hey, I'm going to veg out here and watch some TV," and I pretend I'm going to do more worthwhile things, and I end up just watching TV anyway.

Perhaps these two women, with their honesty to
755 themselves, their sensitivity to each other, and their concern about the ways in which their own behavior is or could be a problem in their relationship, are doing gender, too. They are concerned with the relationship, rather than with getting their own way. This is how
760 women are said to make connection and to demonstrate care, to give what Hochschild (1989) described as a gift of gratitude. Using these strategies, they maximize joint enjoyment of leisure and minimize power imbalances. Rather then reproducing structural hierarchies,
765 they create a bond of equality and provide a different course for the resolution of inherent conflict within couples.

The results from this study are hardly definitive.

They are based on a small, volunteer sample, albeit one
770 sufficiently diverse to include different types of close, romantic relationships. Additionally, the very small number of lesbian and gay couples suggests a need to exercise caution when generalizing from these findings. Further study with larger, representative samples
775 will be required to extend these findings beyond the couples interviewed here.

Nevertheless, the patterns I identified are similar to those found in other studies of television watching in families and of the intersection of gender and power in
780 close relationships. Mundane activities are important for understanding the intersection of gender and power in close relationships. Indeed, as Lull (1988) noted:

> Television is not only a technological medium that transmits bits of information from impersonal institutions
785 to anonymous audiences, [but] it is a social medium, too—a means by which audience members communicate and construct strategies to achieve a wide range of personal and social objectives. (p. 258)

Others (Morley, 1988; Spigel, 1992) have pointed out
790 that the way men engage with television programming and women watch more distractedly are illustrations of cultural power. Daytime television programming in the 1950s, for example, was designed to be repetitive and fragmented to facilitate joint housework and television
795 watching for women (Spigel, 1992), thus helping to create and reinforce the view that leisure at home is problematic for women. The availability of the RCD does not change the fact that women's leisure is fragmented.
800 Recently, I toured an area of Portland, Oregon, billed as "The Street of Dreams," where there are a half dozen homes costing nearly a million dollars apiece. Each year, such homes are opened temporarily to members of a curious public who will never be able to
805 afford them. Inside one was a theater room with three television sets mounted side-by-side along the back wall. A moment after we arrived, a middle-aged heterosexual couple entered the room. The woman smiled and said to the man, "Look, Dan, you could get rid of
810 the remote!" If three television sets in one room is a solution to the problem of being able to watch only one show at a time, gendered struggles inherent in such mundane, everyday activity as watching television are destined to continue. They will do so until women and
815 men are equal in both their microlevel interactions and in the broader social structure.

References

Bryant. J., & Rockwell, S. C. (1993). Remote control devices in television program selection: Experimental evidence. In J. R. Walker & R. V. Bellamy, Jr. (Eds.), *The remote control in the new age of television* (pp. 73–85). Westport, CT: Praeger.

Copeland, G. A., & Schweitzer, K. (1993). Domination of the remote control during family viewing. In J. R. Walker & R. V. Bellamy, Jr. (Eds.), *The remote control in the new age of television* (pp. 155–168). Westport, CT: Praeger.

Cornwell, N. C., Everett, S., Everett, S. E., Moriarty, S., Russomanno, J. A., Tracey, M., & Trager, R. (1993). Measuring RCD use: Method matters. In J. R. Walker & R. V. Bellamy, Jr. (Eds.), *The remote control in the new age of television* (pp. 43–55). Westport, CT: Praeger.

Coverman, S., & Sheley, J. F. (1986). Change in men's housework and child-care time, 1965–1975. *Journal of Marriage and the Family, 48,* 413–422.

Crawford, D. W., Geoffrey, G., & Crouter, A. C. (1986). The stability of leisure preferences. *Journal of Leisure Research, 18,* 96–115.

Eastman, S. T., & Newton, G. D. (1995). Delineating grazing: Observations of remote control use. *Journal of Communication, 45,* 77–95.

Farrington, K., & Chertok, E. (1993). Social conflict theories of the family. In P. G. Boss, W. J. Doherty, R. LaRossa, W. R. Schumm, & S. K. Steinmetz (Eds.), *Sourcebook of family theories and methods: A contextual approach* (pp. 357–381). New York: Plenum.

Fenstermaker, S., West, C., & Zimmerman, D. H. (1991). Gender inequality: New conceptual terrain. In R. L. Blumberg (Ed.), *Gender, family, and economy: The triple overlap* (pp. 289–307). Newbury Park, CA: Sage.

Ferree, M. M. (1990). Beyond separate spheres: Feminism and family research. *Journal of Marriage and the Family, 52,* 866–884.

Firestone, J., & Shelton, B. A. (1994). A comparison of women's and men's leisure time: Subtle effects of the double day. *Leisure Sciences, 16,* 45–60.

Goodman, E. (1993). Click. In *Value judgments* (pp. 180–182). New York: Farrar Strauss, & Giroux.

Heeter, C., & Greenberg, B. S. (1985). Profiling the zappers. *Journal of Advertising Research, 25,* 15–19.

Henderson, K. A. (1990). The meaning of leisure for women: An integrative review of the research. *Journal of Leisure Research, 22,* 228–243.

Henderson, K. A. (1994). Perspectives on analyzing gender, women, and leisure. *Journal of Leisure Research, 26,* 119–137.

Hill, M. S. (1988). Marital stability and spouses' shared time. *Journal of Family Issues, 9,* 427–451.

Hochschild, A. (with Machung, A.) (1989). *The second shift: Working parents and the revolution at home.* New York: Viking.

Holman, T. B., & Jacquart, M. (1988). Leisure-activity patterns and marital satisfaction: A further test. *Journal of Marriage and the Family, 50,* 69–77.

Huston, T. L. (1983). Power. In H. H. Kelley, E. Berscheid, A. Christensen, J. H. Harvey, T. L. Huston, G. Levinger, E. McClintock, L. A. Peplau, & D. R. Patterson (Eds.), *Close relationships* (pp. 169–219). New York: W. H. Freeman.

Kollock, P., Blumstein, P., & Schwartz, P. (1985). Sex and power in interaction: Conversational privilege and duties. *American Sociological Review, 50,* 34–46.

Komter, A. (1989). Hidden power in marriage. *Gender and Society, 3,* 187–216.

Krendl, K. A., Troiano, C., Dawson, R., & Clark, G. (1993). "OK, where's the remote?" Children, families, and remote control devices. In J. R. Walker & R. V. Bellamy, Jr. (Eds.), *The remote control in the new age of television* (pp. 137–153). Westport, CT: Praeger.

Lindlof, T. R., Shatzer, M. J., & Wilkinson, D. (1988). Accommodation of video and television in the American family. In J. Lull (Ed.), *World families watch television* (pp. 158–192). Newbury Park, CA: Sage.

Lull, J. (1988). Constructing rituals of extension through family television viewing. In J. Lull (Ed.), *World families watch television* (pp. 237–259). Newbury Park, CA: Sage.

McDonald, G. W. (1980). Family power: The assessment of a decade of theory and research, 1970–1979. *Journal of Marriage and the Family, 42,* 841–854.

Mederer, H. (1993). Division of labor in two-earner homes: Task accomplishment versus household management as critical variables in perceptions about family work. *Journal of Marriage and the Family, 55,* 133–145.

Morley, D. (1988). Domestic relations: The framework of family viewing in Great Britain. In J. Lull (Ed.), *World families watch television* (pp. 22–48). Newbury Park, CA: Sage.

Osmond, M. W., & Thorne, B. (1993). Feminist theories: The social construction of gender in families and society. In P. G. Boss, W. J. Doherty, R. LaRossa, W. R. Schumm, & S. K. Steinmetz (Eds.), *Sourcebook of family theories and methods: A contextual approach* (pp. 591–623). New York: Plenum.

Perse, E. M., & Ferguson, D. A. (1993). Gender differences in remote control use. In J. R. Walker & R. V. Bellamy, Jr. (Eds.), *The remote control in the new age of television* (pp. 169–186). Westport, CT: Praeger.

Robinson, J. P. (1990, September). I love my TV. *American Demographics, 12,* 24–27.

Shank, J. W. (1986). An exploration of leisure in the lives of dual-career women. *Journal of Leisure Research, 18,* 300–319.

Shaw, S. M. (1985). Gender and leisure: Inequality in the distribution of leisure time. *Journal of Leisure Research, 17,* 266–282.

Shaw, S. M. (1991). Gender, leisure, and constraint: Towards a framework for the analysis of women's leisure. *Journal of Leisure Research, 26,* 8–22.

Spigel, L. (1992). *Make room for TV: television and the family idea in postwar America.* Chicago: University of Chicago.

Szinovacz, M. E. (1987). Family power. In M. B. Sussman & S. K. Steinmetz (Eds.), *Handbook of marriage and the family* (pp. 651–693). New York: Plenum.

Thompson, L. (1991). Family work: Women's sense of fairness. *Journal of Family Issues, 12,* 181–196.

Thompson, L. (1993). Conceptualizing gender in marriage: The case of marital care. *Journal of Marriage and the Family, 55,* 557–569.

Thompson, L., & Walker, A. J. (1989). Gender in families: Women and men in marriage, work, and parenthood. *Journal of Marriage and the Family, 51,* 845–871.

Walker, J. R., & Bellamy, R. V., Jr. (1991). Gratifications of grazing: An exploratory study of remote control use. *Journalism Quarterly, 68,* 422–431.

West, C., & Zimmerman, D. H. (1987). Doing gender. *Gender and Society, 1,* 125–151.

Note: This is an expanded version of the presidential address presented at the 1995 annual meeting of the National Council on Family Relations, Portland, Oregon. I thank the following individuals for their help: Kinsey Green, for providing funds to support a graduate research assistant for this project; Alan Acock, for releasing me from a course during academic year 1994–1995; Janet Lee and Rebecca Warner, for their assistance with measurement; Linda Eddy and the students enrolled in HDFS 442 in the spring of 1994, for their role in data collection; Lori Schreiner, for coding the quantitative data; and Sally Bowman, Alan Acock, Fuzhong Li, John Bratten, and, especially, Takashi Yamamoto, for their help with data analysis. I am grateful also to Katherine Allen, Mark Fine, and two anonymous reviewers for their careful and thoughtful reading of an earlier draft of this article.

Exercise for Article 23

Factual Questions

1. According to feminist scholars, what bears "an uncanny resemblance to the social structure?"

2. According to the literature review, what reason(s) do women give for changing channels? Do they give the same reason(s) men give?

3. Who was "primarily" responsible for recruiting participants?

4. What percentage of the couples were gay or lesbian?

5. Why was a coin tossed?

6. What was the mean number of hours that television was watched each day by the participants?

7. What percentage of the women reported that RCD use was frustrating to them?

Questions for Discussion

8. The author begins her research article with a personal anecdote. (See lines 1–9.) In your opinion, does this strengthen or weaken the article?

9. In your opinion, did the inclusion of lesbian/gay couples strengthen this study? Weaken it? Explain.

10. The interviews were audiotaped. Are there advantages and disadvantages of doing this? Explain.

11. Are the quantitative results or the qualitative results more convincing to you? Do the two types of results complement each other? Explain.

12. To what population(s), if any, would you be willing to generalize the results of this study?

13. If you were to conduct another study on the same topic, what changes in the research methodology would you make?

Quality Ratings

Directions: Indicate your level of agreement with each of the following statements by circling a number from 5 for strongly agree (SA) to 1 for strongly disagree (SD). If you believe an item is not applicable to this research article, leave it blank. Be prepared to explain your ratings.

A. The introduction establishes the importance of the study.

SA   5   4   3   2   1   SD

B. The literature review establishes the context for the study.

SA   5   4   3   2   1   SD

C. The research purpose, question, or hypothesis is clearly stated.

SA   5   4   3   2   1   SD

D. The method of sampling is sound.

SA   5   4   3   2   1   SD

E. Relevant demographics (for example, age, gender, and ethnicity) are described.

SA   5   4   3   2   1   SD

F. Measurement procedures are adequate.

SA   5   4   3   2   1   SD

G. All procedures have been described in sufficient detail to permit a replication of the study.

SA   5   4   3   2   1   SD

H. The participants have been adequately protected from potential harm.

SA   5   4   3   2   1   SD

I. The results are clearly described.

SA   5   4   3   2   1   SD

J. The discussion/conclusion is appropriate.

SA   5   4   3   2   1   SD

K. Despite any flaws, the report is worthy of publication.

SA   5   4   3   2   1   SD

Article 24

Research on Religion-Accommodative Counseling: Review and Meta-Analysis

MICHAEL E. McCULLOUGH
National Institute for Healthcare Research

ABSTRACT. The present meta-analysis examined data from 5 studies (N = 111) that compared the efficacy of standard approaches to counseling for depression with religion-accommodative approaches. There was no evidence that the religion-accommodative approaches were more or less efficacious than the standard approaches. Findings suggest that the choice to use religious approaches with religious clients is probably more a matter of client preference than a matter of differential efficacy. However, additional research is needed to examine whether religion-accommodative approaches yield differential treatment satisfaction or differential improvements in spiritual well-being or facilitate relapse prevention. Given the importance of religion to many potential consumers of psychological services, counseling psychologists should devote greater attention to religion-accommodative counseling in future studies.

From *Journal of Counseling Psychology*, *46*, 92–98. Copyright © 1999 by the American Psychological Association, Inc. Reprinted with permission.

The United States is a highly religious country; 92% of its population are affiliated with a religion (Kosmin & Lachman, 1993). According to a 1995 survey, 96% of Americans believe in God or a universal spirit, 42% indicate that they attend a religious worship service weekly or almost weekly, 67% indicate that they are members of a church or synagogue, and 60% indicate that religion is "important" or "very important" in their lives (Gallup, 1995).

In addition, many scholars acknowledge that certain forms of religious involvement are associated with better functioning on a variety of measures of mental health. Reviews of this research (e.g., Bergin, 1991; Bergin, Masters, & Richards, 1987; Larson et al., 1992; Pargament, 1997; Schumaker, 1992; Worthington, Kurusu, McCullough, & Sandage, 1996) suggested that several forms of religious involvement (including intrinsic religious motivation, attendance at religious worship, receiving coping support from one's religious faith or religious congregation, and positive religious attributions for life events) are positively associated with a variety of measures of mental health. For example, various measures of religious involvement appear to be related to lower degrees of depressive symptoms in adults (Bienenfeld, Koenig, Larson, & Sherrill, 1997; Ellison, 1995; Kendler, Gardner, & Prescott, 1997) and children (Miller, Warner, Wickramaratne, & Weissman, 1997) and less suicide (e.g., Comstock & Partridge, 1972; Kark et al., 1996; Wandrei, 1985).

Koenig, George, and Peterson (1998) reported that depressed people scoring high on measures of intrinsic religiousness were significantly more likely to experience a remission of depression during nearly a 1-year follow-up than were depressed people with lower intrinsic religiousness, even after controlling for 30 potential demographic, psychosocial, and medical confounds. Other studies have shown that religious involvement, as gauged through single-item measures of frequency of religious worship and private prayer as well as more complex measures of religious coping, is related to positive psychological outcomes after major life events (e.g., Pargament et al., 1990; Pargament et al., 1994; Pargament, Smith, & Brant, 1995). This is the case even though several patterns of religious belief and religious coping (e.g., the belief that one's misfortunes are a punishment from God) are associated with greater psychological distress (Pargament, 1997).

Religion in Counseling and Psychotherapy

Some scholars (e.g., Bergin, 1991; Payne, Bergin, & Loftus, 1992; Richards & Bergin, 1997; Shafranske, 1996; Worthington et al., 1996) posited that considering clients' religiousness while designing treatment plans might have an important effect on the efficacy of treatment. Surveys of psychiatrists (Neeleman & King, 1993), psychologists (Bergin & Jensen, 1988; Shafranske & Malony, 1990), and mental health counselors (Kelly, 1995) also indicate that many mental health professionals believe that religious and spiritual values can and should be thoughtfully addressed in the course of mental health treatment. Moreover, a variety of analogue and clinical studies (e.g., Houts & Graham, 1986; T. A. Kelly & Strupp, 1992; Lewis & Lewis, 1985; McCullough & Worthington, 1995; McCullough, Worthington, Maxey, & Rachal, 1997; Morrow, Worthington, & McCullough, 1993) indicate that clients' religious beliefs can influence both (a) the conclusions of clinicians' structured psychological assessments and (b) the process of psychotherapy (cf. Luborsky et al., 1980).

Evidence from Comparative Efficacy Studies

Given the existing research on religion and mental health, an important question for counseling psychologists is whether supporting clients' religious beliefs and values in a structured treatment package yield clinical benefits that are equal to or greater than standard methods of psychological practice. Several empirical studies have addressed this issue. Although the findings of studies that have examined such questions have been reviewed in narrative fashion elsewhere (e.g., W. B. Johnson, 1993; Matthews et al., 1998; Worthington et al., 1996), no researchers have used meta-analytic methods to estimate quantitatively the differential efficacy of such treatments. Meta-analytic reviews that compare religious approaches to counseling with standard approaches to counseling are one of three meta-analytic strategies that can be used to examine whether a given therapeutic approach has therapeutic efficacy (Wampold, 1997).

In the present article, I review the existing research on such religious approaches to counseling using quantitative methods of research synthesis (e.g., Cooper & Hedges, 1994; Hunter & Schmidt, 1990) to estimate the differential efficacy of religious approaches in comparison to standard forms of counseling for depressed religious clients.

Method

Literature Search

The PsycLIT, PsycINFO, Medline, ERIC, and Dissertation Abstracts electronic databases were searched through August 1998 for published and unpublished studies that examined the differential efficacy of a religion-accommodative approach to counseling in comparison to a standard approach to counseling. The reference sections of relevant articles were searched for other studies that would be relevant to this review. This search process continued until no new studies were revealed. In addition, several experts in the field of religion and mental health were contacted to identify unpublished studies.

Studies had to meet four criteria to be included in the meta-analytic sample: They had to (a) compare a religion-accommodative approach to counseling to a standard approach to counseling; (b) randomly assign patients to treatments; (c) involve patients who were suffering from a specific set of psychological symptoms (e.g., anxiety or depression); and (d) offer equal amounts of treatment to clients in the religion-accommodative and standard treatments. Five published studies and one unpublished dissertation (W. B. Johnson, 1991), which was later reported in W. B. Johnson, DeVries, Ridley, Pettorini, and Peterson (1994), met these inclusion criteria. Several studies that investigated religious approaches to psychological treatment (e.g., Azhar & Varma, 1995a, 1995b; Azhar, Varma, & Dharap, 1994; Carlson, Bacaseta, & Simanton, 1988; Richards, Owen, & Stein, 1993; Rye & Par-

gament, 1997; Toh & Tan, 1997) were obtained, but these studies failed to meet all four inclusion criteria. Thus, they were omitted from the meta-analytic sample. A single rater determined which studies met inclusion criteria. This rater's decisions were made without reference to the results or discussion sections of the articles.

The resulting meta-analytic sample included five studies representing data from 111 counseling clients. Descriptions of study populations, measures used, and effect size estimates (with 95% confidence intervals) are given in Table 1.

The Studies

Researchers interested in accommodative forms of religious counseling have taken standard cognitive–behavioral protocols or specific techniques, such as cognitive restructuring (Beck, Rush, Shaw, & Emery, 1979), cognitive coping skills (Meichenbaum, 1985), and appeals to rational thinking (e.g., Ellis & Grieger, 1977), and have developed religion-friendly rationales for and versions of such protocols or techniques (W. B. Johnson & Ridley, 1992b). These adapted protocols or techniques are thought to be theoretically equivalent to standard cognitive–behavioral techniques (Propst, 1996), but more amenable to the religious world view and religious language that religious clients use to understand their lives and their problems. The five studies are described in greater detail next.

Propst (1980). Propst (1980) examined the differential efficacy of a manualized, religion-accommodative approach to cognitive restructuring and imagery modification. Volunteers who scored in the mild or moderate range of depression on the Beck Depression Inventory (BDI; Beck, Ward, Mendelson, Mock, & Erbaugh, 1961) and in at least the moderate range on the King and Hunt (1972) religion scales were randomly assigned to one of two treatments. The standard treatment was an integration of Beck's (1976) cognitive therapy for depression and Meichenbaum's (1973) cognitive–behavior modification. During eight 1-hr sessions conducted over 4 weeks, clients were trained to observe their cognitions and imagery during depressed moods. After clients were convinced of the links between their moods, thoughts, and images, they practiced cognitive restructuring skills for modifying their thoughts and images using imagery and positive self-statements (e.g., "I can see myself in the future coping with that particular situation"). Ten of eleven clients assigned to this condition completed it.

In the religion-accommodative treatment, clients completed the same therapeutic protocol as that used in the standard treatment. The only difference is that participants were trained to replace their negative cognitions and imagery with religious images (e.g., "I can visualize Christ going with me into that difficult situation in the future as I try to cope"). Seven of 9 clients assigned to this condition completed the treatment.

Table 1
Sample Sizes, Effect Sizes, and 95% Confidence Intervals (CI) for the Studies Included in the Meta-Analysis

Study	Religion-accommodative treatment n	Standard treatment n	Effect size (d_+)	95% CI
Propst (1980)	7	10	+0.41	−0.56/+1.39
Pecheur & Edwards (1984)	7	7	+0.53	−0.53/+1.60
Propst et al. (1992)	19	19	+0.51	−0.14/+1.15
W. B. Johnson & Ridley (1992a)	5	5	+0.29	−0.96/+1.53
W. B. Johnson et al. (1994)	16	16	−0.51	−1.22/+0.19

Pecheur and Edwards (1984). Pecheur and Edwards (1984) assessed the differential efficacy of Beck et al.'s (1979) cognitive therapy for depression and a religion-accommodative version of the same therapy. Clients were students from a Christian college who met research diagnostic criteria for major depressive disorder. They also scored in the depressed range on the BDI, the Hamilton Rating Scale for Depression (HRSD; Hamilton, 1960), and a single-item visual analogue scale. In the standard treatment, clients completed eight 50-min sessions of cognitive behavior modification. All 7 clients who were assigned to this treatment completed it.

In the religion-accommodative treatment, clients completed the standard cognitive therapy tasks specified in Beck et al. (1979); however, challenges to negative cognitions were placed in a religious context. For example, rather than replacing negative views of self with statements such as "Our self-acceptance and self-worth are not lost or lessened when we fail," the religion-accommodative approach trained clients to use self-statements such as, "God loves, accepts, and values us just as we are." This treatment was also administered according to a manual, which appears in Pecheur (1980).

Propst, Ostrom, Watkins, Dean, and Mashburn (1992). Propst et al. (1992) compared the efficacy of Beck et al.'s (1979) cognitive therapy for depression with a manualized, religion-accommodative version of the same therapy (see Propst, 1988). Clients were recruited from the community and scored at least 14 on the 28-item version of the HRSD. They also scored at least in the moderate range on standard measures of religious commitment (e.g., Allport & Ross, 1967; King & Hunt, 1972). Clients in the standard treatment completed 18 sessions of individual cognitive therapy for depression. All 19 clients enrolled in this condition completed it.

In the religion-accommodative treatment, clients completed 18 sessions of cognitive therapy that challenged negative cognitions and images by replacing them with positive thoughts and imagery of a religious nature, as in Propst (1980). All 19 clients enrolled in this condition completed it.

W. B. Johnson & Ridley (1992a). Johnson and Ridley (1992) compared the efficacy of rational-emotive

therapy (RET), using Walen, DiGiuseppe, and Wessler's (1980) treatment manual, with a manualized, religion-accommodative version of the same therapy. Clients were theology students and local church members who scored in at least the mildly depressed range on the BDI. They also scored in the "intrinsic" range on a standard measure of religious motivation (Allport & Ross, 1967), suggesting that their religious faith was highly internalized. In the standard RET condition, clients completed six 50-min sessions in 3 weeks, including homework sessions and in-session rehearsal of rational-emotive techniques. All 5 clients assigned to this condition completed it.

In the religion-accommodative treatment, three explicitly Christian treatment components were added. First, clients were directed to dispute irrational beliefs using explicitly Christian beliefs, as in Propst (1980). Second, clients were encouraged to use Christian prayer, thoughts, and imagery in their homework assignments. Third, counselors used brief prayers at the end of each session. All 5 clients assigned to this condition completed it.

W. B. Johnson et al. (1994). W. B. Johnson et al. (1994) compared the efficacy of standard RET and a religion-accommodative form of RET, as in W. B. Johnson and Ridley (1992a). Selection criteria were almost identical to those reported in W. B. Johnson and Ridley (1992a). The standard RET condition was an eight-session protocol delivered over 8 weeks, and was based on two popular RET treatment manuals (Ellis & Dryden, 1987; Walen et al., 1980). All 16 clients assigned to this condition completed it.

The religion-accommodative treatment was based on two treatment manuals discussing Christian versions of RET (Backus, 1985; Thurman, 1989). Although the basic structure of RET was kept intact, clients were encouraged to dispute irrational beliefs based on scriptural beliefs and biblical examples. Homework assignments also used biblical examples and beliefs. All 16 clients assigned to this condition completed it.

Effect Size Estimates

Effect sizes and homogeneity statistics were calculated from means and standard deviations using the DSTAT statistical software, Version 1.10 (B. T. Johnson, 1989), using the formulas prescribed by Hedges and Olkin (1985). Effect sizes were based on the difference between the mean of clients in the standard counseling condition and the mean of clients in the religion-accommodative conditions. This difference was divided by the pooled standard deviation of clients in both conditions. All effect size estimates, expressed as d_+ values, are corrected for the bias that is present in uncorrected g values, as recommended by Hedges and Olkin (1985). Effect sizes can be interpreted as the increased amount of symptom reduction afforded to participants in the religion-accommodative condition, expressed in standard deviation units. In calculating aggregate effect size estimates, individual effect sizes were weighted by the inverse of their sampling error variance, so that studies with larger samples were given greater weight in the calculation of d_+ (Hedges & Olkin, 1985).

The Q statistic was also used to estimate the degree of variability among the effect sizes. The Q statistic is basically a goodness-of-fit statistic with a roughly χ^2 distribution that enables a test of the hypothesis that all observed effect sizes were drawn from the same population. Significant Q values imply a heterogeneous set of effect sizes (Hunter & Schmidt, 1990).

Handling Multiple Dependent Measures

All five studies used the BDI as a dependent measure of depression. Although two of the studies also used the HRSD or a single-item visual analogue measure of depression, or both (Pecheur & Edwards, 1984; Propst et al., 1992), effect size estimates were based exclusively on the BDI for three reasons. First, the BDI has been shown to produce conservative effect size estimates in comparison to rating scales that are completed by clinicians, such as the HRSD (Lambert, Hatch, Kingston, & Edwards, 1986). Second, single-item visual analogue measures of depression (e.g., Aitken, 1969) appear to contain remarkably little true score variance (Faravelli, Albanesi, & Poli, 1986). Third, the aggregation of data across multiple dependent measures requires knowing their intercorrelations, which were not available for all five studies. Thus, the individual and mean effect size estimates reported here can be considered to be somewhat conservative.

Handling Data from Multiple Follow-Up Periods

All five studies collected follow-up data within 1 week of the termination of the trial. Although three of the studies (W. B. Johnson et al., 1994; Pecheur & Edwards, 1984; Propst et al., 1992) also reported follow-up data collected between 1 and 3 months after the termination of the trial, and one study (Propst et al., 1992) reported an effect size for a 24-month follow-up, we based our effect size estimates only on the data from the 1-week follow-up.

Other Problems with Coding Effect Sizes

Some studies reported data on additional experimental conditions, including self-monitoring and therapist contact conditions (Propst, 1980), waiting list control conditions (Pecheur & Edwards, 1984; Propst et al., 1992), and pastoral counseling conditions (Propst et al., 1992). Because none of these conditions were relevant to the central goal of this study, these data were neither coded nor included in the present meta-analytic study.

Two other problems arose in coding effect sizes. First, although Propst (1980) reported posttreatment means on the BDI for both conditions, standard deviations were not reported. On the basis of the assumption that the other four studies in the present meta-analysis would yield similar pooled standard deviations for the BDI, a mean standard deviation for posttest scores on the BDI from these studies (5.81) was used as an imputed standard deviation for Propst (1980). This imputed standard deviation produced a nonsignificant test statistic for the comparison of the religious and standard counseling conditions, as Propst (1980) reported, giving us confidence that our imputed standard deviation was not wholly inaccurate.

Second, Propst et al.'s (1992) results reported treatment effects separately for religious and nonreligious therapists, which was an independent factor in their experimental design. To collapse treatment effects across levels of the therapist religiousness factor, means and standard deviations obtained for religious and nonreligious therapists within each of the two religious counseling conditions were pooled before calculating an effect size for the treatments.

Corrections of Findings for Unreliability in Dependent Measures

Scholars in meta-analysis advise that effect size estimates be corrected for biases (Hunter & Schmidt, 1990, 1994). One of the easiest biases to correct is attenuation resulting from unreliability in the dependent variable. This bias can be corrected by dividing observed effect sizes and standard errors by the square root of the internal consistency of the dependent variable. Because meta-analytic estimates of the BDI's internal consistency were readily available (Beck, Steer, & Garbin, 1988, estimated its internal consistency at $\alpha = .86$), the observed mean effect size and its confidence interval (CI) were divided by the square root of .86, or .927. Corrections for attenuation resulting from unreliability of the dependent variable produce increased effect size estimates but also a proportionate increase in confidence intervals; thus, a nonsignificant effect size will not become significant as a result of this correction (Hunter & Schmidt, 1994).

Estimating Clinical Significance

We were also interested in whether religion-accommodative and standard approaches to counseling yielded clinically significant differences in efficacy (Jacobson & Revenstorf, 1988; Jacobson & Truax, 1991). Thus, we calculated meta-analytic summaries of clinical significance for two studies that reported clinical significance data (using BDI > 9 as a cutoff for "mild clinical depression"; Kendall, Hollon, Beck, Hammen, & Ingram, 1987).

Results

Observed Mean Effect Size and Attenuation-Corrected Effect Size

The mean effect size for the difference between religious and standard counseling during the 1-week follow-up period (number of effect sizes = 5, $N = 111$) was $d_+ = +0.18$ (95% CI: $-.20/+0.56$), indicating that clients in religion-accommodative counseling had slightly lower BDI scores at 1-week follow-up than did clients in standard counseling conditions. This effect size was not reliably different from zero ($p = .34$). The five effect sizes that contributed to this mean effect size were homogeneous, $Q(4) = 5.38$, $p > .10$. The mean effect size after correcting the effects for attenuation resulting from unreliability was $d_+ = +0.20$ (95% CI: $-0.19/+0.61$).

Differences in Clinical Significance

Two studies (W. B. Johnson & C. R. Ridley, 1992a; Propst, 1980) reported the percentage of participants in the religious and standard psychotherapy conditions who manifested evidence of at least mild clinical depression (BDI scores > 9) during the 1-week follow-up period. Aggregation of these data indicated that, among the 20 religion-accommodative counseling clients in the two studies, 4 (20%) were still at least mildly depressed at the end of treatment. Among the 26 standard counseling clients in the two studies, 9 (34.6%) were at least mildly depressed when treatment ended. This difference in clinical significance was not statistically significant, $\chi^2(1, N = 46) = 1.19$, $p > .10$.

Discussion

The goal of the present study was to review the existing empirical evidence regarding the comparative efficacy of religion-accommodative approaches to counseling depressed religious clients. These data suggest that, in the immediate period after completion of counseling, religious approaches to counseling do not have any significant superiority to standard approaches to counseling. Given that the differences in efficacy of most bonafide treatments are surprisingly small (e.g., Lambert & Bergin, 1994; Wampold, 1997), the existing literature on psychotherapy outcomes would have portended the present meta-analytic results. These findings corroborate some narrative reviews that claim equal efficacy for religion-accommodative and standard approaches to counseling (e.g., Worthington et al., 1996), and help to resolve the inconsistencies that others have observed among these studies (e.g., W. B. Johnson, 1993; Matthews et al., 1998).

Although it is true that the religious approaches to counseling were no more effective than the standard approaches to counseling, it is equally true that they were no less effective than the standard approaches to counseling. Thus, the decision to use religion-accommodative approaches might be most wisely based not on the results of comparative clinical trials, which tend to find no differences among well-manualized treatments, but rather on the basis of patient choice (see Wampold, 1997). Not every religious client would prefer or respond favorably to a religion-accommodative approach to counseling. Indeed, the available evidence suggests that all but the most highly religious clients would prefer an approach to counseling that deals with religious issues only peripherally rather than focally (Wyatt & Johnson, 1990; see Worthington et al., 1996, for review).

On the other hand, many religious clients—especially very conservative Christian clients—would indeed be attracted to a counseling approach (or counselor) precisely because the counseling approach (or the counselor) maintained that the clients' system of religious values were at the core of effective psychological change (Worthington et al., 1996). The research reviewed herein indicates that no empirical basis exists for withholding such religion-accommodative treatment from depressed religious clients who desire such a treatment approach.

The Last Word?

There is inherent danger in publishing meta-analytic results. Because of their ability to provide precise-looking point estimates and short CIs (especially when the observed effect size estimates are relatively heterogeneous), meta-analytic summaries can be perceived to be the last word in evaluating research questions. It would be unfortunate if the present results were interpreted as the last word in evaluating the efficacy of religious approaches to counseling, however, because interesting and important questions remain.

For example, although religion-accommodative approaches to counseling do not appear to be differentially efficacious in reducing symptoms (at least depressive symptoms), they might produce differential treatment satisfaction among some religious clients. Also, comparative studies of religion-accommodative therapy are needed with longer follow-up periods. It is possible that religion-accommodative approaches might prove to be superior to standard treatments in longer term follow-up periods, particularly in helping clients from relapsing, for example, back into depressive episodes. The differential effects of religion-accommodative and standard approaches to treatment also need to be investigated for a wider variety of disorders, including anxiety, anger, alcohol and drug problems, and marital and family problems. As well, although religion-accommodative and standard approaches to counseling do not appear to influence clients' religiousness or religious values differentially (Worthington et al., 1996), it is possible that religion-accommodative counseling yields differential improvements in religious clients' spiritual well-being.

Finally, on a technical note, it should be noted that

the studies in this body of literature currently have been seriously underpowered (i.e., in all cases fewer than 20 clients per treatment). This literature would benefit enormously from as few as three or four very high-quality, large-sample (i.e., 30 or more clients per condition) studies that investigated these questions in greater detail. W. B. Johnson (1993) provided other helpful methodological recommendations to which research on religion-accommodative counseling should adhere.

Limitations

The stability of meta-analytic findings comes from the number of studies included in the meta-analysis as well as the number of participants in the constituent studies. Thus, the findings from meta-analyses with small numbers of studies, such as the present study, are more easily overturned than meta-analyses that include larger numbers of studies. Although meta-analytic methods can be used to synthesize the results of as few as two studies (for examples of small-*k* meta-analyses, see Allison & Faith, 1996; Benschop et al., 1998; Kirsch, Montgomery, & Sapirstein, 1995; Uchino, Cacioppo, & Kiecolt-Glaser, 1996), our findings would obviously be considered more trustworthy if more studies had been available.

A second limitation of the present findings relates to the nature of the meta-analytic sample. The five studies reviewed herein all investigated religion-accommodative counseling with depressed Christian clients. We can only speculate whether the present pattern of results would generalize to different religious populations or to people with different sets of presenting problems. Obviously, research is needed to fill in such gaps.

Conclusion

A variety of empirical data now suggest that certain forms of religious involvement can help prevent the onset of psychological difficulties and enhance effective coping with stressors. In addition, the majority of mental health professionals and the general public believe that patients' religious beliefs should be adequately assessed and taken into consideration in mental health treatment. Moreover, data indicate that patients' religious commitments can play a substantial role in counseling processes (Worthington et al., 1996). Data from the present study also indicate that religious approaches to counseling can be as effective as standard approaches to counseling depressed persons. Thus, for some clients, particularly very religious Christian clients, religion-accommodative approaches to counseling could be, quite literally, the treatment of choice. It is hoped that the present study will encourage counseling psychologists to examine whether religion-accommodative approaches yield similar or even superior benefits on other important metrics of therapeutic change and with other common difficulties in living.

References

Aitken, R. C. B. (1969). Measurement of feeling using visual analogue scales. *Proceedings of the Royal Society of Medicine, 62*, 989–993.

Allison, D. B. & Faith, M. S. (1996). Hypnosis as an adjunct to cognitive-behavioral psychotherapy for obesity: A meta-analytic reappraisal. *Journal of Consulting and Clinical Psychology, 64*, 513–516.

Allport, G. W. & Ross, J. M. (1967). Personal religious orientation and prejudice. *Journal of Personality and Social Psychology, 5*, 432–443.

Azhar, M. Z. & Varma, S. L. (1995a). Religious psychotherapy in depressive patients. *Psychotherapy and Psychosomatics, 63*, 165–168.

Azhar, M. Z. & Varma, S. L. (1995b). Religious psychotherapy as management of bereavement. *Acta Psychiatrica Scandinavica, 91*, 233–235.

Azhar, M. Z., Varma, S. L. & Dharap, A. S. (1994). Religious psychotherapy in anxiety disorder patients. *Acta Psychiatrica Scandinavica, 90*, 1–3.

Backus, W. (1985). *Telling the truth to troubled people.* Minneapolis, MN: Bethany House.

Beck, A. T. (1976). *Cognitive therapy and the emotional disorders.* New York: International University Press.

Beck, A. T., Rush, A. J., Shaw, B. F. & Emery, G. (1979). *Cognitive therapy of depression.* New York: Guilford Press.

Beck, A. T., Steer, R. A. & Garbin, M. G. (1988). Psychometric properties of the Beck Depression Inventory: Twenty-five years of evaluation. *Clinical Psychology Review, 8*, 77–100.

Beck, A. T., Ward, C. H., Mendelson, M., Mock, J. E. & Erbaugh, J. K. (1961). An inventory for measuring depression. *Archives of General Psychiatry, 4*, 561–571.

Benschop, R. J., Geenen, R., Mills, P. J., Naliboff, B. D., Kiecolt-Glaser, J. K., Herbert, T. B., van der Pompe, G., Miller, G., Matthews, K. A., Godaert, G. L. R., Gilmore, S. L., Glaser, R., Heijnen, C. J., Dopp, J. M., Bijlsma, J. W. J., Solomon, G. F. & Cacioppo, J. T. (1998). Cardiovascular and immune responses to acute psychological stress in young and old women: A meta-analysis. *Psychosomatic Medicine, 60*, 290–296.

Bergin, A. E. (1991). Values and religious issues in psychotherapy and mental health. *American Psychologist, 46*, 394–403.

Bergin, A. E. & Jensen, J. P. (1988). Mental health values of professional therapists: A national interdisciplinary survey. *Professional Psychology: Research and Practice, 19*, 290–297.

Bergin, A. E., Masters, K. S. & Richards, P. S. (1987). Religiousness and mental health reconsidered: A study of an intrinsically religious sample. *Journal of Counseling Psychology, 34*, 197–204.

Bienenfeld, D., Koenig, H. G., Larson, D. B. & Sherrill, K. A. (1997). Psychosocial predictors of mental health in a population of elderly women. *American Journal of Geriatric Psychiatry, 5*, 43–53.

Carlson, C. R., Bacaseta, P. E. & Simanton, D. A. (1988). A controlled evaluation of devotional meditation and progressive relaxation. *Journal of Psychology and Theology, 16*, 362–368.

Comstock, G. W. & Partridge, K. B. (1972). Church attendance and health. *Journal of Chronic Disease, 25*, 665–672.

Cooper, H. & Hedges, L. V. (1994). *Handbook of research synthesis.* New York: Russell Sage Foundation.

DeVries, R., Ridley, C. R., Pettorini, D. & Peterson, D. R. (1994). The comparative efficacy of Christian and secular rational-emotive therapy with Christian clients. *Journal of Psychology and Theology, 22*, 130–140.

Edwards, K. J. (1984). A comparison of secular and religious versions of cognitive therapy with depressed Christian college students. *Journal of Psychology and Theology, 12*, 45–54.

Ellis, A. & Dryden, W. (1987). *The practice of rational-emotive therapy.* New York: Springer.

Ellis, A. & Grieger, R. (1977). *Handbook of rational-emotive therapy.* New York: Springer.

Ellison, C. G. (1995). Race, religious involvement, and depressive symptomatology in a southeastern U.S. community. *Social Science and Medicine, 40*, 1561–1572.

Faravelli, C., Albanesi, G. & Poli, E. (1986). Assessment of depression: A comparison of rating scales. *Journal of Affective Disorders, 11*, 245–253.

Gallup, G. (1995). *The Gallup poll: Public opinion 1995.* Wilmington, DE: Scholarly Resources.

Hamilton, M. (1960). A rating scale for depression. *Journal of Neurology, Neurosurgery, and Psychiatry, 23*, 56–62.

Hedges, L. V. & Olkin, I. (1985). *Statistical methods for meta-analysis.* Orlando, FL: Academic Press.

Houts, A. C. & Graham, K. (1986). Can religion make you crazy? Impact of client and therapist religious values on clinical judgments. *Journal of Consulting and Clinical Psychology, 54*, 267–271.

Hunter, J. E. & Schmidt, F. L. (1990). *Methods of meta-analysis: Correcting error and bias in research findings.* Newbury Park, CA: Sage.

Hunter, J. E. & Schmidt, F. L. (1994). Correcting for sources of artificial variation across studies. In H. Cooper & L. V. Hedges (Eds.), *Handbook of research synthesis* (pp. 323–336). New York: Russell Sage Foundation.

Jacobson, N. S. & Revenstorf, D. (1988). Statistics for assessing the clinical significance of psychotherapy techniques: Issues, problems, and new developments. *Behavioral Assessment, 10*, 133–145.

Jacobson, N. S. & Truax, P. (1991). Clinical significance: A statistical approach to defining meaningful change in psychotherapy research. *Journal of Consulting and Clinical Psychology, 59,* 12–19.

Johnson, B. T. (1989). *DSTAT: Software for the meta-analytic review of research literatures.* Hillsdale, NJ: Erlbaum.

Johnson, W. B. (1991). *The comparative efficacy of religious and nonreligious rational-emotive therapy with religious clients.* Unpublished doctoral dissertation, Fuller Graduate School of Psychology, Pasadena, CA.

Johnson, W. B. (1993). Outcome research and religious psychotherapies: Where are we and where are we going? *Journal of Psychology and Theology, 21,* 297–308.

Johnson, W. B. & Ridley, C. R. (1992b). Sources of gain in Christian counseling and psychotherapy. *The Counseling Psychologist, 20,* 159–175.

Kark, J. D., Shemi, G., Friedlander, Y., Martin, O., Manor, O. & Blondheim, S. H. (1996). Does religious observance promote health? Mortality in secular vs. religious kibbutzim in Israel. *American Journal of Public Health, 86,* 341–346.

Kelly, E. W. (1995). Counselor values: A national survey. *Journal of Counseling and Development, 73,* 648–653.

Kelly, T. A. & Strupp, H. H. (1992). Patient and therapist values in psychotherapy: Perceived changes, assimilation, similarity, and outcome. *Journal of Consulting and Clinical Psychology, 60,* 34–40.

Kendall, P. C., Hollon, S. D., Beck, A. T., Hammen, C. L. & Ingram, R. E. (1987). Issues and recommendations regarding use of the Beck Depression Inventory. *Cognitive Therapy and Research, 11,* 289–299.

Kendler, K. S., Gardner, C. O. & Prescott, C. A. (1997). Religion, psychopathology, and substance use and abuse: A multimeasure, genetic-epidemiologic study. *American Journal of Psychiatry, 154,* 322–329.

King, M. A. & Hunt, R. A. (1972). Measuring the religious variable: A replication. *Journal for the Scientific Study of Religion, 11,* 240–251.

Kirsch, I., Montgomery, G. & Sapirstein, S. (1995). Hypnosis as an adjunct to cognitive-behavioral psychotherapy: A meta-analysis. *Journal of Consulting and Clinical Psychology, 63,* 214–220.

Koenig, H. G., George, L. K. & Peterson, B. L. (1998). Religiosity and remission of depression in medically ill older patients. *American Journal of Psychiatry, 155,* 536–542.

Kosmin, B. A. & Lachman, S. P. (1993). *One nation under God: Religion in contemporary American society.* New York: Harmony.

Lambert, M. J. & Bergin, A. E. (1994). The effectiveness of psychotherapy. In A. E. Bergin & S. L. Garfield (Eds.), *Handbook of psychotherapy and behavior change* (4th ed., pp. 143–189). New York: Wiley.

Lambert, M. J., Hatch, D. R., Kingston, M. D. & Edwards, B. C. (1986). Zung, Beck, and Hamilton rating scales as measures of treatment outcome: A meta-analytic comparison. *Journal of Consulting and Clinical Psychology, 54,* 54–59.

Larson, D. B., Sherrill, K. A., Lyons, J. S., Craigie, F. C., Thielman, S. B., Greenwold, M. A. & Larson, S. S. (1992). Associations between dimensions of religious commitment and mental health reported in the *American Journal of Psychiatry* and *Archives of General Psychiatry*: 1978–1989. *American Journal of Psychiatry, 149,* 557–559.

Lewis, K. N. & Lewis, D. A. (1985). Impact of religious affiliation on therapists' judgments of patients. *Journal of Consulting and Clinical Psychology, 53,* 926–932.

Luborsky, L., Mintz, J., Auerbach, A., Cristoph, P., Bachrach, H., Todd, T., Johnson, M., Cohen, M. & O'Brien, C. P. (1980). Predicting the outcome of psychotherapy: Findings of the Penn Psychotherapy Project. *Archives of General Psychiatry, 37,* 471–481.

Matthews, D. A., McCullough, M. E., Larson, D. B., Koenig, H. G., Swyers, J. P. & Milano, M. G. (1998). Religious commitment and health: A review of the research and implications for family medicine. *Archives of Family Medicine, 7,* 118–124.

McCullough, M. E. & Worthington, E. L. (1995). College students' perceptions of a psychotherapist's treatment of a religious issue: Partial replication and extension. *Journal of Counseling and Development, 73,* 626–634.

McCullough, M. E., Worthington, E. L., Maxey, J. & Rachal, K. C. (1997). Gender in the context of supportive and challenging religious counseling interventions. *Journal of Counseling Psychology, 44,* 80–88.

Meichenbaum, D. (1973). *Therapist manual for cognitive behavior modification.* Unpublished manuscript, University of Waterloo, Ontario, Canada.

Meichenbaum, D. (1985). *Stress inoculation training.* New York: Pergamon Press.

Miller, L., Warner, V., Wickramaratne, P. & Weissman, M. (1997). Religiosity and depression: Ten-year follow-up of depressed mothers and offspring. *Journal of the American Academy of Child and Adolescent Psychiatry, 36,* 1416–1425.

Morrow, D., Worthington, E. L. & McCullough, M. E. (1993). Observers' perceptions of a psychotherapist's treatment of a religious issue. *Journal of Counseling and Development, 71,* 452–456.

Neeleman, J. & King, M. B. (1993). Psychiatrists' religious attitudes in relation to their clinical practice: A survey of 231 psychiatrists. *Acta Psychiatrica Scandinavica, 88,* 420–424.

Ostrom, R., Watkins, P., Dean, T. & Mashburn, D. (1992). Comparative efficacy of religious and nonreligious cognitive-behavioral therapy for the treatment of clinical depression in religious individuals. *Journal of Consulting and Clinical Psychology, 60,* 94–103.

Pargament, K. I. (1997). *The psychology of religion and coping.* New York: Guilford Press.

Pargament, K. I., Ensing, D. S., Falgout, K., Olsen, H., Reilly, B., Van Haitsma, K. & Warren, R. (1990). God help me: I. Religious coping efforts as predictors of the outcomes to significant life events. *American Journal of Community Psychology, 18,* 793–824.

Pargament, K. I., Ishler, K., Dubow, E., Stanik, P., Rouiller, R., Crowe, P., Cullman, E., Albert, M. & Royster, B. J. (1994). Methods of religious coping with the Gulf War: Cross-sectional and longitudinal analyses. *Journal for the Scientific Study of Religion, 33,* 347–361.

Pargament, K. I., Smith, B. & Brant, C. (1995, November). *Religious and nonreligious coping methods with the 1993 Midwest flood.* Paper presented at the meeting of the Society for the Scientific Study of Religion, St. Louis, MO.

Payne, I. R., Bergin, A. E. & Loftus, P. E. (1992). A review of attempts to integrate spiritual and standard psychotherapy techniques. *Journal of Psychotherapy Integration, 2,* 171–192.

Pecheur, D. (1980). *A comparison of the efficacy of secular and religious cognitive behavior modification in the treatment of depressed Christian college students.* Unpublished doctoral dissertation, Rosemead School of Psychology, La Mirada, CA.

(1980). The comparative efficacy of religious and nonreligious imagery for the treatment of mild depression in religious individuals. *Cognitive Therapy and Research, 4,* 167–178.

Propst, R. L. (1988). *Psychotherapy in a religious framework.* New York: Human Sciences Press.

Propst, R. L. (1996). Cognitive-behavioral therapy and the religious person. In E. P. Shafranske (Ed.), *Religion in the clinical practice of psychology* (pp. 391–408). Washington, DC: American Psychological Association.

Richards, P. S. & Bergin, A. E. (1997). *A spiritual strategy for counseling and psychotherapy.* Washington, DC: American Psychological Association.

Richards, P. S., Owen, L. & Stein, S. (1993). A religiously oriented group counseling intervention for self-defeating perfectionism: A pilot study. *Counseling and Values, 37,* 96–104.

Ridley, C. R. (1992a). Brief Christian and non-Christian rational-emotive therapy with depressed Christian clients: An exploratory study. *Counseling and Values, 36,* 220–229.

Rye, M. S. & Pargament, K. I. (1997, August). *Forgiveness and romantic relationships in college.* Paper presented at the 105th Annual Convention of the American Psychological Association, Chicago.

Schumaker, J. F. (1992). *Religion and mental health.* New York: Oxford University Press.

Shafranske, E. P. (1996). *Religion and the clinical practice of psychology.* Washington, DC: American Psychological Association.

Shafranske, E. P. & Malony, H. N. (1990). Clinical psychologists' religious and spiritual orientations and their practice of psychotherapy. *Psychotherapy, 27,* 72–78.

Thurman, C. (1989). *The lies we believe.* Nashville, TN: Thomas Nelson.

Toh, Y. & Tan, S. Y. (1997). The effectiveness of church-based lay counselors: A controlled outcome study. *Journal of Psychology and Christianity, 16,* 260–267.

Uchino, B. N., Cacioppo, J. T. & Kiecolt-Glaser, J. K. (1996). The relationship between social support and physiological processes: A review with emphasis on underlying mechanisms and implications for health. *Psychological Bulletin, 119,* 488–531.

Walen, S. R., DiGiuseppe, R. & Wessler, R. (1980). *A practitioner's guide to rational emotive therapy.* New York: Oxford University Press.

Wampold, B. E. (1997). Methodological problems in identifying efficacious psychotherapies. *Psychotherapy Research, 7,* 21–43.

Wandrei, K. E. (1985). Identifying potential suicides among high-risk women. *Social Work, 30,* 511–517.

Worthington, E. L., Kurusu, T. A., McCullough, M. E. & Sandage, S. J. (1996). Empirical research on religion and psychotherapeutic processes and outcomes: A ten-year review and research prospectus. *Psychological Bulletin, 119,* 448–487.

Wyatt, S. C. & Johnson, R. W. (1990). The influence of counselors' religious values on clients' perceptions of the counselor. *Journal of Psychology and Theology, 18,* 158–165.

Address correspondence to: Michael E. McCullough, National Institute for Healthcare Research, 6110 Executive Boulevard, Suite 908, Rockville, MD 20852. Electronic mail may be sent to Mike@nihr.org

Exercise for Article 24

Factual Questions

1. In the previous study by Koenig, George, and Peterson, how many potentially confounding variables were controlled for?

2. Which electronic databases were searched to locate relevant studies?

3. How many dissertations met the criteria for being included in the sample for the meta-analysis?

4. To determine effect sizes, the difference between the two means was divided by what?

5. Which of the five studies had the largest sample size?

6. What did the mean effect size (i.e., the mean for all five studies) indicate?

7. Was the mean effect size statistically significant (i.e., was it reliably different from zero)?

Questions for Discussion

8. Only studies in which patients were assigned to treatments at random were included in the meta-analytic sample. Was this a good idea? Explain. (See lines 106–110.)

9. What is your opinion on the researcher's decision to use data on only a one-week follow-up period? (See lines 311–319.)

10. The researcher notes that the five studies analyzed here were "seriously underpowered." Do you regard this as a serious limitation? Explain. (See lines 483–490.)

11. In your opinion, how important are the limitations the researcher discusses in lines 494–516?

12. Are the 95% confidence intervals (CIs) in Table 1 helpful? Explain.

13. In light of this review, what recommendations would you make to a future researcher who plans to conduct a single study (not a meta-analysis of other studies) on this topic?

Quality Ratings

Directions: Indicate your level of agreement with each of the following statements by circling a number from 5 for strongly agree (SA) to 1 for strongly disagree (SD). If you believe an item is not applicable to this research article, leave it blank. Be prepared to explain your ratings.

A. The introduction establishes the importance of the study.

SA   5   4   3   2   1   SD

B. The literature review establishes the context for the study.

SA   5   4   3   2   1   SD

C. The research purpose, question, or hypothesis is clearly stated.

SA   5   4   3   2   1   SD

D. The method of sampling is sound.

SA   5   4   3   2   1   SD

E. Relevant demographics (for example, age, gender, and ethnicity) are described.

SA   5   4   3   2   1   SD

F. Measurement procedures are adequate.

SA   5   4   3   2   1   SD

G. All procedures have been described in sufficient detail to permit a replication of the study.

SA   5   4   3   2   1   SD

H. The participants have been adequately protected from potential harm.

SA   5   4   3   2   1   SD

I. The results are clearly described.

SA   5   4   3   2   1   SD

J. The discussion/conclusion is appropriate.

SA   5   4   3   2   1   SD

K. Despite any flaws, the report is worthy of publication.

SA   5   4   3   2   1   SD

Appendix

A Reader's, Writer's, and Reviewer's Guide to Assessing Research Reports in Clinical Psychology

BRENDAN A. MAHER
Harvard University

Maher, B. A. (1978). A Reader's, Writer's, and Reviewer's Guide to Assessing Research Reports in Clinical Psychology. *Journal of Consulting and Clinical Psychology, 46,* 835–838. Published by the American Psychological Association. This material may be reproduced in whole or in part without permission, provided that acknowledgment is made to Brendan A. Maher and the American Psychological Association.

Many detailed responses to a first draft were reviewed. Particular acknowledgment is due Thomas Achenbach, George Chartier, Andrew Comrey, Jesse Harris, Mary B. Harris, Alan Kazdin, Richard Lanyon, Eric Mash, Martha Mednick, Peter Nathan, K. Daniel O'Leary, N. D. Reppucci, Robert Rosenthal, Richard Suinn, and Norman Watt.

Requests for reprints should be sent to Brendan A. Maher, Department of Psychology and Social Relations, Harvard University, Cambridge, MA 02138.

The editors of the *Journal of Consulting and Clinical Psychology* who served between 1974 and 1978 have seen some 3,500 manuscripts in the area of consulting and clinical psychology. Working with this number of manuscripts has made it possible to formulate a set of general guidelines that may be helpful in the assessment of research reports. Originally developed by and for journal reviewers, the guidelines are necessarily skeletal and summary and omit many methodological concerns. They do, however, address the methodological concerns that have proved to be significant in a number of cases. In response to a number of requests, the guidelines are being made available here.

Topic Content

1. Is the article appropriate to this journal? Does it fall within the boundaries mandated in the masthead description?

Style

1. Does the manuscript conform to APA style in its major aspects?

Introduction

1. Is the introduction as brief as possible given the topic of the article?
2. Are all of the citations correct and necessary, or is there padding? Are important citations missing? Has the author been careful to cite prior reports contrary to the current hypothesis?
3. Is there an explicit hypothesis?
4. Has the *origin* of the hypothesis been made explicit?
5. Was the hypothesis *correctly* derived from the theory that has been cited? Are other, contrary hypotheses compatible with the same theory?
6. Is there an explicit rationale for the selection of measures, and was it derived logically from the hypothesis?

Method

1. Is the method so described that replication is possible without further information?
2. *Subjects*: Were they sampled randomly from the population to which the results will be generalized?
3. Under what circumstances was informed consent obtained?
4. Are there probable biases in sampling (e.g. volunteers, high refusal rates, institution population atypical for the country at large, etc.)?
5. What was the "set" given to subjects? Was there deception? Was there control for experimenter influence and expectancy effects?
6. How were subjects debriefed?
7. Were subjects (patients) led to believe that they were receiving "treatment"?
8. Were there special variables affecting the subjects, such as medication, fatigue, and threats that were not part of the experimental manipulation? In clinical samples, was "organicity" measured and/or eliminated?
9. *Controls*: Were there appropriate control groups? What was being controlled for?
10. When more than one measure was used, was the order counterbalanced? If so, were order effects

actually analyzed statistically?

11. Was there a control task(s) to confirm specificity of results?

12. *Measures*: For both dependent and independent variable measures—was validity and reliability established and reported? When a measure is tailor-made for a study, this is very important. When validities and reliabilities are already available in the literature, it is less important.

13. Is there adequate description of tasks, materials, apparatus, and so forth?

14. Is there discriminant validity of the measures?

15. Are distributions of scores on measures typical of scores that have been reported for similar samples in previous literature?

16. Are measures free from biases such as
    a. Social desirability?
    b. Yeasaying and naysaying?
    c. Correlations with general responsivity?
    d. Verbal ability, intelligence?

17. If measures are scored by observers using categories or codes, what is the interrater reliability?

18. Was administration and scoring of the measures done blind?

19. If short versions, foreign-language translations, and so forth, of common measures are used, has the validity and reliability of these been established?

20. In correlational designs, do the two measures have theoretical and/or methodologies independence?

Representative Design

1. When the stimulus is human (e.g., in clinical judgments of clients of differing race, sex, etc.), is there a *sample* of stimuli (e.g., more than one client of each race or each sex)?

2. When only one stimulus or a few human stimuli were used, was an adequate explanation of the failure to sample given?

Statistics

1. Were the statistics used with appropriate assumptions fulfilled by the data (e.g., normalcy of distributions for parametric techniques)? Where necessary, have scores been transformed appropriately?

2. Were tests of significance properly used and reported? For example, did the author use the p value of a correlation to justify conclusions when the actual size of the correlation suggests little common variance between two measures?

3. Have statistical significance levels been accompanied by an analysis of practical significance levels?

4. Has the author considered the effects of a limited range of scores, and so forth, in using correlations?

5. Is the basic statistical strategy that of a "fishing expedition"; that is, if many comparisons are made, were the obtained significance levels predicted in advance? Consider the number of significance levels as a function of the total number of comparisons made.

Factor Analytic Statistics

1. Have the correlation and factor matrices been made available to the reviewers and to the readers through the National Auxiliary Publications Service or other methods?

2. Is it stated what was used for communalities, and is the choice appropriate? Ones in the diagonals are especially undesirable when items are correlated as the variables.

3. Is the method of termination of factor extraction stated, and is it appropriate in this case?

4. Is the method of factor rotation stated, and is it appropriate in this case?

5. If items are used as variables, what are the proportions of yes and no responses for each variable?

6. Is the sample size given, and is it adequate?

7. Are there evidences of distortion in the final solution, such as single factors, excessively high communalities, obliqueness when an orthogonal solution is used, linearly dependent variables, or too many complex variables?

8. Are artificial factors evident because of inclusion of variables in the analysis that are alternate forms of each other?

Figures and Tables

1. Are the figures and tables (a) necessary and (b) self-explanatory? Large tables of nonsignificant differences, for example, should be eliminated if the few obtained significances can be reported in a sentence or two in the text. Could several tables be combined into a smaller number?

2. Are the axes of figures identified clearly?

3. Do graphs correspond logically to the textual argument of the article? (E.g., if the text states that a certain technique leads to an *increment* of mental health and the accompanying graph shows a *decline* in symptoms, the point is not as clear to the reader as it would be if the text or the graph were amended to achieve visual and verbal congruence.)

Discussion and Conclusion

1. Is the discussion properly confined to the findings or is it digressive, including new post hoc speculations?

2. Has the author explicitly considered and discussed viable alternative explanations of the findings?

3. Have nonsignificant trends in the data been promoted to "findings"?

4. Are the limits of the generalizations possible from the data made clear? Has the author identified his/her own methodological difficulties in the study?

5. Has the author "accepted" the null hypothesis?

6. Has the author considered the possible methodological bases for discrepancies between the results reported and other findings in the literature?

Notes